Agricultural Biotechnology Law

Victoria Sutton, MPA, PhD, JD

ISBN: 978-0-9968186-7-4

Vargas Publishing
P.O. Box 6801
Lubbock, TX 79493

http://vargaspublishing.com

Dedication

*To my children
who continue to inspire me
with their intellect and new adventures*

TABLE OF CONTENTS

Chapter 1

Introduction

This book is a stand-alone casebook and resource for agricultural biotechnology law. It is also arranged with corresponding index numbers with video lectures that cover the material in those same sections for a comprehensive course.

1.1.3 The relationship between law and biotechnology

Law and biotechnology is the application of law to the broad range of activities encompassed within the field of biotechnology.

Biotechnology is defined as the application of biology to human needs. Utilizing the biological sciences and methods of using biology to meet human needs ranges from the need for food to the need for medical technologies to survive. The scientific disciplines, biology, cell biology, molecular biology, immunology, microbiology, chemical engineering, genetics, chemistry, biochemistry, physics, computer science, forensic science and mathematics encompass the range of activities which comprise the underlying scientific principles and knowledge of biotechnology. The integration of these fields of science represent interdisciplinary applications of science among the traditional "hard" sciences. Other fields, such as ethics, bioethics, sociology and psychology — traditional "soft" sciences — have grown to include new specialty areas with interdisciplinary applications to biotechnology.

The relationship of law with biotechnology, as an interdisciplinary study, has scientific, social, political and economic consequences which add to the complexity of the development of this growing body of law addressing the issues of biotechnology in law. Almost every traditional area of law has an application in biotechnology — constitutional law, property law, tort law, criminal law, evidence as well as the specialty fields of international law, intellectual property law, environmental law, indigenous peoples law, patent law and public health law. There are certainly areas of the law which are "behind" in addressing the new issues created by the rapidly growing areas of biotechnology, such as cloning and ownership issues. There are also areas of law which are waiting for biotechnology to "catch up" to the demands of the courtroom, such as the application of reliable biotechnological techniques which can be increasingly relied upon in criminal evidentiary matters. Law drives technology where we have constraints for privacy, for example, with new technologies directed to biodefense surveillance, which must be shaped around those legal constraints.

The study of law and biotechnology encompasses the theoretical and the practical issues of concern to law and biotechnology; and considerations of the current state of the law and biotechnology as well as the future development of law and biotechnology. This understanding is essential for preparation for legal practice, whether in the public sector or private sector.

The growing importance of science in law and the need for more preparation for lawyers has not gone unnoticed by the courts. Justice Breyer, U.S. Supreme Court Associate Justice, in an unusual public advocacy posture, has been actively encouraging and promoting the education of lawyers and judges in the sciences. During a conference at Harvard University's Kennedy School of Government in November 2000, Justice Breyer stated, "Traditionally, some have believed that we need not know science but only law to make decisions. This view is increasingly unrealistic. Since the implications of our decisions in the real world often can and should play a role in our legal decisions, the clearer our understanding of the relevant science, the better..." *USA Today* , 24 Nov 2000, reported, "Although it remains rare for Supreme Court Justices to speak out on public issues, Breyer has publicly urged greater scientific education for judges at least three times this year."

1.1.3.1 **Defining biotechnology**.

Biotechnology's simplest definition is the application of biology to human needs. More specifically, biotechnology is a set of technologies that use biological molecules and cells to make products, solve problems, and do research, based upon an understanding of cellular and molecular structure and processes.

These technologies include: (1) monoclonal antibody technology, which is the use of cells and enzymes to make and breakdown products; (2) cell culture technology which are the techniques used to grow cells in laboratory containers or bioreactors; (3) genetic engineering technology, which is changing an organism's genetic makeup with molecular techniques; (4) biosensor technology, which is the use of biological molecules and transducers for detection and quantification; (5) antisense technology, which is the use of the mechanism of blocking gene expression with oligonucleotides; (6) DNA chip technology, which is the use of DNA probes to detect mutations and monitor gene expression; (7) tissue engineering, which is the techniques used in the growing semi-synthetic tissues and organs synthesis; (8) bioprocessing technology, which are the techniques using cells and enzymes to make and breakdown products; and (9) bioinformatics which is the use of computational tools to organize, access and study information about biology.
(10) CRISPR-CAS9 is in a new class of tools for biotechnology. Using CRISPR-CAS9

for genetic modification is the next generation of biotechnology that allows not only precise replacements and insertions but it is also more accessible with less knowledge and training. Almost all genetically-modified organisms will use CRISPR-CAS9 and successive improved tools that will be developed based on that same technology. It falls into the category "(3)" but is such a quantum leap of technology that it is in a category of its own.

1.1.3.2   **Defining Agricultural Biotechnology and Law.**

The term agricultural biotechnology is all the types of biotechnology that can be applied to the commercialization of biological materials used in agriculture. From wine and cheesemaking to advanced biotechnologies that create genetically modified animals that can produce pharmaceuticals. The entire scope of these activities fall within the range of topics that have legal issues to analyze. Some of these areas already have a line of cases that help to define the law in that area, like GMO labeling laws. Some of these areas are newly emerging ones that have yet to have the interesting legal questions they raise, tested in a judicial court.

The term agricultural biotechnology and law includes domestic law both regulatory and case law, as well as international governance of biotechnology involving international trade, intellectual property and several treaties.

1.2.1.   **The Starlink Incident**

The use of StarLink corn began a controversy about the use of engineered foods in the Fall 2000, when a member of the Friends of the Earth, part of the coalition of groups opposed to genetically engineered foods, went to a Safeway grocery store in Silver Spring, Maryland and collected corn products for analysis. One of the twenty-three products showed the presence of the DNA strand for the production of the Bt protein, Cry9C. While the Cry1A group of Bt proteins had been approved by the U.S. EPA and FDA, Cry9C, in StarLink corn, had been approved only for animal feed use. The presence of Cry9C as well as Cry1A proteins in StarLink gave it added protection against insect pests, but also resulted in a plant with higher levels of toxicity than in previously approved plants.

The finding of the Cry9C DNA in Kraft's Taco Bell taco shells was released to the news media on September 18, 2000 and an investigation ensued. Aventis, the producer of the StarLink variety bought over a million test kits for detecting the presence of StarLink corn, and farmers throughout the nation were contacted and cautioned about the mixing of their corn production.

Attorneys General in the sixteen major corn-growing states including Iowa which made up 39% of the StarLink production in 2000, began to look to Aventis for compensation to the farmers for lost profits. Concerns about liability to farmers for the use of their corn after it is sold is a significant issue which farmers have raised. Further, seed manufacturers require growers agreements which might create further liability for farmers if their crop is used illegally, even after the seed has left their control. In March 2001, EPA issued guidance ending the split registration — approved feed uses for animals, but not for human consumption, stating that StarLink would "no longer be considered a regulator option for products of biotechnology."

StarLink is regulated under both the authority of EPA and the FDA. FIFRA is the statutory authority which is implemented by EPA through the use of labels which denote genetically altered material as "plant-incorporated protectants." "Plant-incorporated protectants" are regulated based upon the definition of a pesticide under FIFRA, which encompasses both chemical or biological methods of insect or pest control. FDA regulates foods based on the presence of these pesticides in the food. Under the Food, Drug and Cosmetic Act, the FDA regulates these GMOs where they result in "pesticide residues in feed and food," because of the inserted genes' continued presence in the food.

The damage caused by the StarLink controversy was litigated in part, on a theory of tort liability, discussed *supra*. The following excerpt describes the regulation of genetically engineered food through the statutory authorities of EPA and FDA:

> In practice, the Coordinated Framework places the burden on USDA to ascertain "whether GMOs are 'safe to grow,'" on EPA to "ensure[] that GMOs are 'safe for the environment,'" and on FDA to "determine[s] whether they are 'safe to eat.'"

> A. *USDA*
> USDA has authority over genetically modified crops under the Plant Protection Act ("PPA"). PPA provides USDA with rather narrow authority to investigate GMOs. Under this Act, USDA can regulate the "movement of organisms that may endanger plant life, and to prevent the introduction, dissemination or establishment of such organisms." USDA deals with genetically modified crops in two different ways. If a genetically modified crop "uses genetic material from a known plant pest," the agency issues a permit. A USDA permit, however, is not required for crops not using "genetic material from a known plant pest." In this second case, the party using the crops is required to give USDA "advance notice of intent to conduct field trials." USDA then has the authority to refuse to grant authorization, but if it fails to act, authorization is presumed.
> USDA also has the authority to identify genetically modified crops as "non-regulated." The developer of the crop can petition USDA for this status. Before granting the petition, the agency must decide that the crop is not a plant pest risk and conduct an Environmental Assessment. There are no USDA restrictions on crops that are "non-regulated." Therefore, USDA's regulation of genetically modified crops extends only to those that use known plant pests. USDA is only obliged to issue permits for, and therefore is only obliged to do a comprehensive examination of, genetically modified crops that use known plant pests.

B. *EPA*

EPA regulates genetically modified organisms primarily under FIFRA. FIFRA regulates pesticide labeling and registration. It authorizes EPA to evaluate genetically modified organisms with "pesticidal properties." FIFRA requires any party intending to market pesticides commercially to register with EPA. This process is supposed to ensure that the product will not cause "unreasonable adverse effects on the environment." . . .

EPA also regulates genetically modified plants that contain pesticide chemicals under the federal Food Drug and Cosmetic Act ("FDCA"). Under FDCA, EPA must either set tolerance levels for pesticide residues in foods or create exemptions from the tolerance levels. EPA, relying on the aforementioned "substantial equivalence doctrine," has created "broad categorical exemptions" for several genetically modified organisms. EPA exempted many genetically modified foods after "concluding that [they] did not endanger public health" and "that there was a reasonable certainty that 'aggregate dietary exposure to these modifications' would not cause harm." Overall, EPA has broad discretion regarding the regulation of genetically modified organisms.

C. *FDA*

FDCA also gives FDA authority to regulate genetically modified organisms. Under FDCA, FDA regulates genetically modified foods through provisions that allow it to prohibit "adulterated foods." An "adulterated food" is a food that "bears or contains any poisonous or deleterious substance which may render it injurious to health." FDA's policy towards genetically modified foods, in line with the "substantial equivalence doctrine," is that they are not inherently dangerous; it regulates genetically modified foods in the same manner as regular foods. Although FDA otherwise would have jurisdiction over genetically modified plants, such as StarLink, that contain pesticidal properties, the agency specifically relinquished this authority in 1992. FDA handed over all regulatory authority concerning genetically modified plants with pesticidal characteristics to EPA. FDA and EPA concluded that "such plants are in fact pesticides and thus subject to EPA's exclusive jurisdiction." The policy statement on the matter admitted that "there may be cases in which the jurisdictional responsibility for a substance is not clear." Confusingly, EPA does not classify plants genetically modified to be resistant to chemical herbicides as pesticides. Therefore, these types of GMOs fall only under FDA's jurisdiction.

Even more confusingly, FDA biotechnology regulation grants a great deal of discretion to manufacturers. FDA regulates genetically modified foods under its authority to regulate food additives. A "food additive," however, is only regulated if the substance "is not generally recognized, among experts qualified by scientific training and experience to evaluate its safety, as having been adequately shown through scientific procedures . . . to be safe under the conditions of its intended use . . . ." Therefore, many ingredients are not reviewed because they are labeled "generally recognized as safe" ("GRAS").

FDA, in determining if a product is GRAS, determines if "there is a consensus of expert opinion regarding the safety of the use of the substance." The manufacturer has significant influence on this determination.

[Linda Beebe, "Symposium Issue II Pesticides: What Will the Future Reap? Note: In re StarLink Corn: The Link between Genetically Damaged Crops and an Inadequate Regulatory Frame Work for Biotechnology," 28 Wm. & Mary Envtl. L. & Pol'y Rev. 511 (Winter 2004).]

NOTES ON STARLINK CORN

Note 1

In 1999, a study was published in the journal NATURE indicating that pollen from *Bt*-corn could kill monarch butterfly larvae in laboratory tests. Although the *Bt*-corn had been shown not to affect many non-target organisms, such as honeybees and ladybugs, the pollen produced by the corn contained crystalline *Bt* endotoxin. In the wild, the corn pollen is dispersed by the wind, causing it to land on other plants, such as the milkweed, which serves as the exclusive food of monarch caterpillars. Although additional data was needed to fully address the seriousness of the risk to wild monarchs, this finding helped fuel the controversy over *Bt*-corn, including the StarLink corn at issue in the case.

Note 2

In 2001, in response to a wave of recalls by corn product manufacturers, Aventis initiated a program in which the StarLink corn, buffer corn, and any corn stored in grain elevators along with StarLink would be bought by Aventis and directed to animal feed and non-food industrial use. The program (known as the StarLink Enhanced Stewardship Program) also included free StarLink test kits and covered costs of cleaning equipment, transport, storage facilities, and transportation. In 2008, the EPA recommended that the Federal Grain Inspection Service cease testing of the US corn supply for the Cry9C protein, which had been in place since the StarLink controversy erupted in 2001. Although StarLink corn has never been shown to be directly harmful to humans, Aventis has not sought to revive use of this brand of corn following its voluntary registration withdrawal in October of 2001. "Starlink" was acquired as a trademark by SpaceX in 2017.

Chapter 2

A History of Agricultural Biotechnology and Law

1.2.2 History of Agricultural Biotechnology Law, Part 1

The History of Biotechnology and Law in Eurasia and the Americas

In many ways, the history of biotechnology is also the history of agriculture. We may not think about the beginnings of agriculture as a technology, but it was a great advancement in human civilization. Time for hunting and gathering was reduced and human thinking turned to technology the arts and entertainment.

Evidence suggests that from two million years ago to 12,000 years ago, humans were hunters and gatherers. [1] Around 10,000 years ago, humans began both the selective crossing of plants for crops and the domestication of animals through selective breeding. Sheep and goats were domesticated around 9,000 B.C.; swine around 7,000 B.C. and cattle around 6,500 B.C. It was in 4,000 B.C. that beer making began with the Sumerians and Babylonians. Then, around 3,200 B.C. (R.K. Robinson, A Colour Guide to Cheese and Fermented Milks, Chapman & Hall (1995)), that microorganisms were utilized for human needs when yogurt and cheese were developed.

In the Americas, Native Americans were developing pharmacological applications of plants and animals to cure illnesses and enhance mood, but also as part of a spiritual connection with the environment. Passing along knowledge was considered a sacred trust and so most of this technology was passed along through oral histories from elders to the next generation.

Based on written records, historical sources indicate that in Asia, the use of plants for medicines and even pesticides developed as early as 500 B.C.. In Sumeria, Babylonia and Egypt, food biotechnology began as early as 4,000 B.C..

---

[1] Hawkes K, O'Connell J, Blurton Jones N. Hunter-gatherer studies and human evolution: A very selective review. *Am J Phys Anthropol.* 2018;165(4):777-800. doi:10.1002/ajpa.23403.

The first law applied to biotechnology was probably the standards for a bioprocessing technology. This first recorded relationship between law and biotechnology was in the writing of the famous Hammurabi law code, which contained the "eye for an eye" code. Contained within that code were precise instructions and regulations for the manufacture of beer in ancient Babylonia. It was around 4,000 B.C. that prehistoric brewing of beer in Sumeria, Babylonia and Egypt began.

The period around 3200 B.C. marks the beginning of the cheesemaking processes. It has been theorized that cheese may have been discovered through the slaughter of unweaned calves with fermented milk remaining in their stomachs. Around 500 B.C., the Chinese recorded the practice of using moldy soybean curds as an antibiotic treatment for pustules and open sores. The use of crop rotation to preserve soil fertility was practiced by the Greeks as early as 250 B.C. The use of pesticides was first recorded around 100 B.C., when the Chinese used Chrysanthemum pollen as an insecticide.

The period from 100-300 A.D. evidenced the Hindu philosophers curiosity about the nature of reproduction and inheritance. Around 1,000 A.D., the Hindus observed that certain diseases may run in families. The laws of Manu set forth the principle that "A man of base descents can never escape his origins." 1,100 to 1,500 A.D. may be the dark ages of biotechnology and law, only because the Black Death swept across the world with much work to try to determine its cause and how to stop it, but it was far too advanced of a scientific question for the body of scientific knowledge of the time and the failure for science to "cure" the plague, probably led to an abandonment of science in favor of spiritual or occult remedies. For example, the ideas of spontaneous generation remained the dominant explanation for the origin of living organisms, such as maggots from horsehair.

A vinegar manufacturing operation in Orleans in the 1500s opened a new age of biotechnology at a larger scale, effectively ending the dark ages of biotechnology development in Europe.

Around 1630 A.D., William Harvey concluded that sexual reproduction existed in the lower organisms, and concluded that males contribute sperm and females contribute an egg to the process. In 1,665 A.D., Robert Hooke observed the cellular structure of cork, and in that same period the idea of spontaneous generation was disproven with the work of Francesco Redi, who with a simple experiment showed that maggots arose from uncovered meat, while covered meat did not produce maggots. Then in 1,680 A.D. Leeuwenhoek observed the fermentation process of yeast through his first microscope.

Prior to the use of cowpox as an inoculation for smallpox, the Moravians, a religious sect, in North Carolina in the early 1700s recorded in their detailed diaries, the use of a small infection of smallpox to guard against a more serious case. This was done by sending smallpox scabs to a community to use to infect the skin of a patient. This resulted in deaths from an unexpectedly serious case, but still the risk of this low level self-infection was less than that from a natural smallpox infection. It was not until 1797, that Edward Jenner, used a different living organisms (e.g., cowpox) to protect people from diseases through inoculation, after observing milk maids (with previous cowpox infections) showing an immunity to smallpox. Louis Pasteur in 1864, proved the existence of microorganisms, and that they reproduced. Thereafter in 1865, Gregor Mendel demonstrated the inheritance of traits from one generation to another in the pea plant, establishing the beginning of the field of genetics. Then in 1869, Johann Meische isolated DNA from the nuclei of white blood cells. It is noteworthy that laws or regulations around the work of these scientists was beyond any regulatory mechanism of the time.

The regulation of cheese has been largely driven by the cultures in which it is produced and consumed. A comparison of European regulation and U.S. regulation illustrates this point:

> The acceptance of raw milk cheeses necessarily implies the rejection of a pasteurization requirement. This rejection has both negative aspects (the possibility of contamination) and positive aspects (better taste). Consumers in Europe generally value the flavor and tradition of raw milk cheeses. Since the cheeses have been produced and eaten for hundreds of years with few public health consequences, consumers do not believe these cheeses present a food safety risk, provided that certain sanitary practices are followed. EC law reflects this view. In contrast, in the U.S., unpasteurized cheeses--products not subjected to modern scientific standards--are considered risky. U.S. law reflects this view by prohibiting fresh raw milk cheeses. Only those products that have been aged for at least sixty days may be imported and sold. Marsha A. Echols, "Food Safety Regulation in the European Union and the United States: Different Cultures, Different Laws," 4 Colum. J. Eur. L. 525, 533 (1998).

The regulation of butter and margarine was a highly charged political issue, and one that would be regulated as some of the first food regulations in the U.S., not for safety but for quality and content. The commercial interests in butter and cheese even led to the establishment of the New York Stock Exchange.

> Butter and margarine became an issue in the United States when margarine was first introduced in 1873. Concern for content of the product was largely driven by politics rather than product quality or content. "New York enacted an antimargarine law in 1877 at the direct urging of the butter interests. Missouri followed suit the same year. Six states adopted labelling laws in 1878: California, Connecticut, Maryland, Massachusetts, Ohio, and Pennsylvania. Three more states passed legislation in 1879: Delaware, Illinois, and Tennessee. Others soon fell into line; by 1886, thirty-four states and territories had enacted some version of margarine labelling legislation." Geoffrey P. Miller, "Public Choice at the Dawn of the Special Interest State: The Story of Butter and Margarine," 77 Calif. L. Rev. 83 (1989).

The strong mercantile, commerce and regulatory interests in butter and cheese led to the development of the New York Stock Exchange. The

Exchange began when members of the Butter and Cheese Exchange of New York created the Butter and Cheese Exchange of New York. On June 1, 1875, this exchange became the American Exchange of New York, and then on April 26, 1880, it became the Butter, Cheese and Egg Exchange of the City of New York. Finally, on June 5, 1882, the Exchange changed its name to the New York Mercantile Exchange. See N.Y. Mercantile Ex. Guide (CCH)PP 51, 61, 65, 59 (1986).

The 1800s began to see synergy from the discoveries of the Enlightenment Era to the new "biology". The word "biology" can be traced back to a beginning in 1802 when biology began to open into a field of science. Appert invented the canning process in 1809, and proteins were discovered in 1830, followed in 1833 with the first isolation of enzymes. Then in 1855, Escherichia coli, a common bacteria, was first isolated, and continues to be an important tool in biotechnology research. The famous work of Gregor Mendel was in 1863, when he discovered the first principles of genetics. From 1881-1900, the first Rabies vaccine was discovered and developed. The promise of an improved quality of life for everyone, not just the wealthy became a real possibility. However, there were negative consequences to this new biotechnology that could be done in great quantities. Alcohol was "ripe" for regulation.

> The possible societal evils of the fermentation of fruit, were recognized, however, and as early as 1855, states were regulating alcohol production. The regulation of alcohol in the United States has a long history, culminating in the twenty-first Amendment to the U.S. Constitution. As Judge Hopkins wrote in a judicial opinion, "Kansas has been one of the pioneers, first, in the regulation, and second, in the prohibition of the beverage liquor traffic. Indeed as early as 1855, her Territorial Legislature passed acts regulating such traffic. Those interested in the subject will find a synopsis of all the liquor laws of Kansas from 1855 to 1933, together with citations pertaining thereto, in a note or appendix to the opinion in Chapman v. Boynton, D.C., 4 F.Supp. 43, 47, from which it appears that prohibition of the beverage liquor traffic had a progressive development in Kansas from regulation of the saloon and tavern down to and including 'bone dry.'" United States v. Robason, 38 F. Supp. 991 at 992 (1941).

In the United States, concern for food safety and regulation began in 1862, the beginning years of the U.S. Civil War. The following excerpt from James Robert Dean, Jr, "FDA at War: Securing the Food That Secured Victory," 53 Food Drug L.J. 453, 456-7 (1998), provides a brief overview of the history of that regulatory agency which was to oversee food safety and the resulting development of regulation:

> The agency now known as FDA began in 1862, when the Chemical Division of the U.S. Department of Agriculture (USDA) was established. The Agriculture Department was charged with undertaking research aimed at

furthering American agriculture. As other divisions of the growing department became more focused on particular lines of research, such as livestock or crop research, the Chemical Division remained a general scientific laboratory. Only because of the growing interest in food adulteration of Harvey W. Wiley, the head of the division, did FDA's predecessor begin to emphasize food and drug matters. After a lengthy legislative fight, the 1906 Pure Food and Drugs Act vested the recently renamed Bureau of Chemistry with regulatory authority. This authority entailed a significant shift in FDA's focus. The pre-1906 Bureau of Chemistry furthered the interests of farmers. The 1906 Act created a new federal consumer protection agency. FDA appropriations jumped from $ 17,100 in 1900 to $ 888,560 in 1910, reflecting these additional responsibilities. The number of FDA personnel also increased from 20 in 1897 to 110 in 1906 and then to 425 by 1908. In the following decades, FDA developed a regulatory model based on frequent seizures and criminal prosecutions of adulterated products.

FDA remained a division of the Agriculture Department until 1940 when it was moved into the Federal Security Agency (FSA). This move ended a long period of institutional conflict between the former Chemical Division and the other divisions of the Agriculture Department. Combined with the new mandate of the 1938 Act, the move marked a new era in FDA's history. Separation from the Agriculture Department that was becoming increasingly concerned with promoting the welfare of farmers, as opposed to the consumer protection mission of FDA, allowed the newly empowered agency to expand fully into its new responsibilities. FSA had fewer institutional biases than the Agriculture Department, making FSA a more suitable home for FDA. President Roosevelt, in his message to Congress explaining the new arrangement, stated that he found it desirable to group together those agencies of the government whose major purpose was to promote social and economic security, educational opportunity, and the health of the citizens of the Nation. FDA, while located in a new home more attuned to its mission, was still a small agency, however, and was allocated only $ 2.5 million from an FSA total budget of $ 1 billion. Despite its strong congressional mandate and history of excellent work, the FDA of 1940 needed to establish its new identity and power quickly. The 1938 Act changed the philosophy behind food and drug regulation. Under the 1906 Act, the agency generally had banned "adulterated" and "misbranded" foods and drugs. The definition of these terms, however, largely remained for the courts to determine. Every violation had to be proven in court to meet the terms of the Act. The 1906 Act could be described as a legal, as opposed to administrative, regime. The 1938 Act reflected a different approach, one more in tune with the emerging New Deal regulatory model. FDA received authority to promulgate standards of identity for common foods, an important exercise of administrative discretion. Where a standard of identity existed, foods sold under the common name established by the standard would be in violation of the FDCA if they did not meet the FDA-established requirements. Furthermore, foods packed in conditions where they might become adulterated were subject to seizure, without a full adjudication of whether the particular item in question was, in fact, adulterated. Another important expansion of FDA's powers was its new authority to review new drugs before they could be marketed legally. While the agency's name remained the same, the 1938 Act provided for the replacement of a traditional police force with an independent regulatory body empowered to create and enforce the law. This marked a significant change for both the regulators and the regulated. FDA was charged with developing a body of law, a task that required both expert knowledge and political deftness.

The regulation of these activities was limited primarily to the recipes and processes as a quality control and public health matter.

World War II produced a need for antimalarial drugs as well as penicillin. The following account describes the role of regulation in the development of these pharmaceuticals:

Malaria was prevalent in the entire Pacific theater and areas in North Africa and Sicily, where millions of American troops soon were to be stationed. While quinine had been used successfully for centuries to treat malaria, supplies of the drug were reduced drastically following the Japanese capture of the East Indies. Although cinchona was native to South America, production was concentrated in the East Indies where the tree grew particularly well. In 1941, ninety-five percent of American quinine came from territory soon to be under Japanese control. To complicate the situation, quinine did not actually cure or prevent malaria; it only relieved the debilitating symptoms. Prolonged use of quinine also produced unpleasant side effects, such as ringing in the ears, blurry vision, and nausea. FDA had recognized some of these problems before the war while investigating how quinine should be marketed under the FDCA. In 1939, FDA had issued a statement requiring that all anti-malarial preparations comply with the requirements of the FDCA, which limited certain labeling claims. . . . .The germicidal properties of penicillin had been reported by Alexander Fleming in 1929, but it had not been used as an antibiotic before World War II. British scientists at Oxford began investigating penicillin for medicinal use in the late 1930s. . . .Penicillin comes from a mold, *Penicillium notatum*. While relatively easy to grow in a laboratory, it proved exceedingly difficult to extract the chemical substance from the organism on a commercial scale. Early attempts involved arrays of large Petri dishes, each harboring an active culture of the penicillin-producing mold. Eventually it proved possible to grow the molds in a solution rather than on the surface of a culture medium, making larger-scale production possible. After considerable effort, the penicillin program proved to be a huge success. By the end of the war all military needs were met and substantial supplies were available for public consumption. . . . .The pattern that emerged during World War II has continued after the war. FDA became a reviewer of scientific research, but not a major patron of science or a research organization itself.

Other nonregulatory agencies, such as the National Institutes of Health and the National Science Foundation, became the primary federal sponsors of scientific research. Soon after the war ended, OSRD canceled FDA's outstanding research projects on synthetic penicillin. The cancellation noted that the major portion of the work in this program has been performed in commercial and academic laboratories, and recent developments require a readjustment of all projects, especially those involving non-governmental groups. Progress in methods of producing penicillin by fermentation and the end of active hostilities have removed the justification for continued governmental sponsorship of this research on its present basis. James Robert Dean, Jr, "FDA at War: Securing the Food That Secured Victory," 53 Food Drug L.J. 453, 497-500(1998).

Penicillin and the development of other drugs coming after the passage of the Food, Drug and Cosmetic Act in 1938, were regulated from development to dispensing of drugs. Foods were also regulated under this Act, too; but many foods such as salt, flour and sugar were classified under the GRAS provision of the Act — generally recognized as safe food products, which meant *de facto* approval for human consumption.

The scientific approach to regulation prevailed at FDA, but it was not without criticism. As one author described the situation:

FDA's "scientific" approach badly served the goal of food and drug regulation. The most famous example is Harvey W. Wiley's crusade against all food additives. The man known for creating the modern system of food and drug regulation also was "seriously deficient" in his grasp of scientific matters. Dupree notes that "although the bureau made steady progress in enforcing pure-food-and-drug standards, it became a correspondingly serious problem to the responsible political chiefs to be sure in the face of pressure that Wiley's facts were straight." This controversy, which developed in food and drug law soon after the turn of the century, was the crux of the late New Deal debate over the future of administrative law. Regulating in the name of expertise can succeed only when the underlying scientific justification generally is accepted as valid. As FDA moved into its broader power granted by the 1938 Act, it frequently approached the edge

13

of scientific knowledge and had correspondingly less legitimating force behind its regulatory plans. . . . The quantum leap in food technology during and after the war eventually led to the food and color additives amendments, which further transformed the agency from Wiley's group of "G-men" into a scientific bureaucracy. James Robert Dean, Jr, "FDA at War: Securing the Food That Secured Victory," 53 Food Drug L.J. 453, 467-8 (1998).

In retrospect, we were in the beginning of the Biotechnology Revolution. The development of biotechnology has been compared to the rapid advances made in the field of physics in the early part of the 20th century, through the 1980s. Almost everything we know about the universe as well as subatomic particles were discovered during this period. But hundreds of years passed between the discoveries of Ptolemy and Newton before the revolution in physics began. The phenomena of revolutions of science have been described by Thomas S. Kuhn in The Structure of Scientific Revolutions 92, 111 (1962), that "scientific revolutions are taken to be those non-cumulative developmental episodes in which an older paradigm is replaced in whole or in part by an incompatible new one. . . .Led by a new paradigm, scientists adopt new instruments and look in new places. Even more important, during revolutions scientists see new and different things when looking with familiar instruments in places they have looked before. Nevertheless, paradigm changes do cause scientists to see the world of their research-engagement differently."

In physics perhaps the two most important discoveries were those of relativity and of quantum mechanics in 1905 and 1925 respectively. In biology the two most important were the structure of the DNA molecule as the blueprint of life and the completion of the mapping of the human genome in 1956 and 2001, respectively.

Similarly, the revolution in biotechnology has created a revolution in the legal field, as well, causing lawyers, legislators and judges to "see different things when looking with familiar laws and political institutions in places they have looked before,"(to apply Kuhn's description of the scientists of a revolution). So, too, biotechnology allows us to ask questions not only in science but in law, which we have never asked before.

The Hungarian engineer, Karl Ereky, is credited with coining the term "biotechnology" in 1919. Ereky used this term to refer to the use of living organisms at some point in the utilization of raw materials to make useful commodities.

The following accounts of the beginnings of modern biotechnology demonstrate the wide range of biological research taking place which produced the synergy that created the development of the biotechnology industry.

From the U.S. Department of Energy's Lawrence Livermore National Laboratory:

The first successful biomolecular project at Livermore took place in the late 1970s with the production of made-to-order monoclonal antibodies. (Antibodies are nature's defender molecules, and monoclonal means that they are produced by a single clone.) [It is possible to] select for and form single clones or copies of immunologically active cells. Such cells make only one antibody, and when isolated, they can be produced infinitely with complete purity and remarkable specificity. Two of Livermore's products are the monoclonal antibodies that recognize the subtle distinction between normal and mutant red blood cells in the glycophorin-A assay. Other Livermore monoclonal antibodies can indicate whether a blood stain is human or whether a child has sickle cell anemia. Still others are useful for making the individual proteins involved in the complex process of repairing DNA.

Perhaps the most important antibodies to come out of this work were those of bromodeoxyuridine in DNA, a substance that can substitute for a normal building block of DNA. A small amount injected into a subject or in a culture will be synthesized into the DNA of any cells that are dividing. When this monoclonal antibody is coupled to a fluorescent marker, all the cells in division become fluorescent and can be seen under a microscope or detected and measured in a a glow cytometer. A Livermore team used this technique. . . to develop methods that revolutionized the study of cell growth and that today are standard procedure worldwide. Cancer patients are routinely evaluated by these methods to see how fast their cancer cells are dividing. . . .

In 1974, Livermore scientists for the first time performed an experiment that successfully measured and sorted Chinese hamster chromosomes using flow cytometry. Not until 1979 did scientist learn how to do the same with human chromosomes, which are much smaller and more varied. . . .

In 1984, Mort Mendelsohn organized a meeting of molecular geneticists from around the world to brainstorm the potential for DNA-oriented methods to detect human heritable mutation in A-bomb survivors. It became clear to those at the meeting that despite the enormous scale of this effort, analysis of the entire human genome was feasible.

In 1986, the Department of Energy was the first federal agency to launch a major initiative to completely decipher the human genetic code. A year later, Livermore researchers began to study all of chromosome 19, which they had earlier learned was the home of several genes important for DNA repair.

In 1990, the Department of Energy joined forces with the National Institutes of Health to kick off the Human Genome Project, the largest biological research project ever.

Early groundbreaking Livermore work in flow cytometry, a technique for separating specific cells from other cells has come to have numerous medical research applications. Some biosensors to detect the specific agents used in biological weapons are based on flow cytometry.

U.S. Department of Energy's Lawrence Livermore National Laboratory, "Research Highlights," Science and Technology Review, 10-13 (January/February 2001).

From the University of California, San Francisco:

In the fall of 1972, there was no such thing as genetic engineering. . . .In the early 1970s, Herbert Boyer's lab at the University of California, San Francisco, isolated an enzyme that cut DNA at specific locations. At the same time, Stanley Cohen's Stanford lab was working out methods for introducing small circular pieces of DNA called "plasmids" into bacteria, which act as living Xerox machines, copying genes each time the microbes divide. At a November 1972 conference in Hawaii, both researchers presented their work — and realized that if they combined their techniques they would have a remarkable tool. . . . within months their labs had jointly proved the possibility of gene "cloning": splicing a gene of interest— say, one that encodes a human hormone — into a microorganism or other cell. The technique is at the heart of DNA sequencing, genetic engineering and indeed , biotechnology.

Stanford seized on the potential of the work, and did something that was quite unusual at the time: They patented the technique. But that might not have happened it if weren't for a 1974 New York Times story on Boyer and Cohen's accomplishment by TR board member Victor K. McElheny, then the Times' technology writer. Clipped by Stanford's news director, the story landed on the desk of the school's director of technology transfer, Niels Reimers. Reimers quickly called Cohen; patents must be filed within a year of the first public disclosure of an invention, and Boyer and Cohen had published their results in 1973. By the time all of the researchers and institutions involved agreed on a strategy, Reimers had only a week to file.

In 1980, Boyer and Cohen received the first of three patents. All told, the patents generated over $250 million in royalties before expiring in 1997.

In 1976, Boyer with venture capitalist Robert Swanson, founded the now-giant Genentech.

"The Birth of Biotech: Herbert Boyer and Stanley Cohen started a revolution," Association of Alumni and Alumnae of the Massachusetts Institute of Technology, Technology Review 120 (July/August 2000).

———————————————

1.2.3.   History of Agricultural Biotechnology Law, Part 2

Genetically Engineered Foods
Food and Drug Administration and the Environmental Protection Agency

1.2.3.1   History of Law and Food Regulation

The following excerpt from Jesse D. Lyon, "OPEN FORUM: Coordinated Food Systems and Accountability Mechanisms for Food Safety: A Law and Economics Approach," 53 Food Drug L.J. 729 (1998) describes the history of law governing food:

> Laws governing the production and marketing of food were recorded from the time of Moses. Moses' book of Leviticus proclaimed that "thou shalt not sow thy field with mingled seed." In addition, in the book of Deuteronomy, Moses' law required "a perfect and just weight, a perfect and just measure." The consequence of disobeying the laws of Moses was God's wrath, often exacted by the offender's enemies: "Thou shalt plant a vineyard, and shalt not gather the grapes thereof. Thine ox shall be slain before thine eyes, and thou shalt not eat thereof." Such rules are consistent with "primitive law's concept of thing responsibility, whereby vengeance was wrought upon the thing itself which caused the damage, as if it were possessed of demons." Imposing this kind of "strict" liability on the products appeased those harmed and prevented tensions from escalating without imposing a subjective finding of fault on the food producer.
>
> As early as the second century B.C., the Han Dynasty in China prohibited "the making of spurious products, and the defrauding of purchasers." This is consistent with the Confucian value of societal harmony, which could be achieved only by universal compliance with the rules of moral behavior. Even at these early stages, Chinese law saw the unsafe or unfair provision of food as an offense against society. An official named the "Supervisor of Markets" and his agents attempted to provide a central mechanism to ensure that societal harmony was not disrupted by debauchery in food-making or marketing. "Because of the enormous importance of food to the Roman Empire, a substantial portion of the Roman civil law was designed to assure a sufficient supply at reasonable prices."
>
> Where food was sold publicly, the government sometimes intervened. The Theodosian Code (A.D. 438) required bread made for pubic sale to be arranged on the steps of a building according to grades. Such rules aimed to protect against fraud, but more often "relied upon the concept of caveat emptor." In the end, this reliance was imperfect. Pliny the Elder's writings particularly evidence the common consumer's inability to detect adulterations during this era, making findings of fault based on objective

standards problematic. Comparative law and economics suggests that food safety rules and institutions originated as general concepts of moral accountability in ancient times, when the food supply chain was not fragmented and individual enterprises were not anonymous. Because exchange frequently was confined within relationships defined not by community, contract, or government, but by a pre-existing familial or parochial bond, food production and marketing norms were most efficiently left to an individual's piety. The provision of food during ancient times was regulated primarily out of prevailing notions of moral obligation. . . .

. . . . . . 2. Food Safety Mechanisms in the Medieval Period (1000 to 1500 A.D.) The food supply chain in the medieval period was composed of farmer-sellers and merchant-manufacturers. "The transformation of agriculture in the eleventh and twelfth centuries created both the opportunity and the need for the rapid expansion of the merchant class. There were large agricultural surpluses to be traded." Food manufacturing became more prevalent during the medieval period. "In the first historical stage of food manufacturing, foods were essentially handmade by farmers or artisans."

"By the Middle Ages over [two hundred] varieties of processed meats were being made commercially by European craftsmen." Because winter feeding of livestock was difficult, most non-breeding animals were slaughtered prior to the onslaught of bad weather, and their meat was salted for safe sale and consumption throughout the winter. "Spices were ground, flour was milled or baked into bread, milk and cheese became articles of commerce. Each offered more opportunity for hidden sophistication," that is food manufacturers could modify or adulterate products to their advantage in increasingly subtle ways that consumers could not detect. Food manufacturers usually were the ultimate seller of their own products. During this period, farm products and manufactured food products were bought and sold at local markets. "Expanded trade in the countryside was initially a result of the 'agricultural revolution' . . . ; indeed, the growth of agriculture was itself a precondition for the growth of the cities." "Methods were known to medieval cultivators which would have increased . . . yields . . . but these methods were simply unprofitable . . . ." Market information during the medieval period was confined to local markets. "Difficulties of communication" and "sparseness of settlement" contributed to the "local character of the economy." The local character of the economy, however, also meant that a merchant's reputation was well known, and much relied on by consumers. . . .

. . . . . . The integrity of the food supply during the medieval period was protected by community extralegal sanctions, reputational constraints, and self-adjudication. Extralegal sanctions discouraged food producers and sellers from adulteration and fraud. In 1315 in France, angry citizens "staged a mass punishment of bakers who had been found guilty of mixing their flour with animal droppings. Sixteen bakers were lashed to wheels in public squares and made to hold bits of rotten bread in outstretched hands, while they were beaten and reviled by the multitude." Additionally, "history records the incident of a butcher being paraded through the streets, his face close to a horse's tail, for selling 'measly' meat . . . [and] of a dishonest brewer who was drawn around town in the garbage cart." Manorial law regulated agricultural production, but soon "merchants constituted a self-governing community." Carrying forward the moral accountability of ancient times, "[a] social and economic morality was developed which purported to guide the souls of merchants . . . ." That morality came to be enforced by "market and fair courts" in Italy and "courts of the staple" in England and Ireland where food sellers were subject to a system of customary merchant law. Mercantile law was transaction-based and arranged to protect the commercial reputation of the merchant class and their need for speedy, informal, and equitable dispute resolution. Its principle of reciprocal rights mandated a fair exchange so that there was a procedural and substantive "equality of burdens or benefits as between the parties to the transaction." The principle of good faith also emerged as a fundamental precept of the mercantile law system. Food adulteration and fraudulent food sales violated both these principles. Because violators risked expulsion from the merchant community, the system ensured fair transactions in food and farm products among parties whose livelihood depended on their perpetually reversing roles as buyers and sellers and on their market access to the merchant community. In England, trade guilds eventually developed among businesspersons in "every important food category." They performed an even narrower regulatory function, at times even exercising "power to search all premises and to seize all unwholesome products."

. . . . Comparative law and economics thus suggests that while moral accountability remained, community accountability was added to protect the integrity of the food supply during the medieval period, when the food supply chain was only minimally fragmented and the relative anonymity of individual players was still quite low. Community accountability comports with "the old 'golden rule' of the Middle Ages -- do unto others as you would wish them to do to you." The behavior of food producers and sellers was constrained most efficiently by their reputation in the local community. . . . . That local ordinances were the most notable and effective medieval legislative attempts to regulate the food supply shows that the food system remained predominantly local, and that its players were constrained most efficiently by accountability to their market community.

C. The Evolution of Traditional Food Safety Mechanisms

The evolution of traditional rules and institutions governing the integrity of the food supply corresponded to increased fragmentation and anonymity as food systems matured. Moral accountability and community accountability remained, but were no longer sufficient. Food system rules and institutions during the development of commerce relied on notions of contractual accountability. As the food supply became widely recognized in the legislative period as a public good, strict societal accountability was added to govern its integrity.

1. Food System Rules and Institutions in Development of Commerce (1500-1800 A.D.)

The sixteenth through eighteenth centuries were marked by the development of commerce and the "era of colonial expansion." Some agricultural historians characterize the first half of this period as a rural economic depression. During this time, food production increasingly separated producers from sellers. During the development of commerce, "urbanization and improved transportation increased the effective demand for even highly perishable foods and beverages." "Colonial America [initially] was an agrarian economy. People consumed the food . . . they produced at home. Even those who lived in small towns kept livestock and maintained their own gardens. [But as] urban centers grew, local food markets were established to serve them." European populations also became increasingly urbanized, in part because of cheaper food supplies brought on by free trade.

. . . . The sixteenth century marked the development of notions of natural law, with its focus on law common to all mankind, essential for human coexistence, and found by reason, not by divine help or the influence of special interests. Any activities of lobbying groups to protect food supply integrity (a noted factor later driving the development of product safety and liability standards) would not result in legislative preference being given to producer or consumer interests. Locke's theories of economic liberalism followed in the seventeenth century; under this view, freedom of contract was revered. Early English common law recognized a civil cause of action for damages for the sale of adulterated food. Civil remedies became prevalent in the sixteenth century when food system rules for the development of commerce became marked by notions of product liability and privity. The concept of product liability "originated in English common law, in which the brewer, butcher, cook, or other person was held responsible for tainted or adulterated drink or food . . . Liability of [such food manufacturers] was limited to the person to whom he or she directly sold a product." Under doctrines of privity of contract, "a contract can generate rights and obligations only for the parties to it." Thus, products liability often depended on a breach of some (often fictional) contractual duty, although liability generally was limited to cases where the manufacturer effectively was held negligent. . . .

Broad, public laws were of little use given the lack of analytical tools to detect subtle adulterations. Nonetheless, regulators strove for effective enforcement. In the mid-1600s, the English Parliament enacted statutes to regulate butter quality. "In order to trace violations [of those statutes], every butter packer was required to brand the container with his full surname and the first initial of his Christian name." The integrity of imported food was more easily protected, for port authorities had incentives to prevent "frauds in the revenue of excise."

. . . . . Centralized government administration had not yet sufficiently evolved to enforce legislated mechanisms to protect the food supply. Rather, societal conviction in the freedom of contract meant that contracts were the favored means for defining relationships and corresponding legal rights and obligations, and food product liability remedies evolved as a corollary to these contractual relationships.

2. Food Safety Mechanisms in the Legislative Period (1800 A.D. to Present)

In the legislative period, the food supply chain became characterized by task specialization and technological efficiencies. "In the agrarian economies of Europe and America, increases in food supplies were obtained in part by bringing marginal lands into cultivation. Production increased, but productivity diminished. Farmers worked harder to extract a smaller crop from stubborn fields of poor productivity. Some people responded to these problems by introducing new methods of farm management. . . . In the process, farming tended to become more intensive. In the early [nineteenth] century there was nearly [five] times as much investment in land improvements as in the middle ages."

"The nineteenth century [also] saw the widespread adoption of machine technologies; craftsmen were replaced by factories using motive power to produce more uniform foods . . . [Subsequent development] brought automation to food manufacturing, but with application to basically physiochemical processes." Most methods of food processing, including "canning, freezing, and chemical preservation (except salting) have all been invented since 1800." Mechanical refrigeration and freezing also were products of nineteenth century ingenuity. "The factory system . . . encouraged increasing specialization within the food industries" and resulted in the "disintegration of food manufacturing functions. As handicrafts [were] replaced by mass production with its great markets and transportation facilities, the close relationship between the producer and consumer of a product [was] altered." During the legislative period, exchange of food products along the supply chain began to take place in multiple, atomistic markets. As a consequence, market information was often incomplete and complicated, resulting in high information search costs. Consumers were wealthier and more highly educated, but now faced "bewildering problems in evaluating products . . . [given] differences of technology, function, price, and promotion on the basis of . . . information that [was] occasionally misleading, often irrelevant, and always imperfect. Manufacturing processes, frequently valuable secrets, are ordinarily either inaccessible to or beyond the . . . general public. The consumer no longer has means or skill enough to investigate for himself the soundness of a product, even when it is not contained in a sealed package." Cost became the primary emphasis of exchange during the legislative period. "Factory production usually lowered costs by the application of mass production techniques on ever larger scales." Quality was correspondingly de-emphasized. The earliest statement of English law concerning the criminal status of food adulteration appeared in the mid-1600s. It was not until the legislative period, however, that food markets became intensely regulated, and food system rules were enforced by sanctions beyond the community level. The public clamored against food adulteration. Food regulation in the modern era was made possible by the introduction of the microscope into food analysis in the 1850's, providing unprecedented detection of germs in adulterated food. The nineteenth century saw the first enactment of general nationwide statutes prohibiting food adulteration, directing penalties for violations, and establishing administrative responsibility for enforcement. "France passed a general food law rather early -- 1851. In 1855, it was amended to include beverages."

The English Parliament enacted its first general food laws in 1860, and the German Empire followed suit in 1879. The United States enacted the comprehensive Pure Food and Drugs Act in 1906. President Woodrow Wilson in 1913 acknowledged that "the first duty of law is to keep sound the society it serves. Sanitary laws [and] pure food laws. . . are intimate parts of the very business of justice and legal efficiency." In 1959, the New York state court deciding Linn v. Radio Center Delicatessen, held that it was "against natural justice and good morals to permit an individual or corporation to manufacture food containing dangerous foreign substances and escape the consequences of his acts . . . ." Linn evidenced that the unsafe provision of basic human needs in the legislative period was viewed as an offense against society, requiring criminal punishment where civil remedies were insufficient to protect the public. Accordingly, food safety regulation is highly representative of the aspects of law protecting the public good. "Under customary law [such as the medieval period's merchant law systems], offenses are treated as torts (private wrongs or injuries) rather than crimes (offenses against the state or the 'society')." Nineteenth-century lawmakers, however, decided that the provision of foods that threaten the integrity of our food supply should be treated as a crime against society. This development occurred after there was a centralized system capable of enforcing national food laws. Once general standards for food production and handling were in place, the government agencies enforcing them could not exclude select individuals from the protection that those rules afforded. All citizens benefitted from food manufacturers' incentive to provide safe food for consumption, while developing general standards essentially are sunk costs. Thus, the marginal costs of food regulation are negligible with increases in food production and consumption.

2.1.3   Defining biotechnologies and synthetic biology

Defining Biotechnology

Biotechnology's simplest definition is the application of biology to human needs. More specifically, biotechnology is a set of technologies that use biological molecules and cells to make products, solve problems, and do research, based upon an under- standing of cellular and molecular structure and processes.

These technologies include:

(1) monoclonal antibody technology, which is the use of cells and enzymes to make and break down products; (2) cell culture technology, which comprises the techniques used to grow cells in laboratory containers or bioreactors; (3) genetic engineering technology, which involves changing an organism's genetic makeup with molecular techniques (this would include CRISPR-CAS9 next generation tools); (4) biosensor technology, which is the use of biological molecules and transducers for detection and quantification; (5) antisense technology, which is the use of the mechanism of blocking gene expression with oligonucleotides; (6) DNA chip technology, which is the use of DNA probes to detect mutations and monitor gene expression; (7) tissue engi- neering, which comprises the techniques used in the growing of semisynthetic tissues and organs; (8) bioprocessing technology, which consist of techniques using cells and enzymes to make and break down products; and (9) bioinformatics, which is the use of computational tools to organize, access, and study information about biology.

2.1.1.1 Monoclonal Antibody Technology

Monoclonal antibody (MCAb) technology uses cells of the immune system that make proteins called antibodies. The immune system is composed of a number of cell types that work together to locate and destroy substances that invade the body. One type of immune system cell, the B lymphocyte, responds to invaders by producing anti- bodies that bind to the foreign substance with extraordinary specificity. The technology to harness the ability of B lymphocytes to make these very specific antibodies is being developed.

The substances that an MCAb detects, quantifies, and localizes are remarkably varied and are limited only by the substance's ability to trigger the production of antibodies. Home pregnancy kits use an MCAb that binds to a hormone produced in the placenta. Many of these antibodies are currently being used to diagnose a number of infectious diseases such as strep throat and gonorrhea. Because cancer cells differ biochemically from normal cells, we can make monoclonal antibodies that detect cancers by binding selectively to tumor cells. In addition to diagnosing diseases in humans, such antibodies are being used to detect plant and animal diseases, food contaminants, and environ- mental pollutants .

This technology has the potential to be used with a radioisotope or toxin tag to a cancerous tumor antibody, and then these tumor-killing agents are delivered directly to the target cells, while bypassing the healthy cells. Monoclonal antibodies can also be used to treat autoimmune diseases, such as multiple sclerosis and lupus, and to prevent complications following heart bypass surgery.

2.1.1.2 Cell Culture Technology

This technology involves the growing of cells in appropriate nutrients in laboratory containers or in large bioreactors in manufacturing facilities.

Plant cell culture technology is based upon the potential of one differentiated cell to generate an entire multicellular plant. This is called the cell's totipotency, or the poten- tial to generate an entire organism.

Animal cell culture technology, using, for example, an insect cell culture, could iso- late viruses that infect insects and then might be grown and used as an insect control agent to protect the treated plant or animal. Mammalian cell culture technology is also being used in livestock breeding. Large numbers of bovine zygotes from genetically su- perior bulls and cows can be produced and cultured before being implanted into surro- gate cows. In its medical application, animal cell culture is used to study such areas as the safety and efficacy of pharmaceutical compounds, the molecular mechanism of viral infection and replication, the toxicity of compounds and basic cell biochemistry.

Embryonic stem cell culture has been recently developed as having major potential medical benefits. Embryonic stem cells in their development eventually grow into a dif- ferentiated cell. However, early in the development they have the potential to differenti- ate into several different kinds of cells. This complete developmental plasticity sets them apart from other stem cells and opens the possibility of using them therapeutically. For example, if we develop the capability to control the differentiation of human embryonic stem cells, we may be able to produce replacement cells to treat diabetes, Parkinson's disease, and many other diseases.

2.1.1.3 Genetic Engineering Technology

Genetic engineering is often referred to as recombinant DNA (rDNA) technology and is carried out by joining or recombining genetic material from two different sources. DNA recombines naturally during the crossing over of chromosomes that oc- curs in gamete formation, during egg fertilization, and when bacteria exchange genetic material through conjugation, transformation, and transduction . The result of the re- combination of DNA is increased genetic variation.

The early domestication of animals through selective breeding is an approach to al- tering the genetic makeup of an organism to adapt to human needs. As a result of this genetic selection, the animals were dramatically changed over time.

The recombination of DNA refers to the specific recombination of DNA through the use of restriction enzymes designed to cut and join DNA in predictable ways at the mol- ecular level. To accomplish this process, bacteria and viruses are used to transport the

DNA segments. The use of this technology allows the transfer of genetic material across species, something which was not possible through selective breeding.

2.1.1.4 Biosensor Technology

A biosensor is a detecting device composed of a biological substance linked to a transducer. The biological substance might be a microbe, a single cell from a multicellu- lar animal, or an enzyme or an antibody . Biosensors can detect substances at extremely low concentrations .

Biosensors generate digital electronic signals by exploiting the specificity of biologi- cal molecules. When the substance we want to measure collides with the biological de- tector, the transducer produces a tiny electrical current. This electrical signal is propor- tional to the concentration of the substance.

These biosensors are being developed to measure nutritional value, safety of food, analyses of blood gases, electrolyte concentrations, and blood-clotting capability in emergency rooms. Monitoring industrial processes and locating and measuring pollu- tants will also utilize biosensors. For example, by coupling a glucose biosensor to an in- sulin infusion pump, the correct blood concentration of glucose could be maintained at all times in those with diabetes. Currently under development are biosensor chips that combine the sensor element with an arithmetic analysis and a wireless transmitter so that a wide range of biological systems can be remotely monitored. In many cases these chips can be permanently implanted in the human body and powered for indefinite pe- riods by the voltage normally present in the body.

2.1.1.5 Antisense Technology

Blocking or decreasing the production of certain proteins is the specific process of antisense technology. Blocking is achieved by using small nucleic acids (oligonucleotides) that prevent translation of the information encoded in DNA into a protein.

The potential applicability of this technology includes circumstances where blocking a gene would be beneficial. For example, antisense technology may be used to slow food spoilage, control viral diseases, inhibit the inflammatory response, and treat asthma, cancers, and thalassemia, a hereditary anemia.

Metabolic engineering is another use for antisense technology. Many compounds in nature that have commercial application are not proteins; for example, most com- pounds produced by plants to deter insect feeding could be useful as crop protectants but are not proteins. By using antisense technology to block the production of enzymes in certain pathways, the plant's metabolism is altered to favor the production of these compounds.

2.1.1.6 DNA Chip Technology

DNA chip technology is a hybrid of semiconductor technology and molecular biol- ogy technology. This technology can perform genetic analysis of tens of thousands of genes through a single "microchip." The manufacturing processes of microchips and DNA chips are similar in principle, but instead of shining light through a series of masks to etch circuits into silicon, automated DNA chip makers use a series of masks to create a sequence of DNA probes on a glass slide.

The DNA is removed from cells, tagged with fluorescent markers, and placed on the chip. Hybridized sequences attach to the probes, and unmatched bits of DNA are then washed away. Using a laser reader, computer, and high-powered microscopes, scientists can analyze thousands of sequences at a time and determine where the tagged DNA finds a match with a chip-mounted DNA probe.

This DNA chip technology is being used to detect mutations in disease-causing genes, to monitor gene expression in yeast and cancer cell lines, diagnose infectious dis- eases, and tell us whether a pathogen is resistant to certain drugs. DNA chips are con- tinuing to develop for crop biotechnology, to improve screening for microbes used in bioremediation, and to hasten drug discovery. DNA chip technology is one of the scientific research priorities in the development of biodefense technologies and has been used experimentally to detect the presence of pathogens in the ambient air through existing air monitoring stations in major cities.

2.1.1.7 Tissue Engineering

Tissue engineering combines the technologies of cell biology with those of materials science to create semisynthetic tissues in the laboratory. These tissues are made up of living cells held together with biodegradable scaffolding material, usually collagen.

One of the first products was the two-layer skin, made by infiltrating a collagen gel with fibroblasts, allowing them to grow, multiply, and become the dermis, then by adding a layer of deratinocytes to serve as the epidermis. In other tissue engineering methods, the scaffolding, made of a synthetic polymer, is shaped and then placed in the body where new tissue is needed. Adjacent cells stimulated by the appropriate growth factors invade the scaffolding, which is eventually degraded and absorbed.

The simple tissues of cartilage and skin were the first to be engineered, successfully. The goal is to create more complex organs made up of a number of tissue types to serve as replacement organs.

2.1.1.8 Bioprocessing Technology

Bioprocessing technology uses living cells or components of living cells to synthesize products, to break down substances, and to release energy. These living cells are typi- cally one-celled organisms, such as bacteria or yeasts or mammalian cells; and the cellu- lar components most often used are enzymes, which are proteins.

Enzymes catalyze all cellular biochemical reactions, which create energy in the break- ing down of molecules and the creation of chemical building blocks to assemble new molecules.

Fermentation and mammalian cell culture are two types of bioprocessing technolo- gies that rely on cellular enzymes. The oldest bioprocessing technology is microbial fer- mentation. In the process of metabolizing glucose in fruits, microbes synthesize by-products which are useful: carbon dioxide for leavening bread, ethanol for brewing wine and beer, lactic acid for making yogurt, and acetic acid (vinegar) for pickling foods. Microbial fermentation is used to synthesize antibiotics, amino acids, hormones, vitamins, industrial solvents, pesticides, food processing aids, pigments, enzymes, en- zyme inhibitors, and pharmaceuticals.

Biodegradation, bioremediation, and phytoremediation are biotechnological processes that are utilized for useful processes. Biodegradation can be useful by utilizing microorganisms to dissolve oil from oil spills or toxic waste. Bioremediation is the result of such cleanups of the environment. Phytoremediation is the use of plants to remove toxic sub- stances and contaminants from the environment through the utilization of plant-specific enzymes.

Many advances in manufacturing are also expected. In manufacturing, for example, use of enzymes can lead to chemical products produced without the high temperatures and pressure characteristics of current chemical technology and with enormous savings in energy.

2.1.1.9 Bioinformatics

Computer technology manages the extraordinary volume of information of gene se-quences, protein structure, carbohydrate structure, and genetic maps for many species.

Methods for organization and utilization of this information involve computational tools, such as algorithms, graphics, artificial intelligence, statistical software, simulation, and database management technologies to map and compare genomes, structures, and functions. It is essential to remember that data do not become knowledge until the data are analyzed.

Bioinformatics for Lawyers

This is a field which is of particular interest to both lawyers and scientists. Although it is primarily technical in identifying catalogs of DNA information in computer searchers among scientists, it is also a useful data base which can be utilized in legal research.

At Argonne National Laboratory, the Computational Biology Group devel- oped WIT3, an interactive database that stores genomics and metabolic infor- mation and provides tools for users to access the data and construct their own models of the sequences of [bases] As, Cs, Gs and Ts. The researchers origi- nally developed a computer program called WIT, or What Is There, to store and compare genomics information on the World Wide Web. The new WIT3 is automated, speeding the process of retrieving data and constructing models. WIT3 is available to researchers on the World Wide Web. The site has about 20,000 users and receives between 3,000 and 5,000 visits a day. The success of Argonne's structural genomics program depends on the technological advances of synchrotron facilities such as the APS [Advanced Proton Source], molecular biology and crystallography methods, robotics, and computer hardware and software. But the process begins with two time-consuming, vital tasks in a more traditional laboratory.

First biologists clone a protein by snipping pieces out of its genome and placing them in "expression bacteria;' which make many protein copies. Ar- gonne researchers created a modern production line using robots to automate this time-consuming cloning task. The Robotic Molecular Biology Facility can produce 400 to 800 protein clones each week; manual methods produce only 20 to 40. Then biologists coax these purified proteins to form crystals for X-ray crystallography in the Structural Biology Center [SBC].

Argonne researchers continue to refine the structural genomics process to make it even faster. For example, the robotic lab plans to quadruple production in 2001 by increasing from 96 to 384 the number of miniature test-tube- like wells the robot can handle at a time. Also, the SBC will take advantage of the APS's brighter X-rays using new larger, faster X-ray detectors that provide information in greater detail. In the future Argonne maybe able to offer a structural genomics assembly line to many users and researchers can send their crystals to be placed in the beamline using robots and have the data re- motely collected and processed in real time.

Scientific Excellence, FRONTIERS (U.S. Dep't of Energy, Argone Nat'l Lab.) 2001 at 4-5.

These biotechnology descriptions are summarized from HELEN KREUZER, PH.D. AND ADRIANNE MASSEY, PH.D., RECOMBINANT DNA AND BIOTECHNOLOGY: A GUIDE FOR TEACHERS, (2d ed. 2001).

2.1.1.10   Synthetic biology.

The Federal Register establishing the screening protocol for synthetic biology describes it as follows:

> Synthetic biology, the developing interdisciplinary field that focuses on both the design and fabrication of novel biological components and systems as well as the re-design and fabrication of existing biological systems, is poised to become the next significant transforming technology for the life sciences and beyond. Synthetic biology is not constrained by the requirement of using existing genetic material. Thus, technologies that permit the directed synthesis of polynucleotides have great potential to be used to generate organisms, both currently existing and novel, including pathogens that could threaten public health, agriculture, plants, animals, the environment, or material. [74 Fed. Reg. 62319 (Nov. 27, 2009)]

2.2.1   The Scientific Method Compared to Legal Methods

2.1.1.1 Introduction to the scientific method and biotechnology

The scientific method is the development of scientific principles based upon scientific observational evidence that is reliable and within a statistically confident range of certainty.

Basic biotechnology research involves the research in the relevant basic sciences — physics, chemistry, biochemistry, biology and other interdisciplinary areas — to discover principles of science which have application in biotechnology processes. Research that is presented in the courtroom must survive the scrutiny of admissibility and reliability based upon the proper application of the scientific method. Conclusions of science must be based upon plausible and reliable scientific evidence gathered using an acceptable scientific process. The use of scientific evidence is discussed in Chapter Eight.

Biotechnology, involves the application of these principles and the solving of problems for human needs. Biotechnology requires the skill and experience of the expert and the application of scientific principles which are generally accepted in the relevant fields.

2.2.1.2 Differences between law and science and technology

Interdisciplinarity and finding ways to merge and infuse disciplines to address complex problems remains an important challenge. However, there are still important differences that must be recognized between the fields that make them what they are.

The American Bar Association invited the former President's Science Advisor and National Medal of Science awardee, the Honorable D. Allan Bromley to deliver the keynote address to the annual meeting in 1998. The address focuses on some of the differences between the fields of science and the study and practice of law.

Keynote Address, 1998 Annual Meeting of the American Bar Association
[excerpt]
D. Allan Bromley
Sterling Professor of the Sciences and Dean of Engineering
Yale University[2]

Prepared for delivery at the 1998 Annual Meeting of the American Bar Association, Toronto, Canada, August 2, 1998.

INTRODUCTION

Science and the law were among the earliest and the most fundamental foundations on which our nation was established. Thomas Jefferson was a lawyer and a self-trained scientist, while Benjamin Franklin was a scientist and a self-trained lawyer; both were ranked among the leading scientists of their age and both clearly had an enormous impact on the development of law in the United States. Their science, of course, was highly applied and would today have been called technology—what both then and now constitutes the engine of the burgeoning economy that in the early days fostered the growth and stability of the young nation.

We sometimes forget that in the early days in North America, there were parallel Spanish, French, and English colonies. Only the latter prospered more or less from the beginning, and historians credit this to the fact that the English colonies, from their very founding, had a particular penchant for resolving political controversies and achieving social order through legal means and legal structures. This was not the case in the Spanish and the French colonies.

As the nation grew and prospered, science and law went their separate ways, developing unique characteristics and institutions, but both solidly rooted in European traditions. There are fundamental differences, however, but the time available to us this afternoon I can only caricature a few of them....In my own area of physics and the physical sciences, for example, we have the arrogance to believe that with less than 20 natural laws, and the tools of mathematics, we can aspire to eventually understand the entire natural

---

[2] Reproduced with permission from the author (2001).

universe and its evolution. I have no idea how many laws the average lawyer deals with on a normal basis, but most certainly that number is vastly greater than 20. It is important, however, to recognize that scientists and lawyers mean quite different things when they use the word law. To a lawyer, law means rules established by properly constituted social authority whereas to a scientist, as I shall discuss presently, a law is a statement, normally expressed in mathematical language, that is distilled from a great many observations of how nature functions and that is assumed to be both permanent and universal.

Mathematics is, in many ways, the universal and international language of science, and of particular importance for our discussion today are the subfields of statistics and probability. This follows because a great many scientific measurements and observations are necessarily, to some degree, uncertain. Scientists generally use both statistics and probability theory and are particularly interested in a quantitative estimate of the probability that a particular experimental finding did not occur merely by chance. Mathematics also allows us to see the essential simplicity and, indeed, beauty in what would otherwise appear capricious or complex, for example, that the shape of the arms of a spiral glazy, the shape of Cape Cod, and the shape of the whirlpool that develops in your bathtub—when you have occasion to observe it—are all governed by the same natural law.

I recognize that all too many legal viscera tighten perceptibly even at the mention of the words "physics" or "mathematics", and this is unfortunate; but you should not forget that mathematicians and scientists return the reaction when faced with any sort of legal action.

In the early days, it might have been possible for science and the law to remain in splendid isolation, but in today's increasingly technological society, science, technology, and the law are inexorably drawn together, and the time has surely come when we need to better understand one another and how we work.

THE SCIENTIFIC METHOD

As I have mentioned, and as all of you are well aware, there are fundamental differences. In law, by definition—and I simplify almost to the point of caricature—there is always an answer, and at a time certain—at the end of the court action; in science, there may well never be an answer, and certainly no answer within any given time frame. And while both science and law seek to arrive at conclusions based on rational reasoning from evidence, the two disciplines define evidence in quite different ways. It is always somewhat jarring to scientists that lawyers consider evidence to be the words that a witness (perhaps a scientific expert) says under oath. A scientist would not consider mere words as constituting evidence, no matter how prestigious and respected was the speaker. Instead, the scientist defines evidence as the observational data on which the expert draws a conclusion.

In, again, simplistic terms, the goal of science is truth, and of law, justice, but the approach to fact-finding in the two fields is very different, indeed. In addressing a question scientists make observations or measurements, and on that basis develop an hypothesis that explains what they observe; unless they can use their mathematical toolkits to derive testable predictions from the hypothesis, however, it is worthless. To the extent that such predictions continue to be confirmed by new observations and measurements, the hypothesis is refined and eventually merits the title of "theory". The worst thing that can happen to a valid theory is that it finally fails to reproduce some carefully established experimental fact, and must be further refined. It is, however, not discarded. It is simply modified so that it can be considered as a special case of a more general and all-encompassing theory that explains not only the new results, but also all of the old. This, for example, is what happened when Newton's dynamics were recognized as a very special case of Einstein's theory of general relativity. Scientists now recognize that Newtonian dynamics are entirely adequate for all situations involving low velocities but when the velocities in the problem become comparable to that of light—as is the case when dealing with elementary particles and large, powerful accelerators— Newtonian dynamics can no longer explain what is observed and Einstein's general theory of relativity is required. A theory that cannot, in principle, be tested until one of its predictions is found to be false is, in fact, not even considered as part of science.

There are, of course other ways of thinking that also attempt to get at the truth, e.g., religion, art, intuition, and even law. But scientific knowledge differs from ordinary day-to-day knowledge, in that science seeks not only to explain how events take place, but also why they take place, and then attempts to organize that knowledge systematically.

Scientific knowledge is cumulative and progressive, and builds continuously on past understanding. As Isaac Newton pointed out, "the fact that I can see farther than others simply reflects the fact that I stand on the shoulders of giants."

Most people are aware of science only through its applications—what we would loosely refer to as the applications of technology; these have had an enormous impact on our entire society, on the quality of our lives, and indeed their duration. In 1955 the average life expectancy of Americans was 58 years, and today it is 82 years. Much of that extension can be directly credited to new scientific understanding and new technologies that allow us to respond constructively to the new understanding. Many of today's medical procedures would have been considered miraculous even a decade ago, and developments in electronics have brought about a revolution in computation and in communication that has literally shrunk our world into a global village.

What I have described is what is generally referred to as the scientific method, but it bears emphasis that there is no single scientific method that adequately describes the work of all scientists. For example, some scientists do controlled experiments; others, such as astronomers are generally unable to control the phenomena that they study, and rely instead on rigorous observations to test their ideas. For all scientists, however, experimental or observational information must be coupled with explanation—with answers to the question "Why?." As the Nobel Laureate François Jacob once wrote, science is an "endless dialogue between imagination and experiment."

Although science strives for orderly investigations, I would be far from candid were I not to admit that the scientific enterprise often does not proceed in any neat or tidy fashion. Many lines of investigation turn out to be blind alleys, and many hypotheses must be abandoned. Perhaps even more important, we have often implemented technologies as soon as they became available without any adequate understanding of what some of the unwanted side-effects might be; as a specific example, our global environment has been the victim of many of these premature technological implementations.

Scientists and engineers do make errors, and sometimes are entirely wrong. Sometimes even the best scientists fail to follow proper procedures, and some scientists, like all humans are, to put it bluntly, sloppy at times. Nevertheless, if a scientific idea is considered to be an important one, future researchers will usually find any errors that may be in it and will rectify them. This, indeed, is why the British philosopher, John Ziman, insists that, "Knowledge that is not public knowledge, accessible to testing by anyone who might so wish—in any way, and with any type of measurement or technology that might be available—is not, in fact, science, but rather priestly lore."

THE JUDICIAL METHOD

In contrast, a judicial inquiry is always bounded in time, because closure is needed. Moreover there is a striking difference in the way the questions are selected; the Article III Courts (the federal court system for my purposes) will hear only an "actual case or controversy", whereas in science any scientific question is open to research. The judicial inquiry stops when all the evidence has been presented and the conclusion must be based on that evidence, even if from a scientific point of view, the evidence is far from complete or has been presented in a light most favorable to the proponent...

In an increasingly technological and litigious society, it is becoming ever more the case that the facts presented to the court have large elements of science and of technology. How are the judges and the lawyers to decide on the validity and reliability of what is being claimed, and whether it should be admitted as evidence, given that very few of them have any formal training or experience in either science or technology?

Before even attempting to discuss possible responses to this question, let me mention a few examples of legal situations where the science was either ignored or misused.

THE MISUSE AND DISUSE OF SCIENCE

A famous case discussed by Ayala and Black, is the 1944 Charlie Chaplin paternity one where the court ruled that Chaplin was indeed the father of a girl whose blood type made his parentage totally impossible. Presumably this judgment was made on the ground that despite the scientific impossibility, the judge had decided that the girl would have a better life with Chaplin as her father, than with someone with much less deep pockets. This was a case where the definitive scientific evidence was simply ignored.

There has been much litigation regarding the alleged cancer-producing effects of low-frequency electromagnetic radiation from power lines, for example—so called EMF effects. It has repeatedly been concluded, however, by the National Academy of Sciences, and by other senior scientific bodies, on the basis of all available evidence that not only is there no evidence for such effects, but also no known aspects of either physics or of biology that could produce such effects. Perhaps the most compelling common-sense argument is that the use of electricity in the U.S. has increased by a factor of about 30 since 1950, while the incidence of all cancers (except those specifically linked to smoking) and most specifically, leukemia in children (the cancer most frequently attributed to EMF), have decreased systematically over the same period. There is no evidence, to the best of any scientific judgment, that any power line or electrical apparatus has ever caused a human cancer.

Nevertheless, in 1993, New York State's highest court held that a claimant could seek damages for a drop in property value caused by public fear of a right-of-way for a high voltage power line. The claimant was not required to prove that there were medically or scientifically reasonable grounds for the phobia concerning the effects of electromagnetic fields. The court felt that the economic question of the loss in market value could be resolved without being, "magnified and escalated by a whole new battery of electromagnetic power engineers, scientists, or medical experts." Phobia, here, is the operative word, and the conclusion is simply that if it is sufficiently widespread, then the fact that it has been shown scientifically to be baseless is irrelevant. In the same year, 1993, when I left the White House, we as a nation had already spent over $32 billion dollars responding to this EMF phobia and it is still alive and well.

Sometimes the fault is not with the court, but rather with the Congress that passed the law in the first place. The Delaney Clause of the Federal Food, Drug, and Cosmetic Act is a case in point. It requires that any substance that has been shown to be carcinogenic in animals must be removed from the market place. Pyrimidone is an organic chemical that has been shown to be mildly carcinogenic in such animal test, but since it had never been detected in food-stuff, there had been no problem. One morning in 1992, however, I received a frantic phone call from Bill Reilly, then the Administrator of the U.S. Environmental Protection Agency. Scientists in the chemistry department at Columbia University had just discovered how to detect pyrimidone at concentrations one thousand times lower than had ever been possible before, and Reilly's problem was that every bottle of red wine contained pryrimidone at this new, lower concentration. His question was, "What the hell do I do now?", since the law now required that all such wine be removed from the marketplace—despite the fact that the pyrimidone had been present since pre-history in all red wine without any harm to humans. Fortunately, I was able, working with the FDA, to get an effective waiver of the Delaney clause in this particular case, but it is an example of laws written with the best of intention, but which fail to recognize that science and technology move on.

Sometimes, too, the court can be more impressed by the scientific messenger—the expert witness—than by the scientific message. In the case of *Wells v. Ortho Pharmaceutical Corporation*, it was alleged that an Ortho spermicide had resulted in severe birth defects in a baby girl. In his award of some $5 million dollars to the mother and daughter, the judge stated openly that his ruling was based largely on this opinion of the opposing scientific experts rather than on any of the scientific evidence itself. With respect to one of the scientific experts testifying on behalf of the plaintiff, the judge said:

"His opinion at trial was the same as the opinion that he previously had offered in his deposition...his detailed explanation of how he had ruled out other possible cause demonstrated that his opinion was the product of a careful, methodical reasoning process and not mere speculation. His demeanor as a witness was excellent; he answered all questions fairly and openly in a balanced manner, translating technical terms and findings in a common, understandable language, and he gave no hint of bias or prejudice."

In contrast, with respect to one of Ortho's major scientific witnesses, the judge said: "His criticisms of plaintiff's attorneys and of expert witnesses who testify for plaintiffs in malformation lawsuits, as well as the absolute terms in which he expressed his conclusions, severely damaged his credibility."

So much for the scientific evidence itself! The judge could have asked how extensive had been the testing of the spermicide in question; how many peer reviewed investigations had found it to have teratogenic (birth defect causing) effects and how many had found none. He could have asked whether this spermicide was a close relative to any other chemicals proved to be teratogenic in humans, and the list goes on...

––––––––––––

The differences between the fields of science and law can be formally examined from the perspective of the theories of logic and reasoning that each uses. The approach to problem solving gave rise to the reasoning methods used, by the nature of the inquiry as well as the required end result. The forms of reasoning and logic that we will discuss in relation to law and science are: inductive reasoning, deductive reasoning and abductive reasoning.

Inductive reasoning is a form of reasoning that makes generalizations based on particular instances. For example, if you have a finite sample size of 1 to n, and for case 1 you find that is red, and for case 2 you find it is red, then n will be red. So the logical conclusion is that all cases are red. This is an example of going from the particular cases to a generalization.

Another form of inductive reasoning goes from the general to the particular. For example, most humans have Blood Type O, and Joe is a human; so, therefore Joe has Blood Type O. There are many other forms of inductive reasoning but not all of them are useful in science.

Deductive reasoning is a form of logic that makes particular conclusions based on generalizations. The opposite of inductive reasoning. This kind of reasoning is what you may recognize as the Sherlock Holmes detective work. For example, in the recent re-interpretation of the Sherlock Holmes classic character by BBC, Sherlock, he makes the observation that the victim had to be murdered and it was not suicide because he was shot on the right side of his head, yet Sherlock Holmes identifies a list of clues that he is left-handed—plugs in the wall on the left side, coffee cup sitting on the table with the handle turned to the left, bread buttered by someone holding a knife in his left hand -- and could not have shot himself in the right side of his head. This is taking a number of particular incidents and all together they lead to a conclusion about a person or an event.

Abductive reasoning is a form of logic that begins with an incomplete set of observations and makes the most likely explanation based on the composite of the observations. For example, abductive reasoning is used to develop a diagnosis from a set of a patient's symptoms. A judge or jurors would also use this form of logic to reach a decision about the guilt or innocence of a defendant based on the evidence before them. The use of circumstantial evidence to convict a defendant of murder is possible using this form of reasoning.

One of the most high profile cases in America and certainly one of the most expensive investigations by the FBI in U.S. history was the Amerithrax case was highly controversial primarily because of this difference in reasoning methods between law and science.

The Amerithrax investigation spanned almost a decade from 2001-2008. In 2008, Bruce Ivins, an army biodefense researcher, was the sole suspect. Right before he was to be arrested, he committed suicide leaving doubt about his guilt, but also scrutiny of the evidence, none of which constituted the "smoking gun" or the defining bit of evidence that would make Ivins the certain perpetrator suspect.

The evidence against Ivins included that he had the knowledge to make the weapons grade anthrax and he had checked out equipment that could be used for that purpose in his laboratory during the few weeks in September before the anthrax attacks. In addition, he worked overtime late in the laboratory during those two weeks – the only time he had worked overtime. Further, he had a vindictive obsession with a sorority which had its headquarters within a block from where the anthrax letters were mailed in New Jersey. Ivins had made long drives there, before the mailings and had made other long drives presumably to mail the letters there. He was also said to have provided false samples of anthrax to the FBI to throw them off and he also suggested they investigate a colleague. One of the return addresses on one of the anthrax-laced envelopes was to a school with the same name as where the Ivins family had provided money and support for a legal battle against the school for not respecting the parents control over their children. But the most decisive bit of evidence was the major investment in analyzing the genome of the anthrax that was used in the attacks. The anthrax could be traced back to a flask which was under the custodial care of Bruce Ivins, known as RMR-1029. But even this was a problem because hundreds of people had access to the anthrax in RMR-1029. None of these bits of evidence was the conclusive "smoking gun" that the FBI hoped to find, but based on the totality of the evidence they were prepared to arrest him and believed they would get a conviction for murder based on this evidence. The case was based completely on circumstantial evidence which would lead to the conclusion that Bruce Ivins was the perpetrator if you used abductive logic.

However, as discussed above, scientists use inductive logic and the proof that is required to make a conclusion must be consistent and linked to every fact. This caused the scientific community to become quite verbal about the conclusion that it was Bruce Ivins and challenge the evidence and even the science that was used to come to that conclusion. This led to the FBI asking the National Academies (formerly the National Academy of Science) to examine the science used in the case and evaluate whether it was reliable or not. The panel took almost two years examining 9600 pages of information from the FBI and raised many questions about the scientific technique but mainly about the conclusion that this all led to Bruce Ivins as the perpetrator.

Another factor that makes these choices of logic for each of these fields of study the necessary ones is the constraint of time. In a legal decision, a trial has a specific amount of time. In fact, the "speedy trial" provision of the Constitution requires some vigilance about how long someone must remain a suspect before resolving the case. A case or an opinion must be decided or reached based on the evidence that is available at the time.

Science discoveries or experiments do not have deadlines in the sense that an answer must be reached. The scientific method requires enough evidence to reach statistically significant confidence levels for certainty for as long as that might take and only then, can a conclusion be made.

Certainty is another factor that has different meanings in law and science. For science, a confidence level of 99% for a statistically significant finding is essential to making a conclusion. Something less may be acceptable in life sciences (95%) and social sciences (90%) where the test subjects are much fewer than the data available in chemistry and physics. (More data is more likely to provide statistically significant results.)

There are some equivalent expressions for levels of certainty in law as they would be interpreted in science. For example, "beyond a reasonable doubt" is a standard for a criminal conviction, which might be translated to a 99% certainty. The standard in many tort cases is "more likely than not" which might be translated to a 51% certainty. The standard for obtaining a warrant, probable cause, may be anywhere above zero, but not zero, in terms of certainty.

The Methods of Law and Science

The "scientific method" has a very structured approach that originated with Francis Bacon around 1620 when he devised a way for people to make correct conclusions about their observations. The approach is to set up an experiment to prove something wrong. This process begins with a hypothesis, which can often be stated as an "if-then" statement. An example of a hypothesis is, "if I expose these mice to chemical XYZ, they will get liver cancer." So the order of inquiry follows this structure:

1. Hypothesis
2. Methods
3. Collect Data
4. Analyze Data
5. Discussion
6. Conclusions
7. Re-formulate hypothesis
     (and repeat)

Scientific articles follow this format and no article that is peer-reviewed will be published in reputable scientific journals without the author following the standard scientific method specific to their field of study. This model is a general model which all studies can fit, except those that are purely observational like astronomy or Freudian psychology.

The legal method is also important to following the field of law or opinions and conclusions of law are not recognized as valid. It differs from the scientific method because the subject matter is available evidence, not generated data collected from a carefully designed experiment. Nevertheless, constant structure for reading and analyzing law is regulated by the application of these:

- Canons of construction
- Principles of law
- Precedent
- Rules from precedent applied to new cases

The concept of *stare decisis* means that the case is finished once it is decided and will never be reopened to decide that same set of facts again. This is almost the opposite of the scientific method which challenges previous norms and principles looking for breakthrough knowledge that might shatter the previously held scientific truths.

The structure of a legal opinion or a legal answer follows a very specific order. The form has come to be known by its acronym, the "IRAC" method. This stands for issue, rule, application and conclusion. This is the order that a logical basis for the conclusion must be laid down in the reasoning. First, the analysis starts with the issue or question of law that is presented. Second, the rule of law is stated which applies to that issue or question. The third step is to apply the rule to the set of facts presented in the question and from that and only then, can a conclusion be reached, the fourth step.

In the case of emerging technologies regulation, law and risk, the approaches to logic and reasoning in the respective fields of law and science can lead to misunderstanding and even distrust on both sides where issues like the Amerithrax case presents questions that challenges the very logical basis of the fields. In all areas of emerging technology because of the novelty that it presents in various areas of law and because of the pressure to be ever protective of the public for unknown or predictable risks, the tension between law and science continues to drive new knowledge that will make both law and science more interdisciplinary.

Chapter 3

Federal Regulation of Agricultural Biotechnology

3.1.1 Federal Regulation of Biotechnology

3.1.1.1 Federal Government

The United States federal government has traditionally funded emerging technologies which are too new and undeveloped to be supported by private sector research, but which are promising enough to merit federal funding in anticipation of their contribution to the national economy, public well-being and international trade.

Twelve agencies and departments in the federal government have been formally identified as having critical roles in the development of biotechnology: Department of Agriculture (USDA); Department of Commerce (DOC); Department of Defense (DOD); Department of Energy (DOE); Department of Health and Human Services (DHHS); Department of the Interior (DOI); Department of Veterans Affairs (DVA); Agency for International Development (AID); Environmental Protection Agency (EPA); National Aeronautics and Space Administration (NASA); and the National Science Foundation (NSF). The understanding of the roles of these agencies and the federal government in biotechnology policy and law is addressed in this section.

The federal government is also expected to regulate and control unwanted effects of technologies, and to rely upon ethical and legal constraints to protect the public. Biotechnology has been challenged with existing laws as it affects the environment, as well as human health. This chapter includes those legal challenges and the direction from the judiciary as these new technologies continue to develop.

3.1.1.2 Executive Branch

In 1992, the leadership of the federal government in biotechnology was first realized when President Bush made Biotechnology one of his five Presidential Initiatives in scientific research. This involved the coordination of twelve federal agencies in order to coordinate both research strategies and budget resources to accelerate the developments in biotechnology in a synergistic manner. This Presidential Initiative was coordinated by the White House Science Office, or the Office of Science and Technology Policy as it is more formally known. This involved a year-long effort to coordinate the budget items with the research programs across all twelve agencies prior to submission of the budget to Congress. The ultimate success of the coordinated budget was then dependent upon Congressional approval by each of the Congressional Committees, having budget authority for each of the twelve agencies or departments.

In 1992, the President proposed a budget of $4.03 billion, representing an 18% increase over the preceding two years of federal investment — $3.76 billion in FY 1992, and $3.38 billion in FY 1991. The majority of the funding (80%) was for basic science and health; reflecting the early federal support for the National Institutes of Health research; a smaller fraction (12%) of the total supported environmental, agricultural and manufacturing/bioprocessing research; about the same fraction was dedicated to infrastructure in biotechnology, such as personnel training (about 12%); and a very small percentage (less than 1%) was for the support of research in marine biotechnology. In the letter of transmittal to the Congress with this Presidential Initiative in biotechnology, the President's Science Adviser, D. Allan Bromley, wrote the following:

This Presidential Initiative [Biotechnology] recognizes the critical role of biotechnology in our nation's future technological strength, economic growth, and the health and quality of life of its people. This country has been the world leader in biological research for the past thirty years which has provided the foundation for the current U.S. pre-eminence in biotechnology research. This leadership, however, is clearly being challenged as the field changes and expands rapidly.

The strategic framework . . . is a coordinated, interagency effort intended to develop and implement a national Biotechnology Research Program to assure the nation of a vigorous base of science and engineering for future development of this critical technology. If aggressively exploited, this effort will maintain the momentum of U.S. leadership in health-directed biotechnology research and will expand research in critical areas where applications of biotechnology research promise significant breakthroughs including agriculture, energy and environment. Executive Office of the President, Federal Coordinating Council for Science, Engineering and Technology, "Biotechnology for the 21st Century," (February 1992).

There was a serious concern that if the United States did not support the emerging biotechnologies, it would loose its world lead in this field. Remaining the world leader in biotechnology research and applications was a matter of securing the future of the national economy as well as one of national security.

During the Bush Administration (1989-1993), Vice President Quayle chaired the Council on Competitiveness, whose mission it was to remove unnecessary or outdated regulatory barriers and to maximize national productivity and quality of life. The Vice President appointed a Biotechnology Working Group with the directive to ensure that regulatory barriers did not prevent the successful development of biotechnologies.

3.1.1.3. Regulation of Biotechnology

(1) Early Developments in Modern Biotechnology Regulation

The rapid development of biotechnology in the 1970s spurred questions about the need to regulate the science, the technology, and even the scientists themselves. The following excerpt from Stuart Auchincloss, "Does Genetic Engineering Need Genetic Engineers?: Should the Regulation of Genetic Engineering Include a New Professional Discipline?" 20 B.C. Envtl. Aff. L. Rev. 37 (Fall 1993), provides an overview of biotechnology regulation by the federal government, beginning with the 1973 Gordon Research Conference on Nucleic Acids:

. . . .III. THE CURRENT REGULATION OF BIOTECHNOLOGY

A. The Historical Roots

When scientists in the early 1970s realized the power of biotechnology, they agreed on collective self-restraint in conducting experiments which might be hazardous. . . When the scientists' concern became public, the safety of their work became a political issue. This Section describes those early actions and the political debate that took place as a result, showing that with the exception of the participation of a few non-governmental organizations, the scientists themselves have created all the federal regulation of biotechnology primarily on the basis of technical considerations, with only grudging acknowledgment of the existence of social issues.

1. The 1973 Gordon Research Conference

In 1973, Maxine Singer, a biochemist with NIH, was one of the two co-chairs of the Gordon Research Conference on Nucleic Acids, a meeting of professional molecular biologists. . . . On the last day of the conference, after the announcement of the powerful new technology of using restriction enzymes to combine the DNA of unrelated organisms, there was an unscheduled debate on the question of the potential hazards from dangerous synthetic mutant germs made possible by this process. . . .A large majority of those scientists who participated in this discussion favored expressing their concern to the National Academy of Sciences. . . .Just a little over half of these scientists also favored making their concerns known more widely in the scientific community. . . .

Acting on this vote, Maxine Singer and her co-chair wrote to the president of the National Academy of Science and to the president of the National Institute of Medicine, 181 SCIENCE 1114, 1114 (1973). The letter announced the scientists' concern that certain hybrid molecules may be hazardous to laboratory workers and the public. . . .The letter requested the National Academy of Sciences to establish a committee to consider the problem and recommend specific actions or guidelines. . . . As a result of the letter, the National Academy of Sciences established a committee of scientists to consider the matter in the Fall of 1973.

A year later, on July 26, 1974 Science published an open letter from the National Academy of Sciences Committee to all scientists throughout the world suggesting a voluntary moratorium on certain genetic engineering experiments because the experiments were too risky for currently available laboratory containment technology, Paul Berg et al., Potential Biohazards of Recombinant DNA Molecules, 185 SCIENCE 303, 303 (1974). Although the concerned scientists intended only to encourage voluntary self-restraint among molecular biologists, the scientists' letter began to alert journalists and the general public to the potential dangers of genetic engineering. . . . Six months after the publication of the letter, an international conference of molecular biologists convened at Asilomar, California on February 24-27, 1975 to consider what the scientists themselves should do next. . .

2. The 1975 Asilomar Conference
    Maxine Singer and four other concerned scientists organized the pivotal Asilomar Conference of molecular biologists in February 1975 to discuss the future of biotechnology. . . .The organizers proclaimed the following two principles to guide genetic engineering experiments: containment as an essential consideration in the design of experiments, and the containment's effectiveness equaling the experiment's estimated risk, Paul Berg et al., Asilomar Conference on Recombinant DNA Molecules, 188 SCIENCE 991, 992 (1975). Even bearing these principles in mind, the conferees agreed that there were certain experiments which ought not to be conducted with the then available containment facilities. . . .
    Beginning at Asilomar, eminent molecular biologists disagreed among themselves about the risk of the genetic engineering experiments, see generally, Michael Rogers, The Pandora's Box Congress, 189 ROLLING STONE 36 (1975). . . While most molecular biologists believed that raising the issues and warning each other was enough, a few molecular biologists felt that the experiments should be halted altogether. . .

B. The Beginning of Federal Regulation
1. The NIH Guidelines

On October 7, 1974, four months before the Asilomar conference, the NIH's director already had formed the Recombinant DNA Molecule Program Advisory Committee (RAC) to consider three aspects of the new genetic engineering technology: potential hazards, the spread of genetically modified organisms in the environment, and guidelines for scientists working with such organisms. . . After the Asilomar conference, however, RAC focused almost exclusively on its third task, preparing guidelines for researchers, see 41 Fed. Reg. 27903 (1976); Collin Norman, Genetic Manipulation: Guidelines Issued, 262 NATURE 2, July 1, 1976.

On June 23, 1976, the Director of the NIH formally issued the guidelines which effectively halted experiments using DNA from warm blooded animals and viruses, 41 Fed. Reg. 27,902-43 (1979); Norman, supra note 82, at 2. NIH, the main source of federal funds for biotechnology research, required an institutional biosafety committee to review proposed experiments before the applicant could receive his or her grant to perform certain experiments. 41 Fed. Reg. 27,920-21 (1976); WATSON & TOOZE, supra note 5, at 63. The regulations also specified the degree of containment necessary for certain particularly dangerous genetic engineering experiments.

Despite their strict limitations on biotechnology experiments, the guidelines appear to apply only to entities receiving research grants from NIH, see generally 41 Fed. Reg. 27,920 (1976). In addition, the only sanction the guidelines imposed was cutting off funding for institutions that did not follow the guidelines. . . .

As scientists around the world have carried out safely many laboratory experiments with genetic engineering, RAC steadily relaxed the guidelines until now most experiments require no more than local peer review, see, NIH Section of the Coordinated Framework, 55 Fed. Reg. 23,349 (1990). Thus, early in the regulation of biotechnology, the NIH guidelines established the pattern of making compliance voluntary for laboratories operating without government funds, most notably industrial and commercial laboratories. . . .

2. Congressional Study and Inaction

Two months after the Asilomar conference, on April 22, 1975, Senator Edward Kennedy, as Chairman of the Subcommittee on Health, held a hearing on the relationship of a free society to its scientific community. . . . The hearing used genetic engineering as a case study to consider the public's role in both the direction of scientific research and the application of the research's results. . .

The April 22 hearing was followed by another hearing on September 22, 1976 on the same subject. . . . In his opening remarks, Senator Kennedy drew particular attention to the problem of industry's "voluntary" compliance with the NIH guidelines. . . . Senator Kennedy singled out General Electric for its unwillingness to participate in the hearing as an example of industry's unwillingness to follow the NIH guidelines (Opening Statement of Senator Edward M. Kennedy at a Hearing of the Senate Health Subcommittee on Recombinant DNA Research and the NIH Guidelines, Wednesday, Sept. 22, 1976 . . .)

Following these hearings, efforts to adopt a biotechnology control act continued in both the United States Senate and the House of Representatives until March 1978 when legislative action ceased. . . . Academic scientists opposed biotechnology regulation by taking the extreme position that the proposed government regulation was similar to the subjugation of Russian biological science to communist ideology during the middle of the Twentieth Century.

Congressional interest in a biotechnology bill disappeared in the Fall of 1978 for many reasons including a lack of support from the executive branch, NIH's relaxation of its guidelines thereby implying that the threat of biotechnology was less than feared, and the complexities of congressional politics. At the same time, Secretary of Health, Education and Welfare (HEW), Joseph Califano stated that his agency, which controlled NIH, did not intend to invoke existing statutory authority to regulate DNA activities, preferring to continue with voluntary control of industry based on NIH's guidelines. . . Over the next five years RAC steadily relaxed the NIH guidelines by determining that ever more classes of experiments posed no special hazard. . . .

C. The Coordinated Framework
In the Spring of 1984 the Council on Natural Resources and the Environment formed a Working Group on Biotechnology, 49 Fed. Reg. 50,856 (1984). The Working Group prepared and published the Coordinated Framework as a proposal for the regulation of biotechnology by existing agencies, under existing statutes, 49 Fed. Reg. 50,856 (1985) (proposed Dec. 31, 1984).

On October 31, 1985, the [Reagan] Domestic Policy Council formed the Biotechnical Science Coordinating Committee (BSCC), 50 Fed. Reg. 47,174 (1985); see also 51 Fed. Reg. 23302 (1986), to establish for all regulatory agencies common definitions of "intergeneric organism" and "pathogen," and to limit federal regulation to these entities. (The Coordinated Framework's definitions are intended to determine what organisms should be appropriate for certain types of review, 51 Fed. Reg. 23302 (1986)).

The BSCC ruled that an intergeneric organism is a microorganism that is "deliberately formed to contain an intergeneric combination of genetic material." . . . Basing a regulatory definition on the location of microbes in the taxonomic system, however, is questionable because of the lack of scientific agreement on the taxonomic classifications and the categories' relation to each other, see, "Principles for Federal Oversight of Biotechnology: Planned Introduction into the Environment of Organisms with Modified Hereditary Traits," 55 Fed. Reg. 31118, (1990) [hereinafter referred to as the "Proposed Refinement"] ". . . Taxonomy . . . is imprecise for microorganisms." Id. at 31119.

Likewise, a pathogen is a "virus or microorganism . . . [broadly defined] that has the ability to cause disease in other living organisms," 51 Fed. Reg. 23,302 (1986). This is followed by a long gloss stating, in effect, that an organism is a regulated pathogen when the organism is dangerous, see, 51 Fed. Reg. 23,306-07 (1986). Up until July 31, 1990 the Coordinated Framework used these two definitions to describe reviewable genetically modified organisms, see 51 Fed. Reg. 23,307 (1986) (Coordinated Framework).

After an eighteen month comment period, the Working Group published the final Coordinated Framework on June 26, 1986, 51 Fed. Reg. 23,301 (1986). The Coordinated Framework expressed the Executive Branch's opinion that the existing statutes provide a basic network of agency control over biotechnology's research and products sufficient for the regulation of the plants, animals, and microorganisms created by the new genetic engineering techniques, 51 Fed. Reg. 23,302-03 (1986) The White House Office of Science and Technology Policy (OSTP) reaffirmed this opinion when the agency issued its "Principles for Federal Oversight of Biotechnology." 55 Fed. Reg. 31,118 (1990). The Coordinated Framework provides a chart which summarizes agency jurisdiction and authority over the approval of biotechnology products, Chart 1, 51 Fed. Reg. 23,304 (1986).

3.1.1.4 Federal regulations – what is regulated?

The regulation of genetically modified organisms is controlled through the regulations developed by the Office of Science and Technology Policy in 1990. In addition to these regulations, recipients of funding from the National Institutes of Health are also subject to NIH regulations for researchers and the release of genetically modified organisms. The publication of the biotechnology regulatory framework used a chart format to identify the responsible agency for the subject biotechnology. Here is Chart I of the Regulatory Framework (51 Fed. Reg. 23,304 (1986):

SUBJECT	RESPONSIBLE AGENCY(IES)
Foods/Food Additives	FDA,[*] FSIS.[a]
Human Drugs, Medical Devices and Biologics	FDA.
Animal Drugs	FDA.
Animal Biologics	APHIS.
Other Contained Uses	EPA.
Plants and Animals	APHIS,[*] FSIS,[a] FDA.[b]
Pesticide Microorganisms Released in the Environment All	EPA,[*] APHIS.[c]
Other Uses (Microorganisms): Intergeneric Combination	EPA,[*] APHIS.[c]
Intrageneric Combination:	

17. The current role of the BSCC under the Coordinated Framework is described at 51 Fed. Reg. at 23,306. The BSCC was originally established on Oct. 31, 1985 and was announced to the public on Nov. 14, 1985 in 51 Fed. Reg. 47,174.
18. 51 Fed. Reg. at 23,306.
19. 51 Fed. Reg. at 23,303.
20. 51 Fed. Reg. at 23,304. Charts appearing in the Coordinated Framework notice which show the assignment of particular federal agencies to review particular products are reprinted in part in Tables 1 and 2 in the text.
21. 51 Fed. Reg. at 23,303.
22. 51 Fed. Reg. at 23,306.
23. This table is reprinted from 51 Fed. Reg. at 23,304.

Jurisdiction over the varied biotechnology products is determined by their use, as has been the case for traditional products. The detailed description of the products and their review are found in the individual agency policy statements contained in this Federal Register Notice. The following is a brief summary of jurisdiction as described in Chart I.

Foods, food additives, human drugs, biologics and devices, and animal drugs are reviewed or licensed by the FDA. Food products prepared from domestic livestock and poultry are under the jurisdiction of the USDA's Food Safety Inspection Service (FSIS).

Animal biologics are reviewed by the Animal and Plant Health Inspection Service (APHIS). APHIS, also reviews plants, seeds, animal biologics, plant pests, animal pathogens and "regulated articles," i.e., certain genetically engineered organisms containing genetic material from a plant pest. An APHIS permit is required prior to the shipment (movement) or release into the environment of regulated articles, or the shipment of a plant pest or animal pathogen.

"Other continaed uses" refers to the closed system uses of those microorganisms, subject to the TSCA, that are intergeneric combinations, i.e., deliberately formed microorganisms which contain genetic material from dissimilar source organisms.

These are subject to EPA's PMN requirement. EPA is considering promulgating a rule to exempt certain classes of microorganisms from this requirement.

Microbial pesticides will be reviewed by EPA, with APHIS involvement in cases where the pesticide is also a plant pest, animal pathogen, or regulated article requiring a permit. (FDA may become involved in implementing pesticide tolerances for foods.)

"Other uses (microorganisms)" include uses involving release into the environment. For these, jurisdiction depends on the characteristics of the organism as well as its use.

"Intergeneric combination" * microorganisms will be reported to EPA under PMN requirements, with APHIS involvement in cases where the microorganisms is also a regulated article requiring a permit.

"Intrageneric combinations" are those mircroorganisms formed by genetic engineering other than intergeneric combinations. For these, when there is a pathogenic source organism, and the microorganism is used for agricultural purposes, APHIS has jurisdiction. If the microorganism is used for nonagricultural purposes, then EPA has jurisdiction, with APHIS involvement in cases where the microorganism is also a regulated article requiring permit. Intrageneric combinations with no pathogenic source organisms are under EPA jurisdiction although EPA will only require an informational report.

These very broad categories gave the biotechnology industry some guidance as to which agency they should consult when developing a new biotechnology. This also brought some certainty where there was no guidance or regulation, frightening "angel investors" who had fueled the biotech industry into holding back until the regulatory landscape was more certain. Although it is often thought that industry does not want to be regulated, that is quite often not the case where complete uncertainty leaves investors without confidence to invest. This simple regulatory action may have saved the fledgling biotech industry when they needed investment the most.

The Auchincloss article, cited above, includes a note on the development and refinement of the Framework by the Office of Science and Technology Policy in 1990:

> Regulatory authority under the Framework, however, extends only to risks from the use or misuse of biotechnology products which are regulated already in the stream of commerce. As an example of the Framework's maintenance of the status quo, the Department of Labor declared that its regulations under the Occupational Safety and Health Act were adequate and that the new biology did not require new regulations to

protect workers. Thus the Occupational Safety and Health Act does nothing to narrow the class of unregulated organisms or to regulate releases not covered by the Framework.

The Coordinated Framework does not cover animals which are not insects, plants which are not parasites, or insects which are not plant pests, Even though the FDA regulates the use of plants and animals for food and medicine, the FDA and United States Department of Agriculture regulate veterinary medicine; Virus, Serum, Toxin Act, and the Public Health Service regulates the interstate movement of etiologic agents, a considerable range of transgenic plants and animals are still free of federal regulation.

The residual class of life forms which are not regulated under any federal program will be referred to in this Article as "unregulated organisms." As examples of unregulated organisms, an industrial enterprise might engineer transgenic fish for weed and mosquito control, or oysters for pearl production and release them to the environment without any intent that people would use the organisms for food. If the genetic engineering work did not have government funding, the organisms' release would be unregulated even if the release occurred in the waters of the United States. No reported case or lawsuit has suggested that such a release might be covered by § 404 of the Clean Water Act or the Rivers and Harbors Appropriations Act of 1899.

Furthermore, the Coordinated Framework does not apply to a large amount of biotechnology work because research does not have a product. . . Most genetically modified organisms that scientists release to the environment are experiments, not commercial products, therefore the Framework does not apply to the resulting organisms unless experimenters receive government funding, or come under the experimental use permit section of the laws. For experiments involving unregulated organisms and carried on without government funding, reporting and peer review are only voluntary. . . . While some such research on future commercial products might fall under the experiment provisions of, for example, Toxic Substance Control Act (TSCA). . . one can imagine uses which might escape even these definitions.

D. The Proposed Refinement of the Coordinated Framework
In hopes of clarifying the Framework, the President's Office of Science and Technology Policy (OSTP), the parent body of the BSCC, referred the problem of what organisms the Coordinated Framework covered to the White House Council on Competitiveness. In late July 1990,

on the basis of the Council on Competitiveness's recommendation, OSTP proposed a refinement of the Coordinated Framework for regulation of biotechnology. . . .As the refinement itself declares, the "Coordinated Framework was expected to evolve in accordance with the experience of the industry, and, thus, modifications to the framework were anticipated." . . . This modification, however, goes to the heart of the Coordinated Framework -- the definition of organism and the need for government supervision of releases to the environment of genetically modified organisms.

The Coordinated Framework limited its application to two classes of organisms -- organisms formed by the combination of genetic material from sources in different genera and microorganisms containing genetic material from pathogenic species -- with each class having several exceptions. The proposed 1990 refinement declares that the Coordinated Framework now applies to all "organisms with deliberately modified hereditary traits." Because regulation under the refinement requires deliberate modification, regulation is limited to the products of genetic engineering and does not include the products of selective breeding and intentional mutation. . . .[See id. Because the Framework is based on risk rather than on strict classifications, only those organism introductions for which safety data already exist, or for which there are existing, adequate safety regulations will be excluded from oversight.

For years scientists and representatives of industry have maintained that the regulation of biotechnology products should be no different from the regulation of hybrids because the risks from genetically modified organisms are comparable to the risks from organisms modified by conventional breeding techniques and possibly less risky because the genetic changes are so specific. . . . Now, the refined Coordinated Framework reflects this view, and all such organisms will be brought within its purview [see 55 Fed. Reg. 31120 (1990)]. The refined Framework discloses the principle that planned introductions "should not be subject to oversight . . . unless information concerning the risk posed by the introduction indicates that oversight is necessary.". . . The refinement thus has something for everyone -- a broader definition of genetically modified organisms and a vaguely worded prohibition on their regulation.

The refinement's definitions feature a no-oversight-until-risk-is-known approach, implying that the burden is on the regulator to demonstrate the risk and bear the cost of showing the risk's existence. . . .The problem is that regulation turns on the existence of "information concerning the risk posed," information which in most cases today does not exist yet. . . .

_____

Jeremy Rifkin, an activist opposed to genetic engineering and biotechnology in general began initiating a number of complaints against the federal government for actions taken which might lead to the release of the genetically-engineering plant into the environment. His actions and the publicity he received raised the public awareness of biotechnology and perpetuated many of his "scientific" ideas which were not science-based principles, at all.

3.1.2   Synthetic Biology Regulation

The regulation of synthetic biology began with the small community of producers self-regulating. The policy that they created was focused on biosecurity to prevent synthetic biology products that they sold from being acquired by nefarious and/or foreign actors.

In 2007, the small group of synthetic biology producers published a report, "Synthetic Biology: Options for Governance," and it focused on three areas they called "societal" areas: "bioterrorism, worker safety and protection of communities and the environment in the vicinity of research laboratories."

This excerpt from the executive summary provides a good overview of synthetic biology and what is at stake in this proposal for governance and their efforts at self-governance:

Introduction to Synthesis
    Researchers have had the basic knowledge and tools to carry out the de novo synthesis of gene-length DNA from nucleotide precursors for over 35 years. At first, however, these "from scratch" synthesis techniques were extremely difficult, and constructing a gene of just over 100 nucleotides in length could take years. Today, using machines called DNA synthesizers, the individual subunit bases adenine (A), cytosine (C), guanine (G), and thymine (T) can be assembled to form the genetic material DNA in any specified sequence, in lengths of tens of thousands of nucleotide base-pairs using readily accessible reagents.
    Synthetic genomics combines methods for the chemical synthesis of DNA with computational techniques to design it. These methods allow scientists to construct genetic material that would be impossible or impractical to produce using more conventional biotechnological approaches.

For instance, synthetic genomics could be used to introduce a cumulative series of changes that dramatically alter an organism's function, or to construct very long strands of genetic material that could serve as the entire genome of a virus or, some time in the near future, even of more complex organisms such as bacteria.

Scientists have been improving their ability to manipulate DNA for decades. There is no clear and unambiguous threshold between synthetic genomics and more conventional approaches to biotechnology. Chemical synthesis can be used to make incremental changes in an organism's genome, just as non-synthetic techniques can generate an entirely new genome. Nevertheless, the combination of design and construction capabilities gives synthetic genomics the potential for revolutionary advances unmatched by other approaches.

Synthetic genomics allows scientists and engineers to focus on their goals without getting bogged down in the underlying molecular manipulations. As a result, the breadth and diversity of the user community has increased, and the range of possible experiments, applications, and outcomes has been substantially enlarged.

Such revolutionary advances have the potential to bring significant benefits to individuals and society. At the same time, the power of these technologies raises questions about the risks from their intentional or accidental misuse for harm. Synthetic genomics thus is a quintessential "dual-use" technology—a technology with broad and varied beneficial applications, but one that could also be turned to nefarious, destructive use. Such technologies have been around ever since the first humans picked up rocks or sharpened sticks. But biology brings some unique dimensions: given the self-propagating nature of biological organisms and the relative accessibility of powerful biotechnologies, the means to produce a "worst case" are more readily attainable than for many other technologies.3

The four authors embarked on this study of synthetic genomics to assess the current state of the technology, identify potential risks and benefits to society, and formulate options for governance of the technology.

This report was closely watched by federal regulators and in this case, the Department of Energy was the agency with oversight for this area, in part, because of the type of processes and equipment for working with synthetic biology was a the molecular level which matched the expertise of the U.S. Department of Energy.

In November 2009, the Department of Health and Human Services issued a policy for synthetic biology producers and guidelines for ensuring safety. These guidelines involved checking sequences ordered from customers against a database of known pathogens to ensure these sequences were not dangerous, and then to also check the customers names against a known database of prohibited individuals on any list including the list of previous violators of any laws.

Here is the policy as it reads in the Federal Register:

DEPARTMENT OF HEALTH AND HUMAN SERVICES
Office of the Secretary
Screening Framework Guidance for
Synthetic Double-Stranded DNA Providers
AGENCY: Department of Health and Human Services, Office of the Secretary.
ACTION: Notice.

Authority: Public Health Service Act, 42 U.S.C. 241, Section 301; HSPD–10.
SUMMARY: To reduce the risk that individuals with ill intent may exploit the commercial application of nucleic acid synthesis technology to access genetic material derived from or encoding Select Agents or Toxins, the U.S. Government has developed recommendations for a framework for synthetic nucleic acid screening. This document is intended to provide guidance to producers of synthetic genomic products regarding the screening of orders so that these orders are filled in compliance with current U.S. regulations and to encourage best practices in addressing potential biosecurity concerns. Following this guidance is voluntary, though many specific recommendations serve to remind providers of their obligations under existing regulations. The target audience for this guidance is the gene and genome synthesis industry, because the technical hurdles for *de novo* synthesis of Select Agents and Toxins from double-stranded DNA are much lower than for *de novo* synthesis of these agents from single-stranded oligonucleotides. This guidance proposes a screening framework for commercial providers of synthetic double-stranded DNA 200 base pairs (bps) or greater in length to address concerns associated with the potential for misuse of their products. The framework includes customer screening and sequence screening, follow-up screening as necessary, and consultation with U.S. Government contacts, as needed.

This guidance is submitted for public consideration and comment for a period of 60 days. The Office of the Assistant Secretary of Preparedness and Response (ASPR) within the Department of Health and Human Services (HHS) is submitting this document for public consideration as the lead agency in a broad interagency process to draft the guidance.

DATES: The public is encouraged to submit written comments on this proposed action. Comments may be submitted to HHS/ASPR in electronic or paper form at the HHS/ASPR e-mail address, mailing address, and fax number shown below under the heading
FOR FURTHER INFORMATION CONTACT. All comments should be submitted by January 26, 2010. All written comments received in response to this notice will be available for review by request.

FOR FURTHER INFORMATION CONTACT:
Jessica Tucker, Ph.D., Office of
Medicine, Science, and Public Health, Office of the Assistant Secretary for Preparedness and Response, U.S.

Department of Health and Human Services, 330 C Street, SW., Room 5008B, Washington, DC 20201; phone: 202–260–0632; fax: 202–205–8494; e-mail address: *asprfrcorrespondence@hhs.gov.*

SUPPLEMENTARY INFORMATION:
Screening Framework Guidance for Synthetic Double-Stranded DNA Providers
I. Summary
Synthetic biology, the developing interdisciplinary field that focuses on both the design and fabrication of novel biological components and systems as well as the re-design and fabrication of existing biological systems, is poised to become the next significant transforming technology for the life sciences and beyond. Synthetic biology is not constrained by the requirement of using existing genetic material. Thus, technologies that permit the directed synthesis of polynucleotides have great potential to be used to generate organisms, both currently existing and novel, including pathogens that could threaten public health, agriculture, plants, animals, the environment, or material. To reduce the risk that individuals with ill intent may exploit the commercial application of nucleic acid synthesis technology to access genetic material derived from or encoding Select Agents or Toxins, the U.S. Government has developed recommendations for a framework for synthetic nucleic acid screening. This document is intended to provide guidance to producers of synthetic genomic products regarding the screening of orders so that these orders are filled in compliance with current U.S. regulations and to encourage best practices in addressing potential biosecurity concerns.

Following this guidance is voluntary, though many specific recommendations serve to remind providers of their obligations under existing regulations. The target audience for this guidance is the gene and genome synthesis industry, because the technical hurdles for *de novo* synthesis of Select Agents and Toxins from double-stranded DNA are much lower than for *de novo* synthesis of these agents from single-stranded oligonucleotides. This guidance proposes a screening framework for commercial providers of synthetic double-stranded DNA 200 base pairs (bps) or greater in length to address concerns associated with the potential for misuse of their products. The framework includes customer screening and sequence screening, follow-up screening as necessary, and consultation with U.S. Government contacts, as needed. Briefly, upon receiving an order for synthetic double-stranded DNA, the U.S. Government recommends that the provider perform *customer screening.* If the information provided by the customer raises any 'red flags,' providers should perform *follow-up screening.* If no customer identity concerns or other 'red flags' are raised in *customer screening, sequence screening* is recommended. If *sequence screening* raises any concerns, providers should pursue *follow-up screening* to clarify the end-use of the ordered sequence. If *follow-up screening* does not resolve concerns about the order or there is reason to believe a customer may intentionally or inadvertently violate U.S. laws, providers should contact designated entities within the U.S. Government for further information. This guidance also provides recommendations regarding proper records retention protocols and screening software.

II. Introduction
Synthetic biology is distinct from traditional recombinant DNA technology in some key aspects: (1) It is not constrained by the requirement for using existing genetic material, and (2) it is an interdisciplinary field that includes biologists, engineers, chemists, and computer modelers. It is the former novel feature, along with rapid advances in DNA synthesis technology and the

open availability of pathogen genome sequence data, that has raised concerns in the scientific community, the nucleic acid synthesis industry, the U.S. Government, and the general public. Within the U.S., microbial organisms and toxins that have been determined to have the potential to pose a severe threat to public health and safety, animal health, plant health, or animal or plant products are regulated through the Select Agent Regulations (SAR), administered by the Department of Health and Human Services/Centers for Disease Control and Prevention (CDC) and the U.S. Department of Agriculture/ Animal and Plant Health Inspection Service (USDA/APHIS). The SAR sets forth requirements for the possession, use, and transfer of listed agents. Technologies that permit the directed synthesis of polynucleotides, which underlie synthetic biology and more specifically synthetic genomics, could enable individuals not authorized to possess Select Agents to gain access to them through their *de novo* synthesis. Such synthesis obviates the need for access to the naturally occurring agents or naturally occurring genetic material from these agents, thereby greatly expanding the potential availability of these agents.

The National Science Advisory Board for Biosecurity (NSABB) was charged with identifying the potential biosecurity concerns raised by the ability to synthesize Select Agents and providing advice on whether current U.S. Government policies and regulations adequately cover the *de novo* synthesis of Select Agents. Their report entitled *Addressing Biosecurity Concerns Related to the Synthesis of Select Agents* was formally transmitted to the U.S. Government in March 2007. Federal Departments and Agencies with equities relevant to life science research and/or security deliberated over the NSABB recommendations and

identified a series of relevant policy actions targeted to promote risk management, while seeking to minimize negative impacts upon scientific progress or industrial development.

One of the formal policy actions in regard to Synthetic DNA and Biological Security charged Federal Departments and Agencies to "engage stakeholders in industry and academia to identify, evaluate and support the establishment of a screening infrastructure for use by commercial providers and users of synthetic nucleic acids." Toward this end, this document provides guidance to synthetic nucleic acid providers regarding a screening framework for synthetically derived double-stranded DNA orders that are 200 bps or greater in length. Specific recommendations are in bold type throughout the text.

III. Goals of Guidance

The primary goal in developing guidance for synthetic nucleic acid providers is to minimize the risk that unauthorized individuals or individuals with malicious intent will gain access to toxins and organisms of concern through the use of nucleic acid synthesis technologies, while at the same time minimizing any negative impacts on the conduct of research and business operations. These guidelines were developed to be easily integrated within providers' existing protocols with minimal cost, and to be globally extensible, both for U.S.-based firms operating abroad and for international companies.

Providers of synthetic nucleic acids have two overriding responsibilities in this context: • Providers should know to whom they are selling a product
- Providers should know if the nature and identity of the product that they are selling poses a hazard to public health, agriculture, or security

To help providers meet these responsibilities, this guidance outlines a screening framework that addresses both customer screening (customer identity) and sequence screening (product identity). Though certain guidance provided in this document is necessarily framed by U.S. policy and regulations, the guidelines were composed so that fundamental goals, provider responsibilities, and the screening framework could be considered for application by the international community. In particular, though the Select Agents and Toxins that are a primary focus of these guidelines may not be relevant for all countries, the sequence screening framework has been developed so that it could be applied to other categories of agents that may be relevant for other regions.

IV. Overall Process: Synthetic Nucleic
Acid Screening Framework

Providers should consider establishing a comprehensive and integrated screening framework that includes both customer screening and sequence screening.

• Customer Screening—The purpose of customer screening is to establish the legitimacy of customers ordering synthetic nucleic acid sequences, both at the level of the individual and the organization. Providers should develop customer screening mechanisms to verify customer identities, to identify potential 'red flags,' and to conform to U.S. trade restrictions and export control regulations.

• Sequence Screening—The purpose of sequence screening is to identify when sequences of concern are ordered. Identification of a sequence of concern does not necessarily imply that the order itself is of concern. Rather, when a sequence of concern is ordered, further customer screening procedures should be used to determine if filling the order would raise cause for concern. Sequence screening is currently being recommended for all double-stranded DNA 200 bps or greater in length.

Many customers will likely volunteer information about their identity or the sequence they are ordering. Providers should corroborate this information as part of their screening framework. The following overall screening methodology is recommended:

1. Upon receiving an order for synthetic double-stranded DNA, the U.S. Government recommends reviewing the information provided by the customer to verify their identity and identify potential 'red flags' (referred to as *customer screening*). If the information provided raises any concerns, providers should ask the customer for additional information to clarify the customer's need for the order and its intended end-use (referred to as *follow-up screening*). Providers should also check customers and their affiliated organizations against lists of denied or blocked persons and entities maintained by the Departments of Commerce, State, and Treasury.

2. If no concerns or 'red flags' are raised during *customer screening,* the U.S. Government recommends screening the ordered sequence to identify sequences derived from or encoding Select Agents and Toxins[1] (referred to as *sequence screening*). For international customers, providers should also screen the ordered sequence to identify sequences derived from or encoding the agents and toxins on the Export Administration Regulation's (EAR's) Commerce Control List (CCL).[2] Scenarios of concern may include:

a. If an ordered nucleic acid can be classified as a Select Agent or Toxin based on the SAR[3] or is identified as a sequence of concern (defined in Section V.B.1.), additional customer verification steps should be performed and may in some cases be required.

---

[1] Please see *http://www.selectagents.gov* to access the most recent Select Agents and Toxins List.

[2] Visit *http://www.access.gpo.gov/bis/ear/ ear_data.html* to access the most recent Commerce Control List and review the Export Administration Regulations.

[3] The CDC/APHIS national Select Agent registry Web site (*http://www.selectagents.gov*) contains a guidance document entitled ''Applicability of the Select Agent Regulations to Issues of Synthetic Genomics'' to assist providers in identifying synthetically derived Select Agent materials that would fall under the current regulations. The regulation of Select Agents and Toxins currently includes (1) Nucleic acids that can produce infectious forms of any Select Agent viruses and (2) Recombinant nucleic acids that encode for the functional form(s) of any of the regulated toxins if the nucleic acids: (i) Can be expressed in vivo or in vitro, or (ii) Are in a vector or recombinant host genome and can be expressed in vivo or in vitro.

b. If an ordered nucleic acid can be classified as a Select Agent or Toxin based on the SAR, providers must be registered under the SAR to possess the nucleic acid. Transfer of the material from the producer must be done in accordance with USDA APHIS and CDC procedures using the APHIS/CDC Form 2 to obtain authorization for and to document the transfer. Additional information on the transfer of select agents and toxins is available at *http://www.selectagents.gov*.

c. If an order is defined as a genetic element that is listed on the CCL, additional restrictions or licensing requirements may exist for international orders.

3. If *sequence screening or customer screening* raises any concerns, providers should pursue *follow-up screening* to clarify the end-use of the ordered sequence. The goal of *follow-up screening* is to assist the provider in determining whether to fill the order. If the provider encounters a scenario where they would benefit from additional assistance in assessing an order, the provider is encouraged to seek advice from the relevant U.S. Government Departments and Agencies by contacting the nearest FBI Field Office Weapons of Mass Destruction (WMD) Coordinator. The WMD Coordinator can be reached by contacting the local FBI Field Office and asking to be connected to the FBI WMD Coordinator.

V. Pertinent Screening Definitions and Details

This section reviews pertinent definitions and provides details of the steps involved in the recommended screening framework. These steps include *customer screening, sequence screening*, and *follow-up screening.*

A. Customer Screening

Customer screening encompasses two overarching responsibilities of providers: Customer verification and identification of any 'red flags.'

1. Customer Verification

To ensure compliance with U.S. regulations concerning exports and sanctioned individuals and countries, the U.S. Government recommends that, for every order, synthetic nucleic acid providers:

(1) Gather the following information to verify a customer's identity: • Customer's (and end-user's, if different) full name and contact information • Billing address and shipping address (if not the same) • Customer's institutional or corporate affiliation (if applicable) • Name of institution's Biological Safety Officer (if applicable)

(2) Screen customers against several lists of proscribed entities (described in Section VI). Lack of affiliation with an institution or firm does not automatically indicate that a customer's order should be denied. In such cases, the U.S. Government recommends conducting *follow-up screening.*

The U.S. Government recommends that companies retain electronic copies of customer orders for at least eight years based on the statute of limitations set forth by U.S. Code Title 18 Section 3286.[45]

The U.S. Government recommends archiving the following information: Customer (and end-user, if different) information (name, organization, address, and phone number), order

---

[4] The eight-year statute of limitations in Section
[5] applies to the offense defined by Title 18 Section 175(b) (possession of biological agents with no reasonable justification).

sequence information, and order information (date placed and shipped, shipping address, and receiver name).

2. 'Red Flags'

In reviewing the customer's order information, providers should take into account any circumstances in the proposed transaction that may indicate that the order may be intended for an inappropriate end-use, end-user or destination. These are known as 'red flags.'
The following is an illustrative list of indicators that can help in identifying suspicious orders of synthetic double- stranded DNA:

• A customer whose identity is not clear, who appears evasive about their identity or affiliations, or whose information cannot be confirmed or verified (*e.g.*, addresses do not match, not a legitimate company, no Web site, cannot be located in trade directories, etc.).

• A customer or intermediary agent who would not be expected in the course of their normal business to place such an order (*e.g.*, no connection to life science research, biotechnology or requirement for DNA synthesis services).

• An unusually large order of DNA sequences, including larger than normal quantities, the same order placed several times, or several orders of the same sequence made in a short timeframe.

• A customer that requests unusual labeling or shipping procedures (*e.g.*, requests to misidentify the goods on the packaging, requests to deliver to a private address, or requests to change the customer's name after the order is
placed, but before it is shipped).

• A customer proposing an unusual method of payment (*e.g.*, arranging payment in cash, personal credit card or through a non-bank third party) or offering to pay unusually favorable payment terms, such as a willingness to pay a higher than expected price.

• A customer that requests unusual confidentiality conditions regarding the order, particularly with respect to the final destination or the destruction of transaction records.
If a review of customer information reveals one or more 'red flags,' the U.S. Government recommends that providers exercise due diligence, inquire regarding the circumstances, and verify the end-use and end-user (*see follow-up screening*). If providers are unsure about whether to fill an order, they should contact the U.S. Government for further information.

B. Sequence Screening

Sequence screening is intended to elicit information detailing the characteristics of the ordered nucleic acid sequence and to determine whether the customer has placed an order for a sequence of concern, based on the product identity. Providers should screen ordered sequences that are 200 bps in length or greater.

1. Identifying Sequences of Concern

The U.S. Government recommends that nucleic acid sequences be screened for nucleic acids derived from or encoding Select Agents and Toxins and, for foreign orders, for nucleic acids derived from or encoding pathogens and toxins on the Commerce Control List. The U.S. Government chose the agents and toxins identified by HHS and USDA as "Select Agents and Toxins" as the most appropriate list of agents of concern against which providers should screen orders since:

• The list is comprised of high consequence pathogens and toxins that have the potential to pose a severe threat to human, animal, or plant health or to animal or plant products

• Their possession, use, and transfer are managed through Federal regulations.

A list of biological agents and toxins that affect humans has been promulgated by HHS/CDC (HHS Select Agents and Toxins, 42 CFR 73.3). A list of biological agents that affect animals and animal products has been promulgated by USDA/APHIS/ Veterinary Services (USDA Select Agents and Toxins, 9 CFR 121.3). A list of agents that affect plants and plant products has been promulgated by USDA/APHIS/Plant Protection and
Quarantine (USDA Select Agents and Toxins, 7 CFR 331.3). Additionally, HHS and USDA promulgated a list of "overlap" agents that affect both humans and animals (42 CFR 73.4 and 9 CFR 121.4). The Select Agent and Toxins lists are reviewed biennially and updated as needed to include additional agents or toxins that may pose a biosecurity concern. Therefore, for the purposes of this guidance, "agents of concern" are classified as Select Agents and Toxins, and "sequences of concern" are sequences derived from or encoding Select Agents and Toxins. For foreign orders, "agents of concern" also include pathogens and toxins on the EAR's CCL, and "sequences of concerns" includes those nucleic acids derived from or encoding those pathogens and toxins.[6]

If a customer orders a synthetic nucleic acid that can be classified as a Select Agent or Toxin, the provider must abide by the CDC and USDA/ APHIS Select Agent Regulations (42 CFR 73, 7 CFR 331, and 9 CFR 121). The CDC/APHIS national Select Agent registry Web site (*http:// www.selectagents.gov*) contains a guidance document developed by the national Select Agent regulatory programs to assist providers in identifying synthetically derived Select Agent materials that would fall under the current regulations. Providers of regulated nucleic acids must be registered with CDC or APHIS in order to synthesize these materials.

The U.S. Government acknowledges that there are synthetic nucleic acid sequences from non-Select Agents or Toxins that may pose a biosecurity concern. Synthetic nucleic acid providers may choose to investigate such sequences as part of their best practices. However, due to the complexity of determining pathogenicity and because research in this area is ongoing, a list of additional non-Select Agent or Toxin sequences or organisms to screen against would not be comprehensive and consequently are not provided by the U.S. Government in this guidance.

Because the CCL and the Select Agents and Toxins list are not identical, separate screening for those sequences on the CCL is recommended for international orders.

2. Technical Goals and Recommendations for Sequence Screening
The reliable and accurate detection of synthetic nucleic acid sequences derived from or encoding sequences or agents of concern is the primary goal of sequence screening. In considering various sequence screening methodologies, the U.S. Government developed the following list of specific technical goals and recommendations for a sequence screening methodology:

The U.S. Government recommends that the sequence screening method should identify sequences *unique* to Select Agents and Toxins. Many DNA sequences encode genes that are required to maintain normal cellular physiology, otherwise known as "house- keeping genes." These "house-keeping genes" are highly conserved between pathogenic and non-pathogenic species. Screening methodologies that recognize highly conserved sequences such as "house-

---

[6] The EAR provisions are subject to change, as they are regularly updated pursuant to multilateral agreements.

60

keeping genes" as positive hits for sequences of concern not only offer little to no biosecurity benefit, but may impede the screening efforts. Such methodologies would produce a larger number of hits adding extra burden for screeners and potentially resulting in actual sequences of concern being overlooked. Additionally, such a system may hamper scientific research by falsely assigning sequences from closely related microbes as sequences of concern.

The U.S. Government recommends that sequence screening be performed for both DNA strands and the resultant polypeptides derived from translations using the three alternative reading frames on each DNA strand (or six- frame translation). Each amino acid is encoded by a codon, a three nucleotide sequence of DNA. The correspondence from codon to amino acid is not unique. A given amino acid may be encoded by one to six distinct codons, which means that an amino acid polypeptide can be encoded by many different DNA sequences. Consequently, to determine whether a nucleotide sequence encodes for a sequence or agent of concern, it is necessary to screen the six-frame translation polypeptides encoded by the DNA sequences in addition to the DNA sequences themselves.

The U.S. Government recommends that sequence alignment methods should permit the detection of "sequences of concern" of 200 bps that may be hidden within larger sequence orders. Genes vary widely in length. If a sequence screening system assesses only the overall sequence length without any local checks, a sequence of concern can go undetected if inserted within a larger, benign sequence. The screening routine should be capable of local sequence alignments to ensure that potentially harmful sequences, embedded within larger sequences, are not overlooked. 200 bps is set as the limit for sequences of concern since synthetic nucleic acids smaller than 200 bps can be readily ordered as oligonucleotides, and gene synthesis companies are the target audience for this guidance.

3. Sequence Screening Methodology

The U.S. Government considered two distinct screening approaches, one based on a curated database of known sequences of concern and another utilizing a method called "Best Match." The first approach requires the creation of databases identifying specific features such as known pathogenic sequences, virulence factors, house-keeping genes, etc. While the acquisition of such knowledge is progressing, at this time customized database approaches are unable to provide a robust solution that can be implemented by DNA synthesis providers. Consequently, the U.S. Government recommends a "Best Match" approach for sequence screening. In this approach, a query sequence is deemed to be unique to a Select Agent or Toxin if the sequence (amino acid) is more closely related to a Select Agent or Toxin sequence than to a non-Select Agent or Toxin sequence. Sequences that are equally related to both a Select Agent or Toxin and a non-Select Agent or Toxin will not produce a sequence hit. As a result, the number of hits for sequences that can be obtained from non-Select Agents and Toxins will be reduced. To meet the goals and recommendations stated above, the U.S. Government recommends that each sequence be broken into a six-frame translation of 200 bp nucleotide segments. Each resulting 66 amino acid sequence should be compared to the GenBank protein sequence database using a sequence alignment tool. The "Best Match" is the sequence or sequences with the greatest percent identity over the entire 66 amino acid sequence. If the "Best Match" is to a Select Agent or Toxin sequence, with no equivalent hits to a non-Select Agent or Toxin, the order should be further investigated by the provider as a potential sequence hit.

The "Best Match" approach is intended to minimize the number of sequence hits due to genes that are shared among both Select Agents or Toxins and non-Select Agents or Toxins.

Nonetheless, some harmless sequences in Select Agents or Toxins or those that are routinely used in scientific research may result in a hit during this sequence screen.

The U.S. Government recommends that providers develop, maintain, and document protocols to determine if a sequence hit qualifies as a true sequence of concern. Additionally, providers should keep records of all hits even if the order is deemed acceptable. In cases where the provider is unable to make the determination, advice can be sought from the relevant U.S. Government Departments and Agencies by contacting the nearest FBI Field Office Weapons of Mass Destruction Coordinator.

The provider may deem some sequences from non-Select Agents and Toxins to be a biosecurity concern. The U.S. Government recommends that providers continue to exercise their due diligence in the investigation of screening hits against non-Select Agents and Toxins that may raise a biosecurity concern.

These sequence screening methodology recommendations do not preclude the use of curated databases in addition to the "Best Match" approach. The development of such databases is encouraged as an additional screening tool that will improve with time as additional data becomes available. Providers may choose to use other screening approaches that they assess to be equivalent or superior to the "Best Match" approach. The U.S. Government recommends that providers develop, maintain, and document their sequence screening protocol within company records.

The U.S. Government recognizes that continued research and development may lead to new and improved screening methodologies. As new methods are developed, U.S. guidance may change accordingly.

C. Follow-Up Screening

Follow-up screening may be warranted if *customer screening* reveals any 'red flags' or *sequence screening* results in a hit. In any case where there are abnormal circumstances surrounding the order or the customer has ordered a sequence of concern, the U.S. Government recommends that providers ask for information regarding the customer's proposed end-use of the order to help assess their need and the scientific legitimacy of their work. Sample end-uses of ordered synthetic nucleic acids could include, but are not limited to:
- Identification of pathogenicity genes via marker-deletion mutagenesis
- Training for threat agent detection
- Production of organism for experimental research studies

If the customer is associated with an institution or firm, providers should also contact the customer's biological safety officer, supervisor, lab director or director of research in order to verify the customer's identity and need. If the customer is not affiliated with an institution or firm, providers should also conduct a literature review of the customer's past research to verify his or her identity and need.

VI. Recommended Processes for Domestic and International Orders

This section outlines recommendations for specific screening processes for orders from domestic and international customers. The *customer screening*, *sequence screening*, and *follow-up screening* protocols that are referenced in this section are defined and described in Section V. Most of the information provided in this section serves as a reminder to providers to ensure they are meeting their legal obligations not to conduct unapproved business transactions with certain proscribed entities.

A. Domestic Orders

Once a domestic customer order is received, the provider should conduct *customer screening.* In addition to verifying the customer identity and identifying any 'red flags,' providers should be aware of regulatory and statutory prohibitions for U.S. persons from dealing with certain foreign persons, entities and companies. In order to avoid violating U.S. law, providers are encouraged to check the individual placing the order and the individual's affiliated institution (when applicable) against several lists of proscribed entities before filling each order, including the:

- Department of Treasury Office of Foreign Assets Control (OFAC) list of Specially Designated Nationals and Blocked Persons (SDN List).
- Department of State list of persons engaged in proliferation activities. • Department of Commerce Denied

Persons List (DPL).

According to U.S. regulations, no U.S. persons or entities may conduct business transactions with individuals or entities on the SDN List without a license from OFAC. This list is maintained by OFAC. OFAC only provides a license to deal with individuals on the SDN List in extremely limited circumstances.[7]

According to U.S. regulations, no U.S. persons or entities may conduct business transactions with individuals sanctioned by the Department of State for engaging in proliferation activities.[8] Additionally, the U.S. Government recommends that providers screen customers against the DPL for domestic orders. This list includes those firms and individuals whose export privileges have been denied. While the Department of Commerce only regulates exports and therefore does not require that companies screen their domestic customers against the list, it recommends that they do so, to avoid unwittingly passing on sensitive technology or materials to U.S. residents known to be involved in proliferation activities.[2]

Because the updated lists are available online, providers should ensure they are using the most recently updated lists when screening customers against these lists.

If no concerns are raised after consulting these lists, the provider should proceed to *sequence screening.* If a sequence of concern is identified, providers should conduct *follow-up screening.* If there are concerns after consulting these lists, providers should consider seeking assistance from the U.S. Government as outlined in Section VII.

B. Foreign Orders

Once an order from a foreign customer is received, the provider should conduct *customer screening.* In addition to complying with the rules described for domestic orders, all providers who export products from the United States to international customers must comply with the U.S. export laws, including the International Emergency Economic Powers Act,[9] the Trading with the Enemy Act,[10] and any implementing U.S. Government regulations or Presidential Executive

---

[7] Additional information, including the SDN List, is available at: *http://www.treas.gov/offices/ enforcement/ofac/sdn/.*

[8] Announcements of such sanctions determinations are printed in the **Federal Register** and are maintained on the Department of State's Web site (*http://www.state.gov/t/isn/c15231.htm*).

[9] Visit *http://www.treas.gov/offices/enforcement/ ofac/legal/statutes/ieepa.pdf* for additional information.

[10] Visit *http://www.treas.gov/offices/enforcement/ ofac/legal/statutes/twea.pdf* for additional information.

orders. Certain transactions with sanctioned countries may be permitted but may require a license from OFAC and/or the Department of Commerce's Bureau of Industry and Security (BIS). Most transactions involving Cuba, Iran, and Sudan are prohibited. In order to comply with the U.S. export laws and regulations, providers must first determine whether a given transaction with a sanctioned country is permitted, and, if not permitted, obtain any appropriate export licenses or other U.S. Government permissions prior to exporting any product to sanctioned countries. According to U.S. regulations, no U.S. persons or entities may conduct transactions with individuals or entities on the SDN List without a license from OFAC. This list is maintained by OFAC. OFAC only provides a license to deal with individuals on the SDN List in extremely limited circumstances.[6]

According to U.S. regulations, no U.S. persons or entities may conduct business transactions with individuals sanctioned by the Department of State for engaging in proliferation activities.[7] If no concerns are identified during *customer screening* or the checks against the lists delineated above, the provider should perform *sequence screening*. In addition to performing sequence screening for Select Agents and Toxins, providers are also encouraged to perform sequence screening of orders from foreign customers to determine whether they are governed by the EAR. As a member of the Australia Group, the United States requires exporters through the EAR to obtain export licenses for exports of reading-frame length nucleic acid sequences from pathogens listed under Export Control Classification Numbers (ECCNs) 1C351, 1C352, 1C353, and 1C354. The EAR also requires exporters to obtain licenses for exports of reading-frame length nucleic acid sequences from pathogens on the Select Agent list not listed elsewhere on the CCL (ECCN 1C360). The EAR requirements specifically apply to genetic elements that encode toxins or sub-units of controlled toxins or genetic elements associated with pathogenicity of controlled microorganisms. Because the EAR's CCL and the Select Agents and Toxins list are not identical, separate screening for those sequences on the CCL is necessary for international orders. The U.S. Government recommends that in addition to screening for Select Agents and Toxins, providers use a "Best Match" approach to identify pathogens and toxins on the CCL when an order is placed by an international customer. If the ordered synthetic nucleic acid is controlled under ECCN 1C353 and is capable of encoding a protein, an export license is necessary for all international orders, according to the EAR.[2]

Even for exported items that do not have a specific entry on the CCL and are considered under EAR 99 (for which a license is not required to most destinations), certain individuals and organizations are prohibited from receiving U.S. exports and others may only receive goods if they have been licensed. As a result, before filling an international order for *any* synthetic nucleic acid that cannot be classified under an ECCN, providers must consult several lists of such individuals and organizations according to the EAR. If the customer appears on any of these lists, additional action is required and an export license may be necessary, depending on the list.[11] These lists include the DPL, the Entity List (EL), and the Unverified List (UL).

In addition to the SDN List and proliferation sanctions notifications, providers must not conduct business with persons and entities on the DPL based on the EAR.[2] The DPL includes parties that have been denied export and reexport privileges.

---

[11] A general review of export control basics is available at *http://www.bis.doc.gov/licensing/ exportingbasics.htm.*

In accordance with the EAR, exports to persons or entities on the EL require an export license.[2] The EL contains a list of names of certain foreign persons—including businesses, research institutions, government and private organizations, individuals, and other types of legal persons—that are subject to specific license requirements for the export, reexport and/or transfer (in- country) of specified items. On an individual basis, the persons on the EL are subject to licensing requirements and policies supplemental to those found elsewhere in the EAR.

The presence of a party on the UL in a transaction is a "red flag" that should be resolved before proceeding with the transaction.[2] The UL includes names and countries of foreign persons who in the past were parties to a transaction with respect to which BIS could not conduct a pre-license check (PLC) or a post-shipment verification (PSV) for reasons outside of the U.S. Government's control. Additional "red flags" can be found in Supplement No. 3 to Part 732 of the EAR.

To avoid violating U.S. laws and regulations, providers should consult these lists whenever an international customer places an order. Because the updated lists are available online, providers should ensure they are using the most recently updated lists when screening customers against these lists. The U.S. Government recommends that the provider check the individual placing the order and the individual's affiliated institution (when applicable) against these lists.

Additionally, U.S. persons or entities may not export, reexport, or transfer (in- country) an item subject to the EAR without a license if, at the time of export, reexport, or transfer (in-country) the exporter knows that the item will be used in the design, development, production, stockpiling, or use of biological weapons in or by any country or destination, worldwide.

If any of these checks reveals cause for concern, the provider should proceed according to the details provided in Section VII. Additionally, if a sequence of concern is identified after *sequence screening, follow-up screening* should occur.

If an order involves an export, according to the EAR, both the provider and customer are required to maintain documentary evidence of the transaction and are prohibited from misrepresenting or concealing material facts in licensing processes and all export control documents.[2]

VII. Contacting the U.S. Government

In cases where *follow-up screening* cannot resolve an issue raised by either *customer screening* or *sequence screening,* the U.S. Government recommends that providers contact one of the following agencies for further information:

Federal Bureau of Investigation (FBI)

If an order turns up 'red flags' or includes a sequence of concern and *follow-up screening* does not sufficiently clarify the customer's identity and the order's intended end- use, providers should contact the Weapons of Mass Destruction (WMD)

Coordinator at their nearest FBI Field

Office. Providers should also contact the WMD Coordinator if the *follow-up screening* reveals that the customer has no legitimate need for the order.

CDC and APHIS Select Agent Regulatory Programs (Select Agent Programs)

If necessary, the CDC and APHIS Select Agent regulatory programs can be contacted through the national Select Agent Web site (*http:// www.selectagents.gov*). The CDC program can be contacted directly via e- mail at *lrsat@cdc.gov* or by fax at 404– 718-2096. The APHIS program can be contacted directly via e-mail at *Agricultural.Select.Agent.Program@ aphis.usda.gov* or by fax at 301–734– 3652.

Department of Commerce

If *sequence screening* reveals that an order from an international customer contains a Select Agent or sequence of concern, providers should contact the nearest field office of the Department of Commerce's Office of Export Enforcement. Providers should also contact the Office of Export Enforcement if they receive an international order from a country currently subject to a U.S. trade embargo or a customer that is on one of the proscribed lists described in Section VI. The Department of Commerce will contact other U.S. Government agencies as necessary. The supervisory office is in Washington, DC and the phone number is 202–482–1208. Locations and contact information for all field offices are available at *http://www.bis.doc.gov/ about/programoffices.htm*. Assistance from an export counselor at the Department of Commerce is available by calling 202–482–4811.

Scenarios

If providers encounter one of the following scenarios and are unable to resolve issues raised by customer screening or sequence screening, they can contact one of the following U.S. Government agencies for assistance, using the contact information provided above:

1. Provider receives double-stranded synthetic DNA order and a customer flag (suspicious customer) is identified in *customer screening*. Recommend the provider contact the nearest FBI Field Office WMD Coordinator. FBI contacts other Departments and Agencies, as appropriate.

2. Provider receives a double-stranded synthetic DNA order that is for a Select Agent or Toxin. Provider should refer to the Select Agent Regulations and follow necessary protocols. If necessary, the provider should contact the appropriate Select Agent Program (CDC or USDA/ APHIS).

a. CDC or APHIS may contact FBIHQ as appropriate.

3. Provider receives a double-stranded DNA order that incorporates a sequence of concern; *follow-up screening* reveals no legitimate purpose[11] for order or research requirement. Provider contacts the FBI WMD Coordinator. FBI contacts the CDC or APHIS as appropriate.

4. Provider receives an international double-stranded DNA order incorporating a Select Agent or Toxin or a sequence of concern and DOC denies the export license. DOC contacts the FBI as appropriate.

5. Provider receives a double-stranded DNA order from a customer that is listed on one or more restricted lists, which prohibits the fulfillment of the order. Provider contacts the FBI WMD Coordinator. FBI contacts DOC as appropriate.

VIII. Customer and Sequence Screening Software and Expertise

There are a variety software packages that can assist with the verification of customers and screening against the necessary lists of proscribed entities. Providers should be aware that commercially available software packages may not necessarily address all aspects of customer screening recommended by the U.S. Government.

----

[11]18 U.S.C. 175(b) defines criminal prohibitions with respect to biological weapons as "Whoever knowingly possesses any biological agent, toxin, or delivery system of a type or in a quantity that, under the circumstances, is not reasonably justified by a prophylactic, protective, bona fide research, or other peaceful purpose, shall be fined under this title, imprisoned not more than 10 years, or both."

In addition to a sequence database and screening method, appropriate sequence screening software must be selected by synthetic nucleic acid providers. The U.S. Government recommends that synthetic nucleic acid providers select a sequence screening software tool that utilizes both a global and local sequence alignment technique; the most popular algorithm that meets both requirements is the BLAST search tool. BLAST is available for download for free at the NCBI site. Similar tools are also freely or commercially available, or could be designed by the provider to meet their sequence screening needs. By utilizing such a tool, similarity over the length of the sequence being screened and the identification of regions that are similar within longer segments that are not alike are both encompassed in the sequence screening approach. Specific criteria for the statistical significance of the hit (BLAST's e-values) or percent identity values will not be recommended because these details depend on the specific screening protocol. By utilizing the "Best Match" approach, the sequence with the greatest percent identity over the entire 66 amino acid sequence should be considered the "Best Match," regardless of the statistical significance or percent identity.

The U.S. Government recommends that synthetic nucleic acid providers have the necessary expertise in-house to perform the sequence screenings, analyze the results and conduct the appropriate follow-up research to evaluate the significance of dubious sequence matches. Such follow-up research could include comparing the ordered sequence to information found in the published literature about Select Agents and Toxins or with information found in other databases of Select

Agents and Toxins.

The U.S. Government recognizes that continued research and development on new and improved bioinformatics tools is desirable. As new methods are developed, U.S. guidance may change accordingly.

IX. Records Retention

The U.S. Government recommends that companies retain electronic copies of customer orders for at least eight years based on statutory limitations set forth by U.S. Code of Federal Crimes and Procedures, Title 18 Section 3286.[4]

The U.S. Government recommends archiving the following information: Customer (and end-user, if different) information (name, organization, address, and phone number), order sequence information, and order information (date placed and shipped, shipping address, and receiver name).

The U.S. Government recommends that providers develop, maintain, and document their sequence screening protocol within company records.

The U.S. Government recommends that providers develop, maintain, and document protocols to determine if a sequence hit qualifies as a true sequence of concern.

The U.S. Government recommends that providers keep records of any *follow-up screening*, even if the order was ultimately filled.

If an order involves an export, according to the EAR, both the provider and customer are required to maintain documentary evidence of the transaction and are prohibited from misrepresenting or concealing material facts in licensing process and all export control documents.[2]

X. Appendix to Screening Framework
Guidance for Synthetic Double- Stranded DNA Providers
Summary of Recommendations

The field of synthetic genomics is evolving rapidly. This document is intended to provide guidance to producers of synthetic genomic products regarding the screening of orders to ensure that these orders are filled in compliance with current U.S. regulations and encourage best practices in addressing any potential biosecurity concerns. The U.S. Government recommends that all orders for synthetic double-stranded DNA 200 base pairs (bps) in length or greater be subject to a screening framework that incorporates both sequence screening and customer screening.

Customer Screening

The U.S. Government recommends that, for every order, synthetic nucleic acid providers:

(1) Gather the following information to verify a customer's identity:

- Customer's (and end-user's, if different) full name and contact information
- Billing address and shipping address (if not the same)
- Customer's institutional or corporate affiliation (if applicable)
- Name of institution's Biological

Safety Officer (if applicable)

(2) Screen customers against several lists of proscribed entities (described under the *Domestic Orders* and *Foreign Orders* sections).

In cases where the customer is not affiliated with an institution or firm, the U.S. Government recommends that the provider conduct *follow-up screening*.

If a review of customer information reveals one or more 'red flags,' the U.S. Government recommends that providers exercise due diligence, inquire regarding the circumstances, and verify the end-use and end-user (see the *Follow-Up Screening* section).

Sequence Screening

The U.S. Government recommends that:

- Nucleic acid sequences be screened using a "Best Match" approach to identify nucleic acids that are unique to Select Agents and Toxins.
- For foreign orders, nucleic acids be screened using a "Best Match" approach to identify nucleic acids that are unique to pathogens and toxins on the Commerce Control List.
- Sequence screening be performed for both DNA strands and the resultant polypeptides derived from translations using the three alternative reading frames on each DNA strand (or six-frame translation).
- Sequence alignment methods should permit the detection of hidden "sequences of concern" as small as 200 bps.

If a customer orders a synthetic nucleic acid that can be classified as a Select Agent or Toxin, the provider should consult and must abide by the CDC and USDA/APHIS Select Agent Regulations (42 CFR 73, 7 CFR 331, and 9 CFR 121). In order to produce a regulated Select Agent or Toxin nucleic acid, the producer must be registered with CDC or USDA/APHIS.[12]

The U.S. Government recommends that providers continue to exercise their due diligence in the investigation of screening hits against non-Select Agents and Toxins that may raise a biosecurity concern.

Follow-up Screening

When customer screening reveals any 'red flags' or sequence screening identifies a sequence of concern, the U.S. Government recommends that providers ask for information regarding the customer's proposed end-use of the order to assess their need and the scientific legitimacy of their work. If the customer is associated with an institution or firm, providers should also contact the customer's biological safety officer, supervisor, lab director or director of research to verify their identity and need. If the customer is not affiliated with an institution or firm, providers should also conduct a literature review of the customer's past research to verify his or her identity and need.

---

[12] Additional information regarding the CDC and USDA/APHIS Select Agent Regulations is available at *http://www.selectagents.gov.*

Domestic Orders

The U.S. Government reminds providers of the following:

- According to U.S. regulations, no U.S. persons or entities may conduct transactions with individuals or entities on the list of Specially Designated Nationals and Blocked Persons (SDN List) without a license from the
Department of the Treasury Office of Foreign Assets Control (OFAC).[13]
- According to U.S. regulations, no U.S. persons or entities may conduct business transactions with individuals sanctioned by the Department of State
for engaging in proliferation activities.[14]

The U.S. Government recommends that providers check domestic customers against the most recent Department of Commerce Denied
Persons List (DPL).[15]

In order to avoid violating U.S. law, providers are encouraged to check the individual placing the order and the individual's affiliated institution (when applicable) against the most recent versions of these lists of proscribed entities before filling each order.

Foreign Orders

The U.S. Government reminds providers of the following:

- All providers who export products from the United States to international customers must comply with the U.S. export laws, including the International Emergency Economic Powers Act
(IEEPA),[16] the Trading with the Enemy Act,[17] and any implementing U.S.
Government regulations or Presidential Executive Orders. Certain transactions with sanctioned countries may be permitted, but most require a license from OFAC and/or the Department of Commerce's Bureau of Industry and Security (BIS). Most transactions involving Cuba, Iran, and Sudan are prohibited. In order to comply with the U.S. export laws and regulations, providers must first determine whether a given transaction with a sanctioned country is permitted, and, if not permitted, obtain any appropriate export licenses or other U.S. government permissions prior to exporting any product to sanctioned countries.
- According to U.S. regulations, no
U.S. persons or entities may conduct business transactions with individuals and entities on the SDN List without a license from OFAC.[13]
- According to U.S. regulations, no U.S. persons or entities may conduct business transactions with individuals sanctioned by the Department of State
for engaging in proliferation activities.[14] • The Export Administration Regulations (EAR) require that providers have an export license from BIS prior to exporting a synthetic nucleic acid that is

---

[13] Additional information, including the SDN List, is available at: *http://www.treas.gov/offices/ enforcement/ofac/sdn/*.

[14] Announcements of such sanctions determinations are printed in the **Federal Register** and are maintained on the Department of State's Web site (*http://www.state.gov/t/isn/c15231.htm*).

[15] Visit *http://www.access.gpo.gov/bis/ear/ ear_data.html* to access the most recent Commerce Control List and review the Export Administration Regulations.

[16] Visit *http://www.treas.gov/offices/enforcement/ ofac/legal/statutes/ieepa.pdf* for additional information.

[17] Visit *http://www.treas.gov/offices/enforcement/ ofac/legal/statutes/twea.pdf* for additional information.

controlled by an Export Control Classification Number (ECCN) and is capable of encoding a protein.[15]

•	U.S. persons or entities may not export, reexport, or transfer (in-country) an item subject to the EAR without a license if, at the time of export, reexport, or transfer (in-country) the exporter knows that the item will be used in the design, development, production, stockpiling, or use of biological weapons in or by any country or destination, worldwide.[15]

•	In accordance with the EAR, providers must not conduct business with persons and entities on the DPL.[15]

•	In accordance with the EAR, exports to persons or entities on the Entity List are subject to licensing requirements and policies in addition to those elsewhere in the EAR.[15]

•	The presence of a party on the UL in a transaction is a "red flag" that should be resolved before proceeding with the transaction.[15]

In order to avoid violating U.S. laws and regulations, providers are encouraged to check the individual placing the order and the individual's affiliated institution (when applicable) against the most recent versions of these lists of proscribed entities before filling each order.

The U.S. Government recommends that providers utilize a "Best Match" approach to identify sequences of pathogens and toxins on the Commerce Control List for international orders. This screen is in addition to the "Best Match" sequence screen for Select Agent and Toxin sequences.

Contacting the U.S. Government

In cases where *follow-up screening* cannot resolve concerns raised by *customer screening* or *sequence screening, or when providers are otherwise unsure about whether to fill an order*, the U.S. Government recommends that providers contact relevant agencies as described in Section VII of "Screening Framework

Guidance for Synthetic Nucleic Acid Providers."

Customer and Sequence Screening Software and Expertise

Providers should be aware that commercially available customer screening software packages may not necessarily address all aspects of customer screening recommended by the U.S. Government.

The U.S. Government recommends that:

•	Synthetic nucleic acid providers select a sequence screening software tool that utilizes both a global and local sequence alignment technique.

•	Synthetic nucleic acid providers have the necessary expertise in-house to perform the sequence screenings, analyze the results, and conduct the appropriate follow-up research to evaluate the significance of dubious sequence matches.

Records Retention

The U.S. Government recommends that:

•	Companies retain electronic copies of customer orders for at least eight years based on the statute of limitations set forth by U.S. Code Title 18 Section 3286.[18] The following information should be archived: Customer (and end- user, if different) information (name, organization,

---

[18] Section 3286 specifies that no person shall be prosecuted, tried, or punished for any noncapital offense involving certain violations unless the indictment is found or the information is instituted within 8 years after the offense was committed. This statute of limitations applies to Title 18 Section 175(b) (possession of biological agents with no reasonable justification).

address, and phone number), order sequence information, and order information (date placed and shipped, shipping address, and receiver name).

•	Providers develop, maintain, and document their sequence screening protocols within company records.

•	Providers develop, maintain, and document protocols to determine if a sequence hit qualifies as a true sequence of concern.

•	Providers keep records of hits that required follow-up screening, even if the order was ultimately filled.

If an order involves an export, according to the EAR, both the provider and customer are required to maintain documentary evidence of the transaction and are prohibited from misrepresenting or concealing material facts in licensing processes and all export control documents.[15]

Dated: November 19, 2009.

Nicole Lurie,
Assistant Secretary for Preparedness and Response.
[FR Doc. E9–28328 Filed 11–25–09; 8:45 am]
BILLING CODE 4150–37–P

## 3.1.3	DIY Regulation

The DIY or Do-It-Yourself community is broadly defined. The term includes organized activities like iGEM, the international genetically engineered machine competition that draws high school students to graduate students in teams to compete for the best application of biotechnology in genetic engineering. The term also includes the independent individual or gathering of individuals to develop genetically modified organisms as a hobby in their garage or warehouse group space.

Citizen science has always been a strong thread in U.S. history and it is a form of free expression protected by the First Amendment as long as it does not endanger the health of the public or pose any other public threat. As long as organisms that are not on lists of potential biological weapons or select agent lists, then there is no regulation of these materials, except potentially for shipping through a common carrier.

The term "biohacker" has become the name for these individuals and their process of "biohacking" biology. The term comes from "hacking" computers by writing code to achieve a particular result, like writing code with DNA.

Only when citizens began genetically engineering animals, did FDA become concerned about the DIY activities. But the guidance developed by FDA in 2009 and again in 2017 imposed commercially driven standards for this process. So FDA asked for voluntary disclosure of activities to FDA and a letter that demonstrates the individual cannot pay for a permit process sufficed for the individual to practice animal genetic modification. One biohacker, David Ishee, received a good bit of notoriety when he began a process of editing out disease-causing genes in Dalmations and Mastiffs that he breeds, based on the identification of the disease-causing gene in the scientific literature.

Ishee is not the only biohacker pushing the limits of regulations. Biohacking has become a worldwide phenomena and many are pushing the limits of regulations in their countries. Here, David Ishee explains in his interview for the *MIT Technology Review* the kinds of regulatory changes that he faces.

A Biohacker's Plan to Upgrade Dalmatians Ends Up in the Doghouse

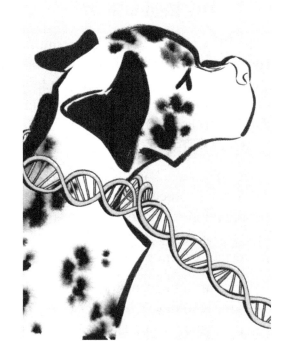

The FDA wants to regulate animals altered using the gene-editing technique CRISPR.

by Andrew Rosenblum
MIT Technology Review

February 1, 2017

David Ishee is a Mississippi kennel operator with a passion for dogs and a plan to improve them using a gene-editing technology called CRISPR from a modest laboratory he's built in a plywood shed.

Sound unlikely? It's serious enough that the U.S. Food and Drug Administration, in a phone call last week, told Ishee he wouldn't be able to sell any edited dogs without its approval.

Ishee, a member of what's called the "biohacker" movement, says he is hoping to use inexpensive new gene-editing techniques to modify the genes of Dalmatians. By repairing a single DNA letter in their genomes, Ishee believes, he can rid them of an inherited disease, hyperuricemia, that's almost as closely associated with the breed as their white coats and black spots.

In early January, Ishee sent the agency a sketch of his plans to fix Dalmatians, expecting to be told no approval was needed. He didn't immediately hear back—and soon found out why. On January 18, the agency released a sweeping new proposal to regulate cattle, pigs, dogs, and other animals modified with gene editing.

The federal health agency already regulates transgenic animals—those with DNA added from a different species. But what about a dog whose genome has been tweaked to repair a disease gene? Or to endow it with the gene for a trait, like fluffy fur, already found in another canine?

According to the newly proposed regulations, such creations will also need federal approval before entering the marketplace.

That was a blow to breeders like Ishee, who think gene-editing technology can quickly help them make better, healthier animals, and reverse some of the damage done to specialized breeds. "I think it will be easier to teach dog breeders CRISPR than it will be to teach dog breeders why pure breeding is a bad thing," he says.

Yet the potential ease of making modifications is raising questions about how CRISPR will be controlled. Last year, the U.S. director of national intelligence, James Clapper, ominously declared that genome editing was a potential "weapon of mass destruction."

Ishee says he had a phone call with the FDA last week and didn't get the impression the agency was enthusiastic to see people like him altering dogs. "I was hoping they would be there with me, trying to come up with creative solutions, to try to serve their needs and the animals' needs," he says. "But I didn't get that feeling. They seemed pretty nervous, like I was out to get them."

According to the agency's new regulatory proposal, it plans to treat the edited portion of the animal's genome as a veterinary drug. That means that just like a new pill, edited dogs can't be sold, or even given away, without first proving they are safe and work as intended, a process likely to incur costly studies and piles of paperwork. For instance, it took the creators of GM "Aquabounty" salmon around 20 years to win approval to commercialize their faster-growing fish.

The new rules have larger companies concerned, too. Last December, a Minnesota biotechnology startup called Recombinetics fired off a letter to the FDA saying that it planned to start selling Holstein milk cows that it had genetically edited so that they wouldn't develop horns. But now Recombinetics's sizable investments are in doubt. Scott Fahrenkrug, the company's founder, says he is ready to fight what he thinks are irrational rules.

"Trump isn't letting those regs [get] enacted," he wrote MIT Technology Review in an e-mail.

Ishee, based in the small town of Mendenhall, also wonders whether the regulations from Washington should be disobeyed. During a conference call webcast on YouTube last week, he and another biohacker mulled what would happen if they just started curing dogs anyway, in an act of civil disobedience.

"I feel like maybe the best thing is to just go ahead and produce the healthy animals and then just tell people," says Ishee. "We cured this disease, but the FDA won't let us."

Humans have been shaping the DNA of dogs for millennia. But the breeding efforts that produced the Dalmatian's spots, or the pug's flat snout, have also led to serious health problems. Certain prized bulldogs can't even give birth without human assistance. "Dogs have more genetic diseases than any other species on the planet," says Ishee. "So that's us. We did that."

A problem for Dalmatians is that the breed lacks a working copy of a gene needed to clear uric acid, causing stones that can block the urethra and can lead to a burst bladder. After several centuries of inbreeding, few Dalmatian have a normal copy of the gene. Although you could introduce a healthy gene by mating a Dalmatian with another dog, then you'd dilute the famous dog's signature look. "Dog breeders are kind of obsessed with pure breeding," says Ishee.

David Ishee

Ishee's plan is to purchase or build DNA that has the correct gene, as well as the molecular ingredients needed to perform the CRISPR gene editing. He would then add it to Dalmatian sperm before artificially inseminating a female. Hopefully, the mutated DNA letter would be repaired in at least some of the resulting litter of dogs.

Whether Ishee can pull it off isn't at all clear. In the past year, Ishee says, he's tried to make "bioluminescent" mastiff puppies by adding DNA from glowing bacteria. Those experiments, intended as a test run for curing canine genetic diseases, have no so far been successful.

Samantha Nicole Lotti, an animal science researcher at the University of Illinois at Urbana-Champaign, says the sperm technique Ishee wants to use can be unpredictable and still hasn't been paired with CRISPR to repair a gene, the kind of gene editing he needs to do. "This does not mean it is not possible," she notes.

Just like researchers at large universities who modify animals for research, Ishee says, he was told the FDA will allow him to edit Dalmatians so long as he keeps the resulting puppies on his property, in a kind of quarantine, and doesn't sell them or give them to other breeders.

Ishee isn't sure he sees the point in fixing just a couple of dogs. He wants to spread the improvement far and wide. "Now that the technology exists, we have an ethical obligation to do something about the genetic problems we created," he says. "It's a horrible disease, they all have it, and nobody seems to be willing to fix it."
https://www.technologyreview.com/s/603530/a-biohackers-plan-to-upgrade-dalmatians-ends-up-in-the-doghouse

Chapter 4

The Genetically-Modified Organisms Controversy

4.1.1.   Overview of NEPA and ESA

The following excerpts are agency overviews of both of these major federal statutes. The National Environmental Policy Act is administered primarily by the Council on Environmental Quality; and the Endangered Species Act is administered by the U.S. Fish and Wildlife Service in the U.S. Department of the Interior.

Both of these statutes are important to many programs in agricultural biotechnology.

4.1.1.1 History and Purpose of NEPA

Congress enacted NEPA in December, 1969, and President Nixon signed it into law on January 1, 1970. NEPA was the first major environmental law in the United States and is often called the "Magna Carta" of environmental laws. Importantly, NEPA established this country's national environmental policies. To implement these policies, NEPA requires agencies to undertake an assessment of the environmental effects of their proposed actions prior to making decisions. Two major purposes of the environmental review process are better informed decisions and citizen involvement, both of which should lead to implementation of NEPA's policies. Who is Responsible for Implementing NEPA? Every agency in the executive branch of the Federal Government has a responsibility to implement NEPA. In NEPA, Congress directed that, to the fullest extent possible, the policies, regulations, and public laws of the United States shall be interpreted and administered in accordance with the policies set forth in NEPA.2

To implement NEPA's policies, Congress prescribed a procedure, commonly referred to as "the NEPA process" or "the environmental impact assessment process." NEPA's procedural requirements apply to all Federal agencies in the executive branch. NEPA does not apply to the President, to Congress, or to the Federal courts.3 Because NEPA implementation is an important responsibility of the Federal Government, many Federal agencies have established offices dedicated to NEPA policy and program oversight. Employees in these offices prepare NEPA guidance, policy, and procedures for the agency, and often make this information available to the public through sources such as Internet websites. Agencies are required to develop their own capacity within a NEPA program in order to develop analyses and documents (or review those prepared by others) to ensure informed decisionmaking.4

The Congress, recognizing the profound impact of man's activity on the interrelations of all components of the natural environment, particularly the profound influences of population growth, high-density urbanization, industrial expansion, resource exploitation, and new and expanding technological advances and recognizing further the critical importance of restoring and maintaining environmental quality to the overall welfare and development of man, declares that it is the continuing policy of the Federal Government, in cooperation with State and local governments, and other concerned public and private organizations, to use all practicable means and measures, including financial and technical assistance, in a manner calculated to foster and promote the general welfare, to create and maintain conditions under which man and nature can exist in productive harmony, and fulfill the social, economic, and other requirements of present and future generations of Americans.

(b) In order to carry out the policy set forth in this Act, it is the continuing responsibility of the Federal Government to use all practicable means, consistent with other essential considerations of national policy, to improve and coordinate Federal plans, functions, programs, and resources to the end that the Nation may — 1. fulfill the responsibilities of each generation as trustee of the environment for succeeding generations; 2. assure for all Americans safe, healthful, productive, and aesthetically and culturally pleasing surroundings; 3. attain the widest range of beneficial uses of the environment without degradation, risk to health or safety, or other undesirable and unintended consequences; 4. preserve important historic, cultural, and natural aspects of our national heritage, and maintain, wherever possible, an environment which supports diversity, and variety of individual choice; 5. achieve a balance between population and resource use which will permit high standards of living and a wide sharing of life's amenities; and 6. enhance the quality of renewable resources and approach the maximum attainable recycling of depletable resources.

(c) The Congress recognizes that each person should enjoy a healthful environment and that each person has a responsibility to contribute to the preservation and enhancement of the environment. 4 A Citizen's Guide to the NEPA the Federal Register for public review and comment when first proposed and some are later codified and published in the Code of Federal Regulations.5 If you experience difficulty locating an agency's NEPA procedures, you can write or call the agency NEPA point of contacts and ask for a copy of their procedures.6 To What Do the Procedural Requirements of NEPA Apply? In NEPA, Congress recognized that the Federal Government's actions may cause significant environmental effects. The range of actions that cause significant environmental effects is broad and includes issuing regulations, providing permits for private actions, funding private actions, making federal land management decisions, constructing publicly-owned facilities, and many other types of actions. Using the NEPA process, agencies are required to determine if their proposed actions have significant environmental effects and to consider the environmental and related social and economic effects of their proposed actions. NEPA's procedural requirements apply to a Federal agency's decisions for actions, including financing, assisting, conducting, or approving projects or programs; agency rules, regulations, plans, policies, or procedures; and legislative proposals.7 NEPA applies when a Federal agency has discretion to choose among one or more alternative means of accomplishing a particular goal.8 Frequently, private individuals or companies will become involved in the NEPA process when they need a permit issued by a Federal agency. When a company applies for a permit (for example, for crossing federal lands or impacting waters of the United States) the agency that is being asked to issue the permit must evaluate the environmental effects of the permit decision under NEPA. Federal agencies might require the private company or developer to pay for the preparation of analyses, but the agency remains responsible for the scope and accuracy of the analysis. 5 The draft agency implementing procedures, or regulations, are published in the Federal Register, and a public comment period is required prior to CEQ approval. Commenting on these agency regulations is one way to be involved in their development. Most agencies already have implementing procedures; however, when they are changed, the agency will again provide for public comment on the proposed changes. 6 See Appendices A and D for information on how to access agency points of contact and agency websites. 7 CEQ NEPA Regulations, 40 C.F.R. § 1508.18. Note that this section applies only to legislation drafted and submitted to Congress by federal agencies. NEPA does not apply to legislation initiated by members of Congress. 8 CEQ NEPA Regulations, 40 C.F.R. § 1508.23.

When Does NEPA Apply? NEPA requires agency decisionmakers to make informed decisions. Therefore, the NEPA process must be completed before an agency makes a final decision on a proposed action. Good NEPA analyses should include a consideration of how NEPA's policy goals (Section 101) will be incorporated into the decision to the extent consistent with other considerations of national policy. NEPA does not require the decisionmaker to select the environmentally preferable alternative or prohibit adverse environmental effects. Indeed, decisionmakers in Federal agencies often have other concerns and policy considerations to take into account in the decisionmaking process, such as social, economic, technical or national security interests. But NEPA does require that decisionmakers be informed of the environmental consequences of their decisions.

The NEPA process can also serve to meet other environmental review requirements. For instance, actions that require the NEPA process may have an impact on endangered species, historic properties, or low income communities. The NEPA analysis, which takes into account the potential impacts of the proposed action and investigates alternative actions, may also serve as a framework to meet other environmental review requirements, such as the Endangered Species Act, the National Historic Preservation Act, the Environmental Justice Executive Order, and other Federal, State, Tribal, and local laws and regulations.9

Who Oversees the NEPA Process?
There are three Federal agencies that have particular responsibilities for NEPA. Primary responsibility is vested in the Council on Environmental Quality (CEQ), established by Congress in NEPA. Congress placed CEQ in the Executive Office of the President and gave it many responsibilities, including the responsibility to ensure that Federal agencies meet their obligations under the Act. CEQ oversees implementation of NEPA, principally through issuance and interpretation of NEPA regulations that implement the procedural requirements of NEPA. CEQ also reviews and approves Federal agency NEPA procedures, approves of alternative arrangements for compliance with NEPA in the case of

emergencies, and helps to resolve disputes between Federal agencies and with other governmental entities and members of the public. 9 CEQ NEPA Regualtions, 40 C.F.R. § 1502.25. 6

In 1978, CEQ issued binding regulations directing agencies on the fundamental requirements necessary to fulfill their NEPA obligations.10 The CEQ regulations set forth minimum requirements for agencies. The CEQ regulations also called for agencies to create their own implementing procedures that supplement the minimum requirements based on each agency's specific mandates, obligations, and missions.11 These agency-specific NEPA procedures account for the slight differences in agencies' NEPA processes.

The Environmental Protection Agency's (EPA) Office of Federal Activities reviews environmental impact statements (EIS) and some environmental assessments (EA) issued by Federal agencies.12 It provides its comments to the public by publishing summaries of them in the Federal Register, a daily publication that provides notice of Federal agency actions.13 EPA's reviews are intended to assist Federal agencies in improving their NEPA analyses and decisions.14 Another government entity involved in NEPA is the U.S. Institute for Environmental Conflict Resolution, which was established by the Environmental Policy and Conflict Resolution Act of 1998 to assist in resolving conflict over environmental issues that involve Federal agencies.15 While part of the Federal Government (it is located within the Morris K. Udall Foundation, a Federal agency located in Tucson, Arizona), it provides an independent, neutral, place for Federal agencies to work with citizens as well as State, local, and Tribal governments, private organizations, and businesses to reach common ground. The Institute provides dispute resolution alternatives to litigation and other adversarial approaches. The Institute is also charged with assisting the Federal Government in the implementation of the substantive policies set forth in Section 101 of NEPA.16 10 CEQ NEPA Regulations, 40 C.F.R. parts 1500-1508, available at www.nepa.gov. 11 CEQ NEPA Regualations, 40 C.F.R. § 1507.3. 12 Clean Air Act, 42 U.S.C. § 7609.

Navigating the NEPA Process Each year, thousands of Environmental Assessments (EAs) and hundreds of Environmental Impact Statements (EISs) are prepared by Federal agencies. These documents provide citizens and communities an opportunity to learn about and be involved in each of those environmental impact assessments that are part of the Federal agency decisionmaking process. It is important to understand that commenting on a proposal is not a "vote" on whether the proposed action should take place.

Nonetheless, the information you provide during the EA and EIS process can influence the decisionmakers and their final decisions because NEPA does require that federal decisionmakers be informed of the environmental consequences of their decisions.

4.1.1.2 Overview of the Endangered Species Act (ESA)

U. S. Fish and Wildlife Service, Endangered Species Program at http://www.fws.gov/endangered/(January 2013)

ESA Basics

40 Years of Conserving
Endangered Species

When Congress passed the Endangered Species Act (ESA) in 1973, it recognized that our rich natural heritage is of "esthetic, ecological, educational, recreational, and scientific value to our Nation and its people." It further expressed concern that many of our nation's native plants and animals were in danger of becoming extinct.

The purpose of the ESA is to protect and recover imperiled species and the ecosystems upon which they depend. The Interior Department's U.S. Fish and Wildlife Service (FWS) and the Commerce Department's National Marine Fisheries Service (NMFS) administer the ESA. The FWS has primary responsibility for terrestrial and freshwater organisms, while the responsibilities of NMFS are mainly marine wildlife such as whales and anadromous fish such as salmon.

Under the ESA, species may be listed as either endangered or threatened. "Endangered" means a species is in danger of extinction throughout all or a significant portion of its range. "Threatened" means a species is likely to become endangered within the foreseeable future. All species of plants and animals, except pest insects, are eligible for listing as endangered or threatened. For the purposes of the ESA, Congress defined species to include subspecies, varieties, and, for vertebrates, distinct population segments.

As of January 2013, the FWS has listed 2,054 species worldwide as endangered or threatened, of which 1,436 occur in the United States.

How are Species Listed?

Section 4 of the ESA requires species to be listed as endangered or threatened solely on the basis of their biological status and threats to their existence.

When evaluating a species for listing, the FWS considers five factors: 1) damage to, or destruction of, a species' habitat; 2) overutilization of the species for commercial, recreational, scientific, or educational purposes; 3) disease or Bart Gamett/USFWS predation; 4) inadequacy of existing protection; and 5) other natural or manmade factors that affect the continued existence of the species. When one or more of these factors imperils the survival of a species, the FWS takes action to protect it. The Fish and Wildlife Service is required to base its listing decisions on the best scientific information available.

Candidates for Listing

The FWS also maintains a list of "candidate" species. These are species for which the FWS has enough information to warrant proposing them for listing but is precluded from doing so by higher listing priorities. While listing actions of higher priority go forward, the FWS works with States, Tribes, private landowners, private partners, and other Federal agencies to carry out conservation actions for these species to prevent further decline and possibly eliminate the need for listing.

Protection

The ESA protects endangered and threatened species and their habitats by prohibiting the "take" of listed animals and the interstate or international trade in listed plants and animals, including their parts and products, except under Federal permit. Such permits generally are available for conservation and scientific purposes.

What is "Take"?

The ESA makes it unlawful for a person to take a listed animal without a permit. Take is defined as "to harass, harm, pursue, hunt, shoot, wound, kill, trap, capture, or collect or attempt to engage in any such conduct." Through regulations, the term "harm" is defined as "an act which actually kills or injures wildlife.

Such an act may include significant habitat modification or degradation where it actually kills or injures wildlife by significantly impairing essential behavioral patterns, including breeding, feeding, or sheltering." Listed plants are not protected from take, although it is illegal to collect or maliciously harm them on Federal land. Protection from commercial trade and the effects of Federal actions do apply for plants. In addtion, States may have their own laws restricting activity involving listed species.

Recovery

The law's ultimate goal is to "recover" species so they no longer need protection under the ESA. Recovery plans describe the steps needed to restore a species to ecological health. FWS biologists write and implement these plans with the assistance of species experts; other Federal, State, and local agencies; Tribes; nongovernmental organizations; academia; and other stakeholders.

Federal Agency Cooperation

Section 7 of the ESA requires Federal agencies to use their legal authorities to promote the conservation purposes of the ESA and to consult with the FWS and NMFS, as appropriate, to ensure that effects of actions they authorize, fund, or USFWS carry out are not likely to jeopardize the continued existence of listed species.

During consultation the "action" agency receives a "biological opinion" or concurrence letter addressing the proposed action. In the relatively few cases in which the FWS or NMFS makes a jeopardy determination, the agency offers "reasonable and prudent alternatives" about how the proposed action could be modified to avoid jeopardy. It is extremely rare that a project ends up being withdrawn or terminated because of jeopardy to a listed species.

The ESA also requires the designation of "critical habitat" for listed species when "prudent and determinable." Critical habitat includes geographic areas that contain the physical or biological features that are essential to the conservation of the species and that may need special management or protection. Critical habitat designations affect only Federal agency actions or federally funded or permitted activities.

Federal agencies are required to avoid "destruction" or "adverse modification" of designated critical habitat. Critical habitat may include areas that are not occupied by the species at the time of listing but are essential to its conservation. An area can be excluded from critical habitat designation if an economic analysis determines that the benefits of excluding it outweigh the benefits of including it, unless failure to designate the area as critical habitat may lead to extinction of the listed species.

The ESA provides a process for exempting development projects from the restrictions if a Cabinet-level "Endangered Species Committee" decides the benefits of the project clearly outweigh the benefits of conserving a species. Since its creation in 1978, the Committee has only been convened three times to make this decision.

Working with State

Partnerships with States are critical to our efforts to conserve listed species. Section 6 of the ESA encourages States to develop and maintain conservation programs for threatened and endangered species. Federal funding is available to promote State participation. Some State laws and regulations are more restrictive than the ESA in granting exceptions or permits.

Working with Landowners

Two-thirds of federally listed species have at least some habitat on private land, and some species have most of their remaining habitat on private land. The FWS has developed an array of tools and incentives to protect the interests of private landowners while encouraging management activities that benefit listed and other at-risk species.

Habitat Conservation Plans

Section 10 of the ESA may be used by landowners including private citizens, corporations, Tribes, States, and counties who want to develop property inhabited by listed species. Landowners may receive a permit to take such species incidental to otherwise legal activities, provided they have developed an approved habitat conservation plan (HCP). HCPs include an assessment of the likely impacts on the species from the proposed action, the steps that the permit holder will take to avoid, minimize, and mitigate the impacts, and the funding available to carry out the steps.

HCPs may benefit not only landowners but also species by securing and managing important habitat and by addressing economic development with a focus on species conservation.

Safe Harbor Agreements

Safe Harbor Agreements (SHAs) provide regulatory assurance for non-Federal landowners who voluntarily aid in the recovery of listed species by improving or maintaining wildlife habitat. Under SHAs, landowners manage the enrolled property and may return it to originally agreed-upon "baseline" conditions for the species and its habitat at the end of the agreement, even if this means incidentally taking the species.

Candidate Conservation Agreements

It is easier to conserve species before they need to be listed as endangered or threatened than to try to recover them when they are in danger of extinction or likely to become so. Candidate Conservation agreements (CCAs) are voluntary agreements between landowners— including Federal land management Agencies— and one or more other parties to reduce or remove threats to candidate or other at-risk species. Parties to the CCA work with the FWS to design conservation measures and monitor the effectiveness of plan implementation.

Candidate Conservation Agreements with Assurances

Under Candidate Conservation Agreements with Assurances (CCAA), non-Federal landowners volunteer to work with the FWS on plans to conserve candidate and other at-risk species so that protection of the ESA is not needed. In return, landowners receive regulatory assurances that, if a species covered by the CCAA is listed, they will not be required to do anything beyond what is specified in the agreement, and they will receive an enhancement of survival permit, allowing incidental take in reference to the management activities identified in the agreement.

Conservation Banks

Conservation banks are lands that are permanently protected and managed as mitigation for the loss elsewhere of listed and other at-risk species and their habitat. Conservation banking is a freemarket enterprise based on supply and demand of mitigation credits. Credits are supplied by landowners who enter into a Conservation Bank Agreement with the FWS agreeing to protect and manage their lands for one or more species. Others who need to mitigate for adverse impacts to those same species may purchase conservation bank credits to meet their mitigation requirements. Conservation banking benefits species by reducing the piecemeal approach to mitigation that often results in many small, isolated and unsustainable preserves that lose their habitat functions and values over time.

International Species

The ESA also implements U.S. participation in the Convention on International Trade in Endangered Species of Wild Fauna and Flora

(CITES), a 175-nation agreement designed to prevent species from becoming endangered or extinct due to international trade. Except as allowed by permit, CITES prohibits importing or exporting species listed on its three appendices. A species may require a permit under the ESA, CITES, or both.

U.S. Fish and Wildlife Service at *http://www.fws. gov/endangered/*.

4.1.2   Controversy over GE foods, Part 1

4.1.2.1.   The controversy over genetically engineered foods

Rachel Carson, the famous environmentalist/author of the 1960s, authoring the book, Silent Spring, which started a nationwide awareness of the destructive use of pesticides, identified the use of a bacteria, *Bacillus thuringiensis* (Bt), as a promising alternative to pesticides. Again, Carson was prophetic.

By 1980, scientists had isolated the proteins in Bt bacteria that were poisonous to insects. Specifically, the genes for producing the crystalline proteins Cry1A group and Cry9C have been isolated for splicing into the DNA of crop plants. This new characteristic of the crop plant, which includes the crystalline protein, protects the plant from insects. Once ingested by the insect, the crystalline protein binds to specific sites in the insect stomach, causing death.

1988 witnessed the first field test of an engineered Bt tomato, and 1990 was the first successful Bt field test, which was with a cotton plant. By 1995, the first commercial use of a Bt potato was underway and by 1998, 25% of U.S. corn was genetically engineered.

This new characteristic in our food, indicated that either the Food and Drug Administration, which regulates food safety, or the Environmental Protection Agency, which regulates the use of pesticides, were the agencies most likely to begin regulatory oversight for these products. The U.S. Environmental Protection Agency initially took responsibility for regulating the engineering of food, because of the pesticide component. The Food and Drug Administration classified these foods as generally accepted as safe (GRAS), needing no regulation. Developers of these genetically engineered foods were required only to consult with the FDA before marketing, to demonstrate the safety of the new food. No labeling requirements were imposed on genetically engineered foods.

The test data to determine safety of these genetically engineered foods focuses on any allergenicity properties which might have been created. Food allergies are reactions to protein molecules. When new proteins are created at the direction of the engineered plants for food, the potential for a food allergy exists. The approach to determining whether these proteins might be allergenic is simply by comparing the structure of the new protein to proteins that are known to cause food allergies, such as those in peanuts. Once it is demonstrated that the new protein has no properties or structure similar to known allergenic proteins, the food is assumed to be safe. The second part of the test for safety, is simply whether the plant is toxic to humans, which can be determined by toxicity tests.

Specifically, a U.S. EPA Science Advisory Board Panel in November 2000 wrote that "To have a high likelihood of allergenicity the protein could be expected to have an amino acid sequence similar to known allergens." The Panel specified that it also would have three or more of the presumed risk factors: relative resistance to acid treatment, relative resistance to protease digestion, general molecular weight range of 10 to 70 kilodalton, probably would be a glycoprotein, with the ability to induce an immunologic response in Brown Norway rats, and have the ability to be found intact in the bloodstream.

Although the protein is present in the engineered crop, the processing of the food destroys fragile proteins which are sensitive to heat. The DNA, however, remains and provides a way of identifying the presence of engineered food, although the protein has been destroyed by processing. The destruction of the protein also precludes the allergic reaction possibility. There have been no confirmed allergic reactions to these proteins which have been approved by the FDA. However, approximately 34 complaints (as of 2000) have been filed with the FDA regarding reported incidences of allergenic reactions.

———————

Using the legal tools to address biotechnology issues, a number of cases have been brought for resolution to the courts. The theories used to challenge federal governmental actions have been based upon existing environmental statutes, consumer information or food labeling statutes. The following case raises issues concerning the labeling of genetically engineered foods, utilizing claims under the Food, Drug and Cosmetic Act, the National Environmental Policy Act, as well as the Administrative Procedure Act.

In 1995, the court heard a challenge to the use of Bovine Somatotropin (rBST) in cows for increased production of milk, because milk producers were not disclosing its use on the consumer label.

4.1.2.2   Stauber

Stauber v. Shalala and Kessler
895 F. Supp. 1178 (W.D. Wisc., 1995)

Opinion by Barbara B. Crabb, District Judge:

This is a civil action for declaratory and injunctive relief brought pursuant to the Food, Drug and Cosmetic Act, the National Environmental Policy Act, and the Administrative Procedure Act. Plaintiffs are American consumers of commercially sold dairy products. Defendants are Donna Shalala, Secretary of the Department of Health and Human Services, and Dr. David Kessler, Commissioner of the Food and Drug Administration. Plaintiffs challenge defendants' approval of intervenor-defendant Monsanto Company's new drug application for Posilac®), a milk production-enhancing, synthetic bovine growth hormone drug. Specifically, plaintiffs contend that: 1) the approval was arbitrary and capricious because the FDA failed to consider health and safety issues related to the use of Posilac; 2) defendants failed to require mandatory labeling of products from cows treated with Posilac; and 3) defendants failed to conduct an adequate environmental assessment or issue an environmental impact statement assessing the environmental effects of Posilac's approval. Plaintiffs request both a declaration that defendants failed to perform their statutory duties in approving Posilac and a permanent injunction suspending the approval of Posilac until defendants comply with their statutory obligations.

The case is before the court on the parties' cross-motions for summary judgment. After a close review of the parties' submissions, I find that plaintiffs have offered no admissible, relevant evidence putting any material facts into dispute. Plaintiffs have not shown that defendants acted arbitrarily and capriciously in approving Posilac or in declining to require product labeling and they have not shown that defendants' environmental assessment was inadequate. Therefore, plaintiffs' claims must be dismissed.

From the proposed findings of fact of the parties, I find that the following material facts are undisputed.

UNDISPUTED FACTS

Bovine somatotrophin (bST), a bovine growth hormone, is a naturally occurring protein hormone produced in the pituitary gland of all cattle. In the 1930s, scientists discovered that injecting dairy cows with bovine growth hormone from other cattle could increase the cows' milk production but the discovery was not pursued on a wide scale because extraction of the hormone from cattle was not cost effective. In the 1980s, however, scientists developed a synthetic recombinant bovine growth hormone. Scientists can now isolate the gene responsible for natural bovine growth hormone, transfer that genetic material into bacterial cells called a "recombinant fermentation organism" and "program" the bacterial cells to produce a synthetic version of the hormone.

In the early 1980s, the FDA approved intervenor-defendant Monsanto Company's investigative new animal drug application for Posilac, a synthetic recombinant bovine somatotrophin. In 1987, Monsanto submitted a new animal drug application for Posilac to the FDA. Over the next several years, Monsanto supported the application with studies and reports documenting the safety and effectiveness of the drug. After reviewing those materials, the FDA approved Monsanto's application for the subcutaneous (injectable) use of Posilac on November 5, 1993. Posilac is the first genetically engineered animal drug to be approved for use in dairy cows and the first milk production enhancement drug to be approved for sale by the FDA.

The FDA approved Posilac despite criticism that the drug would have a significant negative effect on the health of dairy cows and despite concern about potential negative health effects on human consumers of dairy products derived from cows treated with rbST. Scientists, economists, farmers, and environmental and animal welfare organizations have questioned the safety and quality of rbST-derived products. In addition, the FDA received thousands of letters from consumers asking it either to deny approval of rbST or to require labeling of rbST-derived products. The General Accounting Office advised the FDA to withhold approval of Posilac until further research of rbST's potential negative impact on human health could be conducted. After the FDA approved Posilac for marketing, Congress delayed sale of the drug for 90 days while an inter-agency task force supervised by the Office of the President reviewed the data upon which the FDA based its decision. In January 1994, the task force concluded that the FDA's position was adequately supported. The FDA made available to the public a summary of the safety and effectiveness data submitted by Monsanto on which the agency relied in approving Posilac for mass marketing.

A. Cow Safety

Use of Posilac may affect cows adversely in several ways. Posilac increases the risks of reduced pregnancy rates, ovarian cysts and uterine disorders, decreased lengths of gestation periods and lower birth weight of calves. Posilac increases the risk of retained placentas and twinning rates in cows. It may cause increased bovine body temperatures, indigestion, bloating, diarrhea, enlarged hocks, enlarged lesions and injection site swellings. Additionally, use of Posilac increases the risk of clinical and subclinical mastitis, a bacterial infection of the udder. In absolute terms, rbST increases the risk of mastitis by about 0.1 case per cow per year. This risk is less than the risk of mastitis posed by seasonal change.

Before approving Posilac, the FDA reviewed the data submitted by Monsanto as part of its new drug application and considered Posilac's effects on animal health, including: 1) the acute and chronic toxicity of the drug; 2) its effects on reproduction; 3) calf birth traits, growth and health; 4) increased incidence of mastitis; 5) musculoskeletal effects; 6) digestive disorders including indigestion, bloating and diarrhea; 7) injection site reactions; 8) nutrient intake, body weight and body condition; 9) general cow health; and 10) miscellaneous health variables, including circulating anti-somatotrophin binding, blood variables, body temperature and urinalysis results. The agency determined that the risks to cows associated with the use of Posilac could be managed properly under a "manageable risk" criteria and that the risks to animal health were not significant enough to warrant denial of the drug application. (The FDA has never applied a zero risk standard when assessing the safety of new animal drugs.) Monsanto conducted a 14-day drug tolerance study that involved injecting a herd with dosages of rbST up to thirty times the normal dosage. Analysis of both cow and fetal blood and tissue revealed only one health side effect: slight swelling at the injection site.

B. Human Consumer Safety

Before approving Posilac, the FDA considered Posilac's possible negative effects on human health, including the possible effects of 1) increased levels of rbST in milk; 2) increased levels of insulin growth factor in milk; and 3) increased amounts of antibiotic drug residues in milk. 1. RbST BST and its synthetic counterpart rbST are protein hormones that are orally inactive in humans. Upon ingestion, protein hormones (unlike steroid hormones) are broken down by enzymes in the intestines and digested. BST and rbST are orally inactive in cows as well. Like insulin, which must be injected to take effect, bST and rbST must be injected to stimulate milk production in cows. Even if injected into humans, however, rbST would not stimulate growth because human somatotrophin has a significantly different amino acid sequence from that of rbST and human receptors will not bond with rbST. Furthermore, heat destroys rbST, so that pasteurizing milk and cooking meat would tend to destroy at least 90% of the rbST in milk or beef. The FDA found that even at exaggerated doses the ingestion of rbST poses no significant risk to human safety. 2. Mastitis and antibiotics

Antibiotics are used to treat bovine mastitis. Trace residues of the antibiotics can appear in the milk of dairy cows. The level of antibiotic residue in milk is regulated, however. Forty-nine states have adopted the Grade A Pasteurized Milk Ordinance, established by the FDA and the Public Health Service in cooperation with state and local regulatory agencies and members of the milk industry. The ordinance defines standards for milk purity, establishes standards for production of pasteurized milk and milk products, details the method of inspections of farms and processing plants and provides that only producers, haulers, processors and distributors who meet the requirements of the ordinance shall be given permits. Under the milk ordinance, milk that is inspected and found to contain drug residues in excess of the standard must be discarded and the responsible producer is subject to regulatory sanctions.

Although states test milk routinely for drug residues in accordance with the milk ordinance, they generally test only for the presence of four of the antibiotics most commonly used to treat bovine infection, the beta-lactams, which are penicillin-like antibiotics. It has been estimated, however, that over fifty different drugs are used to treat bovine infections, some not approved for use on dairy cows, and the presence of residues from these other drugs would go undetected by most current testing procedures. The General Accounting Office has concluded that there is currently no means of assessing the degree to which current milk supplies are contaminated by these other drugs. One concern surrounding Posilac is that its use will increase the frequency of bovine infection, particularly mastitis, which will in turn lead to an increased need for antibiotics to treat dairy cow infections. Because the current regulatory scheme does not detect the presence of all drug residues in dairy products, there is a risk that greater amounts of antibiotic drug residue will be ingested by human dairy consumers.

To date there have been no long term studies of the impact on human health of increased antibiotics in milk. However, the FDA determined that the increased risk of bovine mastitis caused by Posilac did not present a risk to human health because 1) the increased risk of mastitis from the use of Posilac is not great, and in fact is much lower than the increased risk caused by the many other factors that contribute to mastitis; 2) milk is tested for beta-lactam drugs, and any milk found to contain illegal residues is discarded; and 3) the beta-lactams are the most commonly used antibiotics to treat mastitis. The FDA and its Veterinary Medicine and Food Advisory Committees determined that state and local regulation of milk production and distribution ensures that milk is free from the most widely used antibiotics and that introduction of Posilac to the market would not cause a statistically significant increase in the amount of antibiotic residues found in milk.

3. Somatic cell count

Mastitis brings with it an increase in the amount of somatic cells (i.e., white blood cells) present in dairy milk. Studies by Monsanto showed a significant increase in the somatic cell count in milk from rbST-treated cows in some herds, although the increase was not found in all herds studied. When the various studies conducted by Monsanto on somatic cell count were pooled, the results demonstrated no significant increase in somatic cell counts attributable to rbST treatment. The FDA did not consider somatic cell count from the standpoint of human safety. However, the agency did conclude from Monsanto's studies that rbST did not increase somatic cell count any more than factors such as lactation stage and cow parity. (Cow "parity" is a term that refers to whether and how many times a cow has given birth.) 4. Insulin-like growth factor

Insulin-like growth factor (IGF-1) is protein hormone whose production is regulated at least in part by somatotrophin. It has the same biochemical composition in humans and cows and is present in all milk, human saliva and human digestive juices. RbST increases the amount of IGF-1 in milk. IGF-1 is denatured in the process of making baby formula, but it is not destroyed by pasteurization.

At the time Monsanto filed its new drug application for Posilac, not much was known about the hormone. Defendants have done no long term studies on the effects of increased levels of IGF-1 on human health. However, Monsanto did conduct a two week study of rats administered IGF-1 either by gavage (forced feeding) or systemically by implanted pump. The study indicated no

90

negative health impact on the esophagus, stomach and intestines of the rats from increased levels of IGF-1 administered orally.

The FDA considered IGF-1 when it evaluated the safety and effectiveness of Posilac and concluded that any increase in IGF-1 levels posed no significant health risks to consumers. This conclusion was based on the FDA's determinations that: 1) IGF-1 levels in milk from rbST-treated cows were not significantly higher than milk from untreated cows; 2) IGF-1 was not orally active; 3) even if IGF-1 from milk was absorbed intact, levels of IGF-1 in the human bloodstream are so much higher (100 to 1000 times) than the levels found in cows' milk that the addition of small amounts of IGF-1 from cows' milk would be physiologically insignificant; and 4) the manufacturing process for infant formula denatures almost all of the IGF-1 in cows' milk. The agency concluded that IGF-1 was unlikely to affect either the gastrointestinal track of adults or infants in general.

C. Labeling
The FDA determined that the risks of Posilac to dairy cows could be addressed adequately by labeling the drug itself. The Posilac label contains a "precautions and side-effects" section that lists the potential adverse effects on cows, including reduced pregnancy rates, cystic ovaries, disorders of the uterus, decreases in length of gestation, increased twinning rates, decreased calf birth weight, an increased risk of clinical and subclinical mastitis, digestive disorders and infection site reactions. In bold letters, the warning section informs the dairy farmer that "use of Posilac should be preceded by implementation of a comprehensive and ongoing herd reproductive health program," and "mastitis management practices should be thoroughly evaluated prior to initiating use of Posilac."

The FDA considered whether special labeling should be required for milk and milk products derived from rbST-treated cows in addition to the drug's packaging label. In May 1993, the FDA's Veterinary Medicine and Food Advisory Committees held a meeting to address the issue. The committees received testimony from doctors, scientists, dietitians, dairy farmers, veterinarians, members of medical and scientific organizations and universities, dairy organizations and farm and agricultural groups. On the basis of testimony from the hearings and the data submitted by Monsanto, the FDA concluded that there is no significant difference between milk from cows treated with Posilac and milk from untreated cows. The agency concluded also that rbST had no significant effect on the organoleptic properties of milk or on the lactose, fat, protein, ash, phosphorous and vitamin content of milk. On February 3, 1994, the FDA issued interim guidance on voluntary labeling of milk from untreated cows, concluding that such milk cannot be labeled as "BST free" because BST occurs naturally in milk, but that farmers may label their milk "from cows not treated with rbST," if the statement is placed in proper context. 59 Fed. Reg. 6279-80

91

(February 10, 1994). D. Environmental Issues

The FDA approved Monsanto's new drug application for Posilac without preparing an environmental impact statement, concluding that no statement was necessary because approval of Posilac would not have a significant impact on the environment within the meaning of the National Environmental Policy Act. The FDA based this conclusion on an environmental assessment prepared by Monsanto that addressed Posilac's potential impact on the environment.

The FDA assumes responsibility for the scope and content of the environmental assessment prepared by Monsanto. Agency officials have reviewed the information contained in that document. The environmental assessment refers to studies that evaluated the impact Posilac was likely to have on the dairy industry and concluded that its introduction to the market would not do fundamental damage to current structural trends. The environmental assessment addressed the possibility of shifts in land use patterns as a result of the use of Posilac, concluding that the drug would be unlikely to have any significant effect on land use. The assessment also addressed two alternatives to the current approval of Posilac: 1) additional controls on production; and 2) use of the drug, including labeling. Both alternatives were addressed only with regard to the environmental concerns surrounding the biotechnological aspects of the drug's preparation. Neither the environmental assessment nor the finding of no significant impact addressed consumer health risks posed by increased IGF-1 levels and antibiotic residue levels in milk derived from rbST-treated cows, the impact of Posilac on the health of dairy cows or the potential risks to consumers caused by increases in IGF-1 and antibiotic residues. However, the agency's policy is not to reexamine issues under the National Environmental Policy Act already considered as part of its evaluation of a new animal drug application. The assessment failed to address the impact of Posilac on family dairy farms. Finally, the environmental assessment did not address possible alternatives of 1) approving the drug at lower doses; 2) approving Posilac only as a prescription drug; or 3) approving the drug for use only when accompanied by detailed instructions or educational seminars regarding methods to minimize health risks. . . .

OPINION

. . . 1. Standing under the Food, Drug, and Cosmetic Act   Defendants raised their standing argument once before in this litigation in a motion to dismiss. In an opinion and order entered September 1, 1994, I concluded that standing could be premised on plaintiffs' allegations that they were unable to consume dairy products known to be free of milk from rbST-treated cows. Defendants do not challenge plaintiffs' alleged inability to consume milk products known to be free of milk from rbST-treated cows. Rather, they attack the minor premise of plaintiffs' allegation, that consuming dairy products derived from rbST treated cows is harmful. This argument misconstrues plaintiffs' rights under the Food, Drug, and Cosmetic Act.

The federal Food, Drug, and Cosmetic Act, 21 U.S.C. §§§§ 301-394, is intended to protect American consumers from the risks of consuming unsafe or ineffective food and drugs and thus requires new drug applicants to demonstrate the safety and effectiveness of new drugs before they may be marketed. One aspect of plaintiffs' challenge to the FDA's approval of rbST is that the agency did not hold Monsanto to its burden under the act of demonstrating the safety of Posilac. If this allegation is true, plaintiffs' injury is their exposure to a potentially dangerous drug whose safety has not been demonstrated in accordance with the act.

2. Standing under the National Environmental Policy Act
To have standing under the National Environmental Policy Act, plaintiffs must show that an agency's alleged noncompliance with the act has adversely affected them and that they are within the zone of interests protected by the act. Under the act, individuals are aggrieved by an agency's failure to prepare an environmental impact statement if they can show that the failure creates a reasonable risk that "'environmental impacts will be overlooked'" and that they have a "sufficient geographical nexus to the site of the challenged project that [they] may be expected to suffer whatever environmental consequences the project may have."
Defendants contend that plaintiffs have failed to allege an injury cognizable under the National Environmental Policy Act and have made no showing of a sufficient nexus between the agency's decision not to prepare an environmental impact statement and the alleged harm. Defendants do not challenge plaintiffs' allegations that they are consumers of milk. Rather, defendants' challenge assumes that plaintiffs must prove that rbST is actually harmful. This assumption is flawed, however, because it collapses the standing inquiry into the merits of plaintiffs' claims.

Plaintiffs have introduced evidence tending to show that rbST creates an increased risk of mastitis that will increase dairy farmers' reliance on antibiotics in the treatment of their dairy cows. Plaintiffs offer additional evidence that over 50 drugs are used to treat infections in cows, only 4 of which are seriously regulated. (I note that in analyzing standing, I am able to consider evidence that is outside the administrative record and for that reason may not be considered when assessing plaintiffs' claims of violations of the Food, Drug, and Cosmetic. See infra, section C.) For standing purposes, I conclude that this evidence demonstrates a reasonable risk that 1) farmers will rely increasingly on illegal or otherwise unregulated drugs to treat the higher incidence of mastitis, which in turn will 2) increase the levels of drug residues that might show up in consumers' milk. Plaintiffs argue that there is a risk that increased exposure to drug residues may affect human bioimmune systems and the bacteria living in our digestive systems. Whether plaintiffs are likely to succeed on this claim does not determine whether they have standing under the National Environmental Policy Act. The evidence they have proffered demonstrates a reasonable risk of serious environmental harm caused by the proposed agency action that would clearly affect them as dairy product consumers, were it ever to come to fruition. Therefore, I conclude that the consumer plaintiffs satisfy the requirements for Article III standing under the National Environmental Policy Act. . . .

D. The FDA's Approval of Posilac

The FDA is the federal agency responsible for assuring that new animal drugs are safe and effective for their intended use. Before approving a new animal drug application, the FDA requires a new drug sponsor to demonstrate that the food products from the subject animals will be safe for human consumption, that the drug is safe and effective for the animals in question and that the manufacture and use of the drug will not harm the environment. Approval proceeds in two steps. First, the drug sponsor seeks approval of its investigative new animal drug application, which outlines how the sponsor will conduct the necessary research. This research covers human food safety, animal safety and drug efficacy and includes clinical and field trials, laboratory studies, on-site inspections and other investigative methods. Second, upon completion of the studies, the sponsor submits a new animal drug application that employs investigational studies to establish the safety and efficacy of the drug. Throughout the application process, the burden is on the applicant or drug sponsor to show that the new animal drug is both effective and safe under the proposed conditions of use. Effectiveness must be demonstrated on the basis of "substantial evidence" that the drug "will have the effect it purports or is represented to have under the conditions of use prescribed, recommended, or suggested in the proposed labeling thereof." The Food, Drug, and Cosmetic Act does not indicate the standard an applicant must meet to demonstrate a new drug's safety or the evidence upon which the FDA must base its safety determination. However, the act requires the FDA to consider four specific factors when assessing safety: 1) the likelihood that the drug or a substance formed in food because of the drug will be consumed; 2) the cumulative effect that the drug will be likely to have on man or other animals; 3) safety factors that experts consider appropriate for extrapolating from animal experimentation data; and 4) whether it is likely that the conditions of use proposed or suggested in the labeling will be followed. The FDA is required to take into account the drug's effect on the health of the target animal. A new drug application must contain "full reports of adequate tests by all methods reasonably applicable to show whether or not the drug is safe for use under the conditions prescribed, recommended, or suggested in the proposed labeling." Such testing includes preclinical acute, subacute and chronic toxicity testing, clinical studies and filed investigations.

Plaintiffs contend that the FDA should not have approved Posilac because of safety concerns. For the reasons set out above in section C, supra, none of plaintiffs' proffered evidence indicating that rbST poses a danger to human health may be considered because it is outside the administrative record. The focus narrows, therefore, to plaintiffs' arguments that are grounded properly on the administrative record. Despite the limited amount of evidentiary support plaintiffs have collected, they continue to maintain that Monsanto failed to meet its burden under the Food, Drug, and Cosmetic Act. To survive summary judgment, plaintiffs must raise a genuine issue on the reasonableness of the FDA's conclusion that Monsanto met its burden of showing the safety of Posilac.

In identifying what they consider to be arbitrary and capricious FDA determinations, plaintiffs begin with the assertion that the Posilac label does not adequately counteract the health risks to cows associated with the drug's use. The FDA approved Posilac, notwithstanding its admitted risks of side effects to cows, on the theory that this safety risk is "manageable" if farmers adopt herd management techniques and ongoing herd reproductive health programs as the Posilac label recommends. Plaintiffs contend that this manageable risk criterion is arbitrary and capricious because the drug's label is vague and farmers will not know how to interpret it. Defendants respond by noting that mastitis is not a new problem to dairy farmers and that the increased incidence of mastitis caused by Posilac is not significantly great (0.1 per cow per year). It was on these two findings that the agency grounded its conclusion that the risk was "manageable," and in any event not so great as to warrant denying approval of the drug. Defendants note also that under the Food, Drug, and Cosmetic Act, neither the sponsors of new animal drugs nor the FDA is held to a "zero risk" standard.

Although plaintiffs raise valid concerns about the manageable risk approach, I cannot conclude that the agency's decision was arbitrary and capricious. First, nothing in the record indicates that the agency overlooked some aspect of cow health when reviewing the Posilac application. To the contrary, the record demonstrates that the agency evaluated the target animal's safety as it was required to do, considering each and every one of the known side effects associated with Posilac. Second, I cannot say it was irrational for the agency to conclude that the increased risk of mastitis caused by Posilac is not sufficiently great to warrant denying approval of the drug. This conclusion was based on the agency's determination that the risk of mastitis caused by Posilac is much less than the risk caused by other variables such as seasonal change. Finally, although mastitis is a serious health concern, it is one familiar to dairy farmers, who know how to detect and treat it. I add, however, that in the future it would be helpful to reviewing courts for the FDA to set out the factors it looks at in determining whether a particular risk is a manageable one.

Plaintiffs argue that defendants' decision to approve Posilac was arbitrary and capricious because defendants did not adequately consider the risk of higher levels of antibiotic drug residues in milk that could have an adverse impact on human health because of the greater resistance of certain bacteria, particularly human digestive bacteria. The FDA determined that the risk of exposure to increased amounts of antibiotics was slim because, among other things, the risk of increased mastitis is slight and the level of antibiotic drug residues in milk is highly regulated. Plaintiffs characterize this decision as arbitrary and capricious because many of the drugs used to treat bovine infections are not tested routinely under the current regulatory scheme. Defendants counter that the four antibiotics most commonly screened are also the ones most commonly used to treat bovine infection. The controversy boils down to whether it was proper for the FDA to rely on the current regulatory mechanism to assure that drug residues will be kept out of the milk supply.

Although plaintiffs have raised valid concerns about the adequacy of the current regulatory scheme to assure the purity of the nation's milk supply, they have not shown the agency's reliance on that scheme to be arbitrary and capricious. First and most important, the agency determined that the increased risk of mastitis was not overly great and on that basis concluded that the rise in the use of antibiotics would not be overly great either. Given these conclusions, it was rational for the agency to rest a determination of safety on the current milk purity regulatory scheme especially because milk is tested for the drugs most commonly used to treat mastitis, the beta-lactams. Although I understand plaintiffs' concerns, I conclude that the agency considered the relevant factors and that the record contains support for its determination.

Third, plaintiffs are dissatisfied with the FDA's exploration of the potential risks associated with an increased level of IGF-1 in milk from cows treated with Posilac. The FDA concluded that an increased level of IGF-1 in milk presented no significant human health concerns. This conclusion was based on Monsanto's two-week rat study indicating no adverse effects from oral ingestion of IGF-1 and on other evidence indicating that IGF-1 levels rise only slightly when the producing cow is treated with rbST, that IGF-1 exists in the human blood stream at levels much higher than those appearing in milk and that IGF-1 is denatured when milk is boiled. Plaintiffs are correct that no long term studies have been done, but they have presented no admissible evidence that would show either that longer studies were required or that the two-week rat study was not scientifically adequate to permit the FDA to conclude that IGF-1 poses no significant risk to human health. Without any admissible evidence indicating that the two-week study did not support the conclusions that the agency drew from it, I cannot conclude that the agency's decision lacked a rational basis in the record. E. The FDA's Decision Not to Require Labeling of Products Derived from rbST-treated Cows
Under the Food, Drug, and Cosmetic Act, food is deemed misbranded if its labeling is "false or misleading in any particular." provid [ing] further that:

If an article is alleged to be misbranded because the labeling or advertising is misleading, then in determining whether the labeling or advertising is misleading there shall be taken into account (among other things) not only representations made or suggested by statement, word, design, device, or any combination thereof, but also the extent to which the labeling or advertising fails to reveal facts material in the light of such representations or material with respect to consequences which may result from the use of the article to which the labeling or advertising relates under the conditions of use prescribed in the labeling or advertising thereof or under such conditions of use as are customary or usual.

Plaintiffs contend that food products derived from rbST-treated cows must be labeled as such if the products are to comply with these two provisions. They argue that milk derived from rbST-treated cows differs organoleptically from ordinary milk in several respects and that these differences are "material facts" requiring labeling. In addition, they argue that there is widespread consumer desire for mandatory labeling of rbST-derived milk and that such a degree of demand is also a "material fact" requiring labeling. An organoleptic difference is one capable of being detected by a human sense organ. See Webster's Collegiate Dictionary 953 (1991). In a different context from the one presented here, the FDA has stated:

Information disclosing differences in performance characteristics (e.g., physical properties, flavor characteristics, functional properties and shelf life) is a material fact under section 201(n) of the act because it bears on the consequence of the use of the article. Accordingly, this information must be communicated to the consumer on the product label, or labeling would be misleading, and the product would be misbranded under section 403(a) of the act.

58 Fed. Reg. 2431, 2437 (January 6, 1993) (notice of final FDA rule regarding standards for products named with nutrient content claims, i.e., "fat free," and "low calorie"). However, plaintiffs have been able to point to no evidence in the administrative record indicating that milk derived from rbST-treated cows has performance characteristics or organoleptic properties different from milk from untreated cows. The increased incidence of mastitis in cows would not provide a basis for labeling because plaintiffs have provided no evidence that milk that finds its way to the consumer actually will contain higher levels of drug residues. Plaintiffs assert that the increased somatic cell counts and IGF-1 levels in rbST-derived milk are material facts warranting a label. However, they offer no evidence that increased somatic cell counts and increased IGF-1 levels in rbST-derived milk are organoleptic differences or that they alter the performance characteristics of milk. Indeed, plaintiffs have been unable to put into dispute the agency's conclusion that "administration

97

of sometribove [rbST] has no significant effect on the overall composition of milk."

Regarding widespread consumer demand, plaintiffs are incorrect in their assertion that by itself consumer opinion could suffice to require labeling. The FDA does consider consumer opinion relevant when determining whether a label is required to disclose a material fact, but a factual predicate to the requirement of labeling is a determination that a product differs materially from the type of product it purports to be. If there is a difference, and consumers would likely want to know about the difference, then labeling is appropriate. If, however, the product does not differ in any significant way from what it purports to be, then it would be misbranding to label the product as different, even if consumers misperceived the product as different. In the absence of evidence of a material difference between rbST-derived milk and ordinary milk, the use of consumer demand as the rationale for labeling would violate the Food, Drug, and Cosmetic Act. Because plaintiffs have not presented any evidence demonstrating organoleptic differences between regular and rbST-derived milk or of any harmful effects of rbST on consumers, they have failed to carry their burden of demonstrating the arbitrary and capricious nature of the agency's determination. . . . F. The National Environmental Policy Act

The National Environmental Policy Act, 42 U.S.C. §§ 4321-4370, requires federal agencies to prepare an environmental impact statement if the agency plans to undertake a "major" action "significantly affecting the quality of the human environment." . . .

Plaintiffs contend that the FDA failed to comply with the National Environmental Policy Act when it determined that an environmental impact statement was unnecessary. In particular, plaintiffs contend that the decision not to prepare an environmental impact statement was arbitrary and capricious in light of the failure to address Posilac's socioeconomic effects on the dairy farmer and Posilac's likely effects on human and bovine health in either the environmental assessment or the finding of no significant impact. In addition, plaintiffs challenge the failure to discuss feasible alternatives in the environmental assessment and the finding of no significant impact.

Regarding socioeconomic effects, the regulations promulgated under the National Environmental Policy Act provide that "economic or social effects are not intended by themselves to require preparation of the environmental impact statement." 40 C.F.R. §§ 1508.14. Plaintiffs are wrong when they assert that Posilac's socioeconomic effects on the dairy farmer require the preparation of an environmental impact statement. . . . It is true that an environmental impact statement must discuss economic or social effects of the proposed action to the extent those effects interrelate to its natural or physical environmental effects, but the regulations do not contemplate an independent consideration of socioeconomic effects when there is no determination that the proposed agency activity will significantly effect the environment....

Because defendants were not required to include a discussion of socioeconomic effects in their environmental assessment, it was not arbitrary and capricious to omit consideration of those nonenvironmental effects from the environmental assessment.

The next question is whether, to comply with the National Environmental Policy Act, the FDA was required to take an independent and second look at the effects Posilac might have on the health of cows and consumers or whether the agency could rely on the safety evaluations it made pursuant to its statutory duties under the Food, Drug, and Cosmetic Act. Plaintiffs do not seem to argue that the analysis of the human and bovine health issues required under the two statutes differ in some way or that the analysis required under the Food, Drug, and Cosmetic Act is somehow less rigorous than that required under National Environmental Policy Act. Rather, plaintiffs' argument appears to be simply that the agency must review the issues twice to satisfy the requirements of both statutes....

Plaintiffs contend that at a minimum, the agency should have been required to incorporate by reference its health and safety findings into the environmental assessment and the finding of no significant impact. This argument is not without merit. Such incorporation of the health and safety data by reference in the environmental assessment and finding of no significant impact would provide an interested party (or reviewing court) with a complete picture of all analysis bearing on the agency's obligations under the National Environmental Policy Act.

Plaintiffs' argument fails, however, for two interrelated reasons. First, at bottom, their argument is a purely informational one, which fails because they allege no harm stemming from the asserted procedural defect. Cf. Foundation for Economic Trends v. Lyng,.... (D.C. Cir. 1991) (informational injury alone is not enough to satisfy standing requirements under NEPA). Second, environmental assessments and findings of no significant impact are informal agency actions subject to judicial review under the arbitrary and capricious standard....

The final issue plaintiffs raise is the omission of any discussion of feasible alternatives from the environmental assessment and the finding of no significant impact. Plaintiffs argue that the agency should have considered the possibilities of a delay on approving the Posilac application until further studies on health and safety could be conducted, a lower recommended dosage to the cows, or approval of Posilac only as a prescription drug. (Plaintiffs proposed as fact that the environmental assessment did not address the alternative of approving the drug for marketing only when accompanied by detailed instructions or educational seminars regarding methods to minimize health risks, but they have not pursued this argument in their briefs.) The first alternative, a delay in approving the drug, was suggested to the agency. During the review process the Foundation on Economic Trends, a non-profit consumer organization and a former plaintiff in this action, suggested that approval of the drug be postponed until further safety research could occur. However, plaintiffs have failed to offer evidence that the other two alternatives (a lower recommended dosage or prescription drug status) were ever presented to the agency for consideration. If an alternative is not presented to the agency for consideration, the agency cannot be attacked in federal court for not considering it....

Even if I assume that plaintiffs made a presentation of their alternative of delayed approval pending further research into health and safety that was adequate to require the agency to consider the proposal, see *Vermont Yankee Nuclear Power Corp. v. Natural Resources Defense Council*, ... (1978) (proponents of alternatives must make a preliminary showing that proposed alternative merits review before agency required to consider alternative during agency proceedings), plaintiffs would still not meet their burden of showing that an environmental impact statement should have been prepared. When an agency determines that a proposed action poses a significant risk of harm to the environment, the agency must consider alternatives to the proposed action.... However, if the agency determines that a proposed action will not significantly effect the environment, it is required to consider alternatives only when the proposal involves "unresolved conflicts concerning alternative uses of available resources."... In this situation, I cannot perceive any unresolved conflict concerning uses of available resources. Plaintiffs' proposed alternative involves only a delay in approving the drug until further tests have been conducted. This situation does not involve an "available resource" as the term is used in §§ 4332(E)(2).

ORDER

IT IS ORDERED that the motions for summary judgment of defendants Donna Shalala, Secretary of Health and Human Services, and David Kessler, Commissioner of the Food and Drug Administration, and intervenor defendant Monsanto Company's motions for summary judgment are GRANTED. Plaintiffs' motion for summary judgment is DENIED. The clerk of court is directed to enter judgment for defendants and the intervenor defendant and close this case.

———————————

4.1.3   Controversy over GE foods, Pt. 2, *Alliance for Bio-Integrity*

Five years later, the effort to utilize the National Environmental Policy Act and the Food, Drug and Cosmetic Act were again used to raise labeling and environmental concerns, after thirty-six foods, derived from GMOs were released into the market.

Alliance for Bio-Integrity v. Shalala
116 F. Supp. 2d 166 (D.D.C.. 2000)

MEMORANDUM OPINION: Technological advances have dramatically increased our ability to manipulate our environment, including the foods we consume. One of these advances, recombinant deoxyribonucleic acid (rDNA) technology, has enabled scientists to alter the genetic composition of organisms by mixing genes on the cellular and molecular level in order to create new breeds of plants for human and animal consumption. These new breeds may be designed to repel pests, retain their freshness for a longer period of time, or contain more intense flavor and/or nutritional value. Much controversy has attended such developments in biotechnology, and in particular the production, sale, and trade of genetically modified organisms and foods. The above-captioned lawsuit represents one articulation of this controversy.

Among Plaintiffs, some fear that these new breeds of genetically modified food could contain unexpected toxins or allergens, and others believe that their religion forbids consumption of foods produced through rDNA technology. Plaintiffs, a coalition of groups and individuals including scientists and religious leaders concerned about genetically altered foods, have brought this action to protest the Food and Drug Administration's ("FDA") policy on such foods in general, and in particular on various genetically modified foods that already have entered the marketplace. The parties have filed cross-motions for summary judgment on plaintiffs' multiple claims. Upon careful consideration of the parties' briefs and the entire record, the Court shall grant Defendants' motion as to all counts of Plaintiffs' Complaint.

I. BACKGROUND
On May 29, 1992, the FDA published a "Statement of Policy: Foods Derived From New Plant Varieties" (Statement of Policy, 57 Fed. Reg. 22,984). In the Statement of Policy, FDA announced that the agency would presume that foods produced through the rDNA process were "generally recognized as safe" (GRAS) under the Federal Food, Drug and Cosmetic Act ("FDCA"), 21 U.S.C. §§ 321(s), and therefore not subject to regulation as food additives. While FDA recommended that food producers consult with it before marketing rDNA-produced foods, the agency did not mandate such

consultation. In addition, FDA reserved the right to regulate any particular rDNA-developed food that FDA believed was unsafe on a case-by-case basis, just as FDA would regulate unsafe foods produced through conventional means.

The Statement of Policy also indicated that rDNA modification was not a "material fact" under the FDCA, and that therefore labeling of rDNA-produced foods was not necessarily required. FDA did not engage in a formal notice-and-comment process on the Statement of Policy, nor did it prepare an Environmental Impact Statement or Environmental Assessment. At least thirty-six foods, genetically altered through rDNA technology, have been marketed since the Statement of Policy was issued.

Plaintiffs filed a Complaint in this Court challenging the FDA's policy on six different grounds: (1) the Statement was not properly subjected to notice-and-comment procedures; (2) the FDA did not comply with the National Environmental Protection Act (NEPA) by compiling an Environmental Assessment or Environmental Impact Statement; (3) the FDA's presumption that rDNA-developed foods are GRAS and therefore do not require food additive petitions under 21 U.S.C. §§ 321(s) is arbitrary and capricious; (4) the FDA's decision not to require labeling for rDNA-developed foods is arbitrary and capricious . . .

II. DISCUSSION

A. Subject Matter Jurisdiction . . . . Although the Court may not review FDA's policy-laden individual enforcement decisions, the Court has jurisdiction to review whether or not FDA's Statement of Policy comports with Congressional directives.

B. Notice and Comment Plaintiffs argue that the Statement of Policy should be set aside because it was not subjected to notice and comment proceedings, as required under the Administrative Procedure Act ("APA"), 5 U.S.C. §§ 553. While conceding that the Statement of Policy did not undergo a formal notice and comment process, Defendants maintain that the Statement of Policy is a policy statement or an interpretive rule not subject to notice and comment requirements. Plaintiffs contend instead that the Statement of Policy is a substantive rule, and that therefore it was improperly exempted from a formal notice and comment process. . . . A substantive rule, which must undergo a formal notice-and-comment process, is a rule that "implement[s]" a statute and has "the force and effect of law." Policy statements, on the other hand, are "statements issued by an agency to advise the public prospectively of the manner in which the agency proposes to exercise a discretionary power." Although the distinction between these categories is not entirely clear, the Court of Appeals articulated a two-part test for determining when an agency action is a policy statement. Policy statements (1) must not impose any new rights or obligations, and (2) must "genuinely leave the agency and its decision-makers free to exercise discretion." In weighing these criteria, "the ultimate issue is the agency's intent to be bound." An agency's own characterization of its statement deserves some weight, but it is not dispositive. Rather, courts will look to the actual language of the statement.

By its very name, the Statement of Policy announces itself as a policy statement. More importantly, the plain language of the Statement suggests that it does not have a binding effect. For example, the Statement does not declare that transferred genetic material will be considered GRAS; rather, it announces that "such material is *presumed* to be GRAS." This presumption of safety is rebuttable, because FDA will "require food additive petitions in cases where safety questions exist sufficient to warrant formal premarket review by FDA to ensure public health protection." Rebuttable presumptions leave an agency free to exercise its discretion and may therefore properly be announced in policy statements.

In response to the argument that the Policy Statement vests broad discretion with the agency, Plaintiffs contend that the FDA's application of the Statement has given it a "practical effect" that has effectively bound the agency's discretion, as evidenced by the thirty-six genetically engineered foods that are currently on the market and not regulated by the FDA. Although courts will look to the "agency's actual applications" to determine the nature of an agency statement, such an inquiry occurs "where the language and context of a statement are inconclusive." Here, the plain language of the Statement clearly indicates that it is a policy statement that merely creates a presumption and does not ultimately bind the agency's discretion.

Even if, as Plaintiffs argue, FDA has previously used notice-and-comment procedures to determine GRAS status, in the instant case FDA has not determined GRAS status but has rather announced a GRAS presumption. . . . Because the Statement is a policy statement merely announcing a GRAS presumption, the omission of formal notice-and-comment procedures does not violate the Administrative Procedure Act.

C. NEPA Plaintiffs have also alleged that FDA violated the National Environmental Protection Act (NEPA), 42 U.S.C. §§ 4321 *et seq.*, by not performing an Environmental Assessment (EA) or an Environmental Impact Statement (EIS) in conjunction with the Statement of Policy. NEPA requires "all agencies of the Federal Government . . . [to] include in every recommendation or report on proposals for legislation and other major Federal actions significantly affecting the quality of the human environment, a detailed statement . . . on the environmental impact of the proposed action." 42 U.S.C. §§ 4332(2)(c)(I). "Major federal action," as defined in the Code of Federal Regulations, includes actions such as "adoption of official policy . . . adoption of formal plans . . . adoption of programs . . . [and] approval of specific projects." 40 C.F.R. §§ 1508.18(b)(1-4). For major federal actions, agencies must either prepare an EIS examining the environmental impact of the proposed action, prepare an EA determining whether or not to prepare an EIS, or claim that the action falls within a Categorical Exclusion, "a category of actions which do not individually or cumulatively have a significant effect on the human environment." 40 C.F.R. §§ 1508.4 (1999). If the agency is not engaging in a major federal action, NEPA requirements do not apply.

In the Statement of Policy, FDA announces that "the activities [FDA] may undertake with respect to foods from new plant varieties . . . will [not] constitute agency action under NEPA." FDA's determination that the Statement is not a major federal action is essentially an interpretation of the meaning of "major federal action" in 42 U.S.C. §§ 4332(2)©) and 40 C.F.R. §§ 1508.18. Agencies enjoy wide discretion in interpreting regulations, and the agency's interpretation will be upheld unless it is arbitrary and capricious.

The FDA's determination that the Statement was not a major federal action comports with the holdings of this Circuit, and is therefore neither arbitrary nor capricious. While declaring a rebuttable presumption that foods produced through rDNA technology are GRAS, the FDA has neither made a final determination that any particular food will be allowed into the environment, nor taken any particular regulatory actions that could affect the environment. In order to trigger the NEPA requirement of an EIS, the agency must be prepared to undertake an "'irreversible and irretrievable commitment of resources' to an action that will affect the environment." Because the FDA's presumption does not bind its decisionmaking authority, it has neither taken nor prepared to take the irreversible action that is necessary to require preparation of an EIS . . . Evidencing this non-binding effect is the FDA's 1993 decision to open the labeling issue for further discussion, requesting additional public comment on the possible implementation of a general labeling requirement. 58 Fed. Reg. 25,837 (1993).

Moreover, agency decisions that maintain the substantive status quo do not constitute major federal actions under NEPA. Defendants maintain correctly that their actions have not altered the status quo because "rDNA modified foods . . . were regulated no differently before the publication of the Policy Statement than they are now." Because the announcement of a rebuttable presumption of GRAS does not affect the substantive regulatory status quo, it is not a major federal action.

The Statement of Policy is not only reversible and consistent with the status quo ante; it is also not properly an "agency action." The core of Plaintiff's NEPA claim is that FDA has failed to regulate rDNA-modified foods, and that this failure to act engenders environmental consequences. But NEPA applies only to agency actions, "even if inaction has environmental consequences." *Defenders of Wildlife v. Andrus*, 201 U.S. App. D.C. 252, 627 F.2d 1238, 1243 (D.C. Cir. 1980). The *Defenders of Wildlife* court reasoned that Congress did not intend for agencies to perform environmental studies when the agencies were not acting. *See* 627 F.2d at 1244. In certain cases, agencies may take action by authorizing private action, but in such cases the government still must undertake some overt act, such as issuing a permit or affirming a substance as GRAS.

In the instant case, FDA has not taken an overt action, but instead has merely announced a presumption that certain foods do not require special regulation. This presumption against regulation does not constitute an overt action, and is therefore not subject to NEPA requirements.

In sum, because FDA's Statement of Policy is reversible, maintains the substantive status quo, and takes no overt action, the Statement of Policy does not constitute a major federal action under NEPA. FDA was not required to compile an Environmental Assessment or an Environmental Impact Statement in conjunction with the Statement of Policy, and therefore its failure to do so does not violate NEPA....

D. GRAS Presumption In their challenge to the FDA's Statement of Policy, Plaintiffs further claim that the Statement of Policy's presumption that rDNA-engineered foods are GRAS violates the GRAS requirements of the Federal Food, Drug, and Cosmetic Act ("FDCA"), 21 U.S.C. §§ 321(s), and is therefore arbitrary and capricious. The FDCA provides that any substance which may "become a component or otherwise affect[] the characteristics of any food" shall be deemed a food additive. A producer of a food additive must submit a food additive petition to FDA for approval unless FDA determines that the additive is "generally recognized [by qualified experts] ... as having been adequately shown through scientific procedures ... to be safe under the conditions of its intended use." [1]

In the Statement of Policy, FDA indicated that, under §§ 321(s),

---

[1] The term 'food additive' means any substance the intended use of which results or may result, directly or indirectly, in its becoming a component or otherwise affecting the characteristics of any food (including any substance intended for use in producing, manufacturing, packing, processing, preparing, treating, packaging, transporting, or holding food; and including any source of radiation intended for any such use), if such substance is not generally recognized, among experts qualified by scientific training and experience to evaluate its safety, as having been adequately shown through scientific procedures (or, in the case as a substance used in food prior to January 1, 1958, through either scientific procedures or experience based on common use in food) to be safe under the conditions of its intended use ....

it is the intended or expected introduction of a substance into food that makes the substance potentially subject to food additive regulation. Thus, in the case of foods derived from new plant varieties, it is the transferred genetic material and the intended expression product or products that could be subject to food additive regulation, if such material or expression products are not GRAS. Accordingly, FDA reasoned that the only substances added to rDNA engineered foods are nucleic acid proteins, generally recognized as not only safe but also necessary for survival. ("Nucleic acids are present in the cells of every living organism, including every plant and animal used for food by humans or animals, and do not raise a safety concern as a component of food"). Therefore, FDA concluded that rDNA engineered foods should be presumed to be GRAS unless evidence arises to the contrary. The Statement of Policy does acknowledge, however, that certain genetically modified substances might trigger application of the food additives petitioning process. In that vein, FDA recognized that "the intended expression product in a food could be a protein, carbohydrate, fat or oil, or other substance that differs significantly in structure, function, or composition from substances found currently in food. Such substances may not be GRAS and may require regulation as a food additive."

This Court's evaluation of the FDA's interpretation of §§ 321(s) is framed by *Chevron, U.S.A. v. Natural Resources Defense Council*, 467 U.S. 837 (1984). Since "'statutory interpretation begins with the language of the statute itself,'" as a general matter the Court first must determine whether Congress has spoken directly to the issue at hand, a line of analysis that has become known as *Chevron* step one.... The Court answers this inquiry in the affirmative, then "that is the end of the matter; for the court, as well as the agency, must give effect to the unambiguously expressed intent of Congress."

But *Chevron* review also concerns itself with the extent and application of agency discretion in interpreting the statute at issue. In other words, "a reviewing court's inquiry under *Chevron* is rooted in statutory analysis and is focused on discerning the boundaries of Congress' delegation of authority to the agency." To resolve the issue, "the question for the reviewing court is whether the agency's construction of the statute is faithful to its plain meaning, or, if the statute has no plain meaning, whether the agency's interpretation 'is based on a permissible construction of the statute.'" If this interpretation is "reasonable and consistent with the statutory scheme and legislative history."..., then the Court must defer to the agency. This inquiry into the agency's interpretation constitutes *Chevron* step two.

When Congress passed the Food Additives Amendment in 1958, it obviously could not account for the late twentieth-century technologies that would permit the genetic modification of food. The "object and policy" of the food additive amendments, is to "require the processor who wants to add a new and unproven additive to accept the responsibility . . . of first proving it to be safe for ingestion by human beings." S. Rep. No. 85-2422, at 2 (1958). The plain language of §§ 321(s) fosters a broad reading of "food additive" and includes "any substance intended for use in producing, manufacturing, packing, processing, preparing, treating, packaging, transporting, or holding food; and . . . any source of radiation intended for any such use." §§ 321(s).

Nonetheless, the statute exempts from regulation as additives substances that are "generally recognized . . . to be safe under the conditions of its intended use . . . ." §§ 321(s). Plaintiffs have not disputed FDA's claim that nucleic acid proteins are generally recognized to be safe. Plaintiffs have argued, however, that significant disagreement exists among scientific experts as to whether or not nucleic acid proteins are generally recognized to be safe when they are used to alter organisms genetically. Having examined the record in this case, the Court cannot say that FDA's decision to accord genetically modified foods a presumption of GRAS status is arbitrary and capricious. ... this court must proceed with particular caution, avoiding all temptation to direct the agency in a choice between rational alternatives."*Environmental Defense Fund, Inc. v. Costle*, 188 U.S. App. D.C. 95, 578 F.2d 337, 339 (D.C.Cir.1978).

To be generally recognized as safe, a substance must meet two criteria: (1) it must have technical evidence of safety, usually in published scientific studies, and (2) this technical evidence must be generally known and accepted in the scientific community. *See* 21 C.F.R. §§ 170.30(a-b); 62 Fed. Reg. 18940. Although unanimity among scientists is not required, "a severe conflict among experts . . . precludes a finding of general recognition." 62 Fed. Reg. at 18939. Plaintiffs have produced several documents showing significant disagreements among scientific experts.[2] . . .

. . .Moreover, pointing to a 44,000 page record, the FDA notes that Plaintiffs have chosen to highlight a selected few comments of FDA employees, which were ultimately addressed in the agency's final Policy Statement. As a result, Plaintiffs have failed to convince the Court that the GRAS presumption is inconsistent with the statutory requirements.

---

[2] Plaintiff scientist affidavit describing dangers of rDNA technology, Scientist affidavit describing rDNA technology as "inherently risky", Scientist affidavit describing risks of rDNA technology; FDA scientist comments on the Statement of Policy, noting difference between genetic engineering and cross-breeding; FDA scientist criticizing scientific basis of Statement of Policy; FDA scientists arguing that pre-market review of genetically engineered foods is necessary; FDA scientist arguing that Food Additives Amendment should be applied to rDNA engineered foods; FDA toxicology group head warning that genetically modified plants could have high levels of toxins.

E. Labeling Plaintiffs have also challenged the Statement of Policy's failure to require labeling for genetically engineered foods, for which FDA relied on the presumption that most genetically modified food ingredients would be GRAS. Plaintiffs claim that FDA should have considered the widespread consumer interest in having genetically engineered foods labeled, as well as the special concerns of religious groups and persons with allergies in having these foods labeled.

The FDCA, 21 U.S.C. §§ 321(n), grants the FDA limited authority to require labeling. In general, foods shall be deemed misbranded if their labeling "fails to reveal facts . . . material with respect to consequences which may result from the use of the article to which the labeling . . . relates under the conditions of use prescribed in the labeling . . . or under such conditions of use as are customary or usual." Plaintiffs challenge the FDA's interpretation of the term "material." Thus, the question is again one of statutory interpretation. As is apparent from the statutory language, Congress has not squarely addressed whether materiality pertains only to safety concerns or whether it also includes consumer interest. . . .

Because Congress has not spoken directly to the issue, this Court must determine whether the agency's interpretation of the statute is reasonable. Agency interpretations receive substantial deference, particularly when the agency is interpreting a statute that it is charged with administering. Even if the agency's interpretation is not "the best or most natural by grammatical or other standards," if the interpretation is reasonable, then it is entitled to deference.

The FDA takes the position that no "material change," under §§ 321(n), has occurred in the rDNA derived foods at issue here. Absent unique risks to consumer health[3] or uniform changes to food derived through rDNA technology, the FDA does not read §§ 321(n) to authorize an agency imposed food labeling requirement. More specifically irksome to the Plaintiffs, the FDA does not read §§ 321(n) to authorize labeling requirements solely because of consumer demand. The FDA's exclusion of consumer interest from the factors which determine whether a change is "material" constitutes a reasonable interpretation of the statute. Moreover, it is doubtful whether the FDA would even have the power under the FDCA to require labeling in a

---

[3] In other contexts, the FDA has identified that the presence of an increased risk to consumer safety constitutes a "material change." Likewise, should a material consequence exist for a particular rDNA-derived food, the FDA has and will require special labeling. However, the Policy Statement at issue here provides only a very general rule regarding the entire class of rDNA derived foods. Thus, without a determination that, *as a class*, rDNA derived food pose inherent risks or safety consequences to consumers, or differ in some material way from their traditional counterparts, the FDA is without authority to mandate labeling.

situation where the sole justification for such a requirement is consumer demand. *See Stauber v. Shalala*, 895 F. Supp. 1178, 1193 (W.D.Wis. 1995) ("In the absence of evidence of a material difference between [milk from cows treated with a synthetic hormone] and ordinary milk, the use of consumer demand as the rationale for labeling would violate the Food, Drug, and Cosmetic Act.").

Plaintiffs fail to understand the limitation on the FDA's power to consider consumer demand when making labeling decisions because they fail to recognize that the determination that a product differs materially from the type of product it purports to be is a factual predicate to the requirement of labeling. Only once materiality has been established may the FDA consider consumer opinion to determine whether a label is required to disclose a material fact. Thus, "if there is a [material] difference, and consumers would likely want to know about the difference, then labeling is appropriate. If, however, the product does not differ in any significant way from what it purports to be, then it would be misbranding to label the product as different, even if consumers misperceived the product as different." The FDA has already determined that, in general, rDNA modification does not "materially" alter foods, and as discussed in Section II.E, *supra*, this determination is entitled to deference. Given these facts, the FDA lacks a basis upon which it can legally mandate labeling, regardless of the level of consumer demand.

Plaintiffs also contend that the *process* [10] of genetic modification is a "material fact" under §§ 321(n) which mandates special labeling, implying that there are new risks posed to the consumer. However, the FDA has determined that foods produced through rDNA techniques do not "present any different or greater safety concern than foods developed by traditional plant breeding," and concluded that labeling was not warranted. That determination, unless irrational, is entitled to deference. Accordingly, there is little basis upon which this Court could find that the FDA's interpretation of §§ 321(n) is arbitrary and capricious.

CONCLUSION

For the foregoing reasons, the Court determines that Defendant's 1992 Policy Statement did not violate the Administrative Procedures Act, the National Environmental Policy Act, or the procedures mandated by the FDCA and FDA regulations. Furthermore, Defendant was not arbitrary and capricious in its

---

[10] Disclosure of the conditions or methods of manufacture has long been deemed unnecessary under the law. The Supreme Court reasoned in 1924, "When considered independently of the product, the method of manufacture is not material. The act requires no disclosure concerning it." *U.S. v. Ninety-Five Barrels (More or Less) Alleged Apple Cider Vinegar*, 265 U.S. 438 (1924).

finding that genetically modified foods need not be labeled because they do not differ "materially" from non-modified foods under 21 U.S.C. §§ 321(n). . . . Hence, the Court denies Plaintiffs' motion for summary judgment and grants Defendant's motion for same. An appropriate order accompanies this memorandum opinion.

ORDERED that Judgment is hereby entered for Defendant and the case is DISMISSED.

SO ORDERED.

NOTES

1. A list of documents collected during discovery can be found on the Alliance for bio-Integrity website at http://www.bio-integrity.org/list.html . The organization has posted its explanation of the outcome of the preceding case:

> The judge did not rule that GE foods actually have been shown to be safe. Nor did she determine that there ever was a general recognition of safety among the FDA scientists or within the scientific community. Moreover, she did not even say that the FDA could justifiably continue to presume that GE foods are safe. Her decision was limited to the particular exercise of discretion made by the FDA in May of 1992. She ruled that at that specific point in time, the FDA was entitled to have presumed there was a general recognition of safety among scientific experts; but she indicated we had presented evidence showing that there currently is not a general recognition of safety. Further, she emphasized that the FDA's presumption is supposed to be rebuttable by evidence it receives to the contrary. Nonetheless, the FDA continues to pretend that there is an overwhelming consensus among experts that GE foods have been demonstrated to be safe.

Because of the major flaws in the judge's opinion, we filed an appeal in November 2000. Then in January 2001, the FDA proposed new regulations on GE foods. Although these regulations still did not require any safety testing or labeling of GE foods, had they been implemented, they would have replaced the less formal policy decision of May 1992 against which our lawsuit was brought. This appeared to render it a waste of time for us to further pursue our suit, because if the proposed regulations had been enacted, our suit would have become moot and we would have needed to proceed against the new regulations by filing a new lawsuit. Therefore, the Alliance for Bio-Integrity and the other plaintiffs in our lawsuit dropped our appeal, intending to bring a new lawsuit when the regulations took effect.

However, after we dropped our appeal, and after a two year delay in enacting the proposed regulations, the FDA announced it was withdrawing them. So the FDA continues to rely on its policy statement of 1992, and we cannot revive our appeal of the court's decision. Further, because the 1992 policy has already been upheld in a federal court, it is unlikely that anyone else would be able to sustain a new lawsuit against it. This means that GE foods will continue to be unknowingly consumed by most Americans on a daily basis even though they are on the market in stark violation of the food safety laws.

On balance, our lawsuit accomplished a lot by exposing the FDA's fraud and revealing the unsoundness of its policy and the irresponsibility of its behavior. Even though we failed to overturn the FDA's policy, the court's ruling refutes the standard claims of the biotech industry about the rigor of FDA oversight and the proven safety of its own products. It gives the FDA nothing to be proud of nor does it give the biotech industry anything to brag about. But it does give all consumers something to be very concerned about.

4.2.1   Controversy over GE foods, Pt. 3
FET v. Thomas, FET v. Lyng

4.2.1.1. U.S. Environmental Protection Agency and Department of Agriculture: Genetically Engineered Plants

Genetically engineered plants have raised concerns primarily for their use as food, but the other concerns involve the risk to ecological systems.

On May 20, 1999, an article appeared in *Nature* suggesting that there could be a potential environmental problem with genetically engineered crops. John Losey, Cornell University, reported in this article that Bt corn was deadly for Monarch butterfly larvae. This created a new focus for groups who feared the effects of engineered plants placed in the ecosystem.

March 15, 2001, the U.S. Environmental Protection Agency's Independent Panel on Biotechnology released their report on the reassessment of the Bt corn, cotton, and potato plants. The U.S. EPA registrations for corn and cotton Bt products (plant incorporated protectants) expires September 2001. This time-sensitive conditional permit was designed to allow the U.S. EPA to evaluate the effects on human health and the environment.

The report concluded that an environmental impact statement under NEPA should include a consideration of risk and a determination as to whether the methods used are sufficient to mitigate gene flow between feral and Bt crops. Standards for isolation distance were modified and greater borders were recommended for the protection of feral crops from the Bt crops. The Panel also considered whether a Section 7 consultation with the Department of Interior under the Endangered Species Act was necessary. The Panel concluded that the formal consultation was unnecessary but an informal consultation would be recommended. In summary, the Panel found no significant risk to human health or the environment and made recommendations for improvements in the current

111

management scheme.

The following case challenges a federal action based upon the environmental impact statement considered pursuant to the National Environmental Policy Act (NEPA).

4.2.1.2   FET v. Thomas

Foundation on Economic Trends v. Thomas
637 F.Supp. 25 (D.D.C., 1986)

District Judge Thomas F. Hogan. Plaintiffs, various individuals and non-profit environmental organizations, seek injunctive relief against the Environmental Protection Agency's ("EPA") issuance of an experimental use permit ("EUP") to Advanced Genetic Sciences, Inc. ("AGS"), which authorized AGS to conduct a field test of bacteria strains altered by recombinant DNA technology. Plaintiffs contend that the EPA's issuance of the permit violated the requirements of the Federal Insecticide, Fungicide and Rodenticide Act, 7 U.S.C. §§§§ 136-136y ("FIFRA"), the National Environmental Policy Act, 42 U.S.C. §§§§ 4321, et seq. ("NEPA"), and the Administrative Procedure Act, 5 U.S.C. §§ 706(2)(A) ("APA"). Industrial Biotechnology Association ("IBA"), of which AGS is a member, was permitted to intervene as a defendant. The case is before the Court on plaintiffs' motion for preliminary injunction, the motions for summary judgment filed by defendants and IBA, and plaintiffs' motion for relief under Rule 56(f) of the Federal Rules of Civil Procedure. The Court heard oral argument of counsel on the pending motions on February 28, 1986. Upon consideration of the memoranda in support of and opposition to the motions, the arguments and representations of counsel in open court, and the entire record of this case, the Court concludes that the motion for preliminary injunction should be denied and that the Rule 56(f) motion should be denied. The Court withholds decision on the motions for summary judgment filed by defendants and intervenor.

FINDINGS OF FACT

EPA regulates the sale and distribution of pesticides in the United States under FIFRA through the statute's registration scheme, which prohibits the registration, and hence the use and marketing of pesticides which cause "unreasonable adverse effects on the environment." Any person seeking to test an unregistered pesticide may apply to the EPA for an EUP, which will control the conditions under which the testing may take place. EPA may only issue a permit if it finds that the proposed experiment is needed to produce data necessary for registration, and that the experiment will not cause unreasonable adverse effects on the environment. Tests involving genetically engineered microbial pesticides must be presented to the EPA, to determine whether an EUP is necessary. The agency set out this requirement in a policy statement in the Federal Register, on October 12, 1984, as an interim measure to ensure agency supervision of the release of genetically engineered organisms into the environment. Pursuant to their interim policy, EPA began its review of AGS' proposed recombinant DNA experiments involving genetically altered strains of *Pseudonomas Syringae (P. syringae)* and *Pseudonomas Flourescens (P. fluorescens)* late in 1984. The naturally-occurring strains of these bacteria are involved in the formation of ice crystals on plant surfaces, known as "ice nucleation." Ice-nucleating active (INA+) bacteria promote frost formation and non-ice nucleating active (INA-) bacteria inhibit frost formation. Both forms of bacteria coexist in nature, although INA+ predominate. Through recombinant DNA technology, AGS has deleted genetic material from the INA- bacteria to produce INA- bacteria, in an effort to control frost damage on plants.

In August, 1984, following a request by several of the plaintiffs herein, the Hazard Evaluation Division ("HED") of the EPA Office of Pesticide Programs initiated its interim policy with review of several proposed recombinant DNA experiments which had been recommended for approval by the Recombinant DNA Advisory Committee of the National Institutes of Health. When informed of EPA's notification and EUP requirements, AGS submitted its INA- proposal to EPA, with supporting data, and formal EPA review began on October 31, 1984. HED concluded that the test was not likely to pose significant risks to humans or the environment, but determined that AGS would have to provide more information before testing could be conducted under an EUP. HED's specific areas of environmental concern were the dissemination of the mutant bacteria from the test site, the survivability and colonization abilities of the bacteria, and the possible effects from its release on precipitation patterns.. . . .

HED's preliminary conclusions were reviewed by independent scientists on a subpanel of the FIFRA Scientific Advisory Panel ("SAP") in January, 1985. The SAP subpanel generally agreed with HED's conclusions. In February, 1985 HED informed AGS that an EUP would be required for its proposed field test, and that additional data would have to be submitted on the bacteria's competitiveness, ability to colonize, host specificity and pathogenicity. AGS submitted a modified proposal in June, 1985, and included data responsive to the HED's requests. In addition, AGS requested a waiver of some of the EPA's additional standard data requirements. EPA published notice of this application in the *Federal Register* on August 21, 1985, and requested public comments. HED's initial scientific position that the proposal presented no foreseeable risk issued on August 27, 1985, was reviewed by the U.S. Department of Agriculture, the Food & Drug Administration and NIH. Public comments from plaintiff the Foundation on Economic Trends ("FOET") questioned the agency's conclusions about the bacteria's novelty, competitiveness, pathogenicity, and atmospheric role. FOET also urged more laboratory study of the bacteria's effects. . . .

HED responded to FOET's concerns about the bacteria's role in precipitation by contacting the scientists FOET had referenced in their comments, and by contacting other meteorological scientists. The SAP subpanel finally concluded that the experiment was unlikely to pose significant risks and recommended approval of the application. On November 5, 1985 HED summarized their final position, and responded specifically to public comments, concluding that, in light of the evaluated data and the limited scale of the proposed tests, the lack of the mutant's competitive advantage over the natural INA bacteria, AGS' experiment "does not pose a significant risk of adverse environmental impact." HED addressed FOET's concerns about precipitation effect, "novelty" of the mutant, the need for further testing, the toxicology of the bacteria, and EPA's waiver of certain additional data requirements.

The agency issued EUPs to AGS on November 14, 1985, effective December 1, 1985 through November 30, 1986. Plaintiffs filed this suit the same day, alleging that the agency action violated FIFRA, and was arbitrary, capricious and an abuse of discretion. Plaintiffs filed an amended preliminary injunction request on January 26, 1986.

Under the EUP, AGS can conduct a field test of INA- bacteria on a 0.2 acre site, in Monterey County, California, not less than 15 days after it notifies the agency of its intent to begin testing. An interim local ordinance passed in Monterey County prohibits the release of any genetically altered bacteria prior to March 28, 1986, preventing the test from occurring before that time. Additionally, the EPA has begun an investigation of AGS and its research facility following media reports that possible unauthorized open-air tests of the mutant bacteria have occurred. EPA represented to the Court that it will complete its investigation no later than March 24, 1986, and the parties have stipulated that no testing shall occur under the EUP before then.

CONCLUSIONS OF LAW

[P]laintiffs must establish that there was a procedural defect in the agency EUP process, or that the agency's substantive decision to issue the EUP was arbitrary, capricious or an abuse of discretion, based on the record before the agency.

The data submission and agency review requirements for EUPs are set out at 40 C.F.R. §§ 172.4-172.5. The EPA imposed additional data and review procedures for microbial pesticide EUP applications.... These procedures are to ensure that the permit is needed to accumulate information necessary for pesticide registration under FIFRA, and that the proposed testing will not have unreasonable adverse effects on the environment.

Plaintiffs contend that the EPA improperly waived certain data submission requirements for AGS in their EUP application. Data requirements for this type of test are set out at 40 C.F.R. §§ 158, et seq., and may be waived on a case-by-case basis. HED recommended granting the waivers, and upon consideration of the available information, the limited size and scope of the experiment and AGS' proposed safeguards, the EPA concluded that the waivers were appropriate. No further procedure is required in a waiver determination.

Plaintiffs also challenge the substantive result of this EUP procedure, contending that EPA did not adequately consider the potential pathogenicity and toxicity of the bacteria, the likelihood of its dissemination and off-site reproduction, and the impact of release of INA- on atmospheric precipitation patterns. Plaintiffs also claim that the EPA did not give sufficient consideration to alternatives to the proposed test. In reviewing the adequacy of the EPA's consideration of these factors, the Court notes that the stringent procedural and substantive requirements of NEPA's EIS standards do not literally apply to

114

actions of the EPA in this case. The rationale for this exception is that EPA's actions already occur within a substantive regulatory framework that emphasizes the quality of man's environment, and a procedural framework that provides "full opportunity for thorough consideration of the environmental issues and for ample judicial review." This framework is functionally equivalent to NEPA, and to require formal compliance with the statute, when its purpose and policies have been fulfilled, would be "a legalism carried to the extreme." Based upon its review of the record for purposes of the injunction, the procedures in the present case do not appear to the Court to have fallen short of this goal of "functional equivalence" with NEPA. The EPA appears to have considered at each level of review each of the substantive elements plaintiffs raise in their challenge. The administrative record is, at worst, equivocal on these substantive claims, and in light of the deferential "arbitrary and capricious" standard of review applied to this decision, the Court does not find that plaintiffs have made a "strong showing" that they will succeed on the merits of their claims. Further, plaintiffs have not shown that they will be irreparably injured if an injunction does not issue at this stage, since the parties stipulated in open Court that no testing would be conducted under the EUP prior to completion of the EPA's investigation of AGS on March 24. The county ordinance restricting such testing is also in effect until March 28, preventing the release of INA- bacteria by AGS. Accordingly, the motion for preliminary injunction must be denied. . . ..

Plaintiffs have moved under Fed.R.Civ.P. 56(f) for a continuance of the Court's decision on summary judgment to enable them to conduct discovery related to the media reports of AGS' alleged testing violations. Specifically, plaintiffs contend that discovery may provide evidence of the pathogenicity of the mutant bacteria, which they claim is relevant to their challenge to the agency's EUP review. The Court is of the opinion that discovery involving these issues is not warranted, since it would not aid in plaintiffs' challenge to the adequacy of the record before the agency at the time the decision was made or to the adequacy of the agency's procedure. Plaintiffs admit that the evidence they seek to discover was not before EPA during the EUP review. Affidavit of Jeremy Rifkin. When the permit was issued, the EPA had no reason to doubt the accuracy of AGS' data. Plaintiffs have access to the entire record that was before the agency when it decided to issue the EUPs, and additional data not before the agency cannot serve as a basis to challenge the decision. A continuance to permit discovery of such data is therefore not appropriate in light of the present posture of the case. . .

4.2.1.3.   FET v. Lyng

Foundation on Economic Trends v. Lyng
680 F. Supp. 10 (D.C. Cir., 1988)

Opinion by: Thomas F. Hogan, United States District Judge.
MEMORANDUM OPINION

Plaintiffs [1] brought this action on April 23, 1986, seeking to suspend and revoke the license defendants [2] issued permitting marketing of the pseudorabies vaccine "Omnivac." The case is before the Court on the parties' cross-motions for summary judgment. After consideration and review of the motions, oppositions, replies, supporting memoranda, and the entire administrative record, the Court shall grant defendants' motion and deny plaintiffs' motion.

I. BACKGROUND

The United States Department of Agriculture Animal & Plant Health Inspection Service ("USDA-APHIS") controls the production and marketing of veterinary medicines including vaccines through a licensing process under the Virus-Serum-Toxin Act ("VSTA"), 21 U.S.C. §§ 151-158 (1982), and applicable regulations, 9 C.F.R. pt. 102 (1987). USDA-APHIS may grant a license only after reviewing a product and evaluating its safety, efficacy, purity, and potency. 9 C.F.R. § 102.3(b) (2) (ii) (1987). Vaccines and other veterinary biological products that are prepared using biotechnological or "genetic engineering" procedures must comply with these licensing regulations. *E.g.*, Final Policy Statement for Research and Regulation of Biotechnology Processes and Products, 51 Fed. Reg. 23,336 (June 26, 1986).

In addition, USDA-APHIS is subject to the requirements of the National Environmental Policy Act ("NEPA"), and the agency must prepare an environmental impact statement for any major federal action having a significant impact on the human environment. No environmental impact statement is required if the agency finds that the action will have no significant impact. To determine the impact of an action, the agency must prepare an environmental assessment, which summarizes the available environmental evidence and presents the agency's analysis of relevant data. USDA-APHIS guidelines implementing NEPA require preparation of an environmental assessment "for each proposed new action." The parties do not dispute that the licensing of Omnivac was a "proposed new action" requiring an environmental assessment.

The license application at issue was submitted to USDA-APHIS in December, 1984, by Biologics Corporation, a subsidiary of TechAmerica

---

[1] Plaintiffs are the Foundation on Economic Trends ("FET"), a private nonprofit organization active on issues of biotechnology and genetic engineering; Jeremy Rifkin, president of FET and an activist in the area of biotechnology and genetic engineering; and Dr. Michael W. Fox, Scientific Director of the Humane Society of the United States. All plaintiffs reside in the District of Columbia.

[2] Defendants are Richard Lyng, Secretary, United States Department of Agriculture ("USDA"); Bert W. Hawkins, Administrator of the Animal & Plant Health Inspection Service ("APHIS"), USDA; and J.K. Atwell, Deputy Administrator, Veterinary Services, USDA-APHIS. All are sued in their official capacities.

Group Inc. Novagene, Inc., had developed the vaccine in 1982, under the guidance of Dr. Saul Kit. The vaccine was designed to combat pseudorabies, a contagious disease affecting swine and other livestock. In its natural state, the pseudorabies virus may retreat to the nerve cells of a recovered animal and lie dormant, unaffected by the body's immune system. The dormant virus may be reactivated in this outwardly healthy animal and may then spread to other animals as the carrier "sheds" the virus.

Existing pseudorabies vaccines have been prepared from killed or modified live strains of the virus. The modified live virus vaccine is assertedly the most effective, but generally retains the ability to be harbored in the host's nerve cells and then spread to other animals. While these animals are not infected with a disease-producing virus, they will test positive for infection, complicating diagnosis and health programs.

Omnivac was developed by weakening an existing modified live strain of the virus (Bucharest strain). Researchers deleted the gene that produces the enzyme thymidine kinase ("TK"), which is essential for the survival and replication of the virus. As a result, the TK- vaccine virus cannot survive and multiply in nerve cells, unlike the existing wild strain and weakened vaccine virus strain.

The Administrative Record documents the progress of TechAmerica's application through USDA-APHIS's review process. Dr. George Shibley, Senior Staff Microbiologist at the Veterinary Services Division of USDA-APHIS, monitored the license procedure for Omnivac. After a little more than one year of review, testing, and reporting, USDA-APHIS issued a United States Veterinary Biological Product License to TechAmerica on January 16, 1986. USDA-APHIS did not issue or prepare an environmental assessment or environmental impact statement before it granted the license. The Foundation on Economic Trends petitioned USDA-APHIS in early April, 1986, to revoke or suspend the Omnivac license, based in part on USDA-APHIS's failure to comply with NEPA. The agency suspended the license and prepared a lengthy environmental assessment to document the environmental concerns that were "fully identified and reviewed by Department officials prior to licensing the vaccine."

USDA-APHIS concluded that the licensing of Omnivac would not have a significant impact on the environment, based on the following facts:(1) deletion of the genetic element necessary for reproduction prevents the TK-virus from establishing latency; (2) conventional methodology had been used to render the Bucharest virus strain noninfectious prior to the gene deletion; (3) studies on susceptible host animals demonstrated no transmission of the TK- virus; (4) deletion of the TK gene and the consequent inability of the virus to replicate will result in reduced dissemination of the virulent virus through shedding; (5) TK deletion is a stable characteristic, and any reversion and reacquisition of the TK gene would produce latency but not virulency; (6) there is no likelihood of oncogenicity, as the TK- virus contains no new genetic information from the non-oncogenetic wild pseudorabies virus; (7) the TK- virus demonstrated reduced virulence in other animals; (8) like the existing virus strains, the TK- virus is avirulent to humans; and (9) demonstrated inability of the TK- virus to revert to the wild virus strain, as distinct from the weakened strain from which it is crafted. *Id.* The scientific data requested and submitted from which USDA-APHIS drew these conclusions are presented in the environmental assessment and are discussed more fully below.

The belated Omnivac environmental assessment was released on April 22, 1986, and notice of its availability was published in the Federal Register. 51 Fed. Reg. 15,657 (Apr. 25, 1986). The suspension was lifted immediately and Omnivac production resumed. Plaintiffs filed this action on April 23, 1986, seeking declaratory and injunctive relief. Plaintiffs did not apply for temporary or preliminary injunctive relief. Cross-motions for summary judgment were submitted after the Administrative Record was filed. Plaintiffs contend that USDA-APHIS violated the VSTA and applicable regulations in issuing the license, and that the agency failed to comply with NEPA. Defendants challenge plaintiffs' standing, and assert that USDA-APHIS complied with the law in issuing the license.

II. DISCUSSION . . .

B. *Plaintiffs' Claim Under NEPA*
Plaintiff FET has standing to seek review of USDA's compliance with NEPA, based on its claim that the agency's noncompliance affected FET's ability to provide information to the public. *E.g., Scientists' Institute for Public Information, Inc. v. AEC*, 156 U.S. App. D.C. 395, 481 F.2d 1079, 1086-87 n.29 (D.C. Cir. 1973); *see also Foundation on Economic Trends v. Lyng*, 260 U.S. App. D.C. 159, 817 F.2d 882 (D.C. Cir. 1987) (reviewing gravamen of plaintiffs' challenge to USDA's compliance with NEPA; implicitly assuming existence of standing). FET alleges that USDA-APHIS's environmental assessment ("EA") on Omnivac was inadequate. . . .The Court must ordinarily ask four questions in deciding whether an agency's finding of "no significant impact" in an environmental assessment is arbitrary and capricious:

(1) whether the agency took a "hard look" at the problem; (2) whether the agency identified the relevant areas of environmental concern; (3) as to the problems studied and identified, whether the agency made a convincing case that the impact was insignificant; and (4) if there was an impact of true significance, whether the agency convincingly established what changes in the project sufficiently reduced it to a minimum.

Cabinet Mountains Wilderness v. Peterson, 222 U.S. App. D.C. 228, 685 F.2d 678, 682 (D.C. Cir. 1982). Within this framework, review of USDA-APHIS's decision not to prepare an EIS "must be undertaken with a view merely to determine if the agency has taken the 'hard look' at the environmental consequences of the action that NEPA requires." *Foundation on Economic Trends v. Weinberger*, 610 F. Supp. 829, 838-39 (D.D.C. 1985). To survive review, the agency's environmental assessment "must indicate, in some fashion, that the agency has taken a searching, realistic look at the potential hazards and, with reasoned thought and analysis, candidly and methodically addressed those concerns." *Id.* at 841.

The EA prepared on Omnivac found that use of recombinant TK-pseudorabies vaccine would not have significant impact on the environment. The EA discusses the characteristics of existing strains of wild and modified pseudorabies, describing among other factors the transmission, range, pathogenesis, latency, and survival of the pseudorabies vaccine. The EA then presents the agency's review of the same characteristics of the TK-pseudorabies vaccine, and summarizes the data supporting the scientific conclusions. USDA-APHIS concluded that the TK- virus is stable, avirulent, unlikely to be transmitted, and unable to establish latency, and accordingly, would have no significant impact on the environment.

FET initially asserts that USDA-APHIS failed to consult with other agencies, internal advisory committees, and the public, in violation of applicable regulations. None of the regulations, internal memoranda, or policy statements requires the review plaintiffs seek. Applicable APHIS regulations implementing NEPA require public involvement where program changes will have significant adverse effects on the environment, when APHIS intends to prepare an EIS, and when a draft or final EIS or a finding of no significant impact is available. APHIS Guidelines Concerning Implementation of NEPA Procedures, 44 Fed. Reg. 50,381, 50,383 (Aug. 28, 1979). Applicable USDA regulations leave to the agency's discretion when to seek additional public involvement. 7 C.F.R. § 1b.1(a) (1987) (incorporating Council on Environmental Quality ("CEQ") regulations); 40 C.F.R. § 1506.6 (1987) (CEQ regulation concerning public involvement). The guidelines upon which FET relies to establish interagency and advisory committee review requirements apply, if at all, to the licensing process, and are not mandated by NEPA and its implementing regulations....To the extent regulations and protocol required preliminary consultation, USDA-APHIS provided it.

FET challenges the substance of USDA's conclusions in the EA, delineating what it considers to be deficient testing and inadequate review of data submitted in support of the application. FET's principal concern is with the "safety data" USDA received and compiled. FET raises legitimate complaints about the failure of the original researcher, Dr. Saul Kit, to comply with established reporting and notification requirements in the conduct of an open air test of the vaccine. Even if USDA knew of Dr. Kit's transgressions, the Court cannot conclude that it was "arbitrary and capricious" to consider the data collected. . . .

FET finally argues that the tests and data reflected in the EA do not resolve issues it asserts are central to the nature and effect of Omnivac. USDA presents evidence contradicting these claims, rebutting both the assertion that specific issues were not resolved and the claim that the issues are "central" to the nature and effect of the vaccine. [6]FN6 After careful review of the record, the Court notes that some of the testing "deficiencies" FET recounts reflect the nascency of the field of genetic engineering rather than truncated examination of the product by the agency.

The Court is not in the same position as the agency in its review of the scientific data submitted, and cannot replace the agency's judgment with its own. Upon examination of the environmental assessment and the supporting Administrative Record, the Court concludes that the finding of no significant impact was not arbitrary and capricious. Accordingly, summary judgment shall be granted in defendants' favor under the NEPA claim.

An appropriate order accompanies this opinion.

ORDER OF DISMISSAL

NOTES

Vermont enacted legislation in 2003 to require the identification and labeling of genetically engineered seeds that are brought into the state, the Farmer Protection Act. Does this raise questions with the Dormant Commerce Clause?

Vermont enacted S.182 in the 2002-2003 Session adding this provision: § 611. SERVICE FOR CERTIFICATION OF SEED; STANDARDS AND REGULATIONS: Sec. 1. 6 V.S.A. § 611 ©) This chapter requires the identification of seeds modified by the presence of living modified organisms resulting from modern biotechnology and intended for intentional introduction into the environment. The purpose of such identification is to help to avoid through the use of such seeds any adverse effects on the conservation and sustainable use of biological diversity in this state.

(4) For all seed containing genetically engineered material, the manufacturer or processor shall cause the label or labeling to specify the identity and relevant traits or characteristics of such seed, plus any requirements for their safe handling, storage, transport, and use, the contact point for further information and, as appropriate, the name and address of the manufacturer, distributor, or supplier of such seed.. . .

(b) The secretary may develop rules for labeling procedures consistent with the provisions of this section, which take into account: origin, presence of weed seed, mixtures, hermetically sealed containers, coated seed, "crop seeds," genetically engineered material, genetically engineered plant parts, hybrids, germination medium, and preplanted containers. (Added 1989, No. 85, § 2; amended 2003, No. 42, § 2, eff. May 27, 2003; 2003, No. 97 (Adj. Sess.), § 3, eff. Oct. 1, 2004; 2003, No. 149 (Adj. Sess.), § 13, eff. Oct. 2, 2004.)

---

[6] FET's principal concern is the lack of conclusive data on the potential teratogenicity of Omnivac when ingested by pregnant sows. The vaccine was not specifically approved for administration to pregnant sows, however, until teratogenicity data was received and reviewed, after the initial license was granted.

4.2.2   Controversy over GE Foods, Pt. 4
FET v. Heckler, FET v. Block, FET v. Bowen

4.2.2.1 U.S. Environmental Protection Agency, National Institutes
of Health: Genetically Modified Organisms
FET v. Heckler

Foundation on Economic Trends v. Heckler
756 F.2d 143 (D.C. Cir. 1985)

Circuit Judge J. Skelly Wright: Almost 14 years ago, soon after passage of the National Environmental Policy Act (NEPA), this court faced the challenge of ensuring that the Act's " important legislative purposes, heralded in the halls of Congress, [were] not lost or misdirected in the vast hallways of the federal bureaucracy." *Calvert Cliffs' Coordinating Committee v. USAEC*, ... This case poses a no less formidable challenge: to ensure that the bold words and vigorous spirit of NEPA are not similarly lost or misdirected in the brisk frontiers of science. For this appeal presents an important question at the dawn of the genetic engineering age: what is the appropriate level of environmental review required of the National Institutes of Health (NIH) before it approves the deliberate release of genetically engineered, recombinant-DNA-containing organisms into the open environment? More precisely, in the context of this case, the question is whether to affirm an injunction temporarily enjoining NIH from approving deliberate release experiments without a greater level of environmental concern than the agency has shown thus far. In September 1983 three environmental groups and two individuals filed suit against the federal officials responsible for genetic engineering decisions. Arguing that NIH had not complied with the requirements of NEPA, plaintiffs sought to enjoin a proposed NIH-approved experiment by University of California scientists that would represent the first deliberate release of genetically engineered organisms into the open environment. They also sought to enjoin NIH's approval of any other deliberate release experiments. Plaintiffs later added Regents of the University of California as a defendant. On May 18, 1984 the District Court granted the requested relief and enjoined both the University of California experiment and NIH approval of all other deliberate release experiments. We emphatically agree with the District Court's conclusion that NIH has not yet displayed the rigorous attention to environmental concerns demanded by law. We therefore affirm the District Court's injunction prohibiting the University of California deliberate release experiment until an appropriate environmental assessment is completed. We also share the District Court's view that NIH should give greater consideration to the broad environmental issues attendant on deliberate release of organisms containing recombinant DNA, and to its own responsibility for approving these deliberate release experiments. We find, however, that the part of the injunction enjoining NIH from approving all other deliberate release experiments is, at this juncture, overly broad, and we therefore vacate the part of the injunction that prohibits NIH approval of those experiments. We wish to emphasize, however, that if NIH fails to give appropriate environmental consideration to any other experiment, as it has failed to do with the University of California experiment, injunctive relief would be clearly proper.

I. BACKGROUND

This case arises against a backdrop of the National Environmental Policy Act, the emergence of genetic engineering, and federal attempts to regulate genetic engineering. . . .

A. *National Environmental Policy Act* On January 1, 1970 the National Environmental Policy Act became law. Recognizing "the profound impact of man's activity on the interrelation of all components of the natural environment," Congress sought to "fulfill the responsibilities of each generation as trustee of the environment for succeeding generations." The major "action-forcing" provision of NEPA is the requirement that "all agencies of the Federal government" prepare a detailed environmental analysis for "major Federal actions significantly affecting the quality of the human environment." Congress mandated that this detailed statement, long known as an Environmental Impact Statement (EIS), include such considerations as "the environmental impact of the proposed action," "any adverse environmental effects which cannot be avoided should the proposal be implemented," and "alternatives to the proposed action." Realizing that NEPA would be toothless if agencies could merely issue a conclusory statement that the action did not significantly affect the environment (and that therefore no EIS was required), the Council on Environmental Quality (CEQ), an entity created by NEPA, issued regulations establishing that, unless the major federal action falls within an agency-established "categorical exclusion," the agency should support each finding of "no significant impact" with a "concise public document" called an "environmental assessment" (EA). The environmental assessment must "briefly provide sufficient evidence and analysis for determining whether to prepare an environmental impact statement or a finding of no significant impact." CEQ regulations apply to all federal agencies.

Two fundamental principles underlie NEPA's requirements: federal agencies have the responsibility to consider the environmental effects of major actions significantly affecting environment, and the public has the right to review that consideration. . . . . NEPA's dual mission is thus to generate federal attention to environmental concerns and to reveal that federal consideration for public scrutiny.

In passing NEPA Congress emphasized its particular concern with the role of new technologies and their effect on the environment. The statute explicitly enumerates "new and expanding technological advances" as one of the activities with the potential to threaten the environment. The legislative history reveals an underlying concern with "[a] growing technological power. .. far outstripping man's capacity to understand and ability to control its impact on the environment." S.Rep. No. 91-296. One of NEPA's main functions was to bolster this capacity to understand and control the effects of new technology. *See Scientists' Institute for Public Information v. AEC, ...* NEPA thus stands as landmark legislation, requiring federal agencies to consider the environmental effects of major federal actions, empowering the public to scrutinize this consideration, and revealing a special concern about the environmental effects of new technology.

B. *Genetic Engineering*
Genetic engineering is an important development at the very cusp of scientific advances. More than a decade ago scientists discovered a method for transplanting deoxyribonucleic acid (DNA), the principal substance of genes. Although exchanges and mutations of DNA occur in nature, genetic engineering provides the ability to control these fundamental processes of life and evolution. DNA segments can be recovered and cloned from one organism and inserted into another. The result is known as "recombinant DNA."

Recombinant DNA technology has been limited primarily to small organisms, usually bacteria. This production of new bacteria through altering genetic material has been confined to the laboratory; organisms with recombinant DNA have never been released into the general environment.

Broad claims are made about both the potential benefits and the potential hazards of genetically engineered organisms. Use of recombinant DNA may lead to welcome advances in such areas as food production and disease control. At the same time, however, the environmental consequences of dispersion of genetically engineered organisms are far from clear. According to a recent report by a House of Representatives subcommittee, "The potential environmental risks associated with the deliberate release of genetically engineered organisms or the translocation of any new organism into an ecosystem are best described as 'low probability, high consequence risk '; that is, while there is only a small possibility that damage could occur, the damage that could occur is great." *The Environmental Implications of Genetic Engineering*, Report by Subcommittee on Investigations & Oversight to House Committee on Science & Technology, 98th Cong., 2d Sess. 9 (1984) (hereinafter cited as *Genetic Engineering Report*), JA 167. C. *Federal Oversight of Genetic Engineering*

Spurred by scientists involved in genetic research, NIH began efforts to oversee genetic engineering in the mid-1970's. Federal oversight of deliberate release experiments falls into four periods: (1) NIH's 1976 standards, which prohibited deliberate release of organisms containing recombinant DNA; (2) NIH's 1978 revision, which gave the NIH Director power to approve deliberate release experiments; (3) the NIH Director's approval of three such experiments in the early 1980's; and (4) the District Court's injunction prohibiting the University of California experiment and enjoining NIH approval of all other deliberate release experiments.

1. *NIH's 1976 standards: prohibition on deliberate release.* In 1976 the NIH Director issued "Guidelines for Research on Recombinant DNA Molecules." 41 Fed. Reg. at 27902, JA 230. The Guidelines were an historic development, representing the first major federal effort to oversee genetic research and the culmination of intense scientific attention to the possible hazards of genetic research.

In 1974 scientists working in genetic research voluntarily called for a moratorium on certain kinds of experiments until an international meeting could be convened to consider the potential hazards of recombinant DNA molecules. On October 7, 1974 NIH established the Recombinant DNA Advisory Committee (RAC) to consider genetic research issues. And in February 1975 NIH, the National Science Foundation, and the National Academy of Sciences sponsored an international conference at the Asilomar Conference Center in Pacific Grove, California to review the questions posed by the possibility of genetic engineering.

Finally, in the summer of 1976 the NIH Director announced the Guidelines that would govern NIH-supported genetic research experiments. In broad terms, the Guidelines permitted certain laboratory experiments to go forward under carefully specified conditions; certain other types of experiments were flatly prohibited. Deliberate release -- "deliberate release into the environment of any organism containing a recombinant DNA molecule" -- was one of five categories explicitly banned. In announcing the Guidelines the Director noted that deliberate release of organisms with recombinant DNA was not yet feasible and that, if it became feasible, the ban could be reconsidered. But he stressed that, if such reconsideration occurred, environmental concerns should be paramount: " "It is most important that the potential environmental impact of the release be considered."

Significantly, NIH prepared an EIS to accompany its Guidelines — the only EIS NIH has ever completed on the subject of genetic engineering. The EIS did not specifically refer to deliberate release experiments; such experiments were banned. The EIS did, however, note that dispersion of organisms with recombinant DNA molecules loomed as a potential environmental hazard from the permitted experiments:

Should organisms containing recombined DNA be dispersed into the environment, they might, depending on their fitness relative to naturally occuring [*sic*] organisms, find a suitable ecological niche for their own reproduction. A potentially dangerous organism might then multiply and spread. Subsequent cessation of experiments would not stop the diffusion of the hazardous agent.

Thus in 1976 the NIH Guidelines prohibited deliberate release; the Director emphasized the importance of full environmental consideration of any possible future release; and the EIS identified dispersion of organisms with recombinant DNA as a possible environmental hazard.

2. *The 1978 revision: permission to waive the prohibition against deliberate release.* In 1978 the NIH Director undertook an effort to revise the Guidelines "in light of NIH's experience operating under them and in light of [NIH's] increasing knowledge about the potential risks and benefits of this research technique." 43 Fed.Reg. 33042 (July 28, 1978). Proposed in July and adopted in December, the revision changed the Guidelines in several respects. Most importantly for this appeal, the 1978 revision allowed the NIH Director authority to grant exceptions to the five absolute prohibitions in the Guidelines -- including the prohibition on deliberate release of organisms containing recombinant DNA into the environment....

NIH announced that the standard governing the use of this waiver authority would be the standard generally applicable to the Director's exercise of his duties: "The Director shall weigh each proposed action, through appropriate analysis and consultation, to determine that it complies with the Guidelines and presents no significant risk to health or the environment." NIH also declared that the Director would exercise his authority "with the advice of the Recombinant DNA Advisory Committee after appropriate notice and opportunity for public comment." The Director further stated that his "waiver decisions [would] include a careful consideration of the potential environmental impact, and certain decisions may be accompanied by a formal assessment or statement. This must be determined on a case-by-case basis."

On the subject of deliberate release experiments in particular, the Director suggested that clear standards might be necessary to guide his waiver discretion: "Recognizing the need expressed by . . . commentators for more definitive standards [to govern deliberate release waiver decision], I will refer the matter to the Recombinant Advisory Committee (RAC) for its consideration.... The RAC will be asked to address conditions under which exceptions to various prohibited categories of experiments may be granted." 43 Fed. Reg. at 60083. Thus the Director perceived a possible need for more definitive standards and suggested that such standards might be forthcoming.

NIH did not prepare an EIS to accompany its 1978 revision. It prepared two Environmental Assessments -- one for the revision as proposed, and one for the revision as adopted. The assessments said little about the Director's new waiver authority for deliberate release experiments. The first simply declared, "Waiver decisions will include a careful consideration of potential environmental impact;" the second did not mention the waiver authority.

The 1978 revision also extended the coverage of the Guidelines to all experiments at institutions receiving NIH funds for recombinant DNA research, whether or not the particular experiment had received NIH funds. . . .

3. *Approval of deliberate release experiments*. The 1978 revision was the last significant revision of NIH's guidelines regarding deliberate release experiments. A 1982 revision was largely semantic, 47 Fed. Reg. 17186-17187 (April 21, 1982); a 1983 revision establishing slightly different procedures for deliberate release involving certain plants, is not part of this appeal. The "more definitive standards" suggested by the Director never emerged.

Although the guidelines have not changed, NIH's role has begun to change dramatically. For, with the maturation of genetic engineering technology, NIH has been faced with applications for approval of deliberate release experiments.

The NIH Director, acting on the advice of RAC, has approved three deliberate release experiments at institutions receiving NIH funds for recombinant DNA research. On August 7, 1981 the Director approved a request by Dr. Ronald Davis of Stanford University to field-test corn plants containing recombinant DNA molecules. The goal was to increase the corn's dietary value by improving its ability to store protein. However, the field tests were never conducted because feasibility problems developed. *Genetic Engineering Report*. . .

On April 15, 1983 the Director approved a request by Dr. John Sanford of Cornell University to field-test tomato and tobacco plants with recombinant DNA. The goal was to prove that pollen could serve as a "vector" for insertion of recombinant DNA. Again, however, due to feasibility problems, the experiment never went forward. *Genetic Engineering Report* . . .

On June 1, 1983 the Director gave final approval to the experiment at issue on appeal -- the request by Drs. Nickolas Panopoulos and Steven Lindow of the University of California at Berkeley to apply genetically altered bacteria to plots of potatoes, tomatoes, and beans in northern California.. As discussed in greater detail below, the goal was to increase the crops' frost resistance. Because of the cancellation of the previous two experiments, the

Panopoulos-Lindow experiment would be the first NIH-approved deliberate release experiment actually to be conducted. . . .

In February 1984 a congressional subcommittee report sharply criticized NIH's method of reviewing deliberate release experiments. The report concluded that "the current regulatory framework does not guarantee that adequate consideration will be given to the potential environmental effects of a deliberate release." In particular, "the RAC's ability to adequately evaluate the environmental hazards posed by deliberate releases is limited by both its expertise and its jurisdiction." The subcommittee report recommended a moratorium on deliberate release approvals until an interagency review panel was established to consider the potential environmental effects of each deliberate release experiment. "Each [deliberate release experiment] could result in major environmental damage or adverse public health effects.". . .

4. *The injunction.* In September 1983 three public interest organizations and two individuals filed suit against the three federal officials ultimately responsible for NIH deliberate release decisions; they later added Regents of the University of California as a defendant. The University of California experiment was scheduled to begin on or about May 25, 1984. On May 18 the District Court issued an injunction enjoining the University of California experiment and NIH approval of other deliberate release experiments. The District Court found that plaintiffs were likely to succeed in showing that NIH should have completed at least a more complete environmental assessment, and perhaps an EIS, before approving the University of California experiment; it also found them likely to succeed in showing that NIH should have completed an Environmental Impact Statement in connection with both its 1978 policy change and its imminent "program" of deliberate release approvals. . . .

A. *Review of an Agency Decision Not to Prepare an EIS* That courts must play a cardinal role in the realization of NEPA's mandate is beyond dispute. As the Supreme Court recently emphasized, the critical judicial task is "to ensure that the agency has adequately considered and disclosed the environmental impact of its actions and that its decision is not arbitrary or capricious.". . .Since NEPA requires the agency to "take a 'hard look ' at the environmental consequences before taking a major action," *id. (quoting Kleppe v. Sierra Club),* the judiciary must see that this legal duty is fulfilled. Although the "agency commencing federal action has the initial and primary responsibility for ascertaining whether an EIS is required,". . .the courts must determine that this decision accords with traditional norms of reasoned decisionmaking and that the agency has taken the "hard look" required by NEPA. . . .

A. *The Adequacy of the Environmental Review* 1. *The proposed experiment.* On September 17, 1982 Drs. Lindow and Panopoulos, scientists at Berkeley, submitted a request for NIH approval of an experiment that would involve deliberate release of genetically altered organisms in the open environment. NIH approval was required because the University of California receives NIH funds for recombinant DNA research. Lindow and Panopoulos proposed to apply the genetically altered bacteria to various crops, including potatoes, tomatoes, and beans. By changing the bacteria's genetic composition, Lindow and Panopoulos hoped that the bacteria would change from frost-triggering bacteria to non-frost-triggering bacteria; they further hoped that the engineered non-frost-triggering bacteria would displace the natural frost-triggering bacteria. The ultimate goal was to protect the crops from frost and thus to extend their growing season. Such non-frost-triggering bacteria occur in nature as products of natural mutation, but Lindow and Panopoulos apparently hoped that the genetically engineered organisms would be more stable than the natural mutants. They sought to treat crops at six sites; the workers applying the recombinant-DNA-containing bacteria would wear respirators to reduce the risk of inhalation.... 2. *NIH review.* NIH announced the Lindow-Panopoulos request for approval, the RAC meeting at which it would be considered, and the opportunity to comment. No comments were received. At the RAC meeting on October 25, 1982 RAC members raised questions about the number of sites, the lack of adequate information, and the possible effects on rainfall. RAC voted to recommend that the Director approve the project; the vote was seven in favor, five opposed, with two abstentions. The Director decided to postpone approval and suggested further consideration.

Lindow and Panopoulos resubmitted their proposal with some modifications, including a reduction of experiment sites from six to one. On April 11, 1983, after some discussion, RAC voted to recommend approving the proposal by a vote of 19-0, with no abstentions. The Director then approved the experiment.... 3. *NEPA compliance.* NIH's consideration of the Lindow-Panopoulos experiment falls far short of the NEPA requirements. And, despite the government's apparent belief, the deficiency is not a question of which document contains the environmental analysis. Rather, the deficiency rests in NIH's complete failure to consider the possibility of various environmental effects.

Neither the government nor the University seriously disputes that an environmental assessment is necessary. The government has conceded that the approval is a "major action" and that it does not fall into a categorical exclusion to the EIS requirements, Federal Defendants' Response to Plaintiffs' Second Set of Interrogatories at 17, JA 50; *see also Foundation on Economic Trends v. Heckler,* 587 F. Supp. 753, 767 (D.D.C.1984). The University's contention here -- and the government's contention below, as well as its apparent continuing belief -- is that the environmental consideration given by NIH was equivalent to the necessary environmental assessment and that the injunction requires only a document labelled "Environmental Assessment." We thus fear that the University and the government completely misapprehend the District Court's holding and the requirements imposed by NEPA.

The most glaring deficiency in NIH's review of the Lindow-Panopoulos experiment is its treatment of the possibility of dispersion of recombinant-DNA-containing organisms. As noted, NIH's only EIS on genetic engineering specifically identified dispersion as one of the major environmental concerns associated with recombinant DNA research. The consequences of dispersion of genetically altered organisms are uncertain. Some observers believe that such dispersion would affect the environment and the climate in harmful ways. ("the risk presented by the deliberate release of a genetically engineered organism is that it may cause environmental changes that perturb the ecosystem it encounters and/or that the organism itself may have negative effects if it establishes itself outside of the specific environment for which it was intended").

Thus the problem of dispersion would seem to be one of the major concerns associated with the Lindow-Panopoulos experiment, the first experiment that would actually release genetically engineered organisms in the open environment. Yet in the minutes of the RAC meeting -- the only document on appeal that records *any* NIH consideration of the environmental impact of dispersion -- the entirety of the consideration of dispersion is the following statement: according to a RAC evaluator, "Although some movement of bacteria toward sites near treatment locations by insect or aerial transport *is possible*, the numbers of viable cells transported has been shown to be very small; and these cells are subject to biological and physical processes limiting survival." In this sentence, which was taken almost verbatim from the Lindow-Panopoulos proposal, the RAC evaluator thus conceded the possibility of aerial or insect transport, but merely commented that the number of viable cells would be small, and that they were subject to processes limiting survival. Remarkably, therefore, RAC completely failed to consider the possible environmental impact from dispersion of genetically altered bacteria, however small the number and however subject to procedures limiting survival.[6]

---

[6] The University's arguments defending the NIH review are completely unconvincing. For instance, the University emphasizes that the use of chemically induced non-frost-triggering bacteria has produced "no untoward environmental consequences." Brief for appellant Regents at 42. But the Lindow-Panopoulos proposal itself stressed that the genetically engineered bacteria would have greater "genetic stability" and "competitive fitness" than the chemically-induced bacteria. Similarly, the University points to the presence of non-frost-triggering bacteria in nature. At oral argument, however, the University reported that these natural populations, like the chemical mutants, are probably less stable and competitive than the genetically engineered

In light of this complete failure to address a major environmental concern, NIH's environmental assessment utterly fails to meet the standard of environmental review necessary before an agency decides not to prepare an EIS. The argument that this consideration would be adequate if contained in a document labelled "Environmental Assessment" simply misconceives the clear requirements of NEPA as articulated by the courts . . . An environmental assessment that fails to address a significant environmental concern can hardly be deemed adequate for a reasoned determination that an EIS is not appropriate. . . .Appellants also contend that the adequacy of the environmental assessment can be divined from the NIH Director's final approval -- and his accompanying statement of "no significant risk,". . .This contention also reveals a fundamental misunderstanding about the adequacy of an environmental assessment. Simple, conclusory statements of "no impact" are not enough to fulfill an agency's duty under NEPA. . . .

To reiterate, NIH must first complete a far more adequate environmental assessment of the possible environmental impact of the deliberate release experiment than it has yet undertaken. That assessment must "provide sufficient evidence and analysis for determining whether to prepare an environmental impact statement or a finding of no significant impact," 40 C.F.R. §§ 1508.9(a)(1). Ignoring possible environmental consequences will not suffice. Nor will a mere conclusory statement that the number of recombinant-DNA-containing organisms will be small and subject to processes limiting survival. Instead, NIH must attempt to evaluate seriously the risk that emigration of such organisms from the test site will create ecological disruption. Second, until NIH completes such an evaluation the question whether the experiment requires an EIS remains open. The University of California experiment clearly presents the possibility of a problem identified by NIH in its EIS as a potential environmental hazard. This fact weighs heavily in support of the view than an EIS should be completed, unless NIH can demonstrate either that the experiment does not pose the previously identified danger, or that its assessment of the previously identified danger has changed through a process of reasoned decisionmaking. Nor is it sufficient for the agency merely to state that the environmental effects are currently unknown. Indeed, one of the specific criteria for determining whether an EIS is necessary is "the degree to which the possible effects on the human environment are highly uncertain or involve unique or unknown risks." 40 C.F.R. §§ 1508.27(b)(5).

Thus we approve the District Court's determination that, as a matter of law, plaintiffs are likely to prevail in showing that NIH's environmental assessment of the University of California experiment -- and its discharge of

---

bacteria.

its statutory duty to consider the propriety of an EIS -- was wholly inadequate. . . .

Senior Circuit Judge MacKinnon (concurring).
I am of opinion that the Foundation should have made its original application to NIH. I do not agree that the failure to exhaust can be disposed of by the cases cited holding that exhaustion is "ultimately an exercise of judicial discretion." This is not a case of just failure to exhaust in a pending proceeding before an agency, but a case of a complete failure of the Foundation to present any claim or objection whatsoever to the agency -- NIH. Thus, the normal exhaustion cases where the parties have appeared before the agency are not applicable. However, since the issues in this case are of great importance, new and novel I do not dissent because we are remanding the major issues in the case to the agency where what should have been done by all parties will now be done, and we are reversing in other major respects. . . .

Had the Foundation submitted its objections to the agency, it is thus more than likely, given the demonstrated sensitivity of NIH and its scientists to such matters, that the University and the agency would have responded to any objections and the record here, if the Foundation were not satisfied, would have been more complete and useful. I am thus not so concerned about the fairness to the agency and to the litigants as I am that the Foundation's delay deprived this court of the normal administrative record and consideration by the district court that are required to meet the issues raised by the Foundation.

The Foundation's conduct also has delayed this vital experiment for a very considerable period of time. The use of delaying tactics by those who fear and oppose scientific progress is nothing new. It would, however, be a national catastrophe if the development of this promising new science of genetic engineering were crippled by the unconscionable delays that have been brought about by litigants using the National Environmental Policy Act and other environmental legislation in other areas. The protracted litigations involving the Alaska pipeline, nuclear power plants, and the Clean Air Act present only a few examples.

These concerns extend to the court's comments concerning the possibility of a Programmatic EIS. It is my opinion that because the possibilities of genetic engineering, an industry still in its infancy, extend to so many areas, and because the development of a programmatic EIS would be vulnerable to delaying tactics, composing a programmatic EIS at this time would be neither justified, practical, nor prudent.

Two cases followed in the District of Columbia federal district court, again brought by the Foundation on Economic Trends. Both used NEPA to challenge the impact on the environment. The second case was based on a challenge of the consideration of the environmental impact of a genetically engineered plant, which has a bacteria gene that is intended to prevent frost damage to the plant. The court examines the procedural requirements of NEPA, and finds there is no basis to issue a preliminary injunction to prevent the experiment from going forward, based on compliance with NEPA.

4.2.2.2 FET v. Block

Foundation on Economic Trends v. Block
D. District of Columbia, Civ. No. 84-3045
April 29, 1986

An EA or EIS need not be prepared unless a proposal or major federal action may have a significant impact on the environment. 42 U.S.C. § 4322 (1)©).Plaintiffs allege that defendants' animal productivity research is directed solely at producing larger, more productive animals which are best suited to capital intensive breeding operations. According to plaintiffs, this research focus significantly impacts the environment by decreasing the gene pool of farm animals, pollutes air and water resources, erodes the soil, makes the traditional family farm unit economically obsolete and alters the animal husbandry industry.

Most of these effects are indirect. However, NEPA requires that impact statements consider indirect effects, including a proposal's social and economic consequences. Relying on Sierra Club, plaintiffs urge that the social and economic consequences of defendants' animal breeding research put these activities under the reach of NEPA.However, as defendants' correctly note, Sierra Club does not require that "highly speculative or indefinite impacts" be considered. Before an EA or EIS is prepared the Sierra Club court required that the following factors be considered:With what confidence can one say that 'the impacts are likely to occur? Can one describe them 'now with sufficient specificity to make their consideration useful? If the decisionmaker does not take them into account 'now', will the decisionmaker be able to take account of them before the agency is so firmly committed to the project that further environmental knowledge, as a practical matter, will prove irrelevant to the government's decision?

Applying these criteria, it becomes clear that it is premature to require the defendants in this case to prepare an EA or an EIS evaluating the possible direct and indirect consequences of its animal breeding research. As previously discussed, when research has just begun, and when its success is uncertain, discussion of its eventual applications and the consequences of these applications can be no more than speculation. Furthermore, defendants' experiments in animal breeding and reproduction do not set the USDA on a path of no return. The direction this research takes can be changed at any time. Thus, at this stage, an EA or EIS would be, at most, of limited value, and thus is not required by law.Another day, on a different record, the result might be otherwise.Finally, there is a logical rebuttal to plaintiffs' claim of significant environmental impact: Defendants' experiments are only conducted in laboratories and other controlled environments. The animals are not released into the general environment. Thus, by definition, there can be no "environmental impact". Defendants' have detailed the safeguards now being used to insure that the products of genetic engineering remain under their control. Moreover, even the products of conventional selective breeding research are isolated. (Cattle used in a current USDA breeding experiment in Montana are descended from cattle involved in this same experiment when it began in 1931 at this same location. Given the controls defendants' place on their experimental subjects and products, allegations of significant environmental impact are now nothing but sheerest speculation.

DEFENDANTS' ALLEGED FAILURE TO CONSIDER ALTERNATIVE APPROACHES TO ITS ANIMAL BREEDING RESEARCH IS NOT A VIOLATION OF THE ADMINISTRATIVE PROCEDURES ACT

Plaintiffs allege that defendants' breeding programs focus almost exclusively on producing larger, more productive, more fecund animals and ignore alternative research approaches which would achieve these objectives without the allegedly harmful effects caused by the current program. Failure to consider such alternatives is, in plaintiffs' opinion, arbitrary agency action in violation of the Administrative Procedures Act (APA).Defendants respond in the alternative: (1) their research is not as limited in direction as plaintiffs say, (2) judicial review of USDA research decisions should be highly deferential and under such a standard the programs must be upheld as rational exercises of agency discretion; and (3) plaintiffs lack standing to raise an APA claim.This Court need not tarry long over plaintiffs' APA claim because defendants also raise a jurisdictional defense which neatly disposes of plaintiffs' argument: the challenged research activities have been "committed to agency discretion by law". This phrase has been interpreted to mean that judicial review is precluded when a statute is so broadly drawn that "a court would have no meaningful standard against which to judge the agency's exercise of discretion". In such cases, agencies have absolute discretion. That is the case here. The relevant statute authorizes the USDA to research agriculture's "basic problems" in their "broadest aspect". The statute does not establish priorities, goals, means or methods. No distinction is made between animal and crop research, basic and applied technology, or producer and consumer needs.This wide ranging statute does not supply a reviewing court with "meaningful standards" against which to measure agency action for possible abuse of discretion. Therefore, USDA research activities are not subject to APA review and plaintiffs' APA claim must fall.CONCLUSIONThe issues raised by plaintiffs' complaint go to the heart of the interrelationships among man, nature, and science. However, the relief plaintiffs seek is not available under either NEPA or the APA. Defendants' animal breeding research is not a "proposal for legislation or other major Federal action significantly affecting the environment". Thus, neither a programmatic EA or EIS is required. And, defendants' choices as to the priorities, means, and ends of its animal productivity research is a matter of absolute discretion and thus not subject to judicial review under the APA. Accordingly, defendants' Motion for Summary Judgment will be granted.This is not the last suit which will challenge some aspect of rDNA research. With this in mind it is prudent to emphasize the exceedingly limited nature of the Court's holding. The Court has determined on the basis of the record now before it that defendants' animal productivity research in general, and its rDNA research in particular, need not be the subjects of either a programmatic EA or an EIS. Plaintiffs have failed to prove either that defendants' independent studies are a cohesive program or that its genetic engineering research is sufficiently mature so that an impact statement would be more than an unfounded hypothesis.

However, science is not a static discipline. The structure of DNA was discovered only three decades ago. Twenty years ago genetic engineering was only performed by authors of science fiction. Eventually (and sooner rather than later) genetic engineering will reach the stage when an impact statement may well be required. Perhaps this will be when whole animal rDNA research is ready to leave the laboratory for field tests. Perhaps future rDNA studies may threaten the environment even when conducted under controlled conditions. Perhaps rDNA research will become so expensive that its pursuit can be legitimately said to foreclose alternative approaches to animal productivity research. When the technology is mature an analysis of the benefits and hazards of the proposed activity can be the product of a calculated and informed estimate of the probabilities and not merely haphazard speculation.

This Opinion should not be taken as deprecating plaintiffs' concerns. These merit serious attention but Congress is the place where they should be addressed in the first instance, not the courts.

An Order in accordance with the foregoing will issue of even date herewith.

ORDER

In accordance with the Opinion issued in the above captioned case of even date herewith and for the reasons set forth therein it is, by the Court, this day of April, 1986,ORDERED, that defendants' Motion for Summary Judgment shall be, and the same is hereby granted, and the case will stand dismissed from the dockets of this Court.

While the previous case was involving biotechnology activities in a laboratory, the next test involved a field test, and the court would have to consider how NEPA applied to biotechnological field tests.

4.2.2.4 FET v. Bowen

Foundation on Economic Trends v. Bowen
722 F. Supp. 787 (D.D.C., 1989)

Opinion by George H. Revercomb, District Judge:

The plaintiffs have sued the chiefs of various federal government entities to enjoin the National Institute of Health (NIH) from supporting any research involving various aspects of genetic, AIDS, and cancer research until NIH completes an Environmental Impact Statement (EIS) on the research, pursuant to the National Environmental Policy Act (NEPA). Oral argument was heard on February 28, 1989. In this Opinion and Order, the Court grants the defendants' motion for summary judgment. *I. The Current Legal Standards* NEPA requires the federal government to create a "detailed" statement on all "major Federal actions significantly affecting the quality of the human environment." Such a statement must discuss:

(I) the environmental impact of the proposed action, (ii) any adverse environmental effects which cannot be avoided should the proposal be implemented, (iii) alternatives to the proposed action, (iv) the relationship between local short-term uses of man's environment and the maintenance and enhacement of long-term productivity, and (v) any irreversible and irretrievable commitments of resources which would be involved in the propose action should it be implemented.

Such statements are to be made available to the public, and are designed to inform the governmental policy-makers and the public about the environmental effects of action undertaken with governmental support.

Once an agency has completed an EIS on a major federal action, the agency must supplement the EIS if (1) the agency makes substantial changes to the action that changes the environmental impact, or (2) there are "significant new circumstances or information relevant to environmental concerns and bearing on the proposed action or its impacts."

There is no hard-and-fast rule regarding when there are significant enough new circumstances to require a new EIS. It is clear to the Court, however, that an agency should not have to generate an EIS every time a researcher develops a new project -- such a requirement would be oppressively burdensome and would effectively prevent a tremendous amount of research from going forward. Rather, a supplementary EIS should be required when new developments have so increased the effects and risks to the environment that the old EIS does not properly address them. It is safe

135

to say, then, that a supplementary EIS should not be required when there are new developments in a field of research that scientists believe either have less effect than preceding research or that reveal that the field of research is likely to have less effect on the environment than originally estimated.

The NIH in 1976 published detailed Guidelines on NIH-sponsored rDNA research. The Guidelines set standards for safety and environmental protection in rDNA research, including physical containment of particular experiments, and discouraged certain experiments. They also established groups to review research and determine whether the Guidelines were being followed properly.

In 1977, NIH published the final draft of an EIS on the 1976 Guidelines after accepting public comments. 41 Fed. Reg. 38425 (1977). The statement evaluated the likely consequences of research under the Guidelines and concluded that although following the Guidelines would guard against many possible environmental harms, they would not and could not guarantee that rDNA research would be free from all risk. The EIS also stated that the Guidelines should remain flexible in order to take account of new biological developments and new evaluations of the environmental impact of certain research.

This Court upheld the adequacy of the 1977 EIS in a lawsuit to enjoin NIH-sponsored rDNA research. *Mack v. Califano*, 447 F. Supp. 668 (D.D.C. 1978). Since *Mack*, NIH has published a number of smaller Environmental Assessments ("EA's") to supplement the 1977 EIS. An EA is a "concise public document" that provides "sufficient evidence and analysis for determining whether to prepare an environmental impact statement of a finding of no significant impact" and aids the agency's compliance with NEPA when a full EIS is not necessary. . . . Like an EIS, an EA must include a discussion of the environmental impact of the topic, as well as alternatives to the action involved. . . .

In the years after the formulation of 1976 Guidelines, the experts at NIH determined that the initial level of concern over the dangers of rDNA research was too high, and that some relaxation of the Guidelines was warranted. This conclusion was based on the fact that there had been little or no environmental harm caused by rDNA research and that additional research showed that rDNA did not pose the level of risk that was once feared. The Guidelines thus have been relaxed somewhat nearly each year since 1976, most recently in 1987. The defendants' position is that there is no need for a new EIS on the revised Guidelines because both the new scientific evidence and the excellent environmental record of rDNA research so far prove that the environmental impact of rDNA research is likely to be less than expected in 1977.

II. The Standard of Review

The Court reviews the decision of an agency that an EIS is not necessary under the deferential "arbitrary or capricious" test, 5 U.S.C. §§ 706, which essentially means that the Court cannot "second-guess" the agency unless it has acted unreasonably. The Court must give a hard and thorough look at the evidence presented to it on the record. Nonetheless, the Court thus must uphold scientific evaluations and conclusions by an agency if the decision was a reasonable one, even if there are good -- or even, in the Court's opinion, slightly more convincing -- arguments made on the other side.

With regard to the question of whether an agency has been reasonable in deciding not to create a supplementary EIS for new information or a new development in major federally sponsored action, the Court should consider the likely environmental impact of the new development and the degree of care that the agency appeared to take in evaluating the new development and making its decision not to create a supplement to the EIS. Moreover, the Court should determine whether it was reasonable to conclude that the new developments have not increased the likelihood or changed the form of environment impact significantly. If the Court finds that it was unreasonable to conclude that the new developments do not significantly change the likelihood of environmental impact, it must overturn the agency decision. When there is a debate among scientists as to the environmental impact of new developments, the Court must defer to the agency's decision if its appears to supported by "substantial evidence."

III. The Plaintiff's Challenges

It is settled that NIH approval of experiments involving rDNA constitute "major federal action" under NEPA and thus is subject to the EIS requirement when appropriate. *FOET v. Heckler*, 244 U.S. App. D.C. 122, 756 F.2d 143 (D.C. Cir. 1985). The plaintiffs in this case allege that certain research and experimentation approved by NIH in the years after the 1977 EIS have triggered the requirement of an EIS supplement, but that NIH has failed to create such a supplement.

An agency may not rest on an EIS if there is significant new information to be gathered that would change the environment evaluation. Moreover, NIH is obligated to create a supplement to an EIS when new scientific developments in a biomedical field make an earlier EIS insufficient to evaluate adequately the environmental impact of the new developments. *See, e.g., FOET v. Heckler*, 244 U.S. App. D.C. 122, 756 F.2d 143 (D.C. Cir. 1985).

The plaintiffs disagree that the 1977 EIS is legally sufficient under NEPA to cover all current rDNA research conducted under the auspices of NIH since 1977. Specifically, plaintiffs argue that there are three new areas of research and experimentation that were not evaluated by the 1977 EIS: (1)

the ability to clone oncogenes into bacteria using shuttle vectors; (2) the cloning of the HIV (human immunodeficiency virus); and (3) the engineering of genetic codes of AIDS (acquired immune deficiency syndrome) into animal species. On each of these three broad points, the Court concludes that it is reasonable to maintain that the new developments are not so significant in their likely impact on the environment that a new EIS is necessary. *A. Oncogenic Cloning*

The first area of debate is over the purported new development of the ability to clone oncogenic -- i.e., tumor-causing -- viruses into bacteria by using shuttle vectors. Vectors are DNA molecules used to introduce foreign DNA into a cell. The plaintiffs fear that this ability could lead to a situation in which oncogenic viruses entered into *E. coli* could reproduce, causing danger to other organisms.

The defendants argue persuasively, however, that the ability to clone oncogenic viruses using shuttle vectors does not create any greater risk or harm than cloning using other methods. Indeed, in 1978 NIH published an Environmental Assessment (EA) on changes in oncogenic research. Noting that the new Guidelines removed the ban on research involving oncogenic viruses classified as moderated risk, the EA stated that the change would not have a significant environmental impact and that cloning oncogenic viruses posed a "conceivable" but "unlikely" biohazard. The principles of basic molecular biology provide that it is virtually impossible for a viral segment to generate a oncogenic virus. . . . This conclusion, and the decision to remove the ban on research involving oncogenic viruses, resulted from an in-depth analysis that included a series of workshops attended by experts from all over the world, n1 various reviews of the workshop conclusions, examination of the guidelines of other countries, hours of public hearings, and various public and scientific comment.

The new technique of using shuttle vectors is still the use of gene or DNA segments and therefore does not increase the risk beyond that was evaluated carefully by the EA in 1978. The Court concludes that there was substantial evidence and that it was reasonable to conclude that the new oncogenic cloning research does not require a supplementary EIS.

B. Cloning the HIV Virus

The second area of new research and experimentation identified by plaintiffs is the ability to genetically engineer the HIV virus into HeLa cells and other types of cells not normally susceptible to HIV. Because these HeLa cells would for the first time be a host to the HIV virus, the plaintiffs argue, this new development would increase the risk of environmental harm.

The defendants note, however, that the new capabilities do *not* extend the host range of the HIV virus. Making HeLa cell lines -- which are human cell lines -- susceptible to the HIV virus does not put any new species at greater risk, the defendants point out, because humans are already susceptible to HIV and AIDS. Because the practical effect of the development does not appear to pose any serious additional threat, the Court concludes that it reasonable not to require a supplement to the EIS for this research.

C. Transgenic Experimentation

Finally, the third area of research and experimentation about which the plaintiffs allege that the government has failed to provide adequate environmental impact statement concerns the engineering of the genetic code for viruses causing human disease into other animals. This transgenic research, the plaintiffs claim, has the potential for serious harm should these animals enter man's environment. Particularly, the plaintiffs point to current experimentation at NIH in which the AIDS DNA has been placed in mice.

NIH approved the mice/AIDS experimentation pursuant to the NIH Guidelines. NIH concluded that if the experimentation was controlled using the highest safety level under the Guidelines, there would be no chance that any of the mice could escape the contained environment.

The plaintiffs argue that NIH is legally required to prepare a supplementary EIS to set forth and assess the possible environmental impact of the experiment and other similar experiments. NIH is in the process, however, of working on amendments to its Guidelines regarding the use of transgenic animals. As part of the Guideline amendments, NIH is preparing an environmental assessment (EA). The Court concludes that this EA should satisfy the legal requirements of NEPA.

The Court also concludes that NIH is acting reasonably in permitting the mice/AIDS experimentation to go forward while the EA is being prepared. First, the Court notes that although the AIDS virus was discovered after the original NIH EIS was published in 1977, the mere existence of a new disease that is being researched does not mean that the analyses, safeguards, and assessments of previous environmental evaluations are worthless.

Second, even if the mice/AIDS research does raise new environmental concerns and problems that have not been addressed satisfactorily to the requirements of NEPA, the Court concludes that the proper legal solution is to await the creation of the EA by NIH, instead of enjoining the mice/AIDS research.

NIH has presented persuasive evidence that mice/AIDS experimentation poses only the smallest possible risk to the environment. Under the highest-level containment pursuant to the NIH Guidelines, the mice are stored in "glove box" -- a completely sealed unit with built-in gloves for handling the mice without having to open the box. The mice area is surrounded by a Clorox-filled dunk tank designed to stop the mice. Even if a mouse somehow did escape the unit, it would then have to work its way out of the high-level contained laboratory, which contains mouse traps, and a screen door to enable scientists to examine the area before entering. The defendant states that each of the safety features is inspected once every 10 days.

NIH also has guarded against the harm to humans should the mice somehow escape the laboratory building altogether. The mice have been blinded, to prevent their escape and to put them at a selective disadvantage in the wild. Mice injected with the viral DNA while still in embryo have all died before reaching sexual maturity. Singer Declaration at para. 5. Finally, the AIDS virus has not been found in the saliva or the urine of the mice -- making further remote the possibility that a mouse biting a human or an escaping mouse could spread the AIDS virus.

In sum, the Court does not subscribe completely to the argument that because the mice are not released to the general environment there is no environmental impact. *See FOET v. Block*, Civ. No. 84-3045 (D.D.C. slip op. April 29, 1986) (concluding that there was no environmental impact to an experiment in which animals were kept in the laboratory), *aff'd sub nom. FOET v. Lyng*, 260 U.S. App. D.C. 159, 817 F.2d 882 (D.C. Cir. 1987). The Court realizes that the environmental impact of an experiment or research should be judged while considering the *possibility* that the experiment could affect the environment, as well as the expected impact. In the NIH's mice/AIDS experimentation, the Court concludes that the EA currently being created appears to satisfy the requirements of NEPA, and that the proven very low possibility of any environmental impact before the EA is complete justifies not enjoining NIH from continuing to sponsor the research pending the publication of the EA.

The defendants' motion for summary judgment is granted.

NOTES

Is the application of the National Environmental Policy Act (NEPA) an effective way to challenge biotechnology? So far, the cases brought by Jeremy Rifkin and other similar groups have not been successful in their challenges using NEPA. *See*, Elie Gendloff, "Stauber v. Shalala: Are Environmental Challenges to Biotechnology Too Difficult?" 4 Wis. Envtl. L.J. 41 (Winter 1997). See also, Paul S. Naik, "Biotechnology Through the Eyes of an Opponent: The Resistance of Activist Jeremy Rifkin," 5 Va. J.L. & Tech. 5 (Spring 2000)(Naik observes that despite all of the litigation by Rifkin, he has had little effect on biotechnology policy.)

Genetically Modified Organisms have been sensationalized in terms of their potential for escaping and destroying the environment. For example, the Smithsonian Institutes in the Museum of American History, designed an exhibit to explain the history of biotechnology. Their designers made the unfortunate decision to greet the museum-goers with a large image of Frankenstein with various products of biotechnology. The scientific community was enraged with this perpetuation of misinformation, and several scientific societies wrote letters to that effect to the Smithsonian Secretary. Within about six months, the exhibit was dismantled, but by that time millions of visitors had passed by the image of Frankenstein.

———————————————

Chapter 5

GMO Labeling Controversy

This chapter follows the controversy around the consumer philosophical preferences against the consumption of genetically modified organisms and the tension with seed developers, food producers and farmers who have goals of maximum production and quality. The controversy centered around the use of labels and a demand that government rather than private sector labeling organizations require disclosure. Part of the problem was simply that the FDCA statute did not permit FDA to require labels for anything other than health purposes, and there was no scientific evidence that GMOs or additives that occurred naturally (rBST) had any negative health effects.

In response to this void, and in the face of increasing consumer demand, states began to develop their own programs to require disclosure of additives. These requirements raise dormant Commerce Clause issues, as to whether they place a burden on interstate commerce. The first case in 1996, had to answer these questions as well as whether requiring companies to label products with disclosures that were simply consumer preferences amounted to a violation of the producers' Constitutional right-not-to-speak.

5.1.1 Constitutional First Amendment Limitations in State Labeling Regulations

State regulation in Vermont requiring the use of labeling to provide information to consumers with regard to milk was used to satisfy public concerns about their fears of biotechnology. The labeling law required milk that contained additional rBST, a hormone that exists naturally but as an additive it increased milk production to be labelled with that disclosure. But because there was no scientific evidence that rBST caused any health impact, producers and sellers challenged its Constitutionality, specifically with regard to the First Amendment "right not to speak" protections.

143

5.1.1.1   IDFA v. Amestoy

International Dairy Foods Association v. Amestoy, Attorney General of the State of Vermont
92 F.3d 67 (2d Cir. 1996)

Judges Altimari, McLaughlin and Leval
Altimari, *Circuit Judge:*

Plaintiffs-appellants International Dairy Foods Association, Milk Industry Foundation (MIF), International Ice Cream Association, National Cheese Institute, Grocery Manufacturers of America, Inc. and National Food Processors Association (collectively "appellants" or "dairy manufacturers") appeal from a decision of the district court (Murtha, C.J.), denying their motion for a preliminary injunction. The dairy manufacturers challenged the constitutionality of Vt. Stat. Ann. tit. 6, §§ 2754©) which requires dairy manufacturers to identify products which were, or might have been, derived from dairy cows treated with a synthetic growth hormone used to increase milk production. The dairy manufacturers alleged that the statute violated the United States Constitution's First Amendment and Commerce Clause.

Because we find that the district court abused its discretion in failing to grant preliminary injunctive relief to the dairy manufacturers on First Amendment grounds, we reverse and remand.

Background
In 1993, the federal Food and Drug Administration ("FDA") approved the use of recombinant Bovine Somatotropin ("rBST") (also known as recombinant Bovine Growth Hormone ("rGBH")), a synthetic growth hormone that increases milk production by cows. It is undisputed that the dairy products derived from herds treated with rBST are indistinguishable from products derived from untreated herds; consequently, the FDA declined to require the labeling of products derived from cows receiving the supplemental hormone.

In April 1994, defendant-appellee the State of Vermont ("Vermont") enacted a statute requiring that "if rBST has been used in the production of milk or a milk product for retail sale in this state, the retail milk or milk product shall be labeled as such." The State of Vermont's Commissioner of Agriculture ("Commissioner") subsequently promulgated regulations giving those dairy manufacturers who use rBST four labeling options, among them the posting of a sign to the following effect in any store selling dairy products: rBST INFORMATION

THE PRODUCTS IN THIS CASE THAT CONTAIN OR MAY CONTAIN MILK FROM rBST-TREATED COWS EITHER (1) STATE ON THE PACKAGE

THAT rBST HAS BEEN OR MAY HAVE BEEN USED, OR (2) ARE IDENTIFIED BY A BLUE SHELF LABEL LIKE THIS

[BLUE RECTANGLE]
OR (3) A BLUE STICKER ON THE PACKAGE LIKE THIS. [BLUE DOT]
The United States Food and Drug Administration has determined that there is no significant difference between milk from treated and untreated cows. It is the law of Vermont that products made from the milk of rBST-treated cows be labeled to help consumers make informed shopping decisions. (6 V.S.A. Section 2754)

Failure to comply with the statute and companion regulations subjects manufacturers to civil, as well as criminal penalties.

Appellants filed suit in April 1994, asserting that the statute was unconstitutional. In June 1995, the dairy manufacturers moved for preliminary injunctive relief, seeking to enjoin enforcement of the statute. The dairy manufacturers alleged that the Vermont statute (1) infringed their protected rights under the First Amendment to the Constitution and (2) violated the Constitution's Commerce Clause, U.S. Const., Art. 1, §§ 8. Following an extensive hearing, the United States District Court for the District of Vermont (Murtha, *C.J.*), denied appellants' motion. The dairy manufacturers now appeal.

Because we find that the dairy manufacturers are entitled to an injunction on First Amendment grounds, we do not reach their claims made pursuant to the Commerce Clause.

Discussion
Generally, preliminary injunctive relief is appropriate when the movant shows "(a) irreparable harm and (b) either (1) likelihood of success on the merits or (2) sufficiently serious questions going to the merits to make them a fair ground for litigation and a balance of hardships tipping decidedly toward the party requesting the preliminary relief.". . .("Before a preliminary injunction will be granted in this Circuit, it must pass one of two tests. Both require a showing of irreparable harm."), However, because the injunction at issue stays "government action taken in the public interest pursuant to a statutory . . . scheme," this Court has determined that the movant must satisfy the more rigorous "likelihood of success prong."

We review the district court's denial of a preliminary injunction for an abuse of discretion, and will reverse the district court only if it relied on clearly erroneous findings of fact, misapprehended the law, or erred in formulating the injunction.*1. Irreparable Harm*

Focusing principally on the economic impact of the labeling regulation, the district court found that appellants had not demonstrated irreparable harm to any right protected by the First Amendment. We disagree.

Irreparable harm is "injury for which a monetary award cannot be adequate compensation." . . . It is established that "the loss of First Amendment freedoms, for even minimal periods of time, unquestionably constitutes irreparable injury." . . . Because the statute at issue requires appellants to make an involuntary statement whenever they offer their products for sale, we find that the statute causes the dairy manufacturers irreparable harm.

[T]he district court rejected this claim, stating that:
"the assertion of First Amendment rights does not automatically require a finding of irreparable injury, thus entitling a plaintiff to a preliminary injunction if he shows a likelihood of success on the merits."

Ordinarily, it is the purposeful suppression of speech which constitutes irreparable harm. Compliance with the Vermont Labeling Law does not prohibit the plaintiffs from disseminating a message. Instead, it requires the plaintiffs to truthfully disclose the method used in producing their product. Under these circumstances, the Court does not find that the plaintiffs' assertion of a First Amendment violation leads ineluctably to the conclusion that they will suffer irreparable harm.

We conclude, however, that the manufacturers have carried their burden of establishing irreparable harm. The wrong done by the labeling law to the dairy manufacturers' constitutional right *not* to speak is a serious one that was not given proper weight by the district court. "We begin with the proposition that the right of freedom of thought protected by the First Amendment against state action includes both the right to speak freely and the right to refrain from speaking at all."; "involuntary affirmation could be commanded only on even more immediate and urgent grounds than silence"; recognizing, along with freedom to express one's views publicly, "'concomitant freedom *not* to speak publicly'". . .

The right not to speak inheres in political and commercial speech alike. . . If, however, as Vermont maintains, its labeling law compels appellants to engage in purely commercial speech, the statute must meet a less rigorous test. *See Central Hudson Gas & Elec. Corp. v. Public Serv. Comm'r*, . . . ("The Constitution . . . accords a lesser protection to commercial speech than to other constitutionally guaranteed expression."). The dairy manufacturers insist that the speech is not purely commercial because it compels them "to convey a message regarding the significance of rBST use that is 'expressly contrary to' their views." . . . Agreeing with Vermont, the district court found that the speech was commercial in nature.

146

We need not resolve this controversy at this point; even assuming that the compelled disclosure is purely commercial speech, appellants have amply demonstrated that the First Amendment is sufficiently implicated to cause irreparable harm. *See* (First Amendment implicated by mandatory assessment on almond handlers to fund almond marketing program); *United States v. Frame...* (3d Cir. 1989) (federal Beef Promotion & Research Act implicated beef producer's right to refrain from speaking because it required that producer help fund commercial message to which producer did not necessarily subscribe), ... *Cf. National Comm'n on Egg Nutrition,...* (modifying remedial order provision that required egg producers "to argue the other side of the controversy, thus interfering unnecessarily with the effective presentation of the pro-egg position."). The dairy manufacturers have clearly done more than simply "assert" their First Amendment rights: The statute in question indisputably requires them to speak when they would rather not.... Because compelled speech "contravenes core First Amendment values," appellants have "satisfied the initial requirement for securing injunctive relief."

In *Central Hudson*, the Supreme Court articulated a four-part analysis for determining whether a government restriction on commercial speech is permissible....We need not address the controversy concerning the nature of the speech in question -- commercial or political -- because we find that Vermont fails to meet the less stringent constitutional requirements applicable to compelled commercial speech.

Under *Central Hudson*, we must determine: (1) whether the expression concerns lawful activity and is not misleading; (2) whether the government's interest is substantial; (3) whether the labeling law directly serves the asserted interest; and (4) whether the labeling law is no more extensive than necessary.... Furthermore, the State of Vermont bears the burden of justifying its labeling law.... As the Supreme Court has made clear, "this burden is not satisfied by mere speculation or conjecture; rather, a governmental body seeking to sustain a restriction on commercial speech must demonstrate that the harms it recites are real and that its restriction will in fact alleviate them to a material degree."...

In our view, Vermont has failed to establish the second prong of the *Central Hudson* test, namely that its interest is substantial. In making this determination, we rely only upon those interests set forth by Vermont before the district court.... As the district court made clear, Vermont "does not claim that health or safety concerns prompted the passage of the Vermont Labeling Law," but instead defends the statute on the basis of "strong consumer interest and the public's 'right to know'...." 898 F. Supp. at 249. These interests are insufficient to justify compromising protected constitutional rights.[1]

Vermont's failure to defend its constitutional intrusion on the ground that it negatively impacts public health is easily understood. After exhaustive studies, the FDA has "concluded that rBST has no appreciable effect on the composition of milk produced by treated cows, and that there are no human safety or health concerns associated with food products derived from cows treated with rBST." . . . Because bovine somatotropin ("BST") appears naturally in cows, and because there are no BST receptors in a cow's mammary glands, only trace amounts of BST can be detected in milk, whether or not the cows received the supplement. Moreover, it is undisputed that neither consumers nor scientists can distinguish rBST-derived milk from milk produced by an untreated cow. Indeed, the already extensive record in this case contains no scientific evidence from which an objective observer could conclude that rBST has any impact at all on dairy products. It is thus plain that Vermont could not justify the statute on the basis of "real" harms. . . .

We do not doubt that Vermont's asserted interest, the demand of its citizenry for such information, is genuine; reluctantly, however, we conclude that it is inadequate. We are aware of no case in which consumer interest alone was sufficient to justify requiring a product's manufacturers to publish the functional equivalent of a warning about a production method that has no discernable impact on a final product. . . .

Although the Court is sympathetic to the Vermont consumers who wish to know which products may derive from rBST-treated herds, their desire is insufficient to permit the State of Vermont to compel the dairy manufacturers to speak against their will. Were consumer interest alone sufficient, there is no end to the information that states could require manufacturers to disclose about their production methods. For instance, with respect to cattle, consumers might reasonably evince an interest in knowing which grains herds were fed, with which medicines they were treated, or the age at which they were slaughtered. Absent, however, some indication that this information bears on a reasonable concern for human health or safety or some other sufficiently substantial governmental concern, the manufacturers

---

[1] Although the dissent suggests several interests that if adopted by the state of Vermont may have been substantial, the district court opinion makes clear that Vermont adopted no such rationales for its statute. Rather, Vermont's sole expressed interest was, indeed, "consumer curiosity." The district court plainly stated that, "Vermont takes no position on whether rBST is beneficial or detrimental. However," the district court explained, "Vermont has determined that its consumers want to know whether rBST has been used in the production of their milk and milk products." 898 F. Supp. at 252 (emphasis added). It is clear from the opinion below that the state itself has not adopted the concerns of the consumers; it has only adopted that the consumers are concerned. Unfortunately, mere consumer concern is not, in itself, a substantial interest.

cannot be compelled to disclose it. Instead, those consumers interested in such information should exercise the power of their purses by buying products from manufacturers who voluntarily reveal it.

Accordingly, we hold that consumer curiosity alone is not a strong enough state interest to sustain the compulsion of even an accurate, factual statement,... (compelled disclosure of "fact" is no more acceptable than compelled disclosure of opinion), in a commercial context. *See, e.g., United States v. Sullivan* ... (1948) (upholding federal law requiring warning labels on "*harmful* foods, drugs and cosmetics") *see also Zauderer.*..(disclosure requirements are permissible "as long as [they] are reasonably related to the State's interest in preventing deception of consumers."). . . Because Vermont has demonstrated no cognizable harms, its statute is likely to be held unconstitutional.

Conclusion
Because appellants have demonstrated both irreparable harm and a likelihood of success on the merits, the judgment of the district court is reversed, and the case is remanded for entry of an appropriate injunction.

DISSENT by Leval, Circuit Judge:
I respectfully dissent. Vermont's regulation requiring disclosure of use of rBST in milk production was based on substantial state interests, including worries about rBST's impact on human and cow health, fears for the survival of small dairy farms, and concerns about the manipulation of nature through biotechnology. The objective of the plaintiff milk producers is to conceal their use of rBST from consumers. The policy of the First Amendment, in its application to commercial speech, is to favor the flow of accurate, relevant information. The majority's invocation of the First Amendment to invalidate a state law requiring disclosure of information consumers reasonably desire stands the Amendment on its ear. In my view, the district court correctly found that plaintiffs were unlikely to succeed in proving Vermont's law unconstitutional.

Background
Because many of the most important facts of this case are omitted from the majority's opinion, I briefly review the facts.

Recent advances in genetic technologies led to the development of a synthetically isolated metabolic protein hormone known as recombinant bovine somatotropin (rBST), which, when injected into cows, increases their milk production. Monsanto Company, an amicus in this action on the side of the plaintiff milk producers, has developed the only commercially approved form of rBST and markets it under the brand name "Posilac." This is, of course, at the frontiers of bio-science. A 1994 federal government study of rBST describes it as "one of the first major commercial biotechnology products to

149

be used in the U.S. food and agricultural sector and the first to attract significant attention." Executive Branch of the Federal Government, Use of Bovine Somatotropin (BST) in the United States: Its Potential Effects (January 1994) [hereafter "Federal Study"]...

The United States Food and Drug Administration ("FDA") and others have studied rBST extensively. Based on its study, the FDA authorized commercial use of rBST on November 5, 1993, concluding that "milk and meat from [rBST-treated] cows is safe" for human consumption.

The impending use of rBST caused substantial controversy throughout the country. The Federal Study reports, based on numerous surveys, that consumers favor the labeling of milk produced by use of rBST. In Vermont, a state highly attuned to issues affecting the dairy industry, use of rBST was the subject of frequent press commentary and debate, and provoked considerable opposition. In response to public pressure, the state of Vermont enacted a law requiring that "if rBST has been used in the production of milk or a milk product for retail sale in this state, the retail milk or milk product shall be labeled as such." 6 V.S.A. §§ 2754©). The statute authorized Vermont's Commissioner of Agriculture to adopt implementing rules. Id. at §§ 2754(d). The Department of Agriculture, Food and Markets (hereafter "the Agriculture Department") proceeded to adopt the regulations described in the majority opinion, which essentially require manufacturers to identify dairy products produced with rBST with a blue dot, and retailers to display a sign telling consumers that the blue-dotted products "contain milk from rBST-treated cows" and that the FDA "has determined that there is no significant difference between milk from treated and untreated cows." The sign concludes that the law of Vermont requires that the information be given "to help consumers make informed shopping decisions."

The interests which Vermont sought to advance by its statute and regulations were explained in the Agriculture Department's Economic Impact Statement accompanying its regulations. The Statement reported that consumer interest in disclosure of use of rBST was based on "concerns about FDA determinations about the product as regards health and safety or about recombinant gene technology"; concerns "about the effect of the product on bovine health"; and "concerns about the effect of the product on the existing surplus of milk and in the dairy farm industry's economic status and well-being." This finding was based on "consumer comments to Vermont legislative committees" and to the Department, as well as published reports and letters to the editors published in the press.

The state offered survey evidence which demonstrated similar public concern. Comments by Vermont citizens who had heard or read about rBST were overwhelmingly negative. The most prevalent responses to rBST use included: "Not natural," "More research needs to be done/Long-term effects

150

not clear," "Against additives added to my milk," "Worried about adverse health effects," "Unhealthy for the cow," "Don't need more chemicals," "It's a hormone/Against hormones added to my milk," "Hurts the small dairy farmer," "Producing enough milk already."

On the basis of this evidence the district court found that a majority of Vermonters "do not want to purchase milk products derived from rBST-treated cows,". . . and that the reasons included:

(1) They consider the use of a genetically-engineered hormone in the production unnatural; (2) they believe that use of the hormone will result in increased milk production and lower milk prices, thereby hurting small dairy farmers; (3) they believe that the use of rBST is harmful to cows and potentially harmful to humans; and, (4) they feel that there is a lack of knowledge regarding the long-term effects of rBST.

The court thus understandably concluded that "Vermont has a substantial interest in informing consumers of the use of rBST in the production of milk and dairy products sold in the state."

Discussion A. The Majority Opinion In the face of this evidence and these explicit findings by the district court, the majority oddly concludes that Vermont's sole interest in requiring disclosure of rBST use is to gratify "consumer curiosity," and that this alone "is not a strong enough state interest to sustain the compulsion of even an accurate factual statement." Maj. Op. at 12. The majority seeks to justify its conclusion in three ways. First, it simply disregards the evidence of Vermont's true interests and the district court's findings recognizing those interests. Nowhere does the majority opinion discuss or even mention the evidence or findings regarding the people of Vermont's concerns about human health, cow health, biotechnology, and the survival of small dairy farms. Second, the majority distorts the meaning of the district court opinion. It relies substantially on Judge Murtha's statement that Vermont "does not claim that health or safety concerns prompted the passage of the Vermont Labeling Law," but "bases its justification . . . on strong consumer interest and the public's 'right to know'." . . . . The majority takes this passage out of context. The district court's opinion went on, as quoted above, to explain the concerns that underlie the interest of Vermont's citizenry. Unquestionably the district court found, and the evidence showed, that the interests of the citizenry that led to the passage of the law include health and safety concerns, among others. In the light of the district judge's further explicit findings, it is clear that his statement could not mean what the majority concludes.[2] More likely, what Judge Murtha meant was that Vermont

_____

[2] Indeed had the judge really intended such a finding, it would be unsupportable in view of the evidence that the concerns of the citizenry were communicated to the legislature. When the citizens of a state express concerns to the legislature and the state's lawmaking bodies then

151

does not claim to know whether rBST is harmful. And when he asserted that Vermont's rule was passed to vindicate "strong consumer interest and the public's right to know," this could not mean that the public's interest was based on nothing but "curiosity," because the judge expressly found that the consumer interest was based on health, economic, and ethical concerns.

Third, the majority suggests that, because the FDA has not found health risks in this new procedure, health worries could not be considered "real" or "cognizable.". . .

I find this proposition alarming and dangerous; at the very least, it is extraordinarily unrealistic. Genetic and biotechnological manipulation of basic food products is new and controversial. Although I have no reason to doubt that the FDA's studies of rBST have been thorough, they could not cover long-term effects of rBST on humans. . . .Furthermore, there are many possible reasons why a government agency might fail to find real health risks, including inadequate time and budget for testing, insufficient advancement of scientific techniques, insufficiently large sampling populations, pressures from industry, and simple human error. To suggest that a government agency's failure to find a health risk in a short-term study of a new genetic technology should bar a state from requiring simple disclosure of the use of that technology where its citizens are concerned about such health risks would be unreasonable and dangerous. Although the FDA's conclusions may be reassuring, they do not guarantee the safety of rBST.

Forty years ago, when I (and nearly everyone) smoked, no one told us that we might be endangering our health. Tobacco is but one of many consumer products once considered safe, which were subsequently found to cause health hazards. The limitations of scientific information about new consumer products were well illustrated in a 1990 study produced at the request of Congress by the General Accounting Office. Looking at various prescription drugs available on the market, the study examined the risks associated with the drugs that became known only after they were approved by the FDA, and concluded:

Even after approval, many additional risks may surface when the general population is exposed to a drug. These risks, which range from relatively minor (such as nausea and headache) to serious (such as

------

pass disclosure requirements in response to those expressed concerns, it seems clear (without need for a statutory declaration of purpose) that the state is acting to vindicate the concerns expressed by its citizens, and not merely to gratify their "curiosity." Vermont need not, furthermore, take the position that rBST is harmful to require its disclosure because of potential health risks. The mere fact that it does not know whether rBST poses hazards is sufficient reason to justify disclosure by reason of the unknown potential for harm.

hospitalization and death) arise from the fact that preapproval drug testing is inherently limited. . . . . In studying the frequency and seriousness of risks identified after approval, GAO found that of the 198 drugs approved by FDA between 1976 and 1985 for which data were available, 102 (or 51.5 percent) had serious postapproval risks, as evidenced by labeling changes or withdrawal from the market. All but six of these drugs . . . are deemed by FDA to have benefits that outweigh their risks. The serious postapproval risks are adverse reactions that could lead to hospitalization . . . severe or permanent disability, or death.

GAO Report, "FDA Drug Review: Postapproval Risks, 1976-85," April 1990, at 2-3. As startling as its results may seem, this study merely confirms a common sense proposition: namely, that a government agency's conclusion regarding a product's safety, reached after limited study, is not a guarantee and does not invalidate public concern for unknown side effects.

In short, the majority has no valid basis for its conclusion that Vermont's regulation advances no interest other than the gratification of consumer curiosity, and involves neither health concerns nor other substantial interests. B. Substantial State Interests Freedom of speech is not an absolute right, particularly in the commercial context. In Central Hudson Gas v. Public Service Comm'n of New York. . . the Supreme Court announced standards for governmental regulation of commercial speech. At the outset, commercial speech enjoys no First Amendment protection at all unless it is not misleading (and relates to lawful activity). If the speech passes that test, it is nonetheless subject to regulation if the government has a substantial interest in regulating the speech, the regulation directly advances that interest, and it is no more intrusive than necessary to accomplish its goal.. . . The Supreme Court later clarified that government's power to regulate commercial speech includes the power to compel such speech. Zauderer v. Office of Disciplinary Counsel (upholding state law requiring attorneys who advertised contingent fee services to disclose specific details about how contingent fee would be calculated and to state that certain costs might be borne by the client even in the event of loss).

Except for its conclusion that Vermont had no substantial interest to support its labeling law, the majority finds no fault with the district court's application of these governing standards. Nor do I. Accordingly, the sole issue is whether Vermont had a substantial interest in compelling the disclosure of use of rBST in milk production.

In my view, Vermont's multifaceted interest, outlined above, is altogether substantial. Consumer worries about possible adverse health effects from consumption of rBST, especially over a long term, is unquestionably a substantial interest. As to health risks to cows, the concern is supported by the warning label on Posilac, which states that cows injected with the product are at an increased risk for: various reproductive disorders, "clinical mastitis [udder infections] (visibly abnormal milk)," "digestive disorders such as indigestion, bloat, and diarrhea," "enlarged hocks and lesions," and "swellings" that may be permanent. As to the economic impact of increased milk production, caused by injection of rBST, upon small dairy farmers, the evidence included a U.S. Department of Agriculture economist's written claim that, "if rBST is heavily adopted and milk prices are reduced, at least some of the smaller farmers that do not use rBST might be forced out of the dairy business, because they would not be producing economically sufficient volumes of milk." Public philosophical objection to biotechnological mutation is familiar and widespread.

Any one of these concerns may well suffice to make Vermont's interest substantial; all four, taken together, undoubtedly constitute a substantial governmental justification for Vermont's labeling law.

Indeed, the majority does not contend otherwise. Nowhere does the majority assert that these interests are not substantial. As noted above, the majority justifies its conclusion of absence of a substantial interest by its assertion that Vermont advanced no interest other than consumer curiosity, a conclusion that is contradicted by both the record and the district court's findings.

The Supreme Court has upheld governmental impositions on commercial speech in numerous instances where the governmental interest was no more substantial than those advanced here by Vermont. See Florida Bar v. Went For It, Inc.. . .(upholding 30-day waiting period for lawyers' solicitation of business from accident victims because of state's interests in promoting privacy . . .). . .

C. Plaintiffs' Contentions
Plaintiffs rely on invalid arguments and authorities that are easily distinguishable. In Ibanez v. Florida Dep't of Business & Professional Regulation, 512 U.S. 136, 129 L. Ed. 2d 118, 114 S. Ct. 2084 (1994), the Supreme Court struck down a disciplinary sanction based on a law requiring one who advertised as a "Certified Financial Planner" to disclose in the advertising that her certification came from an unofficial private organization, rather than from the state. The Court found the state's purported interest -- the likelihood of consumer confusion -- to be "purely hypothetical.". . . Plaintiffs contend that Vermont's health concerns are similarly "hypothetical" because there is no demonstrated health risk in rBST. This misreads the Supreme Court's meaning. The point in Ibanez was that there was no demonstration that Florida's citizenry was confused or cared whether a financial planner's certification was from a private organization or the state.

Here, it was clearly shown that Vermont's citizens want rBST disclosure.[4]...

The milk producers argue that because the sign which Vermont's law requires retailers to post goes beyond disclosure of rBST use and makes statements about it, they, like the fund raisers in Riley, are entitled to the full protection of the First Amendment, rather than the more limited protection afforded to commercial speech. They contend that the disclosure required of them is "inextricably intertwined" with fully protected speech. ..... Because the blue dot they affix to their milk containers is linked to the sign retailers post in the stores, they also contend they are forced to subscribe to a message on that sign with which they do not agree.

This argument is merely a contrivance. In the first place, apart from disclosing use of rBST, Vermont's law imposes no speech requirements on the plaintiff milk producers. It is the retailers who are obligated to post signs containing text that relates to the rBST process....

Second, the text posted by retailers under Vermont's law is innocuous. Apart from enabling the consumer to tell which products derive from rBST-treated cows, the only additional required text states:

The United States Food and Drug Administration has determined that there is no significant difference between milk from treated and untreated cows. It is the law of Vermont that products made from the milk of rBSt-treated cows be labeled to help consumers make informed shopping decisions.

The producers cannot contend they disagree with the first sentence, whose only function is to reassure consumers that the FDA found no health hazard in rBST products.[5]   They focus rather on the second sentence, asserting that they disagree with the proposition that "informed shopping decisions" are advanced by disclosure of rBST treatment because they contend it is irrelevant to any legitimate consumer concern. Their argument

---

[4] The evidence included a cartoon, published in the Burlington Free Press: in frame 1, a man declares his confidence in the safety of rBST milk; in frame 2, he drinks the milk; in frame 3, he turns into a werewolf. Plaintiffs cite this cartoon as a demonstration that the concerns of Vermonters are fantastical. They overlook the fact that the cartoon is a joke. But like most jokes it has a basis in reality. The cartoon does not mean that Vermonters think rBST will turn them into werewolves. What it reflects is that, notwithstanding the FDA's assurances, consumers are worried about the effects of rBST.

[5] Indeed, a statistical sampling shows that this labeling makes milk from rBST-treated cows more acceptable to Vermont consumers. Before reading this sign, 86% of respondents preferred milk from untreated cows; after reading the sign, preference for milk from untreated cows fell to 73%.

has no force. The "informed shopping decisions" statement is clearly identified as made by the state of Vermont, not by the milk producers. Furthermore, the statement is virtually meaningless and harmless, especially following the sentence stating that the FDA found no significant difference between milk from treated and untreated cows. The producers cannot even contend that they are obligated by Vermont's regulation to enter into debate. . . .

It is quite clear that the producers' real objection is to the mandatory revelation of the use of rBST, which many Vermonters disfavor, and not to the bland sentence announcing that products are labeled "to help consumers make informed shopping decisions."

D. Disclosure v. Concealment

Notwithstanding their self-righteous references to free expression, the true objective of the milk producers is concealment. They do not wish consumers to know that their milk products were produced by use of rBST because there are consumers who, for various reasons, prefer to avoid rBST. Vermont, on the other hand, has established a labeling requirement whose sole objective (and whose sole effect) is to inform Vermont consumers whether milk products offered for sale were produced with rBST.[6] The dispute under the First Amendment is over whether the milk producers' interest in concealing their use of rBST from consumers will prevail over a state law designed to give consumers the information they desire. The question is simply whether the First Amendment prohibits government from requiring disclosure of truthful relevant information to consumers.

In my view, the interest of the milk producers has little entitlement to protection under the First Amendment. The caselaw that has developed under the doctrine of commercial speech has repeatedly emphasized that the primary function of the First Amendment in its application to commercial speech is to advance truthful disclosure -- the very interest that the milk producers seek to undermine.

The milk producers' invocation of the First Amendment for the

---

[6] I disagree with the majority's contention, Maj. Op. at 12, that voluntary labeling by producers who do not use rBST can be relied on to effectuate Vermont's purpose. There is evidence that, notwithstanding the FDA's determination to permit such voluntary labeling, certain states, no doubt influenced by the rBST lobby, will "not allow any labeling concerning rBST." Affidavit of Ben Cohen, at 3-4. This effectively prevents multistate distributors from including such labeling on their packaging. Producers complying with Vermont's law do not face the same problem. The blue dot has meaning only in conjunction with the signs posted in Vermont retail establishments. Thus producers can inexpensively affix the blue dot without violating the laws of states that forbid all rBST labeling.

purpose of concealing their use of rBST in milk production is entitled to scant recognition. They invoke the Amendment's protection to accomplish exactly what the Amendment opposes. And the majority's ruling deprives Vermont of the right to protect its consumers by requiring truthful disclosure on a subject of legitimate public concern. . . .

I am comforted by two considerations: First, the precedential effect of the majority's ruling is quite limited. By its own terms, it applies only to cases where a state disclosure requirement is supported by no interest other than the gratification of consumer curiosity. In any case in which a state advanced something more, the majority's ruling would have no bearing. . . .Second, Vermont will have a further opportunity to defend its law. The majority's conclusion perhaps results from Vermont's failure to put forth sufficiently clear evidence of the interests it sought to advance.. . .

NOTES

1. Vermont's Legislature responded and passed legislation making voluntary the labeling of milk that was "BST-free":

6 V.S.A. § 2760. Substantial state interest

(a) Role of state government. The Vermont general assembly finds, as does the U.S. Food and Drug Administration, that the states under our federal system of government have traditionally undertaken the role of overseeing milk production. The Vermont general assembly also finds that the intent of the U.S. Food and Drug Administration is to rely primarily on state governments to validate rbST labeling claims regarding milk and dairy products and to ensure that such claims are truthful and not misleading.

(b) State policy. It is the policy of this state:

(1) that Vermont citizens should have an opportunity to choose to consume milk or dairy products which have not had rbST used in their production ("rbST-free"), based on truthful and nonmisleading product labeling;

(2) that Vermont dairy product manufacturers who want to sell rbST-free products in Vermont or out of state should be able to do so, based on a state-sanctioned process for certifying rbST-free labeling claims;

(3) that the economic health and vitality of the Vermont dairy industry is critical to the health of the overall Vermont economy, which depends in part on the high reputation of Vermont farmers and their dairy products, and the associated goodwill toward other Vermont enterprises, and that this economic asset should not be jeopardized by consumer doubts about the integrity of Vermont milk or dairy products caused by false, misleading or unverifiable rbST-free labeling claims; and

(4) to support the right of Vermont dairy farmers to choose to use rbST, and of rbST manufacturers and suppliers to sell their product to Vermont dairy farmers.

c) Substantial state interest. Therefore, the Vermont general assembly:

(1) finds a substantial state interest in ensuring the availability of milk and dairy product labeling information that is accurate and nonmisleading, and in which Vermont and out-of-state consumers can place their confidence; and

(2) seeks to serve this interest through this subchapter by:

(A) authorizing a program of voluntary labeling of milk and dairy products which have not had rbST used in their production; and

(B) providing for the verification of claims that rbST has not been used in the production of milk or dairy products offered for sale in Vermont; but

c) without unduly intruding into the businesses of Vermont dairy farmers who choose to use rbST, or of rbST manufacturers or suppliers who choose to sell their product to Vermont dairy farmers. (Added 1997, No. 154 (Adj. Sess.), § 1, eff. April 29, 1998.

2. November 16, 1999, the Genetically Engineered Food Right To Know Act was introduced in the House of Representatives. The bill proposed amending FDCA, the Federal Meat Inspection Act, and the Poultry Products Inspection Act to require that food that contains a genetically engineered material, or that is produced with a genetically engineered material, be labeled accordingly. *See* H.R. 3377, 106th Cong. (1999). Is this advisable?

3. A scientist in Germany has created a genetically engineered rice plant, called "yellow rice," to include the DNA code for producing Vitamin A. This rice is intended to supplement the diet of millions of people who primarily eat rice, and have Vitamin A deficiencies. Many groups are opposing the widespread use of this rice. What are the policy and legal issues which might be considered in making a determination as to whether this rice should be used?

5.1.2   The National Organic Program

The modern environmental movement began on the story of a pesticide, DDT, by Rachel Carson in the 1960s, *Silent Spring*, originally written as a series in a consumer magazine.

5.1.2.1 The National Organic Movement

Another movement would also be inspired by another would-be pesticide event in 1989. An episode of 60 Minutes in 1989 reported that the use of daminozide, known by its tradename as "Alar," was causing cancer. The product was not a pesticide, but an additive that prevented the pre-harvest rotting of apples.[1] Correspondent Ed Bradely asserted that daminozide was "the most potent cancer-causing agent in our food supply." His claim was drawn from an EPA report that showed that daminozide would break down into dimethylhydrazine (UDMH) and that it caused premature death in mice. Because apples were fed to children in applesauce and apple juice, widespread panic over apples followed. Apples rotted for lack of a market, but the sale of organics increased.

---

1 Kenneth Smith et al., *An Unhappy Anniversary: The Alar Scare Ten Years Later*, American Council on Science and Health (Feb. 1999), available at http://www.acsh.org/publications/pubid.865/pub_detail.asp

Thereafter, an organic market emerged and Congress was lobbied to create a statute to provide for standards and requirements. One particular focus was on labeling foods and what standards would warrant the "organic" label.

The Organic Food Production Act (OFPA) was passed in 1990. In the Congressional report they found that the growth of the organic market was "hampered by a lack of consistent standards for production" and that it was "time for national standard for organic production so that farmers know the rules, so that consumers are sure to get what they pay for, and so that national and international trade in organic foods may prosper."

The interference in interstate commerce by different standards was striking, in particular with the example of organic milk. Congress found that "minor differences in organic milk standards create havoc for the industry." Organic milk production in New Hampshire and Texas required the use of exclusively organic feed, while production in Kansas, Maine, and South Dakota require only unmedicated feed. Further, California and Oregon require different types of feed at certain times in the cows' milk production cycle. Congress found this to be confusing for the consumer by noting that "[e]ven the most sophisticated organic consumer finds it difficult to know, with certainty, what the term 'organic' really means."

Because of the substantial effect on interstate commerce, Congress had the authority to regulate where inconsistent standards between states created a burden on interstate commerce. The OFPA preempts state programs, so the statute permitted states to develop their own organic certification program as long as it was not inconsistent with the federal program [7 U.S.C. 6507(b)(2)(A)-(B)], but the state standards could be more restrictive than the federal standards. The Senate report reflected their intent with the law to "preserve the rights of the States to develop standards particular to their needs that are additional and complementary to the Federal standards" as long as "that State action [does] not disrupt interstate commerce."

Would genetically-modified-organisms (GMOs) be allowed in organic products? The 1990 statute does not prohibit GMOs, but by 2000 the rule had changed and GMOs would be excluded from the National Organic Program, as USDA explains,

> The Organic Food Production Act (OFPA) of 1990 does not mention biotechnology, genetic engineering or genetically modified organisms. OFPA prohibits synthetics unless they are allowed, allows natural substances unless they are prohibited. The first National Organic Program proposed rule (1997) did not prohibit GE substances or GMOs. There was a huge public outcry against GMOs being considered in organic production and handling. Proposed rule withdrawn. The second National Organic Program proposed rule (2000) excluded the use of GMOs in organic production and handling.

[USDA National Organic Program and GMOs Presentation at file:///F:/Agricultural%20Biotechnology%20Law/Labelling/GMO%20Policy%20Training%202012.pdf].

In 2009, almost ten years later, the program is still being questioned about its effectiveness. This article in the Washington Post summarizes the problems and political tensions with the competing interest groups:

Purity of Federal 'Organic' Label Is Questioned

By Kimberly Kindy and Lyndsey Layton
Washington Post Staff Writers
Friday, July 3, 2009

Three years ago, U.S. Department of Agriculture employees determined that synthetic additives in organic baby formula violated federal standards and should be banned from a product carrying the federal organic label. Today the same additives, purported to boost brainpower and vision, can be found in 90 percent of organic baby formula.

The government's turnaround, from prohibition to permission, came after a USDA program manager was lobbied by the formula makers and overruled her staff. That decision and others by a handful of USDA employees, along with an advisory board's approval of a growing list of non-organic ingredients, have helped numerous companies win a coveted green-and-white "USDA Organic" seal on an array of products.

Grated organic cheese, for example, contains wood starch to prevent clumping. Organic beer can be made from non-organic hops. Organic mock duck contains a synthetic ingredient that gives it an authentic, stringy texture.

Relaxation of the federal standards, and an explosion of consumer demand, have helped push the organics market into a $23 billion-a-year business, the fastest growing segment of the food industry. Half of the country's adults say they buy organic food often or sometimes, according to a survey last year by the Harvard School of Public Health.

But the USDA program's shortcomings mean that consumers, who at times must pay twice as much for organic products, are not always getting what they expect: foods without pesticides and other chemicals, produced in a way that is gentle to the environment.

The market's expansion is fueling tension over whether the federal program should be governed by a strict interpretation of "organic" or broadened to include more products by allowing trace elements of non-organic substances. The argument is not over whether the non-organics pose a health threat, but whether they weaken the integrity of the federal organic label.

Agriculture Secretary Tom Vilsack has pledged to protect the label, even as he acknowledged the pressure to lower standards to let more products in.

In response to complaints, the USDA inspector general's office has widened an investigation of whether products carrying the label meet national standards. The probe is also looking into the department's oversight of private certifiers who are hired by farmers and food producers and inspect products to determine whether they can use the label.

Some consumer groups and members of Congress say they worry that the program's lax standards are undermining the federal program and the law itself.

"It will unravel everything we've done if the standards can no longer be trusted," said Sen. Patrick J. Leahy (D-Vt.), who sponsored the federal organics legislation. "If we don't protect the brand, the organic label, the program is finished. It could disappear overnight."

Organic advocates and food marketing experts said the introduction this month of new "natural" products by an organics division of Dean Foods is the latest sign that the value of the USDA label has eroded. The yogurt and milk products will be distributed under the Horizon label and marketed as a lower-priced alternative to organic products.

Congress adopted the organics law after farmers and consumers demanded uniform standards for produce, dairy and meat. The law banned synthetics, pesticides and genetic engineering from foods that would bear a federal organic label. It also required annual testing for pesticides. And it was aimed at preventing producers from falsely claiming their foods were organic.

The USDA created the National Organic Program in 2002 to implement the law. By then, major food companies had bought up most small, independent organic companies. Kraft Foods, for example, owns Boca Foods. Kellogg owns Morningstar Farms, and Coca-Cola owns 40 percent of Honest Tea, maker of the organic beverage favored by President Obama.

That corporate firepower has added to pressure on the government to expand the definition of what is organic, in part because processed foods offered by big industry often require ingredients, additives or processing agents that either do not exist in organic form or are not available in large enough quantities for mass production.

Under the original organics law, 5 percent of a USDA-certified organic product can consist of non-organic substances, provided they are approved by the National Organic Standards Board. That list has grown from 77 to 245 substances since it was created in 2002. Companies must appeal to the board every five years to keep a substance on the list, explaining why an organic alternative has not been found.

The goal was to shrink the list over time, but only one item has been removed so far.

The original law's mandate for annual pesticide testing was also never implemented -- the agency left that optional.

From the beginning, farmers and consumer advocates were concerned about safeguarding the organic label. In 2003, Arthur Harvey, who grows organic blueberries in Maine, successfully sued the USDA, arguing that the fledgling National Organic Program had violated federal law by allowing synthetic additives.

"The big boys like Kraft realized they could really cash in by filling the shelves with products with the organics seal," Harvey said. "But they were sort of inhibited by the original law that said no synthetic ingredients."

His victory was short-lived. The Organic Trade Association, which represents corporations such as Kraft, Dole and Dean Foods, lobbied for and received language in a 2006 appropriations bill allowing certain synthetic food substances in the preparation, processing and packaging of organic foods, creating conditions for a flood of processed organic foods.

Tom Harding, a Pennsylvania-based consultant for small local farmers and big producers, including Kraft, said that broadening the law has helped meet demand by multiplying the number of organic products and greatly expanded the amount of agricultural land that is being managed organically.

"We don't want to eliminate anyone who wants to be a part of the organic community," Harding said. "The growth we've seen has helped the entire organic food chain."

Organics for Babies

Today, labels on organic infant formula boast that they include DHA and ARA, synthetic fatty acids that some studies suggest can help neural development. But according to agency records, when the issue came before the USDA in 2006, agency staff members concluded that the fatty acids could not be added to organic baby formula because they are synthetics that are not on the standards board's approved list.

The fatty acids in formula are often produced using a potential neurotoxin known as hexane, prompting many organics advocates to conclude that the board would not approve their use if it took up the matter.

In a rare move, Barbara Robinson, who administers the organics program and is a deputy USDA administrator, overruled the staff decision after a telephone call and an e-mail exchange with William J. Friedman, a lawyer who represents the formula makers.

"I called [Robinson] up," Friedman said. "I wrote an e-mail. It was a simple matter." The back-and-forth, he said, was nothing more than part of the routine process that sets policy in Washington.

In an interview, Robinson said she agreed with Friedman's argument that fatty acids were not permitted because of an oversight. Vitamins and minerals are allowed, but "accessory nutrients" -- the category that describes fatty acids -- are not specifically named.

As for hexane, Robinson said the law bans its use in processing organic food, but she does not believe the ban extends to the processing of synthetic additives.

"We don't attempt to say how synthetic products can be produced," she said.

Manufacturers say the fatty acids are safe and provide health benefits to infants.

"We test every lot that comes out for hexane, and there is no residue," said David Abramson, president of Maryland-based Martek Biosciences, which produces the fatty acids used by formula companies.

Several groups have filed complaints with the USDA saying they think that the inclusion of the fatty acids in organic products violates federal rules and laws. And they say that Robinson did not have the authority to make the decision on her own.

"This is illegal rulemaking -- a complete violation of the process that is supposed to protect the public," said Gary Cox, a lawyer with the Cornucopia Institute, an organics advocacy group.

Cox and others make the same argument about other decisions by Robinson and several members of her staff.

In 2004, Robinson issued a directive allowing farmers and certifiers to use pesticides on organic crops if "after a reasonable effort" they could not determine whether the pesticide contained chemicals prohibited by the organics law.

The same year, Robinson determined that farmers could feed organic livestock non-organic fish meal, which can contain mercury and PCBs. The law requires that animals that produce organic meat be raised entirely on organic feed.

After sharp protests from Leahy, Consumers Union and other groups, Ann Veneman, then agriculture secretary, rescinded these and two other directives issued by Robinson.

The orders were signed by a staff member, but Robinson took responsibility, saying she had made the decisions unwisely without consulting organics experts, certifiers or the standards board.

"I failed, and take this as a learning experience and do not want it to happen again," she told board members in 2004.

Earlier this year, however, Robinson issued a series of directives without consulting experts, certifiers or the board. She said that because the issues were urgent, including one on food safety, she had to act quickly.

In an interview, Robinson said she believes the federal program's main purpose is to "grow the industry," and she dismissed controversies over synthetics in organic foods as "mostly ridiculous."

Joe Smillie, a board member, said he thinks that advocates for the most restrictive standards are unrealistic and are inhibiting the growth of organics.

"People are really hung up on regulations," said Smillie, who is also vice president of the certifying firm Quality Assurance International, which is involved in certifying 65 percent of organic products found on supermarket shelves. "I say, 'Let's find a way to bend that one, because it's not important.' . . . What are we selling? Are we selling health food? No. Consumers, they expect organic food to be growing in a greenhouse on Pluto. Hello? We live in a polluted world. It isn't pure. We are doing the best we can."

Waiting for Standards

Under Robinson, the National Organic Program has repeatedly opted not to issue standards spelling out how organic food must be grown, treated or produced. In 65 instances since 2002, the standards board has made recommendations that have not been acted upon, creating a haphazard system in which the private certifiers have set their own standards for what products can carry the federal label.

The agency has not acted, for example, on a 2002 board recommendation that would answer a critical question for organic dairy farmers: how to interpret the law requiring that their cows have "access to pasture," rather than be crowded onto feedlots. The result has been that some dairy farms have been selling milk as organic from cows that spend little if any time grazing in open spaces.

"This is really a case of 'justice delayed is justice denied,' " said Alexis Baden-Mayer, national political director for the Organic Consumers Association. "The truly organic dairy farmers, who have their cows out in the pasture all year round, are at a huge competitive disadvantage compared to the big confinement dairies."

Robinson has blamed the delays on the program's small staff, saying that "we have to prioritize."

Without specific standards, the wide discretion given to certifiers has invited producers and farmers to shop around for the certifiers most likely to approve their product, consumer groups say.

Sam Welsch, president of the Nebraska-based OneCert, said his company this year has lost as many as a dozen fruit and vegetable farmers seeking other certifiers that allow the use of certain liquid fertilizers, which most organics experts believe are prohibited by organics laws because they are unnaturally spiked with high levels of nitrogen.

"The rules should be clear enough that there is just one right answer," Welsch said.

Consumer groups and organics advocates are hopeful that the Obama administration will bolster the program. In his proposed budget, the president has doubled resources devoted to organics and installed USDA leaders who support change.

Vilsack's deputy, organics expert Kathleen A. Merrigan, told consumer groups three weeks ago that she intends to heighten enforcement. Merrigan helped write the original organics law and get the federal program off the ground in 2002.

And Vilsack said he wants to protect the organic label. "That term, 'organic,' needs to be pure," he said in an interview. "You can't allow the definition to be eroded to where it means nothing. . . . We have to fight against that kind of pressure."

Still, at the standards board's meeting last month, Chairman Jeff Moyer noted the growing tension. "As the organic industry matures, it is becoming increasingly more difficult to find a balance between the integrity of the word 'organic' and the desire for the industry to grow."

http://www.washingtonpost.com/wp-dyn/content/article/2009/07/02/AR2009070203365_pf.html

After the USDA lost on all counts in the Harvey case, the Congressional Research Service analyzed the case and whether the changes were just due to failure to follow the Administrative Procedure Act or were the changes destructive to the organic program. Here is what they found:

The OFPA also requires the Secretary to promulgate regulations "to carry out" the Act. The Secretary published the National Organic Program Final Rule (Final Rule) in December 2000 and it became effective on October 21,

2002 (codified at 7 C.F.R. pt. 205). Among other things, the Final Rule sets forth a four-tier labeling system for organic foods. Under this system, the type of labeling permitted on a product varies according to the percentage of organic ingredients it contains. The labeling scheme distinguishes: products containing 100% organic ingredients, which may be labeled "100 percent organic"; (2) products containing 94 to 100% organic ingredients, which may be labeled "organic"; (3) products containing 70 to 94% organic ingredients, which may be labeled "made with organic (specified ingredients or food group(s))"; and (4) products containing less than 70% percent organic ingredients, which may identify each organic ingredient on the label or in the ingredient statement with the word "organic."3 Harvey v. Veneman In October 2002, Mr. Arthur Harvey filed a pro se suit against the USDA in the U.S. District Court for the District of Maine, alleging that multiple provisions of the Final Rule were inconsistent with the OFPA and the Administrative Procedures Act.4

The district court ruled in favor of the USDA (i.e., granted summary judgment) on all nine counts brought by Harvey. [Harvey v. Veneman, No. 02-216-P-H, 2003 U.S. Dist. LEXIS 18162 (D. Me., Oct. 10, 2003) accepted and rejected in part by 297 F. Supp. 2d 334 (D. Me., Jan. 7, 2004)]. Harvey subsequently appealed the case to the First Circuit [Harvey v. Veneman, 396 F.3d 28 (1st Cir. 2005)]. and was supported by a number of public interest groups that filed "friends of the court" or Amici Curiae briefs. The First Circuit sided with Harvey on three counts and remanded the holdings to the district court for further action. In brief, the court found that:

- nonorganic ingredients not commercially available in organic form but used in the production of items labeled "organic" must have individual reviews in order to be placed on the National List of Allowed and Prohibited Substances;
- synthetic substances are barred in the processing or handling of products labeled "organic"; and
- dairy herds converting to organic production are not allowed to be fed feed that is only 80% organic for the first nine months of a one-year conversion.

CRS Report on *Harvey v. Veneman* at
https://nationalaglawcenter.org/wp-content/uploads/assets/crs/RS22318.pdf

Congress amended the statute which addressed some of the concerns, but further rulemaking was required to comply with concerns about animals.

January 19, 2017, the USDA published a final rule that would address requirements for the National Organic Program (NOP) with regard to livestock and poultry. The rule provides this summary of the action:

B. Summary of Provisions:

Specifically this final rule:
1. Clarifies how producers and handlers participating in the NOP must treat livestock and poultry to ensure their wellbeing.

2. Clarifies when and how certain physical alterations may be performed on organic livestock and poultry in order to minimize stress. Additionally, some forms of physical alterations are prohibited.

3. Sets maximum indoor and outdoor stocking densities for organic chickens, which vary depending on the type of production and stage of life.

4. Defines outdoor space and requires that outdoor spaces for organic poultry include soil and vegetation.
5. Adds new requirements for transporting organic livestock and poultry to sale or slaughter.

6. Clarifies the application of USDA Food Safety and Inspection Service (FSIS) requirements regarding the handling of livestock and poultry in connection with slaughter to certified organic livestock and poultry establishments and provides for the enforcement of USDA organic regulations based on FSIS inspection findings.

7. AMS has only established indoor space requirements fsor chickens in this final rule. AMS may propose space requirements for other avian species in the future. Other avian species must meet all other indoor requirements including exit doors, ammonia levels, and lighting. [82 Fed. Reg. 7042 (Jan. 19, 2017)].

An important case that helped to define the tolerances for pesticides in organic products was tested in the next case. The farmer claims damages due to pesticide drift from a neighboring farm, causing damages to his organic products and land. However, the tolerances allowed for pesticides in the National Organic Program regulations, led to the court finding that violation of the law in a negligence per se claim, did not lead to a finding of damages.

Supreme Court of Minnesota.

Oluf JOHNSON, et al., Respondents, v. PAYNESVILLE FARMERS UNION COOPERATIVE OIL COMPANY, Appellant.

Nos. A10–1596, A10–2135.
Decided: August 01, 2012

OPINION

This action involves alleged pesticide contamination of organic farm fields in central Minnesota. Appellant Paynesville Farmers Union Cooperative Oil Company ("Cooperative") is a member owned farm products and services provider that, among other things, applies pesticides to farm fields. Respondents Oluf and Debra Johnson ("Johnsons") are organic farmers. The Johnsons claim that while the Cooperative was spraying pesticide onto conventionally farmed fields adjacent to the Johnsons' fields, some pesticide drifted onto and contaminated the Johnsons' organic fields. The Johnsons sued the Cooperative on theories including trespass, nuisance, and negligence per se and sought damages and injunctive relief. The Johnsons claim that the pesticide drift caused them: (1) economic damages because they had to take the contaminated fields out of organic production for 3 years pursuant to 7 C.F.R. § 205.202(b) (2012), (2) economic damages because they had to destroy some crops, (3) inconvenience, and (4) adverse health effects. The district court granted summary judgment to the Cooperative and dismissed all of the Johnsons' claims. The court of appeals reversed. Because we conclude that the Johnsons' trespass claim and claims for damages based on 7 C.F.R. § 205.202(b), fail as a matter of law, we reverse the court of appeals' reinstatement of those claims. But because the district court failed to consider whether the Johnsons' non trespass claims that were not based on 7 C.F.R. § 205.202(b), could survive summary judgment, we affirm the court of appeals' reinstatement of those claims and remand for proceedings consistent with this opinion.

Before discussing the factual background of this case, it is helpful to briefly summarize the organic farming regulations at issue. American organic farming is regulated by the Organic Foods Production Act of 1990, 7 U.S.C. §§ 6501–6523 (2006) ("OFPA"), and the associated federal regulations in the National Organic Program, 7 C.F.R. § 205 (2012) ("NOP"). One of the purposes of the OFPA is "to establish national standards governing the marketing of certain agricultural products as organically produced products." 7 U.S.C. § 6501(1). The states may adopt the federal standards or they may impose "more restrictive requirements governing" products sold as organic. 7 U.S.C. § 6507(b)(1). Minnesota has adopted the OFPA and the NOP as its state organic farming law. Minn.Stat. § 31.925 (2010) (adopting the OFPA and the NOP "as the organic food production law and rules in this state").

168

Under the OFPA and the NOP regulations, a producer cannot market its crops as "organic," and receive the premium price paid for organic products, unless the producer is "certified" by an organic certifying agent. 7 U.S.C. § 6503(d) (stating that the OFPA is implemented by certifying agents authorized through the Secretary of Agriculture); 7 C.F.R. § 205.100, .102 (describing which products can carry the "organic" label). And in order to receive certification, a producer must comply with the NOP. 7 C.F.R. § 205.400. Among numerous other requirements, the NOP provides that land from which crops are intended to be sold as organic must "[h]ave had no prohibited substances . applied to it for a period of 3 years immediately preceding harvest of the crop." 7 C.F.R. § 205.202(b).[1]

Once producers obtain certification to sell products as organic, the OFPA and NOP provide guidelines for certified organic farming operations to ensure continued compliance. See 7 U.S.C. § 6511. Under these guidelines, if a prohibited substance is detected on a product sold or labeled as organic, the certifying agent must conduct an investigation to determine whether there has been a violation of the federal requirements. See 7 U.S.C. § 6511(c)(1). If the investigation indicates that the residue detected on the organic product was "the result of intentional application of a prohibited substance" or the residue is "present at levels that are greater than" federal regulations prescribe, the product cannot be sold as organic. 7 U.S.C. § 6511(c)(2). Under the NOP regulations, crops may not be sold as organic if the crops are shown to have a prohibited substance on them at levels that are greater than 5 percent of the Environmental Protection Agency's tolerance level for that substance. 7 C.F.R. § 205.671

With this regulatory scheme in mind, we turn to the incidents that gave rise to this lawsuit.

In June 2007, the Johnsons filed a complaint with the Minnesota Department of Agriculture ("MDA"), alleging that the Cooperative had contaminated one of their transitional soybean fields[2] through pesticide drift. The subsequent MDA investigation verified that on June 15, 2007, a date when winds were blowing toward the Johnsons' fields at 9 to 21 miles per hour, the Cooperative sprayed Status (diflufenzopyr and dicamba) and Roundup Original (glyphosate) onto a conventional farmer's field immediately adjacent to one of the Johnsons' transitional soybean fields. The MDA informed the Johnsons that there was no tolerance for diflufenzopyr in soybeans (organic, transitional, or conventional) and that, pending chemical testing, the MDA would "determine if there [would] be any harvest prohibitions" on the Johnsons' soybeans. After receiving the results of the chemical testing, the MDA informed the parties that test results revealed that the chemical dicamba was present, but below detection levels. The MDA also reported that the chemicals diflufenzopyr and glyphosate were not present. Because only one of the three chemicals was present based on its testing, the MDA concluded that "it can not be proven if the detections were from drift." And even though the testing did not find diflufenzopyr, the MDA still required that the Johnsons plow down a small portion of the soybeans growing in the field because of "the presence of dicamba" and based on the "visual damage" observed to this crop. In response to this MDA directive, the Johnsons destroyed approximately 10 acres of their soybean crop.

The Johnsons also reported the alleged pesticide drift to their organic certifying agent, the Organic Crop Improvement Association (OCIA), as they were required to do under the NOP. See 7 C.F.R. § 205.400(f)(1). In an August 27, 2007 letter, the OCIA stated that there may have been chemical drift onto a transitional soybean field and that chemical testing was being done. The Johnsons were also told that "[i]f the analysis indicate[d] contamination," they would have to "take this land back to the beginning of 36–month transition." Based on the OCIA's letter, and the dicamba found by the MDA, the Johnsons took the transitional soybean field back to the beginning of the 3–year transition process. In other words, the Johnsons did not market soybeans harvested from this field as organic for an additional 3 years.

On July 3, 2008, the Johnsons reported another incident of alleged contamination to the MDA. In this report, the Johnsons alleged that there was pesticide drift onto one of their transitional alfalfa fields after the Cooperative applied Roundup Power Max and Select Max (containing the chemicals glyphosate and clethodium) to a neighboring conventional farmer's field. The MDA investigator did not observe any plant injury, but chemical testing revealed a minimal amount of glyphosate in the Johnsons' transitional alfalfa. The Johnsons reported another incident of drift on August 1, 2008. The MDA "did not observe any plant injury to the alfalfa field or plants, grass and weeds," but chemical testing revealed the presence, at minimal levels, of chloropyrifos, the active ingredient in another pesticide, Lorsban Advanced. The MDA concluded that drift from the Cooperative's spraying caused both of the positive test results. After receiving these test results, the Johnsons took the affected alfalfa field out of organic production for an additional 3 years. The Johnsons took this action because they believed that the presence of any amount of pesticide on their organic fields prohibited them from selling crops harvested from these fields as organic.

Based on the presence of pesticides in their fields, the Johnsons filed this lawsuit against the Cooperative, alleging trespass, nuisance, negligence per se, and battery. They sought damages and a permanent injunction prohibiting the Cooperative from spraying pesticides within a half mile of the Johnsons' fields.[3] The Johnsons claimed the following types of damages: (1) loss of profits because they had to take the fields onto which pesticide drifted out of organic production for 3 years; (2) loss of profits because they had to destroy approximately 10 acres of soybeans; (3) inconvenience due to increased weeding, pollution remediation, and NOP reporting responsibilities; and (4) adverse health effects.

The district court granted, in part, the Johnsons' motion for a temporary injunction on June 26, 2009, requiring the Cooperative to give the Johnsons notice before it sprayed pesticides on land adjoining the Johnsons' organic farm. Subsequently, the Cooperative moved for summary judgment, and the Johnsons moved to amend their complaint to include claims based on the two 2008 incidents and a claim for punitive damages. After a hearing, the district court granted the Cooperative summary judgment on all of the Johnsons' claims, denied the Johnsons' motion to amend, and vacated the temporary injunction.[4]

The district court concluded that the Johnsons' trespass claim failed as a matter of law, relying on the court of appeals decision in Wendinger v. Forst Farms Inc., 662 N.W.2d 546, 550 (Minn.App.2003), which held that Minnesota does not recognize trespass by particulate matter.[5] The district court also concluded that all of the Johnsons' negligence per se and nuisance claims failed as a matter of law because the Johnsons lacked evidence of damages. This determination was based on the court's conclusion that because there was no evidence that any chemical on the Johnsons' crops exceeded the 5 percent tolerance level in 7 C.F.R. § 205.671, the Johnsons could have sold their crops as organic and therefore the Johnsons did not prove damages. Because the Johnsons did not have any "evidence of damages based on the NOP regulations," the court concluded that all of the Johnsons' claims must be dismissed and the temporary injunction vacated. And because the court concluded that the Johnsons' claims arising from the 2008 incidents would necessarily fail as a matter of law under the same analysis, the court denied the Johnsons' motion to amend their complaint to include claims based on the 2008 incidents.

The court of appeals reversed and remanded. Johnson v. Paynesville Farmers Union Coop. Oil Co., 802 N.W.2d 383 (Minn.App.2011). As to the trespass claim, the court of appeals concluded that the district court "read too much into" Wendinger. Id. at 387. The court of appeals stated that its decision in Wendinger should not be read "to define a unique category of physical substances that can never constitute a trespass." Id. at 388. Instead of focusing on the intangible nature of pesticide drift, the court of appeals focused on the harm caused by it, stating that pesticide drift will "affect the composition of the land." Id. Relying on cases from other jurisdictions that were explicitly distinguished in Wendinger, the court of appeals held that pesticide drift "can interfere with possession" and therefore "a trespass action can arise from a chemical pesticide being deposited in [discernible] and consequential amounts onto one agricultural property as the result of errant overspray during application directed at another." Id. at 389.

As to the negligence per se and nuisance claims based on 7 C.F.R. § 205.202(b), the court of appeals disagreed with the district court's interpretation of the NOP regulations. Johnson, 802 N.W.2d at 390–91. The court of appeals held that the phrase "applied to it" in section 205.202(b) included situations in which pesticides unintentionally came into contact with organic fields. 802 N.W.2d at 390. Based on this conclusion, the court reasoned that the presence of any amount of pesticide on the Johnsons' fields rendered the Johnsons noncompliant with 7 C.F.R. § 205.202(b), and therefore that OCIA had discretion to decertify the Johnsons' fields. 802 N.W.2d at 391 (citing 7 C.F.R. § 205.662(a), (c) (providing that "any noncompliance" with the NOP can lead to decertification)). And because the presence of pesticide on the Johnsons' fields allegedly caused those fields to be decertified, the court of appeals held that the Johnsons had viable claims for damages based on 7 C.F.R. § 205.202(b). 802 N.W.2d at 391. The court of appeals also concluded that the district court erred in failing to separately analyze or discuss the Johnsons' claims that were not based on trespass or on 7 C.F.R. § 205.202(b), before dismissing all of the Johnsons' claims, and that the district court had abused its discretion in denying the Johnsons' motion to amend their complaint to include claims based on the 2008 incidents. 802 N.W.2d at 391–92.

We granted the Cooperative's petition for review, and on appeal, the Cooperative argues that (1) the Johnsons' trespass claim fails as a matter of law; (2) all of the Johnsons' claims fail as a matter of law because the Johnsons have not shown damages; (3) the district court did not err when it denied the Johnsons' motion to amend their complaint; and (4) the district court did not err when it denied the Johnsons a permanent injunction. We consider each of these issues in turn.

. . .

A.
We turn first to the portion of the Johnsons' nuisance and negligence per se claims that are based on 7 C.F.R. § 205.202(b). The Johnsons argue that they had to remove certain fields from organic production for 3 years because pesticides were "applied to" those fields in violation of 7 C.F.R. § 205.202(b). The Johnsons contend that the phrase "applied to it" in the regulation, read in conjunction with other sections of the NOP, means that any application of pesticides to a field, whether intentional or not, requires that the field be taken out of organic production for 3 years.[11] Based on this reading, the Johnsons assert that they were required to take their soybean field back to the beginning of the 3–year transition period because of the 2007 pesticide drift.[12]As a result, the Johnsons claim they lost the ability to market crops from that field as organic, and therefore lost the opportunity to seek the premium prices commanded by organic products.

For its part, the Cooperative argues that the phrase "applied to it" in 7 C.F.R. § 205.202(b), unambiguously means that the organic farmer intentionally applied the prohibited substance to the field. Because the Johnsons did not apply pesticides to the field, the Cooperative argues that section 205.202(b) does not restrict the Johnsons' sale of organic products. In the alternative, the Cooperative argues that if section 205.202(b) is ambiguous, analysis of the relevant canons of construction confirms its interpretation.

The district court adopted the interpretation of the NOP regulation that the Cooperative advances. But the court of appeals reversed, holding that the phrase "applied to it" "implicitly includes unintentional pesticide drift," and that therefore OCIA had discretion to decertify the Johnsons' soybean field under section 205.202(b). Johnson, 802 N.W.2d at 390. And because there was discretion to decertify, the court of appeals concluded that the Johnsons had offered sufficient evidence to survive summary judgment. Id. at 391. We agree with the district court that section 205.202(b) does not regulate the Cooperative's pesticide drift.

In order to resolve the interpretation question presented, we must construe the regulation at issue—7 C.F.R. § 205.202(b). Our first task is to determine whether the regulation is ambiguous. E .g., In re Cities of Annandale & Maple Lake, 731 N.W.2d 502, 516 (Minn.2007) (considering whether a federal regulation was ambiguous). If it is not ambiguous, we apply the plain and ordinary meaning of the words used. See Exelon Generation Co. LLC v. Local 15 Int'l Bhd. Of Elec. Workers, 676 F.3d 566, 570 (7th Cir.2012) (stating that the same rules of construction apply to federal administrative rules as to statutes); Citizens Advocating Responsible Dev. v. Kandiyohi Cnty. Bd. of Comm'rs, 713 N.W.2d 817, 828 n. 9 (Minn.2006) (noting that administrative regulations are governed by the same rules of construction that apply to statutes); cf. Caminetti v. United States, 242 U.S. 470, 485, 37 S.Ct. 192, 61 L.Ed. 442 (1917) (noting that when the meaning of a statute "is plain . the sole function of the courts is to enforce it according to its terms"). In deciding whether the regulation is ambiguous, however, we do not construe the regulation in isolation. Rather, we are to examine the federal regulation in context. See, e.g., Caraco Pharm. Labs., Ltd. v. Novo Nordisk A/S, ---U.S. ----, 132 S.Ct. 1670, 1680, 182 L.Ed.2d 678 (2012) (noting that courts are to consider questions of statutory interpretation by looking at phrases in the context of the entire statute).

The OFPA provides important context for interpretation of the regulation because the NOP regulations were drafted to "carry out" the provisions of the OFPA. 7 U.S.C. § 6521(a). The OFPA focuses on the producers and handlers of the products that are marketed and sold as organic. See 7 U.S.C. § 6503(a) (directing the Secretary of Agriculture to "establish an organic certification program for producers and handlers of agricultural products"). For example, producers must prepare a plan for the operation of their farms in order to obtain certification to sell their products as organic. See 7 U.S.C. §§ 6504, 6513. They must also certify on an annual basis that they have not sold products labeled as organic "except in accordance" with the OFPA, and producers must allow the certifying agent an "on-site inspection" of their farm every year. 7 U.S.C. § 6506(a)(4),(5). Producers also must keep records for 5 years "concerning the production . of agricultural products sold . as organically produced." 7 U.S.C. § 6511(d).

In addition to these general provisions, the OFPA also establishes certain crop production practices that are prohibited when producers seek to sell products as organic. One of these specific practices provides that in order to be sold as organic, the product must "not be produced on land to which any prohibited substances, including synthetic chemicals, have been applied during the 3 years immediately preceding the harvest of the agricultural products." 7 U.S.C. § 6504(2). The OFPA also specifically provides that producers of organic products "shall not apply materials to . seeds or seedlings that are contrary to, or inconsistent with, the applicable organic certification program." 7 U.S.C. § 6508(a).

When we read the phrase "applied to it" in 7 C.F.R. § 205.202(b), within the context of the OFPA's focus on regulating the practices of the producer of organic products, we conclude that this phrase unambiguously regulates behavior by the producer. In other words, in order for products to be sold as organic, the organic farmer must not have applied prohibited substances to the field from which the product was harvested for a period of 3 years preceding the harvest.[13]

The Johnsons urge us, however, to construe the phrase "applied to it" to include actions of third parties, such as the pesticide drift that resulted from the Cooperative's spraying activity at issue here. The Johnsons base their construction on the use of the word "application" in 7 C.F.R. § 205.202(c) and 7 C.F.R. § 205.400(f)(1). Section 205.202(c) provides that any field from which crops are intended to be sold as organic must have distinct boundaries and buffer zones to prevent "unintended application of a prohibited substance." Section 205.400 details the requirements that a producer must meet in order to gain organic certification. Among other things, section 205.400 requires a producer to "[i]mmediately notify the certifying agent concerning any: [a]pplication, including drift, of a prohibited substance to any field . that is part of an [organic] operation." 7 C.F.R. § 205.400(f)(1). Because these regulations specifically include "unintended" applications and "drift" as types of applications, the Johnsons argue that the phrase "applied to it" in section 205.202(b) must similarly be read to include the Cooperative's pesticide drift. We disagree.

As is true for the OFPA and the NOP as a whole, section 205.202(c) is also directed at the producer of organic products, not third parties. In this section, the NOP requires that producers who have been certified as organic create buffers between the fields from which organic products will be harvested and other fields. This provision therefore does not support the conclusion that section 205.202(b) should be read to cover conduct by third parties.

Similarly, section 205.400 does not support the Johnsons' proposed construction of section 205.202(b). In this section, "drift" is the subject of a specific regulation. Section 205.400 confirms that when the NOP regulates "drift," that intention is made explicitly clear. But section 205.202(b) does not regulate "drift"; instead, it provides that prohibited substances are not to be "applied to" organic fields. The use of different words in the two provisions supports the conclusion that the sections address different behavior. See Burlington N. & Santa Fe Ry. Co. v. White, 548 U.S. 53, 62–63, 126 S.Ct. 2405, 165 L.Ed.2d 345 (2006) ("[T]he question is whether Congress intended its different words to make a legal difference. We normally presume that, where words differ as they differ here, Congress acts intentionally and purposely in the disparate inclusion or exclusion." (citation omitted) (internal quotation marks omitted)). The compliance provision in the OFPA statute—7 U.S.C. § 6511—and the corresponding NOP regulation—7 C.F.R. § 205.671–confirm this interpretation.

The compliance provision requires, as a way to enforce the requirements in the OFPA, that "the certifying agent . utilize a system of residue testing to test products sold . as organically produced." 7 U.S.C. § 6511(a). If the agent "determines" that a product intended to be sold as organic "contains any [detectible] pesticide," the producer may be required "to prove that any prohibited substance was not applied to" that product. 7 U.S.C. § 6511(c)(1). Should the agent determine that the residue came from the "intentional application of a prohibited substance," the product may not be sold as organic. 7 U.S.C. § 6511(c)(2)(A). In addition, if "unavoidable residual environmental contamination" is present on the product "at levels that are greater than" those set for the substance at issue, the product may not be sold as organic. 7 U.S.C. § 6511(c)(2)(B). The OFPA thus contemplates that organic products with some amount of prohibited substance residue on them may be marketed and sold as organic. Specifically, if the residue is caused by "environmental contamination," but does not exceed the requisite levels, the product may continue to be sold as organic. Id.

The NOP regulation that specifically implements this compliance provision in the statute—7 C.F.R. § 205.671—confirms this interpretation. Section 205.671 addresses the disqualifying level for "unavoidable residual environmental contamination" referenced in section 6511 of the OFPA. Section 205.671 provides that a crop cannot be sold as organic "[w]hen residue testing detects prohibited substances at levels that are greater than 5 percent of the Environmental Protection Agency's [EPA] tolerance for the specific residue." 7 C.F.R. § 205.671. Under the plain terms of section 205.671, therefore, crops can be sold as organic even if testing shows prohibited substances on those crops as long as the amounts detected do not exceed 5 percent of EPA limits. But if, as the Johnsons contend, any application—including drift—were prohibited by section 205.202(b), then section 205.671 would be superfluous.

As the Johnsons read section 205.202(b), any amount of pesticide, no matter how it came into contact with the field, would require that the field be taken out of organic production for 3 years. There would accordingly be no organic crops left that would be covered under section 205.671 of the NOP or 7 U.S.C. § 6511(c)(2). And the OFPA and NOP would not need a provision allowing crops with minimum levels of pesticide on them (i.e., less than 5 percent) to be sold as organic because such crops would necessarily have been harvested from fields ineligible for organic production. We are not to adopt an interpretation that renders one section of the regulatory scheme a nullity. See Markham v. Cabell, 326 U.S. 404, 409, 66 S.Ct. 193, 90 L.Ed. 165 (1945) (stating that a law will not be strictly read if such reading "results in the emasculation or deletion of a provision which a less literal reading would preserve."). Because the Johnsons' interpretation nullifies part of the OFPA and the NOP, that interpretation is not reasonable, and we decline to adopt it. We instead conclude that "applied to it" used in section 205.202(b), when read in the context of the OFPA and the NOP regulations as a whole, unambiguously refers to prohibited substances that the producer intentionally puts on a field from which crops are intended to be sold as organic.[14]

When the regulation is read in the context of the NOP and the OFPA as a whole and given the statutory scheme's focus on regulating the practices of producers, we conclude that section 205.202(b) does not cover the Cooperative's pesticide drift. Rather, this section governs an organic producer's intentional application of prohibited substances onto fields from which organic products will be harvested.[15]

Having concluded that "applied to it" refers to situations where the producer has applied prohibited substances to the field, we must consider whether the district court correctly dismissed the Johnsons' nuisance and negligence per se claims based on 7 C.F.R. § 205.202(b). While the district court, both parties, and the court of appeals characterize the dismissal as one based on a lack of prima facie evidence of damages, the Johnsons clearly made a prima facie showing of damages; they actually took their soybean field back to the beginning of the 3–year transition period and lost the opportunity to market crops from that field as organic during that time period. The question therefore is not one of damages but is more properly framed as a question of causation. Cambern v. Hubbling, 307 Minn. 168, 171, 238 N.W.2d 622, 624 (1976) ("If the trial court's rule is correct, it is not to be reversed solely because its stated reason was not correct."). And "[w]hile the existence of [causation] is usually a question of fact for the jury, 'when reasonable minds could reach only one conclusion,' it is a question of law." Lietz v. N. States Power Co., 718 N.W.2d 865, 872 (Minn.2006) (quoting Canada v. McCarthy, 567 N.W.2d 496, 506 (Minn.1997)). In other words, the question presented is whether the Johnsons created an issue for trial that the Cooperative's pesticide drift required the Johnsons to remove their field from organic production due to 7 C.F.R. § 205.202(b). We conclude that they did not.

Construing the evidence in the light most favorable to the Johnsons, their certifying agent, OCIA, directed them to take their soybean fields out of organic production for 3 years. But any such directive was inconsistent with the plain language of 7 C.F.R. § 205 .202(b). It was also inconsistent with the OFPA because the Johnsons presented no evidence that any residue exceeded the 5 percent tolerance level in 7 C.F.R. § 205.671. The certifying agent's erroneous interpretation of section 205.202(b) and the OFPA was the proximate cause of the Johnsons' injury, but the Johnsons cannot hold the Cooperative liable for the certifying agent's erroneous interpretation of the law. The Johnsons' remedy for the certifying agent's error was an appeal of that determination because it was "inconsistent with the" OFPA. 7 U.S.C. § 6520(a)(2).

Under the plain language of 7 C.F.R. § 205.202(b), a third party's pesticide drift cannot cause a field to lose organic certification. The Cooperative's pesticide drift therefore could not proximately cause the Johnsons' soybean field to be taken out of organic production for 3 years. See Flom v. Flom, 291 N.W.2d 914, 917 (Minn.1980) (noting that to satisfy the element of proximate cause there must be a showing that the defendant's "conduct was a substantial factor in bringing about the injury"). Because the Cooperative was not, and could not be, the proximate cause of the Johnsons' damage, we hold that the district court properly granted summary judgment to the Cooperative on the Johnsons' nuisance and negligence per se claims based on section 205 .202(b)....

IV.
In summary, we conclude that the Johnsons' trespass claim, and nuisance and negligence per se claims based on 7 C.F.R. § 205.202(b), fail as a matter of law. To the extent that the court of appeals' decision would reinstate those claims and allow the Johnsons to amend their complaint to include those claims for the 2008 incidents of pesticide drift, we reverse. But we conclude that the district court erred in (1) dismissing the Johnsons' nuisance and negligence per se claims to the extent those claims are not based on 7 C.F.R. § 205.202(b), and (2) denying the Johnsons' motion to amend their complaint to include claims for the 2008 incidents to the extent those claims are not based on trespass or 7 C.F.R. § 205.202(b).

Affirmed in part, reversed in part, and remanded.

DISSENT

I respectfully dissent....

II.

I also dissent from the court's interpretation of 7 C.F.R. § 205.202(b) (2012). That regulation reads: "Any field or farm parcel from which harvested crops are intended to be sold, labeled, or represented as 'organic,' must: . (b) Have had no prohibited substances, as listed in § 205.105, applied to it for a period of 3 years immediately preceding harvest of the crop [.]" The court concludes that this regulation does not apply to the alleged conduct here because a pesticide is not "applied to" a farm if its presence is caused by drift, as opposed to being directly applied by the organic farmer. Our rules of statutory interpretation (which we apply to regulations) do not permit us to add words to a regulation whether the words were "purposefully omitted or inadvertently overlooked." Premier Bank v. Becker Dev., LLC, 785 N.W.2d 753, 760 (Minn.2010). Rather, when we interpret a rule, we consult "the language itself, the specific context in which that language is used, and the broader context of the [rule] as a whole." Robinson v. Shell Oil Co., 519 U.S. 337, 341, 117 S.Ct. 843, 136 L.Ed.2d 808 (1997). In this case, the court concludes that the OFPA's focus on producers and handlers of organic products informs its interpretation that "applied to" in section 205.202(b) refers only to application of pesticides by the organic farmer. This conclusion flies in the face of our rules of construction as well as common sense.

First, the language of section 205.202(b) is silent with respect to who applied the prohibited substances. The plain language of the phrase—"Any field or farm parcel . must: . (b) Have had no prohibited substances . applied to it"— indicates that the concern is what the land in question was exposed to, not how it was exposed, why it was exposed, or who caused the exposure. Moreover, use of the passive voice generally indicates the focus of the language is "whether something happened—not how or why it happened." Dean v. United States, 556 U.S. 568, 572, 129 S.Ct. 1849, 173 L.Ed.2d 785 (2009).

Further, numerous regulations in Title 7, Part 205, explicitly govern the behavior of producers and handlers. See 7 C.F.R. § 205.200 (2012) ("The producer or handler . must comply with the applicable provisions."); 7 C.F.R. § 205.201(a) (2012) ("The producer or handler . must develop an organic production or handling system plan."); 7 C.F.R. § 205.203(a) (2012) ("The producer must select and implement tillage and cultivation practices."); 7 C.F.R. § 205.203(b) (2012) ("The producer must manage crop nutrients and soil fertility."); 7 C.F.R. § 205.203(c) (2012) ("The producer must manage plant and animal materials."). The distinct language in section 205.202(b) is striking in comparison to these provisions. In contrast to the provisions that specifically regulate the behavior of producers, the language in section

205.202(b) focuses on a characteristic of the field and does not refer to the producer, handler, or farmer. While section 205.202(a) implicitly references producers and handlers, by referring to provisions that specifically prescribe their conduct, section 205.202(b) does not do so in any way.

Evidently, under the court's reading of the regulations, if a third party intentionally applies a prohibited pesticide to an organic farm field in a quantity sufficient to leave a residue that violates the regulation, 7 U.S.C. § 6511(c)(2)(A) (2006) would not prohibit the product's sale as an organic product because the producer had not applied the prohibited pesticide. See 7 U.S.C. § 6511(c)(2)(A) (prohibiting the sale of a product as organic if, upon inspection, it is determined that pesticide or nonorganic residue is present as a "result of intentional application of a prohibited substance"). The court's reading makes no sense because no matter who applies the prohibited pesticide and no matter how the pesticide is applied, whether by drift or otherwise, the end product will be no less contaminated and no less in violation of regulations limiting such contamination.

Therefore, I dissent.

GILDEA, Chief Justice.

5.1.3. National Bioengineered Foods Disclosure Act of 2016

The National Organic Program was successful in excluding GMOs as a requirement for certification as "organic" by 2000, but the controversy still continued that began with the first case in this chapter, *International Diary Foods*.

5.1.3.1 The Return of the Labeling Controvery

In 2016 Congress passed an amendment to the Agricultural Marketing Act of 1946, which required the USDA to promulgate regulations to label food containing genetically modified organisms (GMOs). In order to overcome a Constitutional right not to speak articulated in *International Diary Foods*, a Congressional finding that included a compelling government interest that outweighed the right-not-to-speak was required. In addition, the Congress had to have authority to regulate this area, which it assumed because of the different labeling programs from state to state, making this a burden on interstate commerce.

In 2017, USDA promulgated regulations for labeling bioengineered foods.

These regulations require that food manufacturers, importers and retailers who package and label food for retail sale or bulk sale, are subject to this labeling requirement. Excluded from the scope of this regulation are restaurants and small food manufacturers (defined as having annual receipts less than $2.5 million). Lists of bioengineered foods and their trade names will be used for uniformity and disclosure on labeling. Actual knowledge that the seller has a bioengineered food not on the list, they are still obligated to disclose it.

Detectability is one standard for disclosure. Exemptions for up to five percent that is inadvertent or technically unavoidable the regulated entity must use standard processes. However, if there is an intentional use of bioengineered substance or ingredient a disclosure is required. However, an animal that is fed a bioengineered food, does not require disclosure. Any foods certified under the National Organic Program (NOP), it does not require disclosure.

Disclosures must be made on the display panels at the point of sale so that a consumer can see it. Four options for disclosure include on-pacage text, symbol, electronic or digital disclosure or text message (information on the package that will send an immediate response to a consumer's mobile device). The text should say "bioengineered food" or "contains bioengineered food ingredients". A specific symbol must be used, if the symbol option is selected.

December 21, 2018, the USDA released a final rule with the authority of the National Bioengineered Food Disclosure Act of 2016, regarding the establishment of new national mandatory bioengineered (BE) food disclosure standard (NBFDS or Standard). The rule announces,

> "The new Standard requires food manufacturers, importers, and other entities that label foods for retail sale to disclose information about BE food and BE food ingredients. This rule is intended to provide a mandatory uniform national standard for disclosure of information to consumers about the BE status of foods. Establishment and implementation of the new Standard is required by an amendment to the Agricultural Marketing Act of 1946." Effective Date: This rule becomes effective February 19, 2019. Implementation Date: January 1, 2020. Extended Implementation Date (for small food manufacturers): January 1, 2021. Voluntary Compliance Date: Ends on December 31, 2021. Mandatory Compliance Date: January 1, 2022. [83 Fed. Reg. 65814-65876, December 21, 2018].

The statute continues to update the lists of bioengineered foods that must be disclosed, and that list is certain to grow.

In 2019, the Natural Grocers challenged the regulations in a law suit against USDA for failure to comply with the Administrative Procedure Act, as well as claiming the regulation is beyond the scope of the statute. In the U.S. District Court for the Northern District of California (*Natural Grocers, et al. v. Sonny Perdue, Secretary of USDA, et al.*, No. 3:20-cv-05151) they make four claims: (1) the use of QR codes was arbitrary and capricious and contrary to the NBFDS Act; (2) the USDA's exclusion of the terms "GE" and "GMO" is arbitrary and capricious and confusing to consumers; (3) the exclusion of highly refined foods was arbitrary and capricious and beyond the scope of the NBFDS Act; and (4) the Free Speech right of industry to label foods produced through "genetic engineering" is a violation of the First Amendment.

Chapter 6

Biopharma

6.1.1 Genetically-Engineered Pharmaceutical-Producing Plant Varieties (GEPPVs)

Genetically-Engineered Pharmaceutical-Producing Plant Varieties (GEPPVs) plants that are designed to grow a drug, antibody or other pharmaceutical biologic or even industrial chemicals. The USDA regulates all of these plans as genetically-modified (GM) plants which is normally regulated under a either a permit or notification process; except with GEPPVs a permit is always required. Since GEPPVs carry more risk, they are overseen by USDA/APHIS from the field trials process usually requiring an Environmental Assessment and/or an Environmental Impact Statement under the National Environmental Policy Act.

USDA has not created a different process for biopharming but uses enhanced measures to address the increased risk of biopharming plants. The requirement for buffer zones around field trials is doubled for biopharma crops and the objective is to "minimize" contamination of other crops, because the risk will never be zero in a field trial. USDA also keeps the location of field trials as a trade secret in order to avoid vandalism, and also does not require the disclosure of the type of pharmaceutical or the name of the grower to neighbors or the public.

The FDA must also ensure the pharmaceutical or drug meets the standards under the FDCA for safety and efficacy. If the drug is a "biosimilar" it will follow a shorter regulatory pathway. In 2014, FDA gave a fast track authority for the development of the drug ZMapp for emergency use with Ebola patients. This is discussed later in this section.

This multi-layer process for approval of biopharming has made development more difficult, but the risk-benefit protocol is logically a constraint on the control of biopharma.

6.1.1.1   U.S. Department of Agriculture and BioPharming

BioPharming, or the production of crops which are designed to produce pharmaceuticals and the threat of cross-pollination from these GEPPVs (genetically engineered, pharmaceutical-producing plant varieties) increases their risk in field trials. More than 30 states have permitted biopharming trials and Hawaii is one of the most active states for biopharming, according to permits issued by the USDA.

The following case is a challenge to the continued use of land for biopharming by plaintiffs in Hawaii.

6.1.2   CFS v. Veneman and CFS v. Johanns

6.1.2.1 CFS v. Veneman

Center for Food Safety v. Veneman
364 F. Supp. 2d 1202 (D. Hawaii, 2005)

Plaintiffs allege that Defendants permitted open-air field tests of experimental, genetically engineered, pharmaceutical-producing plant varieties ("GEPPVs") of crops such as corn. These plant varieties are engineered to produce biologically active drugs, hormones, vaccines and industrial chemicals. [Plaintiffs state that Defendants have issued permits allowing companies to grow crops in Hawaii to produce proteins such as cytokines, which suppress the immune system, interferon alpha, which may cause dementia and neurotoxicity, avidin, known to cause Vitamin B deficiency, and trypsin, an inhalant allergen known to cause occupational asthma in workers, amongst others.]

Plaintiffs assert that Hawaii has become a preferred site for field testing genetically engineered crops at thousands of plot locations throughout the islands. Plaintiffs' first through fifth claims involve Defendants' alleged failure to comply with NEPA in the promulgation of the field tests at issue in the instant case. Plaintiffs maintain that Defendants never prepared an Environmental Impact Statement ("EIS") or environmental assessment ("EA") as they claim was required by NEPA before approving the permits at issue. Plaintiffs allege violations of ESA, 16 U.S.C. § 1533 et seq. in their sixth through tenth claims in part for Defendants' failure to consult with the United States Fish and Wildlife Service ("FWS") prior to issuing the permits.

Plaintiffs next assert in their eleventh claim for relief that Defendants violated the Plant Protection Act ("PPA"), 7 U.S.C. § 7701 et seq., and the Administrative Procedure Act ("APA"), 5 U.S.C. 551 et seq., by arbitrarily and capriciously denying their request to promulgate regulations under the PPA to both prohibit the challenged field tests generally and also prohibit the use of food crops affected by the tests. Plaintiffs seek declaratory and injunctive relief to compensate Plaintiffs for the risks Defendants' actions pose to public health, the environment, and the economy.

The "capable of repetition, yet evading review" exception to the general principle that a court must dismiss claims that are rendered moot was first established by the Supreme Court in Southern Pacific Terminal Co. v. ICC. (1911). There are two requirements that must exist for the exception to apply: "(1) the duration of the challenged action is too short to allow full litigation before it ceases, and (2) there is a reasonable expectation that the plaintiffs will be subjected to it again.

In the instant case, the Court finds evidence supporting the existence of both required elements. First, the Court evaluates whether the underlying action is almost certain to run its course before a court can give the case full consideration. Regarding the field test plantings at issue, the period between the first planting and the last harvest ranged from less than a week to more than a year; all terminated in less than two years. Moreover, APHIS announced in a letter dated January 14, 2004, a rule limiting the duration of biopharmaceutical permits and plantings to one growing season, or a maximum of one year. No stretch of the imagination would allow this Court to conclude that one year is sufficient time for a claim to be adjudicated from the trial level through appellate review. Indeed, in the instant case, one year was not sufficient time to allow even the completion of discovery or the litigation of jurisdictional issues. This finding is consistent with Ninth Circuit precedent, which has held that challenges to two-year permits meet the durational requirement for the exception, because two years is not a sufficient period of time to allow full litigation. The second, the Court must assess whether the challenged action will probably affect the Plaintiffs in the future. As Plaintiffs note, Defendants have themselves repeatedly asserted that the activity will recur on these cites. Indeed, Defendants own declarant, Dr. Neil Hoffman, stated the following:

Historically, biotechnology companies have used the same field-test sites repeatedly. This is particularly true in Hawaii where much of their breeding work goes on year round. BRS staff contacted Dow and Garst, two companies that recently had GEPPV trials in Hawaii. Garst has been at the

183

same site since 1985 and has a 30 year lease on the property they are using. Dow has been using the same site since the 1960s. Therefore, it is a certainty that the locations previously used for GEPPVs will be used in the near future for other field trials, both pursuant and subject to future permits.

Moreover, the Court finds that not only is it likely that such testing will continue in Hawaii, but it is also likely that the testing will continue under the circumstances to which Plaintiffs object. During the pendency of this lawsuit, at least 25 applications have been filed seeking permission to conduct biopharmaceutical field tests in other jurisdictions across the nation, and at least 10 have been approved by Defendants without an EIS or EA. As such, the Court finds that the record evidences a probability that the challenged action will affect Plaintiffs in the future.

The Court finds that declaratory and equitable relief is still available to Plaintiffs, regardless of the completion of the testing at issue. As shown in the Ninth Circuit's previous decisions, such equitable relief could include a court order requiring of study of the impact the crop testing ultimately had on the surrounding environment, and if necessary, to take remedial measures. The Court does not reach any ruling regarding the propriety of such a remedy, should Plaintiffs ultimately prevail on the merits of their case; the possibility is only raised hypothetically to show that equitable remedies remain available and the case is not mooted. Moreover, claims ten and eleven of Plaintiffs' complaint, which seek declaratory judgment regarding alleged programmatic violations of the Endangered Species Act, Plant Protection Act, and Administrative Procedure Act, are not affected by Defendants' mootness argument at all.

6.1.2.2   CFS v. Johanns

Center for Food Safety v. Johanns
451 F.Supp.2d 1165 (D.Hawai'i 2006)

J. MICHAEL SEABRIGHT, District Judge.

I.   INTRODUCTION

From 2001 to 2003, four companies-ProdiGene, Monsanto, Hawaii Agriculture Research Center (HARC), and Garst Seed-planted corn and sugarcane that had been genetically modified to produce experimental pharmaceutical products. The companies modified the genetic structure of the corn or sugarcane so that, when harvested, the plants would contain hormones, vaccines, or proteins that could be used to treat human illnesses. For example, one company engineered corn to produce experimental vaccines for the Human Immunodeficiency Virus and the Hepatitis B virus, while another company engineered corn and sugarcane to produce cancer-fighting agents. These techniques are still experimental, and from 2001 to 2003 these four companies con- ducted limited field tests of these genetically engineered pharmaceutical-producing plant varieties ("GEPPVs") on Kauai, Maui, Molokai, and Oahu.

ProdiGene, Monsanto, HARC, and Garst Seed received permits to plant these crops from the United States Department of Agriculture, Animal and Plant Health Inspection Service ("APHIS"). The companies have already planted and harvested these crops, the permits have expired, and the companies are no longer planting crops pursuant to these permits.

The Plaintiffs argue that APHIS2 broke the law in issuing these permits. Because these crops produce experimental pharmaceutical products, the Plaintiffs argue, their effect on Hawaii's ecosystem (especially Hawaii's 329 endangered and threatened species) is unclear. The Plaintiffs contend that these experimental crops could cross-pollinate with existing food crops, thus contaminating the food supply.

The Plaintiffs also argue that animals that feed on corn (as well as animals further up the food chain that feed on corn-eating ani- mals) would become unwitting carriers of experimental pharmaceutical products, causing even more widespread dissemination of these experimental vaccines, hormones, and proteins. According to the Plaintiffs, APHIS was required to evaluate the environmental impact of these genetically engineered crops before issuing the permits. In failing to do so, the Plaintiffs argue, APHIS violated both the National Environmental Policy Act ("NEPA") and the Endangered Species Act ("ESA"). The Plaintiffs also argue that these four permits were part of a broader "GEPPV program": a collection of policies and protocols which, taken together, form a comprehensive program for the promotion and regulation of GEPPV development and testing. The Plaintiffs contend that APHIS was required to consider the environmental impact of the program as a whole and that APHIS's failure to do so constitutes an additional violation of NEPA and the ESA. As a remedy for failing to follow NEPA and the ESA in implementing this "GEPPV program;' the Plaintiffs seek a nationwide ban on all GEPPV open-air field testing until APHIS complies with NEPA and the ESA. APHIS, on the other hand, argues that it fulfilled its statutory obligations. APHIS contends that it placed strict conditions on the permits to ensure that the genetically modified crops would not contaminate the environment, such that it complied with both the ESA and NEPA.

According to APHIS, because the Plaintiffs have failed to demonstrate any environ- mental harm from these open-air field tests, the Plaintiffs' claims necessarily fail. And as for the alleged "GEPPV program;' APHIS argues that its internal policies and protocols do not rise to the level of "final agency action"; consequently, APHIS contends, the Plaintiffs are not entitled to judicial review of this "program."

In addition to the dispute over the four permits and the alleged "GEPPV program;' there is a dispute over a petition for rulemaking submitted to APHIS by the Plaintiffs. The Plaintiffs submitted their Petition to APHIS on December 16, 2002; the Petition sought five specific actions from APHIS, and the Plaintiffs argue that APHIS arbitrarily and capriciously denied the Petition. APHIS contends that the Plaintiffs' claims are not ripe and must be dismissed.

After more than two and a half years of contentious litigation, the court heard the parties' motions for summary judgment on July 7, 2006.

Based on the following, the court GRANTS IN PART and DENIES IN PART the Plaintiffs' motion for summary judgment and GRANTS IN PART and DENIES IN PART the Defendants' motion for summary judgment.

The court concludes that APHIS violated both the ESA and NEPA in issuing the four permits, but concludes that injunctive relief is not necessary to remedy these violations. The court then concludes that APHIS's alleged "GEPPV program" was neither a "final agency action" subject to review under the Administrative Procedure Act nor "agency action" subject to the requirements of the ESA.

II. BACKGROUND
A. Legal Framework
A brief description of the legal framework applicable to the instant case may assist in placing the facts in context. The Plaintiffs allege APHIS violated the ESA, NEPA, and the Plant Protection Act ("PPA"); the court first discusses the Administrative Procedure Act ("APA"), which provides for judicial review of agency action, and then examines the ESA, NEPA, and the PPA.

1. Administrative Procedure Act

The APA allows for judicial review of "[a]gency action made reviewable by statute and final agency action for which there is no other adequate remedy in a court [.]" 5

U.S.C. § 704. The APA defines "agency action" as "includ[ing] the whole or a part of an agency rule, order, license, sanction, relief, or the equivalent or denial thereof, or fail- ure to act[.]" 5 U.S.C. §551(13). As discussed more fully infra,some statutes (such as the ESA) contain provisions allowing for greater judicial review than that provided in the APA, whereas many statutes (such as NEPA) do not contain their own review standards (such that the APA standards control). As set forth in 5 U.S.C. § 706, the "arbitrary and capricious" standard of review applies to judicial review of agency actions:

The reviewing court shall-
(1)   compel agency action unlawfully withheld or unreasonably delayed; and
(2)   hold unlawful and set aside agency action, findings, and conclusions found to be-
(A)   arbitrary, capricious, an abuse of discretion, or otherwise not in accordance with law;
(B)   contrary to constitutional right, power, privilege, or immunity;
(C)   in excess of statutory jurisdiction, authority, or limitations, or short of statutory right; [or]
(D)   without observance of procedure required by law

2.   Endangered Species Act [l]
One of the express policies of the Endangered Species Act, 16 U.S.C. § 1531 et seq., is to ensure "that all Federal departments and agencies shall seek to conserve endangered species and threatened species[.]" 16 U.S.C. § 153l(c)(l). The ESA mandates interagency collaboration, through a series of procedural requirements outlined in the statute, to ef- fectuate Congress's goals of protecting endangered and threatened plant and animal species. 16 U.S.C. §§1532, 1536. Specifically, the ESA requires the following:

[E]ach Federal agency shall request of the Secretary [of the Interior] information whether any species which is listed or proposed to be listed [as an endangered species or a threatened species] may be present in the area of such proposed action. If the Secretary advises, based on the best scientific and commercial data available, that such species may be present, such agency shall conduct a biological assessment for the purpose of identify- ing any endangered species or threatened species which is likely to be affected by such ac- tion. 16 U.S.C. § 1536(c)(l); 50 C.F.R. §402.12(c) (requiring federal agencies to request information regarding listed species and critical habitat from the Department of the Interior) . In other words, whenever an agency is considering taking an "action;' that agency must request a list, from either the United States Fish and Wildlife Service ("FWS") or the National Marine Fisheries Service ("NMFS"), of those endangered and threatened species present in the geographic area of the proposed action .

[T]he APA allows for judicial review of "[a]gency action made reviewable by statute and final agency action for which there is no other adequate remedy in a court[.]" 5

U.S.C. § 704. The ESA falls into the former category, as it contains a broad citizen suit provision allowing suits "to enjoin any person, including the United States and any other governmental instrumentality or agency, who is alleged to be in violation of any provision of this chapter or regulation issued under the authority thereof to enforce the ESA." 16 U.S.C. § 1540(g)(l)(A).

The Plaintiffs allege that APHIS failed to follow the procedures outlined in 16 U.S.C. § 1536. These procedural requirements, however, only apply to "agency action;' a term defined by the ESA as "any action authorized, funded, or carried out by" a federal agency. 16 U.S.C. § 1536(a)(2). The joint regulations (promulgated by the United States Fish & Wildlife Service and the National Marine Fisheries Service) implementing the ESA similarly provide:

"Action" means all activities or programs of any kind authorized, funded, or carried out, in whole or in part, by Federal agencies in the United States or upon the high seas. Examples include, but are not limited to: (a) actions intended to conserve listed species or their habi- tat; (b) the promulgation of regulations; (c) the granting of licenses, contracts, leases, ease- ments, rights-of-way, permits, or grants-in-aid; or (d) actions directly or indirectly causing modifications to the land, water, or air. 50 C.F.R. §402.02. APHIS does not dispute that is- suance of the four permits is "agency action" sufficient to trigger the requirements of the ESA. The parties disagree, however, as to whether APHIS 's purported "GEPPV program" is an "agency action" within the meaning of the ESA. As discussed infra, the court concludes that this "GEPPV program" is not an "agency action" under the ESA.

3.   National Environmental Policy Act
The National Environmental Policy Act, 42 U.S.C. §4321 et seq., states that "each per- son should enjoy a healthful environment and that each person has a responsibility to con- tribute to the preservation and enhancement of the environment:' 42 U.S.C. §4331(c). To that end, NEPA

requires federal agencies to evaluate the impact of their actions on the natural environment. See 42 U.S.C. §4332. Specifically, NEPA requires all federal agencies to "include in every recommendation or report on proposals for legislation and other major Federal actions significantly affecting the quality of the human environment, a detailed statement by the responsible official on the environmental impact of the proposed action[.]" 42 U.S.C. §4332(2)(c). Through NEPA, Congress established the Council on Environmental Quality ("CEQ"), which has promulgated regulations requiring all agencies to comply with certain procedures before acting. 42 U.S.C. §4342; 40 C.F.R. Part 1500. The CEQ regulations require agencies to prepare an "environmental assessment"("EA") and/or an "environmental impact statement" ("EIS") before acting, except in limited circumstances. 40 C.F.R. §§1501.3, 1501.4. An EIS is "a detailed written statement as required by" NEPA, and an EA is "a concise public document" that an agency prepares when deciding whether it needs to prepare a more extensive EIS. 40 C.F.R. §§1508.9, 1508.11.

There are circumstances under which an agency may avoid preparing either an EA or an EIS. The CEQ regulations allow federal agencies to develop "categorical exclusion[s]" to the EA/EIS requirements for routine agency actions that are known to have no significant effect on the human environment:

Categorical exclusion means a category of actions which do not individually or cumulatively have a significant effect on the human environment and which have been found to have no such effect and for which, therefore, neither an environmental assessment nor an environmental impact statement is required . Any procedures under this section shall provide for extraordinary circumstances in which a normally excluded action may have a significant environmental effect. 40 C.F.R . § 1508.4.

APHIS promulgated its own regulations to ensure that its actions complied with NEPA and with the CEQ regulations. In 7 C.F.R . § 372.5, APHIS describes four categories of actions : "Actions normally requiring environmental impact statements"; "Actions normally requiring environmental assessments but not necessarily environmental impact statements"; "Categorically excluded actions"; and "Exceptions for categorically excluded actions." (Italics omitted.) In other words, 7 C.F.R. § 372.5 generally tracks the CEQ's requirements (as set forth in 40 C.F.R. § 1508.4): it allows federal agencies to develop categorical exclusions, but requires agencies to "provide for extraordinary circumstances in which a normally excluded action may have a significant environmental effect."

The APHIS regulations regarding categorically excluded actions provide in relevant part: This class of APHIS actions shares many of the same characteristics as the class of actions that normally requires environmental assessments but not necessarily environmental impact statements. The major difference is that the means through which adverse environmental impacts may be avoided or minimized have actually been built right into the actions themselves. The efficacy of this approach generally has been established through testing and/or monitoring [Types of categorically excluded actions] include: (3) Licensing and permitting (ii) Permitting, or acknowledgement of notifications for, confined field releases of genetically engineered organisms and products[.] 7 C.F.R. §372.S(c). The relevant exception to this categorical exclusion appears in 7 C.F.R. § 372.5(d): Whenever the decision maker determines that a categorically excluded action may have the potential to affect "significantly" the quality of the "human environment;' as those terms are defined at 40 CFR 1508.27 and 1508.14, respectively, an environmental assessment or an environmental impact statement will be prepared.

For example: (4) When a confined field release of genetically engineered organisms or products involves new species or organisms or novel modifications that raise new issues. In sum, APHIS does not need to prepare an EA or an EIS when it issues permits for actions in which "the means through which adverse environmental impacts may be avoided or minimized have actually been built right into the actions themselves" -such as "confined field release[s] of genetically engineered organisms and products" - so long as those field releases do not "involve[ ] new species or organisms or novel modifications that raise new issues." In interpreting the statutes and regulations cited supra, the Ninth Circuit has held that, "[w]hen an agency decides to proceed with an action in the absence of an EA or EIS, the agency must adequately explain its decision." Alaska Ctr. For the Env't v. U.S. Forest Serv., 189 F.3d 851, 859 (9th Cir.1999). "NEPA's proce- dural requirements require agencies to take a 'hard look' at the environmental conse- quences of their actions. A hard look includes 'considering all foreseeable direct and in- direct impacts.'" Earth Island Inst. v. U.S. Forest Serv., 442 F.3d 1147, 1159 (9th Cir.2006) (quoting Idaho Sporting Cong. v. Rittenhouse, 305 F.3d 957, 973 (9th Cir.2002)). '"An agency cannot avoid its statutory responsibilities under NEPA merely by asserting that an activity it wishes to pursue will have an insignificant effect on the environment.'" Alaska Ctr. for the Env't, 189 F.3d at 859 (quoting Jones v. Gordon, 792 F.2d 821, 828 (9th Cir.1986)). To comply with NEPA, '"[t]he agency must supply a convincing statement of reasons why potential effects are insignificant.'" Id. (quoting Steamboa tersv. Fed . Energy Regulatory Comm'n, 759 F.2d 1382, 1393 (9th Cir.1985)) .

There does not appear to be any specific process an agency must follow in determining that a categorical exclusion applies and that an exception to that exclusion does not apply; the agency must simply explain its decision in a reasoned manner. Once again, however, a court may only review an agency's activity if that activity rises to the level of "final agency action." Unlike the ESA, NEPA does not contain its own definition of "agency action." Instead, NEPA uses the definition from the APA, which provides that "'agency action' includes the whole or a part of an agency rule, order, license, sanction, relief, or the equivalent or denial thereof, or failure to act[.]" 5 U.S.C. §551(13). As with the Plaintiffs' ESA claims, APHIS does not dispute that issuance of the four permits is "agency action" sufficient to trigger the requirements of NEPA, but APHIS argues that the alleged "GEPPV program" is not "agency action" within the meaning of NEPA and the APA. As discussed infra, the court concludes that this "GEPPV program" is not a "final agency action" under NEPA.

4.   Plant Protection Act

The Plant Protection Act ("PPA"), 7 U.S.C. § 7701 et seq., was enacted in 2000 to at- tempt to detect, control, eradicate, and suppress plant pests and noxious weeds. 7 U.S.C. § 7701(1). The PPA gives the Secretary of Agriculture the authority to promulgate regulations to prevent the introduction and dissemination of plant pests. 7 U.S.C. §§7702(16), 7711(a). The PPA regulations appear in 7 C.F.R. Part 340.

The Plaintiffs do not claim that APHIS violated the PPA. Instead, as discussed more fully infra, the Plaintiffs contend that they asked APHIS to promulgate rules pursuant to the PPA; that APHIS ignored the Plaintiffs' request for the past three and a half years; and that APHIS's inaction violated the APA. [T] the court concludes that some of the Plaintiffs' claims are unripe inasmuch as they do not address "final agency action"; the court concludes that the remaining claims are ripe but that APHIS's actions were nei- ther arbitrary nor capricious.

IV.   DISCUSSION

In its Second Amended Complaint, the Plaintiffs allege the following: (1) APHIS violated NEPA and the ESA in issuing each of the four permits at issue in this case (Counts One through Four and Six through Nine, respectively); (2) APHIS violated NEPA and the ESA in implementing its "GEPPV program" (Counts Five and Ten, respectively); and (3) APHIS violated the PPA and the APA in failing to respond to the Plaintiffs' Peti- tion (Count Eleven) .

191

Finally, in Section E, the court considers the appropriate remedies in this case and concludes that injunctive relief is not appropriate as to those Counts on which the Plaintiffs prevail.

A.   Endangered Species Act

Hawaii is known not only for its remarkable landscape and beaches, but also for its considerable number of endangered and threatened species. The Fish and Wildlife Service reports on its website that there are 329 endangered and threatened plant and animal species in Hawaii, including thirty-two types of birds. Hawaii has more endangered and threatened species than any other state, and Hawaii's 329 listed species represent approximately twenty-five percent of all listed species in the United States. Although strict compliance with the ESA's procedural requirements is always critically important, these requirements are particularly crucial in Hawaii given Hawaii's extensive number of threatened and endangered species.

APHIS argues that it complied with the ESA in issuing the four permits. APHIS points to 50 C.F.R. § 402.14, which provides that "[e]ach Federal agency shall review its actions at the earliest possible time to determine whether any action may affect listed species or critical habitat"; APHIS argues that it determined that its proposed actions would not affect listed species or critical habitat, such that formal consultation was not required. APHIS's argument misses the mark. The problem is not with APHIS's decision not to conduct a formal consultation: APHIS may ultimately be correct that formal consultation was not required (though the court makes no findings on this point), but this is not the real issue. Instead, the problem is that APHIS skipped the initial, mandatory step of obtaining information about listed species and critical habitats from FWS and NMFS.

Regardless of whether the field tests of the genetically modified crops were "confined" (as discussed more fully infra), and regardless of whether APHIS's actions were in fact innocuous with respect to listed species and habitats, APHIS violated the ESA. APHIS engaged in "agency action"- granting a series of permits to field test genetically modified crops-without fulfilling its congressionally mandated duty to obtain information from FWS and NMFS regarding endangered species, threatened species, and critical habitats.

Even if APHIS is ultimately correct in its assertion that no listed species or habitats have been harmed, APHIS 's actions are nevertheless tainted because APHIS failed to comply with a fundamental procedural requirement. APHIS's utter disregard for this simple investigation requirement, especially given the extraordinary number of endangered and threatened plants and animals in Hawaii, constitutes an unequivocal violation of a clear congressional mandate.

In an apparent effort to mitigate, APHIS turns to its second argument: "No harm, no foul." APHIS argues that, because the Plaintiffs have not provided any evidence to show that a single listed species or habitat was harmed in any way, the Plaintiffs' claims necessarily fail. This argument is absurd. An agency violates the ESA when it fails to follow the procedures mandated by Congress, and an agency will not escape scrutiny based on the fortunate outcome that no listed plant, animal, or habitat was harmed. APHIS's argument essentially asks the court to believe that APHIS is immune from suit, no matter how egregious the violation of the ESA, so long as APHIS does not cause any substantive harm to any listed species or habitat.

In other words, APHIS argues that the Plaintiffs may not proceed with a lawsuit against the agency unless APHIS actually facilitates an organism's extinction. This after-the-fact justification (and good fortune) cannot absolve APHIS of its failure to follow a clear congressional mandate. If a project is allowed to proceed without substantial compliance with those procedural requirements, there can be no assurance that a violation of the ESA's substantive provisions will not result. The latter, of course, is impermissible.

In sum, the Defendants' argument is utterly without merit. The court therefore grants summary judgment in favor of the Plaintiffs as to Counts Six, Seven, Eight, and Nine of the Second Amended Complaint.

B.   National Environmental Policy Act

The court concludes that APHIS violated NEPA because APHIS failed to articulate its reasons for declining to prepare an EA or EIS. There is nothing in the administrative record to indicate that, contemporaneously with the issuance of the four permits, APHIS considered the applicability of NEPA, categorical exclusions, or the exceptions to those exclusions. In other words, APHIS failed to provide a reasoned explanation for its apparent determinations that a categorical exclusion applied and that the exceptions to the exclusion did not apply. Consequently, APHIS's actions-granting the four permits were arbitrary and capricious.

1.   APHIS cannot rely on a categorical exclusion post hoc

The court could find nothing in the administrative record to indicate that APHIS considered NEPA when deciding whether to issue the four permits. Nowhere in the administrative record does APHIS discuss the applicability of the categorical exclusion or the exceptions to that exclusion.

As the Ninth Circuit has explained: It is difficult for a reviewing court to determine if the application of an exclusion is arbitrary and capricious where there is no contemporaneous documentation to show that the agency considered the environmental consequences of its action and decided to apply a categorical exclusion to the facts of a particular decision.

APHIS argues that the four permits fit within its broad categorical exclusion in 7 C.F.R. §372.S(c) (environmental mitigation measures built into the agency action itself) and its own more specific categorical exclusion in 7 C.F.R. §372.5(c)(3)(ii) ("confined field releases of genetically engineered organisms").

APHIS cannot, however, abdicate its responsibilities during the administrative process and expect the court to defer to the agency's post hoc explanations. Furthermore, the fact that a field test is "confined" or "controlled" for purposes of the PPA does not necessarily mean that the field test is "confined" within the meaning of the categorical exclusion within APHIS's NEPA regulations. While there may be substantial or complete overlap between 7 C.F.R. Part 340 and 7 C.F.R. §372.5(c)(3)(ii), there must be some indication in the administrative record that APHIS considered the environmental consequences of its actions. NEPA requires no less. APHIS's effort to justify its actions falls short.

Based on the administrative record, the court concludes that APHIS's issuance of the four permits-without an EA, an EIS, or an explanation as to why neither an EA nor an EIS was required-was arbitrary and capricious. Furthermore, as explained in the following section, APHIS's issuance of the four permits without considering the exceptions to the applicable categorical exclusion was also arbitrary and capricious.

2.   APHIS's failure to consider the exceptions to the categorical exclusion renders APHIS's actions arbitrary and capricious. APHIS also argued that it should be held to a lower standard because this was "informal" rather than "formal" agency action. This argument is similarly without merit. The court agrees with APHIS that no formal NEPA document was required and that, as a general rule, an agency action will survive the arbitrary and capricious standard even if the agency was disorganized in performing its review. Nevertheless, an agency action will not survive judicial review where the administrative record fails to reflect any consideration of environmental harm as required by NEPA. "[w]hen a confined field release of genetically engineered organisms or products involves new species or organisms or novel modifications that raise new issues." The Plaintiffs argue that this

exception applies to the four permits at issue, such that APHIS violated NEPA by failing to prepare an EA or EIS. In the instant case, whether the exception in 7 C.F.R. §372.5(d)(4) does apply is unclear, but there is substantial evidence that it may apply. Applications and correspondence submitted by two of the four permittees state that the proposed field tests involve "novel" proteins. Whether the remaining two permit applications involve "novel modifications" that "raise new issues" is unclear. While the idea of genetically modifying food crops to produce experimental pharmaceutical products may certainly appear "novel" to a layperson, this court lacks the expertise to make this kind of determination.

Whether the proposed field tests involve "novel modifications," and whether these modifications "raise new issues," are questions best left to APHIS; the court will defer to APHIS's judgment on these issues, but APHIS must articulate a reasoned decision based on the information available to it. In the instant case, APHIS has simply failed to provide any explanation for its implied determination that the exceptions to the categorical exclusion do not apply. This is not the type of reasoned decisionmaking required of federal agencies, and it cannot stand. The court finds that there is substantial evidence that an exception to the categorical exclusion may apply and that APHIS was required to provide some explanation as to why, in its view, the exceptions did not apply. Consequently, the court concludes that APHIS's issuance of the four permits, without considering the exceptions to the categorical exclusions, was arbitrary and capricious. Therefore, the court grants summary judgment in favor of the Plaintiffs as to Counts One, Two, Three, and Four of the Second Amended Complaint.

C.   The "GEPPV Program"
The Plaintiffs argue that APHIS did more than just issue a series of individual permits: they argue that APHIS developed and implemented an organized, national pro- gram (with coordinated policies, protocols, and regulations) and that APHIS was required by NEPA and the ESA to study the impact of this program on the environment and endangered species. The Plaintiffs contend that APHIS's failure to consider the cumulative impact of its national GEPPV program constitutes a separate violation of NEPA and the ESA (Counts Five and Ten, respectively, of the Plaintiffs' Second Amended Complaint). APHIS argues that there was no "final agency action" for purposes of the NEPA claim and no "agency action" for purposes of the ESA claim, such that the Plaintiffs' claims necessarily fail. The court agrees with APHIS. The court first examines the NEPA claim and then turns to the ESA claim.

1.   NEPA

The APA provides that "[a]gency action made reviewable by statute and final agency ac- tion for which there is no other adequate remedy in a court are subject to judicial review." 5 U.S.C. § 704. And second, the action must be one by which "rights or obligations have been determined," or from which "legal consequences will flow," Port of Boston Marine Terminal Assn. v. Rederiaktiebolaget Transatlantic, 400 U.S. 62, 71, 91 S.Ct. 203, 209, 27 L.Ed.2d 203 (1970).

The Plaintiffs allege that APHIS has a national "GEPPV program" and that this national program has a substantial environmental impact. The court is not persuaded. [I]t is clear that APHIS has some internal policies and procedures by which it operates. An agency's decision to publicly share its internal guidelines and policies does not automatically mean that "final agency action" exists.

Obviously, federal agencies routinely develop internal procedures and protocols in attempting to fulfill their statutory duties, but ... these procedures and protocols do not rise to the level of "final agency action" for purposes of NEPA unless the agency engages in some activity with some direct impact on the environment. Thus, even if the Plaintiffs are correct that "APHIS, through its program, promotes and oversees the development and testing of GEPPVs," the Plaintiffs have not pointed to any "final agency action," apart from issuance of the four permits, that allows for judicial review.

Similarly, the court is unpersuaded that APHIS's PPA regulations evince a broader "GEPPV program" that, in turn, constitutes "final agency action." The Plaintiffs admit that they are not bringing a facial challenge to the regulations themselves; instead, they appear to argue that the regulations, when viewed in concert with APHIS's internal procedures and protocols, constitute a "final agency action" subject to judicial review. Plaintiffs have failed to demonstrate, in their briefing and in oral argument, how these regulations have transformed internal procedures into a "final agency action." The Plaintiffs' fourth argument-that APHIS's programmatic EIS ("PEIS"), currently underway, demonstrates that APHIS has always had a "GEPPV program" is similarly without merit. The Plaintiffs would have the court believe that, any time an agency decides to conduct a PEIS, all agency activity that preceded the PEIS necessarily violated NEPA (because the agency was "acting" without a PEIS in place). If the court were to agree with the Plaintiffs, agencies would have a tremendous disincentive to prepare programmatic environmental impact statements because, according to the Plaintiffs, initia- tion of the PEIS process is essentially an admission that the agency had been violating NEPA prior to initiating the PEIS process. The law is clear as to when a PEIS must be prepared, and no PEIS was necessary for the agency activity relied upon by the Plaintiffs. The fact that APHIS decided to initiate a PEIS does not demonstrate that APHIS engaged in "final agency action" before beginning the PEIS. The Plaintiffs have failed to produce any evidence or point to any genuine issue of material fact demonstrating that there is a reviewable agency action. None of the four items relied upon by the Plaintiffs-either individually or cumulatively-shows that the "GEPPV program" is "final agency action" sufficient to allow for judicial review under the APA. Because there is no "final agency action" for the court to review, APHIS is entitled to summary judgment as to Count Five.

2.   ESA

[T]he ESA contains a broad citizen suit provision. Consequently, the Plaintiffs' ESA claim is not limited by the "final agency action" restriction applicable to the NEPA claim. 16 U.S.C. §540(g)(l)(A). Nevertheless, federal agencies are only required to comply with the ESA's procedural requirements when an agency proposes an "agency action".

Although ESA provides a slightly broader definition of "agency action" than NEPA, the ESA, like NEPA, still contemplates something more tangible than internal agency protocols and policies. Even if the Plaintiffs are correct that APHIS has established an organized method of running a "GEPPV program," the court fails to see how these coordinated polices and regulations constitute an "agency action" separate and distinct from APHIS's action in issuing the individual permits.

In sum, the Plaintiffs have failed to produce evidence of an "agency action;' and with no "agency action," there can be no violation of the ESA (because an agency is only required to comply with the ESA's procedural requirements where the agency proposes to engage in "agency action"). Consequently, the court grants summary judgment in favor of APHIS as to Count Ten of the Plaintiffs' Second Amended Complaint.

D.   Plant Protection Act

In Count Eleven of their Second Amended Complaint, the Plaintiffs contend that APHIS has essentially denied their December 16, 2002 Petition and that this effective denial was arbitrary and capricious. The Defendants argue that APHIS never denied the Petition, such that the Plaintiffs' claims are unripe. Consequently, the court concludes that [some of] the Plaintiffs' claim is unripe and grants summary judgment in favor of the Defendants.

E. Remedies

The court agrees with Plaintiffs' assessment of the situation: injunctive relief is inappropriate as to Counts One through Four and Six through Nine. The most the court could do is issue an injunction stating that APHIS must comply with NEPA, the ESA, and the APA; given that APHIS is already required to do all those things, and given that the permits have all expired (such that there is no ongoing or pending agency action to enjoin), the court sees no reason to issue an injunction.

V.   CONCLUSION

Based on the foregoing, the court GRANTS summary judgment in favor of the Plaintiffs as to Counts One, Two, Three, Four, Six, Seven, Eight, and Nine of their Second Amended Complaint, and the court GRANTS summary judgment in favor of the Defendants as to Counts Five, Ten, and Eleven of the Plaintiffs' Second Amended Complaint....

IT IS SO ORDERED.
DATED: Honolulu, Hawaii, August 31, 2006.

6.1.3   Golden rice, ZMapp, Vit. A Tomato

6.1.3.1   Golden Rice

Golden Rice is a variety of rice genetically engineered to biosynthesize beta-carotene, a precursor of vitamin A. This rice was developed in an attempt to offer a convenient self-sustaining solution to areas suffering from a shortage of dietary vitamin A. In many developing parts of the world, vitamin A deficiency represents a prominent health problem, with 670,000 children under the age of five estimated to be killed each year. While the primary means of combating vitamin A deficiency involves the use of vitamin supplements, the local cultivation of Golden Rice could offer a simpler and less expensive alternative in areas where rice is a staple food. The company that developed Golden Rice, Syngenta, has offered royalty-free use of the patented product for subsistence farmers who make less than $10,000 per year on the produce. Despite these efforts, Golden Rice has been met with significant opposition from environmental and anti-globalization groups. Some of the primary concerns include the potential contamination of native rice with genetically modified rice; the large amount of Golden Rice required to be ingested to meet the minimum vitamin A daily requirement; and the avoidance of the issue of a lack of green, leafy vegetables in the diet of affected persons. At present, research continues on the feasibility of using Golden Rice as a solution to global vitamin A deficiency.

Note from Fed Reg (2019):

2. Rice: AMS is aware that the Philippine Department of Agriculture approved the safety of bioengineered rice (Event—GR2E, Production of provitamin A carotenoids), also known as golden rice, for use as human food.[8] While this approval has to do with the safety of the rice as human food, the rice is not yet authorized for commercial production. Because this rice has not yet been authorized for commercial release and is not in legal commercial production, it does not meet the criteria identified in 7 CFR 66.7(a)(4) and AMS is not recommending it be added to the List. AMS seeks comment on its understanding of the current status of this rice.

6.1.3.2 ZMapp

ZMapp is a therapeutic that was developed as a rapid response to Ebola in the 2013-2014 epidemic. The World Health Organization and the western hemisphere was slow to respond to the epidemic emerging in three of the countries of western Africa (Ivory Coast, Guinea, Liberia). But once Ebola began to spread beyond Africa, the efforts to develop a vaccine and therapeutics accelerated their development. However, behind the scenes, when there is not a pandemic hundreds of U.S. scientists had been working on researching a vaccine or "cure" for Ebola. In addition, there was an intense distrust among the people of west Africa of the western countries profiting from a vaccine and a distrust of their own corrupt governments.

From, Adnan I Qureshi, "West Saharan Response to Ebola Virus Disease Epidemic," chapter in *Ebola Virus Disease: From Origins to Outbreak (Elsevier,* 2016) at https://www.sciencedirect.com/book/9780128042304/ebola-virus-disease (open source at Science Direct).

The reproduction of cells in the tobacco leaf had been an ongoing research process already for about a decade, when the opportunity arose to apply this urgent need to develop antibodies to Ebola, the company, ZMapp was successful with this biotechnology process using a company in Kentucky for the growing process, Kentucky Bioprocessing, a subsidiary of Reynolds America.

ZMapp was not tried on any human subjects when it was determined to meet the experimental use category (EUA) of FDA for use on Ebola patients in October 2014. The World Health Organization also determined it met the requirements through its emergency use in public health emergencies protocol, Monitored Emergency Use of Unregistered and Investigational Interventions (MEURI). https://apps.who.int/iris/handle/10665/250580.

A brief account of the course of the Ebola epidemic in west Africa is given in a book by Michael B.A. Oldstone and Madeleine Rose Oldstone, in *Ebola's Curse*, 2017:

> At this Doctors Without Borders center where Khan now awaited help were others infected with Ebola and also gravely sick. Yet, the center had barely enough ZMapp for three or four persons. Despite his eminence, Dr. Khan was not told that ZMapp was available. The choice of which patients received ZMapp lay primarily in the hands of a team at the Canadian company that made ZMapp and members of Doctors Without Borders at the Kailahun treatment center. But they were not the only decision makers. Also involved were representatives from the World Health Organization, Center for Disease Control and Prevention, and National Institutes of Health. Despite the danger of progressive disease as time passed, the health officials deliberated while considering that neither the antibody's therapeutic effectiveness nor its side effects were known. In the end, they decided not to tell Khan about ZMapp or ask if it could be used on him. Instead, the ZMapp was transported to Guinea where two Ebola-infected victims were treated: a volunteer American physician, Kent Brantly, and a volunteer American health worker, Nancy Writebol, both from Samaritan's Purse charity. Later a priest, Miguel Pajares, from Spain was also given ZMapp. The first two survived but the priest died.

The WHO approved ZMapp in the 2018-19 Kivu Ebola outbreak in the Democratic Republic of the Congo under the MEURI protocol. However, the newer drug, REGENERON, proved to be much more effective than ZMapp and in August 2019, the Democratic Republic of the Congo's national health authorities, the World Health Organization, and the National Institutes of Health announced ZMapp would no longer be used to treat Ebola because REGENERON was much more effective. REGENERON was developed in response to COVID-19 need for therapeutics, was the first drug to be approved by the FDA as an approved treatment for Ebola, October 2020. (https://www.fda.gov/news-events/press-announcements/fda-approves-first-treatment-ebola-virus.)

The hope of GEPPVs continues and we can expect to see more developments in this area of biotechnology.

Chapter 7

Transgenic Animals

7.1.1 Transgenic animals

Transgenic Animals

Advances in scientific discovery and laboratory techniques in the last half of the twentieth century resulted in the ability to manipulate the deoxyribonucleic acid (D)of organisms and gave rise to transgenic animals. The use of transgenic animals may accelerate classical breeding programs and provide a means for the economical production of life-saving pharmaceuticals.

To understand how a transgenic animal is produced, it is necessary to review the basic components and functions of living organisms.

Genes and the Genome

Animals are made of billions of cells all working together. Every cell of the animal has a complete "instruction manual" or genome (pronounced "JEE-nom") that is inherited from the parents of the animal as a combination of their genomes. The genome resides in the nucleus of the cell.

Making a Transgenic Animal

One way to produce transgenic animals is through a technique called *microinjection*. O nce scientists have identified and isolated the piece of DNA comprising the gene to be transferred, it is injected into a fertilized egg of the desired animal using a very small glass needle visualized under a microscope. In approximately one percent of the injected eggs, the gene becomes a new "word" in the egg's "instruction manual" by physically combining with the egg's genome.

I d eally, the new gene integrates into the genome before the egg begins to divide. If this occurs, every cell in the animal can contain the new protein and the animal will pass the gene on to its offspring. After injection of the gene, the fertilized egg is implanted into a surrogate mother where it fully develops into a transgenic animal.

Traits Being Introduced Into Animals

Currently, the only routine commercial use of transgenic animals (primarily mice) is in the area of human disease research. One way to characterize the range of genetic modifications that are being considered for use in animals is in the three broad areas of input, output, and value-added traits. Examples of each are described below.

Input traits

An "input" trait helps livestock and dairy **ro cers** by increasing production efficiency.

Input traits that are being investigated for use in animals:

I.   Faster, more efficient growth rates
II.   Increased production of milk or wool
III.   Resistance to diseases caused by viruses and bacteria

Output traits

An output trait helps **consumers or downstream processors** by enhancing the quality of the animal product.

Output traits that may prove to be beneficial:

I.   Leaner, more tender beef and pork
II.   Milk that lacks allergenic proteins, or results in increased amounts of cheese and yogurt

Value-added traits

By adding or modifying genes, animals can function in completely new ways.

III.   Producing large amounts of therapeutic proteins in animal milk may be an efficient, relatively low cost method to manufacture many proteins used to treat human diseases or proteins that have industrial value.
IV.   Transplanting animal organs into humans, or xenotransplantation, can be made more successful by genetically modifying the organs so that they are not as readily rejected by the human immune system.

Development of animals that serve as models for human diseases to help scientists better understand prevention and treatment strategies.

Risks and Regulation of Transgenic Animals

One concern of transgenic animal technology is the welfare of the animals. Developmental and health abnormalitites have been reported in conjunction with its use; therefore, researchers must take care to minimize animal suffering.

The inadvertent release or escape of transgenic animals (particularly fish) into the wild where they could breed or compete with the natural population is often cited as a potential risk to the environment. T he actual risk associated with this will depend on the type of animal and the nature of the genetic modification; however, where appropriate, procedures must be in place to alleviate this concern.

The Federal level, the Food and Drug Administration, the Department of Agriculture, and the Environmental Protection Agency are required to regulate transgenic animals and their products to ensure that they are safe for public use and the environment. Depending on the nature of the genetic modification, and the proposed use of the resulting animal or product, more than one agency may be involved in the approval process.

7.1.2 GMO Animals, Intl Center for Tech Ass v. Thompson

7.1.2.1 ICTA v. Thompson, the GloFish case

INTERNATIONAL CENTER FOR TECHNOLOGY ASSESSMENT et al.,
Plaintiffs,
v.
Tommy THOMPSON, Secretary, U.S. Department of Health and
Human Services et al., Defendants.

421 F. Supp. 2d 1 (D.D.C. 2006).

MEMORANDUM OPINION
URBINA, District Judge.

DENYING THE PLAINTIFFS' MOTION TO ALTER OR AMEND JUDGMENT

I.   INTRODUCTION

This matter comes before the court on the plaintiffs' motion to alter or amend judgment. The plaintiffs' suit challenges the defendants' decision to allow unregulated commercialization of a genetically engineered ornamental fish and the defendants' alleged failure to comply with the National Environmental Policy Act ("NEPA"), 42 U.S.C. § 4321 et seq. and the Endangered Species Act ("ESA"), 16 U.S.C. § 1531 et seq. On March 30, 2005, the court granted the defendants' motion to dismiss the case. The plaintiffs now request that the court reverse its decision granting the defendants' motion to dismiss. Because this court did not commit a clear error in dismissing the amended complaint, the court declines to alter or amend judgment.

II.   BACKGROUND

A.   Factual Background

The development and use of genetically engineered animals for food and ornamental purposes has become a fast-growing industry in recent years. Am. Compl. ¶ 31. Genetically engineered animals are subject to a wide array of regulatory authority. Defs.' Mot. to Dismiss at 6–9. Under the New Animal Drug Application ("NADA")1 provisions of the Federal Food, Drug, and Cosmetic Act ("FDCA"), the Food and Drug Administration ("FDA") is responsible for approving new animal drug products. 21 U.S.C. § 360b.

At least one manufacturer, Yorktown Technologies, L.P. ("Yorktown"), has developed a line of genetically engineered ornamental or "pet" fish, hereinafter referred to by its trademarked name GloFish. Am. Compl. ¶ 35. The GloFish is a bright red fluorescent zebra fish that contains inserted genetic constructs from a sea coral, which cause the fish to glow under certain kinds of light. Id. Although GloFish are intended for use in home aquariums, the plaintiffs allege that they "could be put to other uses and readily enter the animal and human food chains through accidental or intentional releases." Id.

In the fall of 2003, Yorktown's CEO, Alan Blake, allegedly contacted one of the defendants, John Matheson, Program Officer at the FDA's Center for Veterinary Medicine, to ask about the FDA's views regarding GloFish. Defs.' Mot. to Dismiss at 11; Pls.' Opp'n to Defs.' Mot. to Dismiss *5 at 4. In response to this inquiry, the FDA reviewed materials provided by Yorktown to the public through its website and consulted directly with staff at the Animal and Plant Health Inspection Service of the USDA. Defs.' Mot. to Dismiss at 12; Pls.' Opp'n to Defs.' Mot. to Dismiss at 4–5. After considering the legal, scientific, and policy issues involved in the commercialization of GloFish, the FDA determined that regulation would be inappropriate. Pls.' Opp'n to Defs.' Mot. to Dismiss at 5; Defs.' Mot. to Dismiss at 12. Accordingly, on December 9, 2003, the FDA issued the following statement (the "GloFish Statement"):

Because tropical aquarium fish are not used for food purposes, they pose no threat to the food supply. There is no evidence that these genetically engineered zebra danio fish pose any more threat to the environment than their unmodified counterparts which have long been widely sold in the United States. In the absence of a clear risk to the public health, the FDA finds no reason to regulate these particular fish.

Am. Compl. ¶ 38; Defs.' Mot. to Dismiss at 12. The next day, Yorktown announced on its website that in response to the FDA's decision not to regulate GloFish and due to unprecedented demand, limited numbers of GloFish would be made available immediately, with nationwide sales commencing shortly thereafter. Am. Compl. ¶ 40.

B.   Procedural History

On March 4, 2004, the plaintiffs, seeking declaratory and injunctive relief, filed an amended complaint. The amended complaint makes the claims that the FDA: (1) arbitrarily and capriciously distinguished between food and non-food uses in the GloFish Statement; (2) failed to review Yorktown's request for approval of the GloFish under the statutorily-prescribed standards; (3) failed to prepare an environmental impact statement ("EIS") or an environmental assessment prior to allowing the proposed commercialization of GloFish, in violation of NEPA; (4) failed to prepare an EIS or an environmental assessment with respect to genetically engineered ornamental fish, and other genetically engineered animals generally, in violation of NEPA; (5) failed to prepare a biological assessment and failed to consult with the Fish and Wildlife Service ("FWS") before allowing the proposed commercialization of GloFish, in violation of the ESA; and (6) violated the ESA through its actions with respect to genetically engineered ornamental fish, and other genetically engineered animals generally. Am. Compl. ¶¶ 56–79.

On April 19, 2004, the defendants responded to the complaint by filing a motion to dismiss. On March 30, 2005, the court granted the defendants' motion to dismiss. The court dismissed the first two claims (the "NADA claims") because the FDA's decision not to regulate GloFish is committed to the agency's discretion. Mem. Op. (Mar. 30, 2005) ("Mem.Op.") at 17–25. The court dismissed the third and fourth claims (the "NEPA claims") because the FDA has not taken a major federal action as required by NEPA. Id. at 25–29. Finally, the court dismissed the fifth and sixth claims (the "ESA claims") because the FDA has not engaged in agency action as required by ESA. Id. at 29–32. The plaintiffs subsequently filed a motion to alter or amend the court's judgment. Pls.' Mot to Alter or Amend Judgment ("Pls.' Mot"). The court now turns to that motion.

III.   ANALYSIS

A.   Standard of Review for Motion to Alter or Amend

Federal Rule of Civil Procedure 59(e) provides that a motion to alter or *6 amend a judgment must be filed within 10 days of the entry of the judgment at issue. FED.R.CIV.P. 59(e); see also Mashpee Wampanoag Tribal Council, Inc. v. Norton, 357 U.S.App. D.C. 422, 336 F.3d 1094, 1098 (D.C.Cir.2003). While the court has considerable discretion in ruling on a Rule 59(e) motion, the reconsideration and amendment of a previous order is an unusual measure. Firestone v. Firestone, 76 F.3d 1205, 1208 (D.C.Cir.1996) (per curiam); McDowell v. Calderon, 197 F.3d 1253, 1255 (9th Cir.1999).

Rule 59(e) motions "need not be granted unless the district court finds that there is an intervening change of controlling law, the availability of new evidence, or the need to correct a clear legal error or prevent manifest injustice." Ciralsky v. Cent. Intelligence Agency, 355 F.3d 661, 671 (D.C.Cir.2004) (quoting Firestone, 76 F.3d at 1208). Moreover, "[a] Rule 59(e) motion to reconsider is not simply an opportunity to reargue facts and theories upon which a court has already ruled," New York v. United States, 880 F.Supp. 37, 38 (D.D.C.1995), or a vehicle for presenting theories or arguments that could have been advanced earlier. Kattan v. Dist. of Columbia, 995 F.2d 274, 276 (D.C.Cir.1993); W.C. & A.N. Miller Cos.

v.   United States, 173 F.R.D. 1, 3 (D.D.C.1997).

B.   The Court's Dismissal of the NADA Claims is Not in Clear Error
The plaintiffs' first two claims allege that the FDA improperly refused to regulate the GloFish, and that the FDA's failure to assert regulatory authority over the GloFish violates the NADA provisions of the FDCA. The court dismissed the two claims, argued in the alternative, because the FDA's "enforcement decisions relating to unapproved new animal drug products are discretionary and are not subject to judicial review under the APA." Mem. Op. at 18.

1.   The FDA Properly Refused to Assert Regulatory Jurisdiction Over the GloFish
The plaintiffs' first claim is that the FDA arbitrarily and capriciously denied regulatory jurisdiction over the GloFish. Am. Compl. ¶¶ 39, 58. In particular, the plaintiffs allege that the FDA "arbitrarily and capriciously advised Yorktown that no NADA was mandated" because the FDA mistakenly

believed it lacked jurisdiction to regulate the GloFish. Pls.' Mot. at 4. The court dismissed the plaintiffs' first claim because this is not a case "where the agency refuses to institute proceedings based solely on the belief that it lacks jurisdiction."2 Mem. Op. at 22 (quoting Balt. Gas & Elec. v. Fed. Energy Reg. Comm'n, 252 F.3d 456, 460 (D.C.Cir.2001)).

The plaintiffs' motion to alter or amend judgment simply reiterates the argument that the FDA refused to assert regulatory authority over the GloFish based on the FDA's mistaken belief that it lacks jurisdiction. The plaintiffs, moreover, do not present any new factual evidence to indicate clear error in the court's original conclusion *7 that the FDA was not acting on the basis of a mistaken belief as to its regulatory jurisdiction.3 Indeed, the evidence available, the GloFish statement, states that the FDA "finds no reason to regulate" GloFish. Am. Compl. ¶ 38. Nowhere does the statement indicate that the FDA believed it did not have the authority to regulate GloFish. As the court previously stated, the "FDA is simply exercising its discretion not to take enforcement actions against these particular fish." Mem. Op. at 22. In short, the plaintiffs do not present any new evidence indicating that the court's conclusion that the FDA was not acting under the mistaken belief that it lacked jurisdiction is incorrect. New York, 880 F.Supp. at 38 (denying a motion to alter judgment because the moving party failed to identify new evidence or a clear error of law). Accordingly, the court denies the plaintiffs' motion to alter the dismissal of their first claim.

2. The Plaintiffs Fail to Show Yorktown Submitted a NADA

The court also rejected the plaintiffs' second claim, which alleges, in the alternative, that Yorktown Technologies did submit a NADA, and that the FDA subsequently reviewed the NADA under the wrong regulatory standard. Mem. Op. at 17–18. The plaintiffs move this court to alter or amend the judgment by arguing that the court's dismissal is based on its assumption that Yorktown Technologies did not submit a NADA.4 The plaintiffs argue that the court was required to treat their allegation that Yorktown Technologies submitted a NADA as true for the purposes of analyzing the defendants' motion to dismiss. Pls.' Mot. at 2–3.

Because subject-matter jurisdiction focuses on the court's power to hear the claim, the court must give the plaintiffs' factual allegations closer scrutiny when resolving a Rule 12(b)(1) motion than would be required for a Rule 12(b)(6) motion for failure to state a claim. Macharia v. United States, 334 F.3d 61, 64, 69 (D.C.Cir.2003); Grand Lodge of Fraternal Order of Police v. Ashcroft, 185 F.Supp.2d 9, 13 (D.D.C.2001). Indeed, district courts are required to resolve factual disputes to its subject matter jurisdiction. Phoenix

Consulting, Inc. v. Republic of Angola, 216 F.3d 36, 41 (D.C.Cir.2000). Although the plaintiffs allege that Yorktown Technologies submitted a NADA for GloFish, nowhere in the pleadings do the plaintiffs allege any facts supporting such a conclusion. Rather, the plaintiffs urge the court to treat informal contacts between Yorktown and the FDA as a submission of a NADA. Looking at the evidence, such as the Matheson Declaration, this court determined Yorktown did not submit a NADA. Mem. Op. at 21 n. 10; see also Defs.' Mot. to Dismiss, Ex. A ("Matheson Decl.") ¶ 26. Based on the court's conclusion that the plaintiffs could not show that Yorktown submitted a NADA, the court determined that there were no statutory "guidelines for the agency to follow in *8 exercising its enforcement power," and accordingly, the court did not have jurisdiction to review the claim. Mem. Op. at 21 (citing Chaney, 470 U.S. 821, 105 S.Ct. 1649, 84 L.Ed.2d 714 (1985))

Assuming arguendo that Yorktown submitted a NADA, the court still declines to alter or amend the judgment because the FDA has the discretion to decline to take any enforcement action once a NADA is approved.5 The FDA's decisions not to prosecute or enforce are presumptively unreviewable by the court because such decisions are committed to the agency's discretion. Jerome Stevens Pharma., Inc. v. FDA, 402 F.3d 1249, 1256–57 (D.C.Cir.2005). Thus, assuming arguendo that Yorktown submitted a NADA and that the FDA approved the NADA, the FDA's determination not to take any enforcement actions in connection with the GloFish NADA is discretionary and not subject to judicial review. In sum, the plaintiffs' motion to alter or amend the judgment dismissing their second claim does not contain any new information or new arguments to support their contention that this court has jurisdiction. The court accordingly denies the plaintiffs' motion to alter or amend the dismissal of the NADA claims.

C.   The Court's Dismissal of the NEPA Claims is Not in Clear Error
The plaintiffs also move the court to alter its dismissal of their allegations that the defendants failed to comply with the NEPA requirements. The plaintiffs contend that two FDA actions amount to "major" federal actions triggering NEPA. First, in their third claim, the plaintiffs assert that the defendants' refusal to regulate GloFish constitutes major federal action. Am. Compl. ¶¶ 64–67. Second, in their fourth claim, the plaintiffs assert that the defendants' broader refusal to regulate genetically engineered ornamental fish is major federal action triggering NEPA requirements. Id. ¶¶ 68–73. The court dismissed both of these claims finding that the FDA's activities did not amount to major federal action. Mem. Op. at 23.

NEPA requires federal agencies to prepare an EIS if the agency plans to undertake a "major" federal action "significantly affecting the quality of the human environment." 42 U.S.C. § 4332(C). If the agency has not engaged in a major federal action, NEPA requirements do not apply. Macht v. Skinner, 916 F.2d 13, 16 (D.C.Cir.1990). To trigger NEPA's requirement that an agency prepare an EIS, the agency must undertake an "irreversible and irretrievable commitment of resources to an action that will affect the environment." Alliance for Bio–Integrity v. Shalala, 116 F.Supp.2d 166, 174 (D.D.C.2000) (quoting Wyoming Outdoor Council v. U.S. Forest Serv., 165 F.3d 43, 49 (D.C.Cir.1999)). Agency decisions that maintain the status quo do not constitute major federal actions. Id. Moreover, "NEPA applies only to agency actions 'even if inaction has environmental consequences,' " id. at 174–75 (quoting Defenders of Wildlife v. Andrus, 627 F.2d 1238, 1243 (D.C.Cir.1980)), because "[n]o agency could meet its NEPA obligations if it had to prepare an environmental impact statement every time the agency had power to act but did not do so," Defenders of Wildlife, 627 F.2d at 1246.

1. The FDA's Refusal to Regulate GloFish is Not a Major Federal Action
The plaintiffs allege this court clearly erred in dismissing the third claim because the court looked beyond the pleadings in ruling against them. Pls.' Mot. at 6. Specifically, the plaintiffs allege that the court's dismissal of their third claim was based on the court's determination that no NADA was submitted. Because the plaintiffs' argument is based on a misunderstanding of the court's reasoning and of the applicable law, the court declines to alter its decision to dismiss the plaintiffs' third claim.

The court, in ruling on a motion to dismiss, need not accept "legal conclusions cast as factual allegations." Warren v. Dist. of Columbia, 353 F.3d 36, 39 (D.C.Cir.2004); Browning v. Clinton, 292 F.3d 235, 242 (D.C.Cir.2002). Therefore, assuming arguendo that the court was required to accept the plaintiffs' allegation that Yorktown submitted a NADA for the purpose of ruling on a motion to dismiss, the court was not required to accept the plaintiffs' legal conclusion that the FDA's refusal to regulate GloFish constituted a major federal action under NEPA.

According to the plaintiffs, the defendants have engaged in a "major federal action" triggering NEPA compliance because they have "authorized the sale of a genetically engineered fish that has the potential to significantly impact public health, animal health, and the environment." Pls.' Opp'n to Defs.' Mot. to Dismiss at 31. But, the FDA never authorized the sale of GloFish. Rather, the agency declined to initiate enforcement proceedings against the GloFish manufacturer. The FDA's decision not to regulate GloFish is not an

209

agency action, but rather, an agency inaction. In addition, the FDA has not made an "irreversible and irretrievable commitment of resources" to the regulation of GloFish or the regulation of genetically engineered animals in general that would trigger NEPA's requirements. Id. at 174. To the contrary, the FDA's GloFish statement indicates that no resources are being committed to regulate GloFish because the GloFish Statement explicitly states that the FDA "finds no reason to regulate these particular fish." Alliance for Bio-Integrity, 116 F.Supp.2d at 174. Because NEPA does not require the FDA to prepare an EIS, the declines to alter or amend its original ruling dismissing the third claim.

2. The FDA's Refusal to Regulate Genetically Engineered Animals is Not a Major Federal Action

The court dismissed the plaintiffs' fourth claim, which alleges that the FDA's failure to prepare an EIS with respect to genetically engineered animals violates the NEPA, because the court concluded that the FDA did not engage in a major federal action. Mem. Op. at 23. In moving the court to alter or amend its judgment, the plaintiffs charge the court with committing clear error for failing to interpret the facts liberally in their favor and for misapplying NEPA regulations. Pls.' Mot. at 10. The court's conclusion, however, remains unchanged because the plaintiffs do not present any new evidence or arguments showing that the court committed a clear error.

The court must "treat the complaint's factual allegations—including mixed questions of law and fact—as true and draw all reasonable inferences therefrom in the plaintiff's favor." Macharia, 334 F.3d at 64. The court, however, need not accept as true inferences unsupported by facts set out in the complaint or "legal conclusions cast as factual allegations." Browning, 292 F.3d at 242; see also Warren, 353 F.3d at 39. Here, the plaintiffs *10 urge the court to accept their legal conclusions that the FDA's activities constitute a major federal action as true. These legal conclusions are not binding on the court. Thus, the court declines to alter or amend its judgment.6

D.   The Court's Dismissal of the ESA Claims is Not in Clear Error

The court dismissed the plaintiffs' fifth and sixth claims because they failed to sufficiently allege an agency action triggering ESA compliance. Mem. Op. at 29. The plaintiffs now argue that the court committed clear error in concluding that the FDA's actions concerning GloFish and other genetically engineered animals do not trigger ESA requirements. Pls.' Mot. at 6. Because the plaintiffs have not presented any new arguments or evidence showing that the court committed a clear error, the court denies the plaintiffs' motion to alter or amend the dismissal of the fifth and sixth claims.7

To trigger ESA requirements, an agency must have engaged in an agency action. 16 U.S.C. § 1536(a)(2); 50 C.F.R. § 402.03 (stating that the consultation requirement in Section 7 of the ESA is limited to agency "action in which there is discretionary Federal involvement or control"); Natural Res. Def. Council v. Houston, 146 F.3d 1118, 1125 (9th Cir.1998). "The standard for 'major federal action' under NEPA and 'agency action' under ESA are much the same." Marbled Murrelet v. Babbitt, 83 F.3d 1068, 1075 (9th Cir.1996). "Agency action" is defined by the ESA as "any action authorized, funded, or carried out by" a federal agency. 16 U.S.C. § 1536(a)(2); see Marbled Murrelet, 83 F.3d at 1073. Examples of agency action "include, but are not limited to ... actions intended to conserve listed species or their habitat; ... the promulgation of regulations; ... [and] actions directly or indirectly causing modifications to the land, water, or air." 50 C.F.R. § 402.02.

The plaintiffs' motion asserts that the court's reasoning in dismissing their fifth and sixth claims is based on facts extraneous to the amended complaint. Pls.' Mot. at 6. Specifically, the plaintiffs allege that *11 the court's ruling is based on its determination Yorktown did not submit a NADA. Id. at 6. The court, however, did not base its ruling on this determination. Mem. Op. at 29–30.

The court concluded that the FDA's actions did not constitute agency action because the plaintiffs failed to allege that the defendants engaged in any type of action. Mem. Op. at 30. As the court stated, the FDA simply decided not to engage in enforcement activity. Mem. Op. at 30. The court, furthermore, was not required to accept the plaintiffs' legal conclusion that the alleged inaction constitutes an agency action. Warren, 353 F.3d at 39; Browning, 292 F.3d at 242. As the court explained previously, the plaintiffs mischaracterized the FDA's refusal to engage in enforcement activity as an affirmative action authorizing and approving Yorktown's commercialization of GloFish. Mem. Op. at 30. Consequently, the defendants did not engage in an "agency action" triggering ESA compliance. Fund for Animals, Inc. v. Thomas, 127 F.3d 80, 84 n. 6 (D.C.Cir.1997) (noting that promulgation of policy to refrain from regulating a particular subject matter "most probably would have been no 'agency action' to trigger the ESA consultation requirement").

IV.   CONCLUSION

For the foregoing reasons, the court denies the plaintiffs' motion to alter or amend its ruling granting the defendants' motion to dismiss. An order consistent with this Memorandum Opinion is separately and contemporaneously issued this 8th day of March, 2006.

Footnotes

1. "The Food, Drug and Cosmetic Act ('FDCA') provides that any new animal drug is considered unsafe prior to receiving FDA approval for its intended use. 21 U.S.C. § 360b(a)(1)(A). To secure such approval, the FDCA requires the applicant to file a New Animal Drug Application ('NADA') that includes information demonstrating both the safety and the efficacy of the drug. Id. § 360b(d)(1)(A)." A.L. Pharma, Inc. v. Shalala, 62 F.3d 1484, 1486 (D.C.Cir.1995).

2. Generally, an agency's decision not to prosecute or enforce is committed to the agency's discretion and courts presumptively do not have subject-matter jurisdiction to review actions committed to agency discretion. Heckler v. Chaney, 470 U.S. 821, 831, 105 S.Ct. 1649, 84 L.Ed.2d 714 (1985); Balt. Gas & Elec. v. Fed. Energy Reg. Comm'n, 252 F.3d 456, 459 (D.C.Cir.2001). The presumption against judicial review may be overcome where the agency refuses to institute proceedings based on the mistaken belief that it lacks jurisdiction. Balt. Gas & Elec., 252 F.3d 456, 460 (quoting Chaney, 470 U.S. at 833 n. 4, 105 S.Ct. 1649). See also Mem. Op. (Mar. 30, 2005) ("Mem.Op.") at 18–19.

3. The plaintiffs' only argument with respect to the dismissal of the first claim is a one-sentence statement that it was an error for this court to conclude that the plaintiffs will not be able to prove that the FDA believed it lacked jurisdiction. Pls.' Mot. to Alter or Amend Judgment ("Pls.' Mot.") at 4.

4. The court reasoned that because Yorktown did not submit a NADA, the defendants' decision not to regulate the FDA was "simply a decision not to exercise enforcement authority." Mem. Op. at 21. The court concluded that such a decision is beyond the reach of judicial review. Id. The plaintiffs do not dispute the court's legal conclusion. Rather, the plaintiffs assert that Yorktown submitted a NADA and that the defendants arbitrarily and capriciously approved the NADA.

5. The defendants make this precise argument in their opposition to the plaintiffs' motion. Defs.' Opp'n to Pls.' Mot. to Alter or Amend Judgment at 5 n. 4. The plaintiffs' reply does not make any arguments regarding this court's ability to review the FDA's decision not to take an enforcement action.

6. The plaintiffs also allege that the court committed clear error in applying the NEPA regulations. Pls.' Mot. at 9. Although the plaintiffs charge the court with ignoring 40 C.F.R. § 1502.4(b), the plaintiffs did not include this argument in their opposition to the defendants' motion to dismiss. District courts are not "required to unearth theories and precedents not cited by a party." Bucheit v. Palestine Liberation Org., 388 F.3d 346, 352 (D.C.Cir.2004) (quoting Ned Chartering & Trading, Inc. v. Republic of Pakistan, 294 F.3d 148, 155 (D.C.Cir.2002)). That responsibility is delegated to the party's attorneys. Id. Given the plaintiffs' failure to raise these challenges in the original motions briefing, the court need not address the arguments the plaintiffs present in the instant motion. Turkmani v. Republic of Bolivia, 273 F.Supp.2d 45, 50 (D.D.C.2002) (citing Sequa Corp. v. GBJ Corp., 156 F.3d 136, 144 (2d Cir.1998)). This court's decisions are "not intended as mere first drafts, subject to revision and reconsideration at a litigant's pleasure." Id. (citations omitted). Neither does a motion to alter or amend judgment provide the plaintiffs a second bite at the juridical apple. Id.; see also All West Pet Supply v. Hill's Pet Prods. Div., 847 F.Supp. 858, 860 (D.Kan.1994) (stating that "[a] party's failure to present his strongest case in the first instance does not entitle him to a second chance in the form of a motion to alter or amend"). Moreover, 40 C.F.R. § 1502.4(b) provides no support for the plaintiffs' argument that the FDA's inaction triggers the NEPA requirements. 40 C.F.R. § 1502.4(b) (stating that an EIS may be required "for broad Federal actions such as the adoption of new agency programs or regulations").

7. The court notes that a motion to alter or amend judgment "is not simply an opportunity to reargue facts and theories upon which a court has already ruled." New York v. United States, 880 F.Supp. 37, 38 (D.D.C.1995).

7.1.3 The AquaAdvantage Salmon Controvery

The AquaAdvantage Salmon, developed by AquaBounty Technologies, contains a gene from the Chinook salmon (combined with a promoter from the ocean pout) that enables the salmon to produce enhanced quantities of growth hormone and rapidly reach market size. Although these genetic modifications provide an obvious competitive advantage over traditional salmon aquaculture, this salmon is also touted as an environmentally sustainable alternative to traditional farming techniques.

Specifically, the rearing of these fish in land-based facilities is claimed to reduce the environmental impact on coastal areas, eliminate the threat of disease transfer between farm fish and wild fish, and produce more fish with less feed. The location of the facilities near major consumer markets may also reduce the environmental impacts associated with long-distance trucking, air freight, and ocean shipping.

At present, the AquaAdvantage Salmon is undergoing review by the FDA as the first genetically modified animal to enter the U.S. food supply. In December 2012, the FDA issued a preliminary finding of "no significant impact" pursuant to an Environmental Assessment (EA), finding that the production and grow-out of these fish in secure facilities outside of the United States minimized the likelihood that the fish could escape captivity, survive and reproduce in the wild, and become established in the environment of the United States.

In 2013, the FDA extended the public comment period for the preliminary EA, and no further formal action has been announced on the approval of this fish. Incredibly, two decades have passed between the time that AquaBounty first applied for approval of the genetically modified salmon and the ongoing review.

In 2015, the FDA completed an Environmental Assessment of the AquAdvantage Salmon and here is an excerpt:

> FDA's approach to analysis in this EA is based on a characterization of hazards, an evaluation of potential exposure pathways, and a consideration of the likelihood of any resulting risk. The environmental analysis of consequences in the EA incorporates the principles described above by the National Research Council (NRC, 2002) as well as the U.S. Environmental Protection Agency's (EPA) approach to ecological risk assessment (EPA, 1992). The potential hazards and harms addressed in this EA center on the likelihood and consequences of diploid ABT salmon, and AquAdvantage Salmon, escaping, surviving, and becoming established in the environment, and then dispersing or migrating such that there might be an exposure pathway to the United States, and subsequently causing an adverse outcome (the risk) to the environment of the United States. These hazards are addressed for the production of eyed-eggs and grow-out to market size, within the framework of a conceptual risk assessment model, and the following series of risk-related questions:

> 1. What is the likelihood that AquAdvantage Salmon will escape the conditions of confinement?
> 2. What is the likelihood that AquAdvantage Salmon will survive and disperse if they escape the conditions of confinement?

3. What is the likelihood that AquAdvantage Salmon will reproduce and establish if they escape the conditions of confinement?
4. What are the likely consequences to, or effects on, the environment of the United States should AquAdvantage Salmon escape the conditions of confinement?

For the purposes of this environmental assessment, although AquAdvantage Salmon that will provide food for export into the United States is an all-female, triploid fish from the EO1α lineage, this EA encompasses risks associated with all other lifestages (i.e., gametes through adults), and all of the zygosities and ploidies associated genotypes and phenotypes (i.e., diploids, triploids, hemizygotes, homozygotes females and masculinized females) that are required for the production of the triploid, all-female AquAdvantage salmon to be used for food. In general, when it is important for the purposes of assessing a specific environmental risk, we specify whether an animal is assumed to be reproductively competent, and the term "diploid ABT salmon" is used.

AquAdvantage Salmon and diploid ABT salmon would be produced and grown-out only in secure facilities with multiple and redundant forms of effective physical containment that have been verified and validated by FDA. Based on this analysis, FDA considers the likelihood that AquAdvantage Salmon and diploid ABT salmon could escape from

containment, survive, and become established in the local environments of either the PEI or Panamanian facilities to be very low. This is consistent with the conclusions of Canadian authorities based on their qualitative Failure Mode Analysis of the physical barriers and operational procedures involving containment at both the PEI and Panamanian facilities. The Canadian officials concluded that the potential for both acute failure of physical containment and chronic release of AquAdvantage Salmon[1] is negligible at the PEI facility and low for the Panamanian facility, with at least reasonable certainty. Given this very low likelihood of escape, survival, and establishment in the

---

[1] The Canadian Science Response (DFO). (2013). Summary of the environmental and Indirect Human Health risk Assessment of AquAdvantage Salmon. DFO Can Sci. Divis. Sec. Sci. Respon. 2013/023) refers to all life stages as AquAdvantage Salmon. ("Although the proposed AquAdvantage Salmon product for export to Panama is all-female triploid eyed-eggs from the EO-1α line….other life stages (gametes through to sexually mature adults), genotypes (i.e., diploids, triloid, hemizygotes, homozyotes) and gender (females and masculinized females) are required for the production of the eyed-eggs and are therefore included in the risk assessment").

environments local to the PEI and Panamanian facilities, it is also highly unlikely that AquAdvantage Salmon could disperse and migrate such that there would be an exposure pathway to the environment of the United States.

Should unintentional release occur, the environmental conditions in the geographic settings of the egg production and grow-out sites and farther afield (e.g., the tropical Pacific Ocean) would afford additional means of containment of any escaped eggs or fish, given that these conditions would be generally hostile to their long-term survival, reproduction, and establishment. In Canada, this is evidenced by the lack of Atlantic salmon in the vicinity of the egg production facility even though these fish are native to this area and have been intentionally stocked there in the past. These environmental conditions greatly limit, or in the case of Panama, essentially preclude the possibility of a complete exposure pathway by which diploid ABT salmon or AquAdvantage Salmon, could reach the United States.

In addition, because the production process for AquAdvantage Salmon ensures that populations produced will be triploid (effectively sterile), all-female animals, the possibility of AquAdvantage Salmon reproducing in the wild is likewise extremely remote. The greatest potential risk to the environment of the United States would occur in the event of the escape of diploid ABT broodstock from the PEI facility. These fish are likely reproductively competent, and some will be homozygous for the *opAFP-GHc2* gene. Given that growth enhanced Atlantic salmon in general do not have a reproductive advantage compared to non-GE Atlantic salmon, and sometimes are disadvantaged (Moreau and Fleming, 2011; Moreau et al. 2011a), it is expected that large numbers of fish would need to escape in order for there to be any potential chance of reproduction and establishment, and there is a very low probability of that occurring at the PEI egg production facility due to the small numbers of broodstock maintained at that facility, and the stringent physical containment at that site. In summary, the evidence collected and evaluated by FDA indicates that the proposed action on the NADA for AquAdvantage Salmon, including development, production, and grow-out of these GE salmon under the conditions specified in the application and as described in this EA, would not result in a significant impact on the quality of the human environment in the United States, including populations of endangered Atlantic salmon.

FDA has considered the no action alternative for this action, that is, a decision not to approve the NADA for AquAdvantage Salmon. There are two general likely scenarios to consider as a result of the no action alternative: (1) the sponsor would cease production of AquAdvantage Salmon, and (2) the sponsor would continue to rear AquAdvantage Salmon at the existing locations outside of the United States, and/or at new suitable locations outside the United States (and could decide to sell the eggs, fish, or the technology to producers outside the United States), with no intent to market food from these fish in the United States. There are no potential environmental impacts arising from the first general scenario. If no AquAdvantage Salmon are produced, there will be no production sites and no potential for escape or release of these fish to the environment, and therefore no effects on the environment of the United States. For the second general scenario, production of AquAdvantage Salmon at locations outside the United States for marketing outside the United States (i.e., outside the jurisdiction of FDA)[2], an assessment of potential effects on the environment becomes highly uncertain as the conditions and effects of those conditions are not reasonably foreseeable. Because production of AquAdvantage Salmon would be possible at any number of locations worldwide, under different containment conditions and levels of regulatory oversight, and potentially within areas where native Atlantic salmon and other salmonid species are present, there are far too many variables and unknowns to define specific scenarios and perform a comprehensive risk assessment for them.

July 2016, Congress passed the National Bioengineered Food Disclosure Law, that directed the U.S. Secretary of Agriculture to establish a mandatory standard for disclosing foods that are or might be bioengineered. The standard was issued on December 20, 2018, and defines bioengineered foods as "those that contain detectable genetic material that has been modified through certain lab techniques and cannot be created through conventional breeding or found in nature", effective January 1, 2020. This includes the AquaAdvantage salmon.

---

[2] This scenario, production of AquAdvantage Salmon outside the jurisdiction of the United States, is possible regardless of whether FDA approves the NADA. It appears more likely to occur if FDA does not approve the NADA because ABT would need to produce AquAdvantage Salmon outside FDA's jurisdiction, i.e., outside the U.S. without importing food from such fish into the U.S., if it wished to market food from its GE salmon without FDA regulation.

7.2.1   Oxitec mosquito and the ATryn Goat

7.2.1.1 Oxitec mosquito regulation

Excerpt from Joel Aldrich, OBTAINING APPROVAL FOR THE RELEASE OF GENETICALLY MODIFIED MOSQUITOES: AN ANALYSIS OF THE REGULATORY FRAMEWORK (2015) (unpublished):

> APHIS regulates biotechnology activities that involve animal biologics, plants, seeds, plant pests, animal pathogens, and "regulated articles." "Regulated articles" encompass certain genetically engineered organisms containing genetic material from plant pests. If the contemplated use involves the shipment or release of such regulated articles into the environment, or the shipment of a plant pest or animal pathogen, a permit issued by APHIS will be required. In addition, APHIS is responsible for the regulation of certain intrageneric pathogenic organisms and nonengineered pathogenic organisms, but only if the use of those organisms is tied to agriculture. For situations involving non-agricultural use, EPA serves as the regulatory authority.

> Issues may arise with respect to life forms that do not neatly fit into one the above circumscribed categories, as well as biotechnology work that does not have an end product. If the experimental release of genetically modified organisms does not involve a commercial product, does not involve the work of scientists receiving government funding, and does not come under an experimental use permit section of the law, the Framework does not apply. In order to address these issues, the President's Office of Science and Technology Policy eventually broadened the application of the Framework to all "organisms with deliberately modified hereditary traits," instead of mere organisms formed by the combination of genetic information from different genera or microorganisms containing genetic material from pathogens. In addition, the OSTP reduced the overall regulatory burden on the scientific community by narrowing the regulatory oversight to situations in which the risk posed by introduction of the organism is established by existing information.

> . . .

> VII.   Proposed Regulation of Genetically Modified Mosquitoes as an Animal Drug
> The FDA defines a new animal drug, in part, as "any drug intended for use in animals other than man, including any drug intended for use in animal feed but not including the animal feed, the composition

218

of which is such that the drug is not generally recognized as safe and effective for the use under the conditions prescribed, recommended, or suggested in the labeling of the drug." The FDCA prohibits the sale of a new animal drug in interstate commerce unless the drug is the subject of an approved NADA, abbreviated NADA, or a conditional approval pursuant to 21 U.S.C. § 360ccc. Although new animal drugs generally must comply with these provisions, unapproved investigational new drugs may be exempt from these requirements if the drug fits within the criteria listed in 51 CFR § 511.

In 2009, the FDA published guidance on the regulation of genetically engineered animals containing heritable recombinant DNA constructs (i.e., a construct that may be passed through the lineage of a genetically modified animal). Under this guidance, the FDA considers the FDCA definition of a "drug" to be met by an ". . . rDNA construct in a GE animal that is intended to affect the structure or function of the body of the GE animal, regardless of the intended use of products that may be produced by the GE animal . . . ." Although the regulated article is the rDNA construct within the animal, the FDA frequently refers to the regulation of the whole animal as a short hand. Any animals derived from the same transformation event (e.g., animals containing the rDNA construct as a result of breeding of the genetically modified animal), are considered to contain the same regulated article and are thus evaluated under a single NADA. In order to demonstrate effectives of the regulated article during the NADA approval process, one would need to show that the genetically modified animal had the claimed altered characteristic. Additionally, for commercially available GE animals, sponsors will need to demonstrate that the ". . . construct and/or phenotype are stably maintained in a representative sample of animals. . ." subsequent to NADA approval and use in commerce. Although all such genetically modified animals would be subject to premarket approval requirements, the FDA has decided not take INAD or NADA enforcement actions with respect to certain genetically modified animals. These animals include: "(1) GE animals of non-food-species that are regulated by other government agencies or entities . . . ; and (2) GE animals of non-food-species that are raised and used in contained and controlled conditions such as GE laboratory animals used in research institutions."

Because the transgenic mosquitoes developed by Oxitec contain a heritable rDNA construct that is designed to affect the animal's structure or function (i.e., the DNA construct containing the fluorescent marker and lethal gene designed to prevent to the production of viable offspring), the inserted rDNA construct would seem to fall squarely within the FDA's definition of a "drug" under the FDCA. Additionally, because this construct is being used in an animal other than man and has not yet been evaluated for safety and efficacy under a NADA, the construct further comes under the definition of a "new animal drug." Although the FDA's guidance indicates that the inserted DNA construct is technically the regulated article, in practice it would appear that the entire animal becomes regulated by the FDA. The transgenic mosquitoes also fail to capture the benefit of a GE animal exemption, as the mosquitoes are not being regulated by another government agency and are not being proposed for use in a controlled or contained environment. Although it may seem curious that a genetically modified insect with the potential to affect its own wild population would fall outside of the jurisdiction of the EPA or APHIS, the limitations imposed by the Framework and the underlying statutes demonstrate why these mosquitoes do not come within the proper regulatory jurisdiction of either of these agencies. EPA's regulatory jurisdiction is limited to certain microorganisms and pesticides.

Additionally, APHIS's regulatory jurisdiction is focused on animal biologics, plants, seeds, plant pests, animal pathogens, and "regulated articles." Mosquitoes are not microorganisms, and would not seem to fall within the EPA's definition of a pesticide, which excludes biological control agents such as ladybugs and other insect predators. Although mosquitoes could likely be considered an animal pest and may harbor some animal pathogens (e.g., dengue fever virus and chikungunya virus), the mosquitoes themselves also do not neatly fit within any of the defined biological product categories regulated by APHIS. Accordingly, the genetically modified mosquitoes would appear to cleanly escape regulation by EPA or APHIS under the present Framework and the associated legislation.

. . .

VIII.   Conclusions and Future Directions
An analysis of the regulatory framework applicable to genetically modified insects reveals a confusing array of statutes, regulations, and official policies. While some insects may become regulated under the authority of APHIS due to their agricultural implications, other insects may fall under a more general net of regulation by the FDA. Additionally, it is conceivable that some genetically modified insects might slip through the cracks of regulation altogether, similar to the situation involving GloFish®.

Of the three major agencies involved in the regulation of biotechnology, it would appear that the EPA has the least amount of primary regulatory authority over insects released into the wild. EPA's biotechnology product and research jurisdiction is largely limited to certain microorganisms and biologically-based pesticides (e.g., pheromones and microbial compositions), which would not encompass insects. In contrast, APHIS appears to have broad regulatory authority over both the resulting transgenic insect and the specific incorporated genetic material if either is amenable to categorization as a "plant pest." The transgenic insects most likely to fall under the jurisdiction of APHIS would thus include those insects identified as plant pests (such as the pink bollworm) or those that contain genetic material derived from plant pests.

Among the major regulatory agencies identified in the Framework, the FDA would appear to have the broadest potential to regulate genetically modified insects. The FDA's authority to regulate transgenic insects stems for the agency's ability to regulate drugs, which includes genetic constructs that affect the structure or function of an organism. Historically, however, the FDA has been reluctant to regulate organisms that do not enter the food supply and that do not pose an apparent risk to public health.

––––––––––––––––––

As the prospect of a future of regulating insects for FDA became evident coupled with the problem that the FDA had no expertise in regulating insects, the negotiated authority to FDA to define these animals as drugs due to their genetic alterations and purposes, was reconsidered in 2017. The U.S. Environmental Protection Agency became the lead, once FDA no longer defined mosquitoes as "drugs" leaving EPA to regulate them as "pesticides" under FIFRA. The New York Times reported:

Officials: GMO Mosquitoes Aren't 'Drugs,' Need EPA Oversight
THE ASSOCIATED PRESS OCT. 4, 2017, 3:37 P.M. E.D.T. MIAMI —
U.S. Food and Drug Administration officials say genetically modified mosquitoes are not "drugs" and should be regulated by environmental authorities. According to guidelines posted online Wednesday, federal officials have decided that mosquitoes engineered by the biotech firm Oxitec will be regulated from now on by the Environmental Protection Agency. The guidelines clarify that products intended to function as

pesticides to control mosquito populations should fall under the EPA. The FDA has authority over mosquito-related products intended to prevent or treat diseases. Oxitec releases nonbiting male mosquitoes modified with synthetic DNA to produce offspring that die before maturing. The method aims to reduce mosquito populations that spread Zika and other viruses. Florida officials have sought federal and public approval to follow Brazil and the Cayman Islands in releasing Oxitec's mosquitoes.

The U.S. EPA developed industry guidance October 2017 to clarify the roles of EPA and FDA.

#236

Clarification of FDA and EPA Jurisdiction Over Mosquito-Related Products

Guidance for Industry

Submit comments on this guidance at any time. Submit written comments to the Dockets Management Staff (HFA-305), Food and Drug Administration, 5630 Fishers Lane, Room 1061, Rockville, MD 20852. Submit electronic comments on the guidance at https://www.regulations.gov/. All written comments should be identified with the Docket No. FDA-2016-D-4482.

For further information regarding this document, contact AskCVM@fda.hhs.gov.

Additional copies of this guidance document may be requested from the Policy and Regulations Staff (HFV-6), Center for Veterinary Medicine, Food and Drug Administration, 7500 Standish Place, Rockville, MD 20855, and may be viewed on the Internet at either https://www.fda.gov/AnimalVeterinary/default.htm or https://www.regulations.gov/.

U.S. Department of Health and Human Services Food and Drug Administration

Center for Veterinary Medicine
October 2017

Clarification of FDA and EPA Jurisdiction Over Mosquito-Related Products

Guidance for Industry

I. INTRODUCTION

This guidance provides information for industry and other stakeholders regarding regulatory oversight of articles, including substances, for use in or on mosquitoes ("mosquito-related products"). We are providing this guidance to clarify circumstances under which such products are regulated by the Food and Drug Administration (FDA) as new animal drugs under the Federal Food, Drug, and Cosmetic Act (FD&C Act) and other circumstances under which such products are regulated by the Environmental Protection Agency (EPA) as pesticides under the Federal Insecticide, Fungicide, and Rodenticide Act (FIFRA).

FDA's guidance documents, including this guidance, do not establish legally enforceable responsibilities. Instead, guidances describe the Agency's current thinking on a topic and should be viewed only as recommendations, unless specific regulatory or statutory requirements are cited. The use of the word *should* in the Agency's guidances means that something is suggested or recommended, but not required.

V. BACKGROUND

Both FDA and EPA regulate products intended for use in or on animals. FDA is charged with protecting the public health by, among other things, ensuring that animal drugs are safe and effective [21 U.S.C. §393(b)(2)(B)]; under FIFRA, EPA is charged with protecting human health and the environment by ensuring registered pesticide products, when used according to the label directions, result in no unreasonable adverse effects to man or the environment. [7 U.S.C. §136a(c)(5)].

A. New Animal Drugs

The FD&C Act defines the term "drug" as, among other things, "articles intended for use in the diagnosis, cure, mitigation, treatment, or prevention of disease in man or other animals" and "articles (other than food) intended to affect the structure or any function of the body of man or other animals." [21 U.S.C. §321(g)(1)]. With very limited exceptions for animal drugs that are generally recognized as safe and effective or are subject to a "grandfather" clause, the FD&C Act defines drugs that are intended for use for animals as "new animal drugs." As such, these drugs

are subject to applicable pre-market approval and/or other review requirements. [21 U.S.C.

223

§321(v); 21 U.S.C. §360b; 21 U.S.C. §360ccc; 21 U.S.C. §360ccc-1].

B.   Pesticides

FIFRA defines the term "pesticide" to mean, in part, "(1) any substance or mixture of substances intended for preventing, destroying, repelling, or mitigating any pest...except that the term 'Pesticide' shall not include any article that is a 'new animal drug' within the meaning of section 321([v]) of title 21..." [7 U.S.C. §136(u)]. Generally speaking, pesticides must be registered with EPA prior to distribution or sale, unless they are otherwise excluded or exempted from regulation (e.g., they meet the specific conditions or criteria in 40 CFR § 152.6; or they qualify for an exemption as, for instance, a minimum risk pesticide under 40 CFR § 152.25(f)).

VI.   DISCUSSION

A.   Scope of Guidance

This guidance provides information for industry and other stakeholders regarding regulatory oversight of mosquito-related products. This guidance is important in light of the public health urgency of countering the spread of mosquito-borne disease, such as that caused by the Zika virus. Vector control is a critical element of the effort to combat the spread of mosquito-borne disease.[1] Novel mosquito control technologies have gained greater attention as an element of this effort; however, there has been some confusion with respect to FDA's and EPA's respective jurisdiction over such mosquito-related products.

Given the public health implications of mosquito control, FDA, working collaboratively with EPA, is providing this guidance to clarify the regulatory oversight of mosquito-related products, including but not limited to those produced through biotechnology.[2]

B.   FDA and EPA Jurisdiction Over Mosquito-Related Products [3]

The FD&C Act's definition of "drug" includes "articles intended for use in the diagnosis, cure, mitigation, treatment, or prevention of disease in man or other animals" and "articles (other than food) intended to affect the structure or any function of the body of man or other animals." 21

---

[1] See "*A Strategy for Integrating Best Practices with New Science to Prevent Disease Transmission by Aedes Mosquito Vectors*," available online at: https://www.hsdl.org/?abstract&did=797520.

[2] We also note that FDA, EPA, and USDA have committed to clarifying how the U.S. Federal Government intends to regulate genetically engineered insects. *National Strategy for Modernizing the Regulatory System for Biotechnology Products*, released by the White House Office of Science

and Technology Policy, September 16, 2016.

[3] Developers may need to comply with additional requirements for import or interstate movement of certain mosquito-related products, including those contained in mosquitoes. To ensure you are in compliance with applicable requirements, contact APHIS at https://www.aphis.usda.gov/aphis/ourfocus/biotechnology/sa_contact_brs/ct_contact_brs; and CDC at https://www.cdc.gov/phpr/ipp/index.htm.

U.S.C. §321(g)(1). However, mosquitoes, which are animals, also fall within the FIFRA definition of "pest."[4]

FIFRA's definition of "pesticide" includes "any substance or mixture of substances intended for preventing, destroying, repelling, or mitigating any pest" and "any substance or mixture of substances intended for use as a plant regulator, defoliant, or desiccant." 7 U.S.C. §136(u).

Pesticide products for mosquitoes, which are intended to prevent, destroy, repel, or mitigate mosquitoes, necessarily affect the structure or function of the body of the mosquito.

Before 1975, FDA and EPA each had authority to regulate substances that controlled mosquito population if they met both the definition of "new animal drug" under the FD&C Act and the definition of "pesticide" under FIFRA. Because of concern that this dual jurisdiction created regulatory burden and confusion about which Agency had primary jurisdiction, Congress amended FIFRA's definition of "pesticide" in 1975 to exclude any article that is a "new animal drug" within the meaning of the FD&C Act. Since the FIFRA definition of pesticide was amended in 1975, EPA has registered, as pesticides, articles that control the population of mosquitoes by killing them or interfering with their reproduction, which is consistent with FDA's and EPA's general agreement that articles or categories of articles that control the population of mosquitoes are most appropriately regulated as pesticides. This general agreement arises from a careful consideration of Congressional intent.

Given this history, FDA is clarifying that the phrase "articles (other than food) intended to affect the structure or any function of the body of man or other animals" in the FD&C Act's drug definition [21 U.S.C. 321 (g)(1)(C)] does not include articles intended to function as pesticides by preventing, destroying, repelling, or mitigating mosquitoes for population control purposes. FDA believes that this interpretation is consistent with congressional intent and provides a rational approach for dividing responsibilities between FDA and EPA in regulating mosquito- related products.

1.   Examples of New Animal Drugs – Regulated by FDA

a. Products intended to reduce the virus/pathogen load within a mosquito, including reduction in virus/pathogen replication and spread within the mosquito and/or reduction in virus/pathogen transmissibility from mosquitoes to humans.

b. Products intended to prevent mosquito-borne disease in humans or animals.

2. Example of Pesticide Products – Regulated by EPA

Products intended to reduce the population of mosquitoes (for example, by killing them at some point in their life cycle, or by interfering with their reproduction or development). [5]

---

[4] FIFRA defines a "pest" broadly to include "(1) any insect, rodent, nematode, fungus, weed, or (2) any other form of terrestrial or aquatic plant or animal life or virus, bacteria, or other micro-organism (except viruses, bacteria, or other micro-organisms on or in living man or other animals)." 7 U.S.C. § 136(t). EPA's regulation at 40 CFR 152.5 expands in more specific detail on precisely what constitutes a pest for purposes of FIFRA.

C. Guidance for Sponsors/Manufacturers of Products Intended for use in Mosquitoes

FDA encourages sponsors of mosquito-related products, other than those that are intended to prevent, destroy, repel, or mitigate mosquitoes by controlling a mosquito population, to contact FDA early in the development process. If a developer has a jurisdictional question, for example, which agency or agencies would have oversight of a mosquito-related product that is expressly intended for both mosquito population control and human disease suppression, the developer may contact either or both agencies via the contacts listed in section IV of this guidance. The agencies will consult with each other on the jurisdictional question, as is already common practice. The agencies may also suggest a joint meeting among EPA, FDA, and the sponsor to discuss appropriate pathways to market.

VII. CONTACT INFORMATION

If you have any questions about how this interpretation may affect your regulated products, or products you have under development, you should contact the following FDA and EPA personnel:

FDA:

Laura R. Epstein
Center for Veterinary Medicine (HFV-1) Food and Drug Administration
7500 Standish Pl. Rockville, MD 20855
301-796-8558

EPA:

Elizabeth A. Milewski, Ph.D.
Biopesticides and Pollution Prevention Division Office of Pesticide Programs
Environmental Protection Agency

1200 Pennsylvania Avenue NW Washington DC 20460 703-347-0400

Christopher A. Wozniak, Ph.D.
Biopesticides and Pollution Prevention Division Office of Pesticide Programs
Environmental Protection Agency
1200 Pennsylvania Avenue NW Washington DC 20460 703-308-4043

This confusion and change of regulatory authority illustrates the problem of emerging technologies and how early regulatory action and even authority may shift as more is learned and more governance experience increases understanding.

7.2.1.2 FDA Approval of ATryn

In 2009, the FDA issued its first approval of a biological product derived from genetically engineered animals. ATryn, produced by GTC Biotherapeutics, Inc., is an anticoagulant used for the prevention of blood clots in patients with hereditary antithrombin (AT) deficiency, a rare blood disorder affecting approximately 1 in 5,000 people in the United States. ATryn is produced from the milk of transgenic goats that have been genetically modified to contain DNA for the production of human antithrombin. The manufacturer of ATryn received approval from two FDA centers that separately evaluated the human orphan drug and animal drug aspects of the biologic. The Center for Biologics Evaluation and Research (CBER) evaluated the biologic's safety and efficacy in human clinical studies, and the Center for Veterinary Medicine (CVM) addressed the safety and stability of the recombinant DNA construct in the transgenic goats.

The CBER evaluated two studies that included 31 patients with hereditary AT deficiency, with only one ATryn-treated patient developing the blood clots that ATryn is designed to prevent. During its review, the CVM determined that introduction of the construct did not cause any adverse outcomes to the health of the transgenic goats and ensured that the manufacturer had adequate procedures in place to prevent food from the goats from entering the food supply.

Furthermore, the CVM specified that the goats could not be used for food or feed and validated a method suitable for identifying the DNA construct in both animals and their products. The CVM also conducted an environmental assessment under NEPA, finding that the goats did not cause any significant impact on the environment.

The issues of the welfare of the animal, as well as the risk to the environment were considered in this Environmental Assessment. Several steps to ensure safety included segregation of the animals. Here is an excerpt from the Environmental Assessment, January 2009:

D. Phenotypic Characterization of the GE Animal

CVM reviewed all of the information submitted by GTC to the agency in order to characterize the phenotype of the GE animals to determine whether the insertion of the Bc6 rDNA construct or its expression may have caused changes resulting in the increased risk of adverse outcomes. This review included the results of both of the FDA inspection and the site visit of the GTC farm in Massachusetts. Particular emphasis has been placed on the visit conducted by a CVM veterinarian and a ruminant animal physiologist in November 2008, in order to observe goat management procedures, review original animal health and husbandry records, and obtain copies of standard operating procedures and internal GTC reports related to the health and husbandry of the GTC 155-92 GE goats.

CVM's review indicated that there were no apparent differences in the health, mastitis, nutrition, and reproductive status of GTC 155-92 goats vs. non-GE goats on GTC's goat farm. Other than the presence of rhAT in the milk of the GE goats, which is the intended outcome, the only difference noted was that rhAT female goats had lower daily milk production and shorter lactations than their non-GE herd mates. This is attributable to genetics that originated from a single male founder vs. their non-GE herd mates that had a more diverse genetic background with increased opportunity to introduce superior dairy genetics vs. the rhAT population.

CVM concluded that the insertion of the Bc6 rDNA construct did not pose an increased risk of adverse outcomes to the health of the GE animals; no effects were noted that are anticipated to have an adverse outcome on the environment.

E. Environmental Assessment

In order to conduct the environmental assessment, the results of the previous four evaluations are combined with an analysis of the husbandry and containment of the GE goats, including a review of the animal production facilities and practices; the conditions under which the animals are housed;

containment and biosecurity, including animal identification; disposition of animal carcasses, and disposal of animal wastes.

a. GE Animal Production Facilities and Practices

GTC's 155-92 GE goat production herd is housed at a farm owned by GTC in central Massachusetts that is a United States Department of Agriculture (USDA)-registered research facility (9 CFR 2.38). As a result, the goat herd is inspected, monitored, and has been certified scrapie-free by Animal and Plant Health Inspection Service (APHIS) veterinary inspectors in the USDA Voluntary Scrapie Flock Certification Program (VSFCP). The herd was closed to the introduction of animals from outside the facility in 2000.

The GTC farm also has an Animal Welfare Assurance on file with the National Institutes of Health, Office of Laboratory Animal Welfare and has been inspected and accredited since

1997 by the Association for Assessment and Accreditation of Laboratory Animal Care International (AAALAC Int.). As mandated under the Animal Welfare Act, all animal activities and related husbandry, facilities and veterinary care are overseen by GTC's Institutional Animal Care and Use Committee (IACUC). All of these certificates and inspection reports have been confirmed by copies submitted to FDA or during site visits performed by FDA staff.

The current 155-92 GE goat production herd includes several hundred male and female goats, whose genetics stem from Alpine, Saanen, Toggenburg, and Nubian breeds. CVM scientists conducted a site visit of the GTC farm in Massachusetts in early November 2008. The conditions and general practices at GTC's farm are described below based on information submitted by GTC in the IND, BLA, and NADA; standard operating procedures (SOPs) and other documents collected during the CVM site visit; and personal observations made by CVM scientists during the site-visit.

GTC also maintains a small 155-92 GE goat herd at a facility in central Pennsylvania. This secondary herd is managed as a source of animals to renew or expand the existing production herd should the need arise. The secondary herd is maintained entirely indoors under secure conditions. It was not inspected by FDA; however, GTC represents that it is maintained under conditions very similar to those for the Massachusetts production herd; the sponsor has provided additional information to support this.

Details on the biosecurity and containment conditions at the Pennsylvania facility are presented in Section *g* below.

b. GTC's Massachusetts Farm, Goat Housing and the Surrounding Environment

Acquisition of the GTC farm site in Massachusetts was governed by a series of strict selection criteria to minimize risks of disease spread and assure containment:

- No occupation by bovine species for at least five years prior to purchase to reduce the risk from environmental pathogens;
- No evidence of occupation by sheep or goats to minimize the risk from scrapie or other species-specific pathogens;
- Suitability of the terrain for agricultural operations;
- No activities on abutting properties that would pose herd safety or health concerns;
- No significant environmental risks on or close to the property; and
- Water that meets National Primary Drinking Water Standards

Once the site was selected and purchased by GTC, animal housing was designed and built to address animal comfort, efficiency of logistical operations, and to comply with animal care and welfare regulations for animal spaces, including USDA's regulations for research facilities (9 CFR 2.38). Additionally, the potential impact of seasonal extremes and weather conditions on goat health and welfare were taken into consideration in the design of the buildings.

Most of the animal housing consists of state of the art large barns, employing dry lot design, and a center alley with internal penning. Surface materials are designed to withstand cleaning with detergents, disinfectants and high-pressure water. Passive ventilation is provided through screened ventilation curtains, and active ventilation is provided in some buildings for which passive ventilation is insufficient to maintain appropriate conditions. Goats can enter fenced outdoor paddocks via doors in each pen; outdoor paddocks are surfaced with gravel and stone dust. Goats are allowed free access to these outside paddock areas unless inclement weather dictates internal housing. No free-range pasturing is allowed for any goats. Pens are equipped with structures and materials to engage the goats, including climbing steps to simulate hills, and various entertainment devices.

All on-site GE goats are contained by duplicate barrier systems. External fencing encompasses the entire campus of buildings, while internal fencing and barriers maintain each group of animals within their barn and the adjoining paddocks. Access to this site is highly restricted with both physical and electronic access restrictions in place. Additional details are provided below in Section *e* on physical security and animal containment.

The GTC farm is surrounded on its four boundaries by a highway and GTC-owned land to the east, by railroad tracks to the west, by a wooded grove to the north, and by a large hill to the south. Outside of the immediate farm perimeter, the surrounding area is rolling, densely wooded, and semi-rural, with a few isolated agricultural fields and open meadows. The area contains many scattered residences along the nearby roads and in a few isolated subdivisions. Many of these residences consist of large homes and relatively large lots. Several large ponds are found in the area, many surrounded by residences.

c. Animal Identification, Segregation, and Husbandry

The following description of animal identification and husbandry is provided to indicate the risk mitigation measures in place to address potential misclassification of GE animals as nonGE, and contributes to an assessment of the overall farm security and the potential for longterm escape and misidentification of animals.

Each goat in the herd is assigned a unique identification number at birth, and a master list of all assigned numbers is maintained at the facility to ensure traceability. That unique number is associated with each animal in three redundant ways:

1.   Permanent ear tattoo applied less than 24 hours after birth;
2.   Subcutaneous transponder (electronic implant); and 3. Physical tag attached to a neck chain or Velcro collar.

Members of GTC's farm staff conduct a monthly herd-wide inventory to identify any animals that have missing or illegible tags, which are then replaced. Farm staff also conduct an annual herd-wide transponder check, which replaces non-functional transponders.

All goats, regardless of their GE status, are segregated before sexual maturity into age and size cohorts to encourage socialization and maintain a healthy juvenile group. Young goats are housed primarily in dedicated nurseries and kid spaces. Male goats are segregated from females before they reach sexual maturity to prevent unplanned pregnancies. When an rhAT GE doe begins lactation, she is moved to a dedicated dairy building on the farm where she is qualified, milked, and housed.

GTC farm staff are trained (with appropriate documentation) to perform all routine animal husbandry activities including, but not limited to, daily feeding, milking, watering, grooming, and breeding of goats. Execution of farm tasks are conducted in accordance with documented procedures that provide guidance of all animal interactions as well as non-animal related activities.

d. Animal Health and Biosecurity

The following description of animal health and biosecurity is part of the assessment that evaluates the potential for environmental risks resulting from the spread of disease due to housing and biosecurity practices at the GTC facilities, or to help determine the potential for disease status in the event that an animal escapes from the facility.

GTC strictly adheres to currently accepted guidelines regarding animal health and welfare.

This includes those outlined in the Animal Welfare Act, *The Guide for the Care and Use of Laboratory Animal* (including all amendments established by the National Institute of Health as combined in the *Public Health Service Policy on the Humane Care and Use of Laboratory*

Animals), and also the *Guide For the Care and Use of Agricultural Animals in Agricultural Research and Teaching* published by the Federation of Animal Science Societies and accepted by the USDA-APHIS-AC and AAALAC Int. GTC also complies with all other federal, state and local requirements for the responsible use and care of animals.

A quarterly review of morbidity and mortality (M&M) data is performed to evaluate the health status of the herd, with the aim improving the overall animal health and welfare of the animals, and decreasing M&M within the general herd. Several full-time veterinarians are employed by GTC to provide 24/7 coverage year round. The veterinarians monitor and track both individual animal and herd health on a daily basis and can detect subtle changes that may be indicative of potential clinical or sub-clinical issues or

232

possible adventitious agent concerns. For each goat, a permanent health record is initiated immediately after birth and is maintained throughout its life. This record contains a complete history including date of birth, sex, breed, results of routine and diagnostic testing, records of vaccinations, preventative care and treatments, surgical procedures and breeding and reproductive data.

Control starts at the level of the farm with extensive, well-documented, written standard operating procedures employed for the majority of operations involved with maintaining the site and for caring of the animals. Similar practices apply to incoming materials, which at a minimum, include all of GTC's hay, grain, and bedding materials. Lastly, this control encompasses monitoring, and restricting where necessary, flow of personnel/visitors and vehicular traffic.

GTC's quality assurance (QA) documentation system utilizes a number of different categories of documents to encompass the activities that occur at the level of the farm and animal; standard farm practices, standard veterinary practices, and other standard operating procedures and good manufacturing practices that are aimed at defining best practice in an agricultural/pharmaceutical setting. These documents provide the exact procedure to be followed by trained personnel. Similar to recombinant production systems established for other rDNA organisms, it is these practices and the documentation system that allows for a highly controlled, well characterized, and consistent product to be produced from the rhAT goat herd.

A variety of general adventitious agent risk minimization (i.e., biosecurity) measures have been implemented at the GTC farm. Many of these measures are derived from generally accepted principles used to minimize risk of adventitious agent introduction into recombinant expression systems, downstream processing operations, and specific recommendations for animal-derived products in regulatory guidance documents. The primary basis for such measures is the definition of an appropriate level of segregation and control at the level of the environment, the equipment, the raw materials and the manufacturing process. A similar approach has been taken for production of rhAT in GE goats.

The risk minimization started at the level of the farm with strict selection criteria for the farm site and the goats. Following establishment of the base herd, closure of the herd reduced any potential for entry of adventitious agents into the herd via outside animal introduction resulting in the current certified scrapie-free and specific-pathogen free goat herd. A comprehensive biosecurity program was implemented which covers both internal and external aspects of farm operations and the overall animal care program.

In the event of the suspected presence of an infectious disease, a goat or group of goats may require isolated to avoid the possible disease spread. Based on the presumptive clinical diagnosis, the goat(s) will be hospitalized, quarantined, or isolated. Several infirmaries are located throughout the GTC farm, and two isolation suites are located in the main clinic.

From the perspective of the introduction of infectious agents from the outside, the program encompasses all personnel and visitors or service personnel/contractors. The program addresses known wildlife that exists in the surrounding environment and appropriate monitoring and controls to limit that population, where possible. The biosecurity program includes an Integrated Pest Management (IPM) Program that monitors and controls incursions by birds, rodents and insects. Extensive use of bird netting, rodent traps, and electronic insect light traps is part of the IPM program.

Internal aspects of the biosecurity program focuses on the goat herd itself and addresses herd closure, evaluation of raw materials provided to the goats (hay, grain, water, bedding, etc.), and the monitoring of overall clinical health as a tool for detecting potential disease entry.

Although focused on maintaining animal health, many of the extensive biosecurity measures in place at the GTC farm also directly or indirectly contribute to animal containment and tracking (i.e., physical security) and reduce the risk of long-term escape.

e. Physical Security and Animal Containment

The GTC farm is surrounded by a double barrier between all 155-92 GE goats in the production herd and the outside environs. The entire farm site is surrounded by a heavy, 6foot high, chain-link perimeter fence with gated access. The fence also extends 18 inches below ground level to prevent the ingress of external wildlife or the egress of farm animals. At locations where there are gates for access to the farm and the fencing cannot be buried, there are additional barriers present. Each barn that houses 155-92 GE goats has an external paddock/exercise yard with wood and wire fencing that limits the goats' access to the farm grounds. Inside each barn there are other physical containment structures preventing escape. The perimeter and paddock fencing was examined during the site visit by CVM staff and found to be appropriately strong and secure with no obvious gaps or openings that would allow entry of large wildlife or the escape of goats.

Access to the farm from the perimeter is highly regulated. The vehicle gates and building entrances are all electronically controlled with video surveillance. All personnel and visitors are required to fill out a detailed biosecurity questionnaire prior to or upon initial entry. Site access may be restricted or denied depending on the person's biosecurity risk. The only vehicles allowed within the perimeter fencing are those essential for servicing the farm as there are already dedicated vehicles on the farm for movement between the buildings on the site. All persons' footwear and vehicle tires must receive an appropriate treatment (e.g., disinfectant foot bath) with a biosecurity solution prior to entry onto the farm site.

A video surveillance system is in place which focuses on key entry points and remote sections of the farm perimeter. Recording is performed around the clock and is available for review as needed. The farm is staffed with non-security personnel around the clock, 7 days a week. In addition, there is a dedicated security force on site all nights, weekends, and holidays. Daily checks by farm staff and veterinarians during feeding and milking operations help insure that the absence of any goats would be quickly identified.

All told, at least five levels of physical containment are considered to be present at the GTC farm including two independent fencing systems, 24-hr staffing/security, multiple daily staff checks, and video surveillance.

Chapter 8

Cloning and Registering Animals

Introduction

Should cloning of farm animals be regulated? In March 2000, PPL Therapeutics made international headlines when it announced that it had finally succeeded in cloning pigs. At the same time, Akira Onishi, an animal breeder at Japan's National Institute of Animal Industry in Tsukuba, Japan reported the cloning of Xena, a pig.

The cloning of pigs creates a capability to provide an unlimited source of organs for transplantation, or xenotransplantation. However, the risks of xenotransplanation carry with it the risk of infection with pig retroviruses which can infect human cells [289 Science 1118 (Aug. 18, 2000)].

This did not affect the possibilities of cloning outstanding animals including horses. But a highly prized horse requires that it be registered, and the next case takes on the question of whether cloned animals can be registered in breed registries, and in this case, the American Quarter Horse registry.

IN THE UNITED STATES COURT OF APPEALS FOR THE FIFTH CIRCUIT
No. 13-11043 United States Court of Appeals
Fifth Circuit

ABRAHAM & VENEKLASEN JOINT VENTURE; ABRAHAM EQUINE,
INCORPORATED; JASON ABRAHAM,
January 14, 2015

Plaintiffs - Appellees
v.
AMERICAN QUARTER HORSE ASSOCIATION,
Defendant - Appellant
Appeal from the United States District Court for the Northern District of
Texas

Before JOLLY and JONES, Circuit Judges, and AFRICK*, District Judge. EDITH H. JONES, Circuit Judge:

Jason Abraham, Abraham Equine, Inc., and Abraham & Veneklasen Joint Venture ("Plaintiffs") filed suit alleging that the American Quarter Horse Association ("AQHA") violated Sections 1 and 2 of the Sherman Act and the Texas Free Enterprise and Antitrust Act.1 The antitrust allegations stem from votes by the Stud Book and Registration Committee ("SBRC") of the AQHA, which had blocked AQHA registration of horses created through somatic cell nuclear transfer ("SCNT"), also known as cloning. At trial, AQHA moved for judgment as a matter of law ("JMOL"), Fed. R. Civ. P. 50(a), which was denied by the district court. AQHA appeals the denial of its motion. 1 Because the Texas Free Enterprise and Antitrust Act utilizes the same standards as the Sherman Act for establishing a violation, the Sherman Act analysis applies to Plaintiffs' state law claims as well.

We REVERSE the denial of AQHA's motion for Judgment as a Matter of Law and RENDER judgment in favor of AQHA.

BACKGROUND

The plaintiffs here include Abraham & Veneklasen Joint Venture, a business formed by Jonathan Abraham and Gregg Veneklasen. Abraham is the sole shareholder of Abraham Equine, Inc., which provides recipient mares that act as surrogate mothers for Quarter Horse embryos. Veneklasen is a veterinarian, owner of a veterinary hospital, and an expert in advanced equine reproductive techniques. The two formed Abraham & Veneklasen Joint Venture to invest in shares of multiple Quarter Horses that were produced by cloning top prize winners in racing and cutting horse competitions. Without access to AQHA's breed registry, however, the cloned horses cannot participate in the lucrative racing, breeding or horse shows that are characteristic of the market for "elite Quarter Horses," as defined by Plaintiffs' expert.

Appellant AQHA is a non-profit association with a general membership of more than 280,000 worldwide that was organized in 1940 to collect and register the pedigrees and protect the breed of the American Quarter Horse. In addition to its breed registry, which has listed millions of horses over the years, AQHA sponsors horse shows that attract international patronage, supports educational activities, and sanctions races in which only AQHA- registered horses may compete. Consequently, "[M]eaningful participation in this multimillion dollar industry is dependent upon AQHA membership and AQHA registration." Hatley v. American Quarter Horse Ass'n, 552 F.2d 646, 654 (5th Cir. 1977).

Strategic decisions for the organization are made by the Board of Directors, the five-member Executive Committee, and a variety of standing committees that report to the general membership and the Board. The Board's membership has ranged from about 280-340 during the years in question, and about 99 new Board members joined the Board during the same period. The Stud Book and Registration Committee is one such standing committee. The SBRC comprises about 30 members, with partial annual rotating membership, and its members are selected by the President with the advice and majority vote of the Executive Committee. The SBRC reviews proposed changes to AQHA's equine registration rules and makes recommendations regarding those proposals to the general membership at the annual convention. During the annual meeting, general members are allowed to address the SBRC and observe its discussions. The SBRC's recommendation is then presented to the general membership, which determines whether that recommendation is submitted to the Board for final approval. Only the Board of Directors may change the breed registration rules.

From its inception, AQHA has maintained rules identifying the characteristics required of any horse sought to be registered as an American Quarter Horse, and the organization's registry has maintained records of the offspring of registered American Quarter Horses. Originally, the records consisted essentially of birth certificates for the offspring. As animal reproductive techniques have evolved, however, AQHA registered horses bred by means of artificial insemination and embryo transfers.

Most recently, AQHA approved registration of horses "bred" by Intracytoplasmic Sperm Injection ("ICSI"). ICSI involves the injection of a single sperm cell into a mature unfertilized egg cell called an oocyte. The fertilized egg is then transferred to a recipient mare. The plaintiffs' cloning techniques, known as Somatic Cell Nuclear Transfer ("SCNT"), create animals without distinct sire and dam bloodlines for registry. Instead, each cloned horse is a "twin separated by time" of only one animal and any other clones of that initial donor horse.

At its annual convention in 2003, the AQHA Board adopted Rule 227(a), which declared cloned horses ineligible for AQHA breed registration. Between 2008 and 2013, the AQHA received four requests to change the rule, two of which were made by Plaintiffs. In 2008, the SBRC responded by recommending further study; in 2009 the SBRC recommended the creation of a cloning task force to study the impact and science of cloning; and in 2010 the SBRC recommended a denial of the rule change proposal. Since 2010, the SBRC has recommended retention of the rule, and the Board has accepted that recommendation.2 [2 In 2013, the Board voted to defend the instant litigation, i.e., to defend the anti- clone-registration rule.] The plaintiffs contend that members of the SBRC and the SBRC conspired with AQHA to prevent cloned horses from being registered as American Quarter Horses and thus excluded their horses from the market for "elite Quarter Horses." Influential members of the SBRC allegedly tainted the committee's deliberations because their personal economic interests would be harmed by competition with cloned horses, especially in breeding and racing. The plaintiffs articulated a plausible motive for anticompetitive activity, but the principal questions on appeal are whether they proved an actual conspiracy to restrain trade in violation of Section 1 of the Sherman Act, or illegal monopolization by AQHA of breed registration for the "elite Quarter Horse" market in violation of Section 2

.

Plaintiffs filed suit in April 2012, and their case was tried to a jury. The court denied AQHA's motion for judgment as a matter of law. After sending two notes asking for clarification, the jury found in favor of the plaintiffs but declined to award damages. To effectuate the verdict, the court entered a sweeping injunction that specified the rule changes AQHA must adopt to permit breed registration of cloned horses. AQHA has appealed, challenging the sufficiency of evidence for each element of the Sherman Act claims and the scope of the district court's injunction. 3 [3 We do not reach issues concerning the injunctive relief.]

STANDARD OF REVIEW

This court reviews a denial of a motion for judgment as a matter of law de novo. Evans v. Ford Motor Co., 484 F.3d 329, 334 (5th Cir. 2007). A motion for JMOL should be granted if the evidence is legally insufficient, such that "the facts and inferences point so strongly and overwhelmingly in favor of one party that the Court believes that reasonable men could not arrive at a contrary verdict." Boeing v. Shipman, 411 F.2d 365, 374 (5th Cir. 1969) (en banc), overruled on other grounds by Gautreaux v. Scurlock Marine, Inc., 107 F.3d 331, 336 (5th Cir. 1997) (en banc). The reviewing court must consider the facts in the light most favorable to the verdict. Giles v. Gen. Elec. Co., 245 F.3d 474, 481 (5th Cir. 2001).

DISCUSSION

I.   Section 1 of the Sherman Act.

As opposed to Section 2 of the Sherman Act, Section 1 is only concerned with concerted conduct among separate economic actors rather than their independent or merely parallel action. Ultimately, "plaintiffs must show that the defendants (1) engaged in a conspiracy (2) that produced some anti-competitive effect (3) in the relevant market." Johnson v. Hosp. Corp. of Am., 95 F.3d 383, 392 (5th Cir. 1996). But not all nominally separate entities are capable of violating Section 1 of the Sherman Act through a conspiracy that restrains trade. AQHA contends, first, that as a "single entity," it could not conspire with its members or with the SBRC. Alternatively, AQHA asserts that the evidence of conspiracy is legally insufficient to support the verdict.

A.   Entities Capable of Conspiring.

As a general rule, Section 1 of the Sherman Act does not apply to single entities. Am. Needle, Inc. v. Nat'l Football League, 560 U.S. 183, 190, 130 S. Ct. 2201, 2207 (2010). The Court reiterated in American Needle, however, that "concerted action under§ 1 does not turn simply on whether the parties involved are legally distinct entities." Id. at 191. Thus, "[a]greements made within a firm can constitute concerted action covered by § 1 when the parties to the agreement act on interests separate from those of the firm itself, and the intra-firm agreements may simply be a formalistic shell for ongoing concerted action." Id. at 200. A functional analysis of the parties' actual participation in the alleged anticompetitive conduct is necessary to draw the inference of illegal concerted action. Pursuant to this functional approach, a corporation and its officers and employees, or a corporation and its divisions or wholly owned subsidiaries have been held to be a "single entity" that is incapable of concerted action that impairs competition in the marketplace. See Copperweld Corp. v. Independence Tube Corp., 467 U.S. 752, 767, 104 S. Ct. 2731, 2739 (1984). Other legal entities, however, when made up of members or entities that maycompete with each other, may conspire illegally. See, e.g., United States v. Sealy, Inc., 388 U.S. 350, 352-56, 87 S. Ct. 1847, 1850-52 (1967); Nat'l Collegiate Athletic Ass'n v. Bd. of Regents of Univ. of Okla., 468 U.S. 85, 104 S. Ct. 2948 (1984); Associated Press v. United States, 326 U.S. 1, 65 S. Ct. 1416 (1945). The "key", according to the Court, is whether the "contract, combination... , or conspiracy" joins together "separate decisionmakers," i.e., "separate economic actors pursuing separate economic interests." Am. Needle, 560 U.S. at 195, 130 S. Ct. at 2205. If so, then the agreement may deprive the marketplace of independent centers of decisionmaking[.]" Id. At 195, 2212.

Following this explanation, the Court in American Needle readily concluded that the joint venture formed by thirty-two NFL teams, "at least" with regard to their decision collectively to license the teams' independently owned intellectual property, was engaged in concerted rather than single entity action and thus potentially violated Section 1. The Court reasoned that apart from the teams' agreement to cooperate in exploiting these assets, they would be competitors in the market to produce and sell team logo wearing apparel and headgear by licensing their intellectual property and dealing with suppliers.

On one hand, the Court held that the justification for the National Football League Properties' ("NFLP") cooperative agreement-the structural necessity of a sports league to produce the "product" of major league football- is irrelevant to whether there was concerted or independent action at the threshold of Section 1 analysis. Am. Needle, 560 U.S. at 199, 130 S. Ct. at 2214. On the other hand, however, the Court recognized that because restraints on competition like those embodied in sports leagues or joint ventures are necessary to make a product available at all, the rule of reason rather than per se rules determines the ultimate question of antitrust violations. Id. at 203.

American Needle's rejection of "single entity" status for organizations with "separate economic actors" does not fit comfortably with the facts before us. AQHA is more than a sports league, it is not a trade association, and its quarter million members are involved in ranching, horse training, pleasure riding and many other activities besides the "elite Quarter Horse" market. The plaintiffs expert claimed that no more than .5% of the yearlings sold each year fall within the plaintiffs' proposed sub-market of AQHA-registered elite Quarter Horses. Under such circumstances, it is difficult to draw the conclusion that because a tiny number of economic actors within AQHA may "pursue their separate economic interests," the organization has conspired with that minority.

American Needle, in contrast, involved membership all of whom owned and profited from the exclusive licensing arrangements entered into by the NFLP joint venture. Similarly, in the other cases cited by the Court in American Needle, the organizations found capable of conspiring with members who were "independent decisionmakers" were trade groups or competitor groups all of whose members directly profited from the exclusionary conduct.

In American Needle, the Court's description of potentially illegal conspiracies involving such organizations is laden with adjectives referring to the members' independent economic interests.   Am. Needle, 560 U.S.

at 196- 97, 130 S. Ct. at 2212-13 (describing members of the NFLP as "independently managed business[es]" and "competing suppliers of valuable trademarks"). Here, there is no such unity of interest among over a quarter million members. Other features appear to distinguish this case from American Needle.

First, no other case has yet held that an animal breed registry organization can violate the antitrust laws by passing on the qualifications for the breed itself. This court in Hatley rejected an antitrust conspiracy claim against AQHA where a horse of undisputed "elite" lineage was denied registration because it had white markings above the permissible places on its legs.

v. Am. Quarter Horse Ass'n, 552 F.2d 646, 654 (5th Cir. 1977). Whenever an organization devoted to the preservation of an animal breed revises its standards, exclusion from the relevant "market" will occur. See, e.g., Jack Russell Terrier Network of N. Cal. v. Am. Kennel Club, Inc., 407 F.3d 1027, 1034 (9th Cir. 2005) (affirming dismissal where organization devoted to those dogs elected not to register dogs that were jointly registered with the American Kennel Club); Jessup v. Am. Kennel Club, Inc., 61 F. Supp. 2d 5 (S.D.N.Y. 1999), aff'd. on dist. ct. op., 210 F.3d 111 (2d Cir. 2000) (granting summary judgment against claims that Labrador dog breed standards were changed in conspiracy to restrain trade or monopolize). Perhaps setting the standards for a breed is relevant under American Needle to rule of reason analysis after the possibility of concerted action has been admitted. If so, then breed standards for these volunteer groups should often be immune from antitrust scrutiny because they are essential to "creating the product." That the organization's purpose is to preserve and enhance the breed's characteristics creates further tension with American Needle's paradigm of a "firm" and "separate economic actors" within the firm whose economic interests diverge from those of the firm. Contrary to the plaintiffs' assertions, AQHA is not narrowly interested in "having more members and more registered horses." If that premise were true, AQHA would not insist on maintaining pure bloodlines and might elect to register the offspring of horses cross-bred with pure Quarter Horses, if the offspring otherwise complied with Quarter Horse characteristics. Alternatively, AQHA's enforcement of its "white rule," which denied registration to Hatley's horse, might have been loosened. See Hatley, 552 F.2d at 646. From this standpoint, AQHA's self-interest as an organization is not limited to profit. The district court recognized the fallacy in the plaintiffs' reasoning when it concluded that, "It is unclear... whether the AQHA would benefit or be harmed by allowing clone registration." Abraham & Veneklasen Joint Venture v. Am.

Quarter Horse Ass'n, No. 2:12-CV-103-J, 2013 WL 2297104, at *3 (N.D. Tex. May 24, 2013). Thus, the divergence of interests between AQHA and the alleged conspirators, which American Needle posits, is not clear. Moreover, an issue not plumbed in American Needle is how to assess the organization's ability to conspire with its members given different types of legal structures. In the NFLP, apparently all the member teams had to agree on the exclusive licensing arrangement, and all the teams owned intellectual property subject to the agreement; there was thus unity of purpose and decisionmaking by the interested economic actors. AQHA, however, makes policy through a Board of Directors with around 300 annually rotating members. The SBRC proposes action on registration rules, but it cannot unilaterally dispose of the issue. Any AQHA member may propose a rule to the Board during its annual meeting.

A functional analysis of an organization's ability to conspire with legally distinct members ought to take these facts into account. It is not clear whether American Needle applies on a more abstract plane that covers any organization with actors who have separate economic interests. See, e.g., Robertson v. Sea Pines Real Estate Cos., Inc., 679 F.3d 278, 285-86 (4th Cir. 2012) (refusing to dismiss Section 1 claim against MLS composed of separate real estate brokerages that were potential competitors). AQHA, however, urges the Court's emphasis on the pursuit of separate economic interests as a cornerstone of its argument that the majority of SBRC members' personal interests were not furthered by the anti-cloning rule.

Given these troubling distinctions, we need not resolve in this opinion the scope of American Needle for animal breed registry organizations. Instead, we will assume arguendo that AQHA was legally capable of conspiring with members of the SBRC in violation of Section 1. The judgment must be reversed, however, for insufficient evidence of a conspiracy. 4 [4 The Court was careful to note that being capable of a Section 1 violation through conspiracy was not the same as proving the existence of a conspiracy or that conspiracy's effect on trade. Indeed, the Court explained that the rule of reason should be applied, ensuring that many entities capable of conspiring would not be ultimately found liable. Am. Needle, 560 U.S. at 203.]

B.   Evidence of a Conspiracy.

To prove a conspiracy in restraint of trade, the Plaintiff must show some kind of "common design and understanding, or a meeting of minds in an unlawful arrangement." Am. Tobacco Co. v. United States, 328 U.S. 781, 810, 66 S. Ct. 1125 (1946); see also Monsanto Co. v. Spray-Rite Serv. Corp.,

465 U.S. 752, 761, 104 S. Ct. 1464, 1469 (1984). If direct evidence is unavailable and the plaintiff relies on circumstantial evidence, the "antitrust plaintiff must present evidence tending to exclude the possibility of independent conduct." Viazis v. Am. Ass'n of Orthodontists, 314 F.3d 758, 763 (5th Cir. 2002) (citing Monsanto, 465 U.S. at 768). Ultimately, any conduct that is "as consistent with permissible competition as with illegal conspiracy" cannot support a conspiracy inference. Matsushita Elec. Indus. Co. v. Zenith Radio Corp., 475 U.S. 574, 588, 106 S. Ct. 1348, 1356 (1986).

Plaintiffs here introduced only circumstantial evidence to prove their theory that certain SBRC members, acting to advance their economic interests, controlled the SBRC, and the Board deferred to them, resulting in a conspiracy with AQHA to exclude the plaintiffs' cloned horses from the elite Quarter Horse market. Whether taken individually or as a whole, the evidence does not raise a substantial issue of conspiratorial activity. In Plaintiffs' appellate brief, a single page is labeled "Evidence: Agreements with and within the SBRC." Plaintiffs there contend that trial testimony "reinforced" the existence of an agreement and provide a string citation to the record without any explanation of the testimony. The testimony captured by the string citation contains three types of evidence: (1) some SBRC members, who own, race, show and/or breed elite Quarter Horses, stand to benefit personally from retaining the ban on clones; (2) those members were "influential"; and (3) such influential members spoke vociferously against cloning at SBRC meetings. In its statement of the case, Plaintiffs' brief also references (1) an alleged concession by a former AQHA president that there was an "agreement" within SBRC to prevent clones from being registered; (2) meeting notes concerning the "strategy" to defeat registration; (3) and "sham" procedures over the course of four years while AQHA discussed and debated registration of cloned horses.5 [5 Curiously, Plaintiffs' string citation also contains a reference to testimony that the SBRC meetings on the science of cloning had fairly presented both sides of the issue. This evidence seems to cut against Plaintiffs' burden of providing evidence that tends to rule out independent action.] Despite Plaintiffs' provocative descriptions, the evidence of a conspiracy to control the SBRC and AQHA is lacking.

The first category of evidence in the string citation-some members of the SBRC stand to gain financially from the clone ban-proved less than Plaintiffs would like. At trial, plaintiff Jason Abraham testified that twenty members of the SBRC bred some type of Quarter Horse or were influential in breeding circles.6 [6 It should be noted that Plaintiff argues that a majority of SBRC members are breeders who stand to gain from the restraint of trade, even though many of those breeders do not participate in the "elite Quarter

Horse market" upon which Plaintiffs base their claim. We do not address the market issue-as this case is resolved under the conspiracy issue- butPlaintiffs admission that non elite Quarter Horse breeders are impacted by cloning bans would have to play some role in determining whether Plaintiffs "elite Quarter Horse market" is a distinct market that actually exists.]
Abraham, however, acknowledged he did not know about their status as elite breeders.

Plaintiff Veneklasen made the same assertion about twenty elite breeders on the SBRC, but he had to change his testimony after being confronted with the membership list. He admitted that the list showed only four or five members of the SBRC who remained active in horse breeding, while the other individuals had either retired or had never participated as breeders in the elite Quarter Horse market. AQHA witness Jeff Tebow, a member of the SBRC, testified that a few of the SBRC members had made a substantial amount of money from the industry and a few of them supported themselves by horse breeding. Tebow referred to these individuals as "the leaders of our industry." SBRC member Butch Wise also testified that quite a few committee members "had some skin in the game" as breeders, but he did not distinguish between breeders of elite and non-elite horses. Wise later testified that it was common for committee members to sell horses for one another, use a common brokerage firm, and breed horses with one another's stock.

The picture that emerges from the testimony and relationship diagram offered by Plaintiffs is that of a committee some of whose members have been financially successful in aspects of Quarter Horse business and some of whom have had extensive, fruitful outside business relationships with each other. This evidence is relevant to the "separate economic interests" test for determining whether a single entity is capable of a conspiracy, but more than the existence of the financial interests of a few is required to prove a conspiratorial agreement among them.

Since Plaintiffs rely on circumstantial evidence, they must show that circumstantial evidence both supports an inference of conspiracy and tends to exclude independent conduct. Viazis v. Am. Ass'n of Orthodontists, 314 F.3d 758, 763 (5th Cir. 2002). Any conduct that is "as consistent with permissible competition as with illegal conspiracy does not, standing alone, support an inference of antitrust conspiracy." Matsushita Elec. Indus. Co. v. Zenith Radio Corp., 475 U.S. 574, 588, 106 S. Ct. 1348, 1356 (1986). It is here critical to note that the SBRC, whose membership altered each year, included about thirty members annually during the relevant period, but only a handful of them were identified by Plaintiffs as profiting in the elite Quarter Horse market. Yet there was a conspicuous lack of evidence concerning the dozens of committee members not financially involved in the elite Quarter Horse market. Whatever the motivations of the breeders who were singled out by Plaintiffs, they were outnumbered in voting strength by the others who were not shown to have such financial interests. Moreover, trial testimony established that SBRC members had ethical concerns about cloning in addition to practical concerns about verifying parentage to maintain the integrity of the registry. At best, the evidence showed that only a vocal minority of SBRC members both opposed cloning and had financial interests that could be injured by registration of cloned elite Quarter Horses.

The second category of testimony contained in Plaintiffs string citation is the alleged disproportionate influence of certain SBRC members, but that, too, cannot support an inference of conspiracy. Plaintiff Gregg Veneklasen's trial testimony labeled a few members of the SBRC as a "good ol' boys club," based on each member's financial success in racing or breeding Quarter Horses. But aside from hollow labels, Plaintiffs have no evidence that any such sub-group exerted a disproportionate influence to affect vote outcomes within the SBRC or the Board. And even if this "boys club" existed to exert influence generally, the only evidence that its members made any kind of agreement to oppose cloning amounts to no more than innuendo.

The third category of testimony contained in the string citation-an AQHA member made unfavorable statements at an SBRC meeting-also fails to support an inference of a conspiracy. In addition to an agreement among the members of the committee, Plaintiffs allege a conspiracy between the committee and AQHA. To support this theory of an agreement between the AQHA and SBRC, Plaintiffs introduced the testimony of Robert "Blake" Russell, the President of ViaGen L.C., the laboratory which conducts business with Plaintiffs. Russell testified that he attended the 2009 AQHA convention and the corresponding SBRC meeting that was addressed by AQHA Executive Committee Member John Andreini. Russell testified that Andreini's impassioned speech against registering clones included the statement, "I will not allow this technology to move forward. I will not have sixty First Down Dashes [a legendarily successful racing Quarter Horse] in every county in this country. And I have put millions of dollars in this industry, and if this is approved, I will take every dime of it out." Russell testified that he believed Andreini was concerned with the competitive effects of lifting the clone ban. AQHA registered clones would be able to compete in lucrative races and take part in the breeding market. Russell believed Andreini did not want to face "sixty First Down Dashes" in competition. Assuming arguendo that Andreini was attempting to restrain competition, the record is devoid of any evidence regarding SBRC member reactions to Andreini. Did they respond favorably or negatively? Were they, in any way, influenced by his speech? Was it given any weight? Without more, Andreini's impassioned speech is simply a one-sided complaint about cloning.

This court has already rejected the inferential value of one-sided complaints in Viazis v. Am. Ass'n of Orthodontists, 314 F.3d 758 (5th Cir. 2002). In Viazis, an orthodontic devices manufacturer contracted with a dentist to manufacture and advertise a product that the dentist had invented and patented. When the dentist aggressively advertised the product himself, the American Association of Orthodontists ("AAO") complained of the dentist's behavior to the manufacturer.

The complaints were coupled with veiled threats of a boycott. This court held that the evidence of AAO complaints to the manufacturer was insufficient to infer the second party's intent to enter into a conspiracy. With circumstantial evidence, this court noted, the plaintiff must present evidence that tends to exclude the possibility of the manufacturer's independent conduct.

Since one-sided complaints could not exclude the possibility of independent action, the manufacturer's actions were as consistent with legal conduct as with conspiratorial conduct, making the evidence insufficient to support a finding of conspiracy.

Andreini's one-sided complaints are factually indistinguishable from Viazis. An agreement requires a meeting of the minds. Like the AAO complaints in Viazis, the only evidence here is a one-sided complaint without any hint of a favorable response from the alleged co-conspirator, the SBRC. Only half of the equation is present. And a one-sided complaint is just not a suitable basis for an inference of conspiracy. Even Andreini's threat to pull his money from the industry cannot distinguish this case from a typical one-sided complaint. The AAO in Viazis also threatened monetary retaliation in the form of a boycott of the manufacturer. And just like the threat of boycott in Viazis, Plaintiffs would have to show some additional evidence that the SBRC responded to that economic threat with some action. Viazis, 314 F.3d at 763. Therefore, no inference of a conspiracy can be drawn from Andreini's one-side complaint. 7 [7 If the plaintiffs intended to use Andreini's speech as indicative of one-sided complaints made by other AQHA members, e.g., Frank Merrill, their brief does not say so. However, mere complaints, without proof of an agreement to exclude cloned horses from registration, are insufficiently probative of concerted, as opposed to independent action by the SBRC or its members.]

In addition to the evidence referenced in the string citation, Plaintiffs' statement of facts alluded to other evidence they consider incriminating. They reference testimony of Frank Merrill, a former AQHA president and sometime SBRC member who was outspokenly opposed to registering cloned horses. Merrill, they contend, admitted that the SBRC "agreed to exclude" cloned horses. This is a mischaracterization. Merrill was referring not to a conspiratorial agreement, but only to the thirty-member committee's official votes on the subject. Cf Tunica Web Advertising v. Tunica Casino Operators Ass'n, 496 F.3d 403, 410 (5th Cir. 2007) (evidence of emails referencing "gentleman's agreement" among competitors sufficient to create fact issue of conspiracy).

Plaintiffs accuse the AQHA and SBRC of "sham procedures" designed to defeat registration of cloned horses. They refer to a "secret meeting" in January 2012 that, behind the back of AQHA's then president, lay the groundwork for SBRC's official rejection of registration for clones. The only evidence of a meeting in January 2012, however, is an email/rom the president inviting certain SBRC members to an official meeting of AQHA's Executive Committee meeting to discuss cloning. There was nothing secret about it. Even more telling, there is no testimony about what transpired at the not-so- secret meeting.

Plaintiffs contend that AQHA "stacked" the SBRC with hand-selected industry leaders with interests in conflict with cloning. As has been noted, the committee was never shown to have a voting majority of members with interests in elite Quarter Horses, although most of its members, unsurprisingly, have been breeders of Quarter Horses. In any event, Plaintiffs failed to explain why the selection of SBRC members was not as consistent with permissible activity as it was with impermissible activity; selecting industry leaders who are knowledgeable about breeding for a committee focused on registration of the breed seems quite reasonable. In regard to Plaintiffs' more general challenges to SBRC's procedures, its relation to decisionmaking by the Board, and its conduct of the cloning task force, Plaintiffs offered nothing more than pejoratives without evidence that the deliberative processes in place deviated from AQHA's standard procedures or failed to offer the plaintiffs an opportunity to make their case for registering cloned horses. As one court explained, "[T]he antitrust laws are not intended as a device to review the details of parliamentary procedure."

Jessup v. American Kennel Club Inc., 61 F.Supp. 2d 5, 12 (S.D.N.Y. 1999), aff'd on dist. ct. op., 210 F.3d 111 (2d.Cir. 2000). Plaintiffs did not produce evidence tending to exclude the possibility of a decision arrived at by independent, not illegally concerted action.

Finally, the plaintiffs focus on a "plan" to delay and ultimately reject cloned horse registration that allegedly appeared in the handwritten notes of AQHA's executive director Don Treadway. The eight pages of random, scrawled notes span nearly two years and derive from various meetings and conversations. While they reveal Treadway's thinking and concerns others expressed about cloning and AQHA's possible reaction to it, they contain no "smoking gun" referencing any agreement within AQHA or its membership to restrain the market for elite Quarter Horses.

Reasonable jurors, in sum, could not draw any inference of conspiracy from the evidence presented, because it neither tends to exclude the possibility of independent action nor does it suggest the existence of any conspiracy at all. In the absence of substantial evidence on the issue of an illegal conspiracy to restrain trade, AQHA's JMOL motion should have been granted.

II.   Section 2 of the Sherman Act
Because Plaintiffs' conspiracy claim is unsustainable as a matter of law, we must consider the alternative verdict that AQHA as a single entity is liable for illegal monopolization under Section 2 of the Sherman Act. "A violation of section 2 of the Sherman Act is made out when it is shown that the asserted violator 1) possesses monopoly power in the relevant market and 2) acquired or maintained that power willfully, as distinguished from the power having arisen and continued by growth produced by the development of a superior product, business acumen, or historic accident." Stearns Airport Equip. Co. v. FMC Corp., 170 F.3d 518, 522 (5th Cir. 1999). Having or acquiring a monopoly is not in and of itself illegal. The illegal abuse of power occurs when the monopolist exercises its power to control prices or exclude competitors from the relevant market for its products. See, e.g., United States v. E.I. DuPont de Nemours, 351 U.S. 377, 391-94, 76 S. Ct. 994, 1005-06 (1956) (discussing Section 2 illegal monopoly power in terms of the potential competitors for the monopolist's product).

Plaintiffs here contend that AQHA monopolized the relevant market for elite Quarter Horses. Assuming arguendo that this is a cognizable relevant market, it is true that AQHA's breed registry rules admit or exclude horses from that market. Nothing in the record, however, shows that AQHA competes in the elite Quarter Horse Market. AQHA is a member organization; it is not engaged in breeding, racing, selling or showing elite Quarter Horses. AQHA was entitled to JMOL because it neither enjoyed nor was attempting to enjoy monopoly power in the elite Quarter Horse market. Beard v. Parkview Hosp., 912 F.2d 138, 144 (6th Cir. 1990) (defendant hospital that signed exclusive radiological services contract could not "monopolize" the radiological services market in which it did not compete).

According to the plaintiffs, competition in the monopolized relevant market is not a requirement of Section 2. This is incorrect. The only two cases they cite are inapposite or distinguishable. One case alleged a group boycott violating Section 1 of the Sherman Act with no claim of a Section 2 abuse of monopoly power. Tunica Web Adver., 496 F.3d at 409; see also Eastman Kodak Co. v. Image Technical Servs., Inc., 504 U.S. 451, 481, 112 S. Ct. 2072, 2090 (1992) ("Monopoly power under § 2 requires, of course, something greater than market power under§ 1."). In the other case relied on by Plaintiffs, an archery manufacturers and distributors trade association that put on an archery trade show acted in concert with association members to drive out of business its only competitor in the market for archery trade shows. Full Draw Prods. v. Easton Sports Inc., 182 F.3d 745 (10th Cir. 1999). The trade association competed directly in the monopolized market, and a motion to dismiss was accordingly reversed. In contrast to Full Draw, the Section 2 claim made in this case challenges only the conduct of AQHA (not concerted monopolization activity), and AQHA is not a competitor of the plaintiffs.

Finally, as case law demonstrates, the essential attributes of illegal monopoly power are judged by the monopolist's participation in the relevant market. See, e.g., American Tobacco Co. v. U.S., 328 U.S. 781, 809, 66 S. Ct. 1125 (1946) (defining monopoly power as the power to "exclude actual or potential competition from the field"); Heatransfer Corp. v. Volkswagenwerk, A. G., 553 F.2d 964, 981 (5th Cir. 1977) ("Such a share of the relevant market is sufficient to establish a monopoly power."); Sheridan v. Marathon Petroleum Co. LLC, 530 F.3d 590, 594 (7th Cir. 2008) ("Monopoly power we know is a seller's ability to charge a price above the competitive level (roughly speaking, above cost, including the cost of capital) without losing so many sales to existing competitors or new entrants as to make the price increase unprofitable.")(emphasis omitted). The ability to extract above-market profits from raised prices, the possession of large market share, and the ability to exclude one's competitors are all factors that could only apply to a party who participates in the relevant market that has been monopolized.

Consequently, the Section 2 claim failed as a matter of law because AQHA is not a competitor in the allegedly relevant market for elite Quarter Horses.

CONCLUSION

For these reasons, we REVERSE and RENDER judgment for the Appellant.

Chapter 9

Indigenous Agriculture & Biotechnology

This chapter looks at the ways that agricultural biotechnology have impacted the interests and needs for genetic preservation with attendant problems of genetic contamination. The chapter concludes with an examination of how indigenous food sovereignty has become a movement to return to a traditional diet that had been displaced with colonization and forced transition to reservation subsistence and how one tribal law is used to ensure that biotechnology does not alter traditional foods.

9.1.1 Genetic Preservation

Genetic preservation of seeds is the goal of the Doomsday Seed Bank, located in a remote area of the globe for exactly that potential global doomsday scenario. (Although climate change has been listed as the danger, an asteroid or other cosmic event could also be on the list.)

Other interests of Congress, such as endangered species have now been re-cast as genetic preservation. One example is a bill introduced by the late Representative from Hawaii (Cong. Patsy Mink):

Vol. 145, No. 9   145 Cong. Rec. 85 (Tuesday, January 19, 1999) HON. PATSY T. MINK of Hawaii in the House of Representatives:
Mrs. MINK of Hawaii. Mr. Speaker, today I am introducing the Plant Genetic Conservation Appropriations Act of 2000 that provides $1.5 million for a genetic plant conservation project that collects and preserves genetic material from our Nation's endangered plants. While the Fish and Wildlife Service continues to make strides in battling the war against further extinction of endangered species, we must do more. As of 1997 when I originally introduced this legislation, there were 513 plants listed as Endangered and 101 as threatened under the Endangered Species Act. Today, there are 567 plants listed as endangered and 135 as threatened. The need to supplement the Fish and Wildlife Services work is critical. I believe a crucial part of the solution to save our endangered species is the genetic plant conservation project, which can help save and catalog genetic material for later propagation. As genetic technology develops, we

will have saved the essential materials necessary to restore plant populations. The Plant Genetic Conservation Appropriations Act of 2000 requests $1.5 million for activities such as rare plant monitoring and sampling, seed bank upgrade and curation, propagation of endangered plant collections, expanded greenhouse capacity, nursery construction, cryogenic storage research, and in-vitro storage expansion. In my home state of Hawaii, the endangered plant population sadly comprises 46 percent of the total U.S. plants listed as endangered. And our endangered plant list continues to grow. We cannot afford to wait any longer. By allocating the resources and allowing scientists to collect the genetic samples now, we can ensure our endangered plants will survive. I strongly urge my colleagues to support the Plant Genetic Conservation Appropriations Act 2000. This necessary bill can lead us to preserving plants that many of our ecosystems cannot afford to lose.

The text of the bill reads as follows: H. R. 398, 106th Cong., 1st Sess.:
PLANT GENETIC CONSERVATION For expenses necessary to carry out a plant genetic conservation program to store material from rare, endangered, and threatened plants in Hawaii and other States and areas of the United States, including expenses for construction and maintenance of a temperature-controlled facility for such purpose, $1,500,000.

A recent article examines the International Treaty on Plant Genetic Resources for Food and Agriculture, as a tool for genetic conservation:

B. The International Treaty on Plant Genetic Resources for Food and Agriculture The Preamble of the Nagoya Protocol recognizes the multitude of international treaties and agreements that work in concert toward the aim of food security and sustainable development; for example, the 16th stanza acknowledging the importance of the International Treaty for Plant Genetic Resources for Food and Agriculture, created by the Food and Agricultural Organization ("FAO"). The Preamble of the International Treaty denotes that due to all countries relying heavily on food and agriculture that originated elsewhere, and the continued depletion of many natural resources, conservation is a common concern for all countries. While the United States signed the treaty in 2002, it has yet to be a contracting party, and thus cannot access the benefits of being a fullfledged member. The objective of this treaty is "the conservation and sustainable use of plant genetic resources for food and agriculture and the fair and equitable sharing of the benefits arising out of their use, in harmony with the Convention on Biological Diversity, for sustainable agriculture and food security." Particularly, the Benefit Sharing Fund, a multilateral system that offers both monetary benefits and non-monetary benefits, can be used for projects that represent innovative partnerships, potentially including seed bank networks. The United States can take advantage of the Multilateral System offered by the treaty and protocols to not only bolster the funds allocated to current domestic seed banks, but also to build additional seed banks. This system increases the chances for innovative solutions to be found to these complex issues around seed banks and regulation, partially due to the International Treaty declaring the genetic resources of 64 important crops, comprising of crops that account for 80% of all human consumption, accessible to everyone. The more minds working on preservation issues, the more likely a solution can be found. The genetic material for those crops can be accessed via gene banks around the world, from small research operations to national and international seed collections. Ratifying also comes with the benefit of funding from the Global Crop Diversity Trust, which is committed to raising funds for gene banks. Finally, in terms of addressing industry intellectual property and commercial competitive fears, agricultural corporations do not have to worry about being mandated to share new developments. In lieu of sharing the new developments, companies can simply pay a percentage of commercial benefits from research to a common fund that supports conservation in developing countries; a business and philanthropic two-in-one. There is also a mandatory Standard Material Transfer agreement that parties utilizing the Multilateral System must use; thus bringing uniformity to the transfer of plant genetic resources for food and agriculture use and ensuring conformity to the Treaty. UN agreements, such as the Standard Material Transfer, also take into account, and act in concert with, other international agreements such as the Rome Declaration on World Food Security and the World Food Summit Plan of Action. The combination of agreements provides a regulatory framework that is sufficient for United States policy makers to concoct cohesive laws on how the nation deals with food security, particularly seed storage and backups.

Patel, Jasmine (2017) "Deep Seeded Problems: A Look At Seed Bank Regulations," Seattle Journal of Environmental Law: Vol. 7 : Iss. 1 , Article 2. Available at: https://digitalcommons.law.seattleu.edu/sjel/vol7/iss1/2

9.1.2 Genetic contamination

One of the early signals that genetic contamination of heritage crops came with a study that showed that 5 of 7 traditional Mexican corn varieties had been contaminated with genetically modified corn. The study had been conducted between a scientist in Mexico and a scientist in California and it was published in Nature magazine, one of the most prestigious publications for new discoveries. (Nature, 2001). This had a tremendous impact and was regarded as hard evidence that GMOs were destined to contaminate the environment, including our protected original heritage crop plants.

The article was published in November 2001, and there was a great amount of controversy in the scientific community disputing these findings because no other examples of corn contamination had been found.

18. Kraus, S. D., Prescott, J. H., Knowlton, A. R. & Stone, G. S. in *Right Whale Past and Present Status* (eds Brownell, R. L. Jr, Best, P. B. & Prescott, J. H.) 145–151 (Rep. Int. Whaling Comm. Special Issue 10, Cambridge, 1986).

19. Knowlton, A. R. in *Shipping/Right Whale Workshop* (eds Knowlton, A. R., Kraus, S. D., Mack, D. T. & Mooney-Seus, M. L.) 31–36 (New England Aquarium Aquatic Forum Series Report 97–3, Massachusetts, 1997).

20. Plánaque, S. & Reid, P. C. Predicting *Calanus finmarchicus* abundance from a climatic signal. *J. Mar. Biol. Ass. UK* 78, 1015–1018 (1998).

21. Holden, C. Whale baby boomlet. *Science* 291, 429 (2001).

22. Hosmer, D. W. & Lemeshow, D. *Applied Logistic Regression* (Wiley, New York, 1989).

Acknowledgements

We thank S. Kraus, A. Knowlton, P. Hamilton and the NEA for data. We also thank S. Brault, M. Hill, P. Kareiva, J.-D. Lebreton, M. Neubert, J. Nichols and the participants of the first Woods Hole Workshop on the Demography of Marine Mammals for discussions and suggestions. This project was funded by the Woods Hole Oceanographic Institution Sea Grant Program, the Rinehart Coastal Research Center, the David and Lucile Packard Foundation and The Robert W. Morse Chair.

Correspondence and requests for materials should be addressed to M.F. (e-mail: mfujiwara@whoi.edu).

....

Transgenic DNA introgressed into traditional maize landraces in Oaxaca, Mexico

David Quist & Ignacio H. Chapela

Department of Environmental Science, Policy and Management, University of California, Berkeley, California 94720-3110, USA

Concerns have been raised about the potential effects of transgenic introductions on the genetic diversity of crop landraces and wild relatives in areas of crop origin and diversification, as this diversity is considered essential for global food security. Direct effects on non-target species[1,2], and the possibility of unintentionally transferring traits of ecological relevance onto landraces and wild relatives have also been sources of concern[3,4]. The degree of genetic connectivity between industrial crops and their progenitors in landraces and wild relatives is a principal determinant of the evolutionary history of crops and agroecosystems throughout the world[5,6]. Recent introductions of transgenic DNA constructs into agricultural fields provide unique markers to measure such connectivity. For these reasons, the detection of transgenic DNA in crop landraces is of critical importance. Here we report the presence of introgressed transgenic DNA constructs in native maize landraces grown in remote mountains in Oaxaca, Mexico, part of the Mesoamerican centre of origin and diversification of this crop[7-9].

In October and November 2000 we sampled whole cobs of native, or 'criollo', landraces of maize from four standing fields in two locations of the Sierra Norte de Oaxaca in Southern Mexico (samples A1–A3 and B1–B3), more than 20 km from the main mountain-crossing road that connects the cities of Oaxaca and Tuxtepec in the Municipality of Ixtlán. As each kernel results from ovule fertilization by individual pollen grains, each pooled criollo sample represents a composite of ~150–400 pollination events. One additional bulk grain sample (K1) was obtained from the local stores of the Mexican governmental agency Diconsa (formerly the National Commission for Popular Subsistence), which distributes subsidized food throughout the country. Negative controls were cob samples of blue maize from the Cuzco Valley in Peru (P1) and a 20-seed sample from an historical collection obtained in the Sierra Norte de Oaxaca in 1971 (H1). Positive controls were bulk grain

samples of Yieldgard *Bacillus thuringiensis* (Bt)-maize (Bt1; Monsanto Corporation) and Roundup-Ready maize (RR1; Monsanto Corporation) obtained from leftover stock for the 2000 planting season in the United States. Using a polymerase chain reaction (PCR)-based approach, we first tested for the presence of a common element in transgenic constructs currently on the market—the 35S promoter (p-35S) from the cauliflower mosaic virus (CMV). The high copy number and widespread use of p-35S in synthetic vectors used to incorporate transgenic DNA during plant transformation make it an ideal marker to detect transgenic constructs[10-12].

We obtained positive PCR amplification using primers specific for p-35S in five of the seven Mexican maize samples tested (Fig. 1). Four criollo samples showed weak albeit clear PCR amplification, whereas the Diconsa sample yielded very strong amplification comparable in intensity to transgenic-positive Bt1 and RR1 controls. The historical negative control (data not shown) and the contemporary sample from Cuzco, Peru, were both invariably negative. Low PCR amplification from landraces was due to low transgenic abundance (that is, a low percentage of kernels in each cob), not to differential efficiency in the reaction, as demonstrated by internal control amplification of the maize-specific alpha zein protein 1 gene (Fig. 1, *zp1*). During the review period of this manuscript, the Mexican Government (National Institute of Ecology, INE, and National Commission of Biodiversity, Conabio) established an independent research effort. Their results, published through official government press releases, confirm the presence of transgenic DNA in landrace genomes in two Mexican states, including Oaxaca. Samples obtained by the Mexican research initiative from sites located near our collection areas in the Sierra Norte de Oaxaca also confirm the relatively low abundance of transgenic DNA in these remote areas. The governmental research effort analysed individual kernels, making it possible for them to quantify abundances in the range of 3–10%. Because we pooled all kernels in each cob, we cannot make such a quantitative statement, although low PCR amplification signal from criollo samples is compatible with abundances in this percentage range.

Using a nested primer system, we were able to amplify the weak bands from all CMV-positive criollo samples (Fig. 1) sufficiently for nucleotide sequencing (GenBank accession numbers AF434747–AF434750), which always showed at least 98% homology with CMV p-35S constructs in commercially used vectors such as pMON273 (GenBank accession number X04879.1) and the K1 sample (accession number AF434746).

Further PCR testing of the same samples showed the presence of the nopaline synthase terminator sequence from *Agrobacterium tumefaciens* (T-NOS) in two of the six criollo samples (A3 and B2; GenBank accession numbers AF434752 and AF434751, respec-

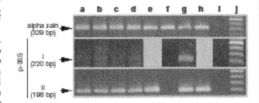

Figure 1 PCR amplification of DNA from the maize-specific alpha zein protein gene (top panel) and the CMV p-35S promoter (centre and bottom panels). The centre panel represents amplification protocol I (single amplification); the bottom panel indicates amplification protocol II (nested priming amplification). a–d, Criollo maize samples. Samples A2 (a), A3 (b), B2 (c) and B3 (d) are shown. e, Sample K1 from Diconsa store. f, Negative control P1, from Peru. g, Roundup-Ready maize RR1. h, Bt-maize Bt1. i, Internal negative control for PCR reaction. j, DNA ladder (100 base pairs (bp)), 500-bp marker at the top in each panel. Expected size for each fragment is marked on the left.

 541

256

In August 2005, in a rare action, Nature magazine withdrew the controversial finding of GMO contamination in Mexican maize. The authors speculate that the reason that no further genetic contamination had been found is because farmers were just getting better had isolating their GMO corn and protecting traditional maize. It remains to be seen if this will be repeated or if GMO corn simply does not contaminate the germ seed of corn, so that it is carried on to future generation. Fortunately, traditional Mexican maize was safe for now.

Four years on, no transgenes found in Mexican maize

Four years ago, the discovery of transgenes from genetically modified (GM) crops in traditional maize varieties in Oaxaca, Mexico, triggered an almighty row. A new survey suggests that measures taken since then to purge the crops of transgenes have been effective.

In the original paper, David Quist and Ignacio Chapela of the University of California, Berkeley, used the polymerase chain reaction (PCR) to detect two genetic sequences from GM maize in harvests from 2000 (D. Quist and I. H. Chapela *Nature* 414, 541–543; 2001). Using a variant of the technique called inverse PCR, they also argued that the transgenes had integrated throughout the genomes of Mexico's maize varieties.

This was a shocking result, as it suggested that the 'contaminated' plants were not sporadic hybrids. Instead, it seemed that the transgenes were entrenched in the traditional varieties at the centre of natural genetic diver-

sity for maize. "It was as if someone had gone to the United Kingdom and started replacing the stained-glass windows in the cathedrals with plastic," says Jorge Soberón, a former Mexican government scientist now at the University of Kansas in Lawrence and a co-author of the new study.

The inverse-PCR methodology used by Quist and Chapela soon came under fire, however, and *Nature* stated that it would not have published the paper if the criticisms had cropped up while the paper was under review. But even so, few experts questioned the basic finding that some transgenes had flowed into Mexican maize.

> "The authors speculate that the fields were cleared of transgenes through education of local farmers and a reduction in GM imports."

Despite an official moratorium on GM planting, this could have resulted from local farmers planting GM maize intended for food use that was imported from the United States. Unpublished work by Mexican government scientists also found transgenes, but a thorough and systematic confirmation was lacking.

That survey has now been done — and to the surprise of the authors, they found no transgenes at all. The sample of more than 150,000 seeds from 2003 and 2004 was negative for the same two transgenic sequences (S. Ortiz-García *et al. Proc. Natl Acad. Sci. USA* doi10.1073/pnas.0503356102; 2005). "I was convinced we were going to verify Quist and Chapela's results," says co-author Exequiel Ezcurra, head of the Biodiversity Research Center of the Californias at the San Diego Natural History Museum and former president of the National Institute of Ecology in Mexico City.

The authors speculate that transgenes were present in the fields in 2000, but dropped out of local maize varieties thanks to a programme of education for farmers and a reduction in GM maize imports. The researchers, led by Allison Snow of Ohio State University in Columbus, did not directly replicate Quist and Chapela's inverse-PCR methods. But Snow says that the apparent failure of the transgenes to persist down the generations contradicts the idea that they were entrenched in the genomes of the traditional maize varieties.

Brian Johnson, who follows developments in agricultural biotechnology for the government conservation agency English Nature, is unsurprised by this finding: "If there are transgenes in Mexico, or anywhere else, I would expect that they would be difficult to find — they would be rather sporadic." Johnson says he never believed they were permanently incorporated into the genes of traditional maize varieties.

Chapela stands by his findings, saying it is "naive" to believe an education programme could have such a dramatic effect. He claims that the commercial labs used by the research team to do the screening used conservative thresholds for declaring a match with the transgene sequences. But Bernd Schoel, director of research at one of those labs — Genetic ID of Fairfield, Iowa — says the screen was as sensitive as possible, given the sample size. ∎

Emma Marris

Maize unmodified: Mexican farmer Lorenzo Rebollo holds some of a recently harvested crop.

258

Meanwhile, Bayer Cropscience was learning that the rice genome was much more susceptible to receiving genetically modified rice fertilization, and traditional rice crops could be contaminated. Bayer Cropscience ended its research with genetically modified rice due to the danger of cross pollination and difficulty controlling potentional environmental contamination.

The following article discusses the ethical issues of protecting traditional crops from genetic contamination, not only because of the interest in biological integrity of the genomes of crops, but because they play such an important role in traditional ceremonies and traditions of indigenous people. The collection of wild rice by Minnesota's tribes is a centuries old tradition with specific techniques of collection and preservation.

Wild Rice and Ethics

By Winona LaDuke
28.3 Cultural Survival Quarterly (Sept. 15, 2004)

For the past five years, the Anishinaabeg community of Minnesota has asked the University of Minnesota to stop its genetic work on wild rice. "We object to the exploitation of our wild rice for pecuniary gain," wrote then Minnesota Chippewa Tribal President Norman Deschampe to the University of Minnesota in an 1998 letter. "The genetic variants of wild rice found naturally occurring on the waters in territories ceded by the Minnesota Chippewa Tribe to the state of Minnesota are a unique treasure that has been carefully protected by the people of our tribe for centuries. Rights to the rice have been the subject of treaty and it is a resource that enjoys federal trust protection. ... We are of the opinion that the wild rice rights assured by treaty accrue not only to individual grains of rice, but to the very essence of the resource. We were not promised just any wild rice; that promise could be kept by delivering sacks of grain to our members each year. We were promised the rice that grew in the waters of our people, and all the value that rice holds ... a sacred and significant place in our culture."

Virtually every tribal government and Native organization in the region has repeatedly called on the University to stop genetic work on wild rice. Finally, after attorneys for the Ojibwe filed a set of Freedom of Information Act requests, Dean Charles Muscoplat at the University of Minnesota began a "dialogue." The research in contention, however, continues unabated.

100 Years of Disagreement

"Academic Freedom" sometimes collides with ethics. In the new millennium, America expects both, and that is somewhat of a challenge.

About 100 years ago the University of Minnesota dispatched its first anthropologists to the reservations in the north. Albert Jenks came, along with his colleague from the Smithsonian Institute, Ales Hrdlicka, a physical anthropologist who specialized in comparing indigenous peoples' heads to monkey heads. The two came to White Earth Reservation and other reservations with scapulars in hand, and measured the heads of the Anishinaabeg. It turns out that Jenks not only measured Anishinaabeg heads, but returned later to study wild rice. In *The Wild Rice Gatherers of the Upper Lakes*, published by the Smithsonian Institution in 1900, Jenks noted with disdain the Ojibwe harvesting practices: "Wild rice, which had led to their advance thus far, held them back from further progress, unless, indeed, they left it behind them, for with them it was incapable of extensive cultivation."

In short, Jenks surmised that Ojibwe production systems were inadequate. This assumption would become the prevailing thought at the University of Minnesota throughout the 20th century. In the 1950s, University of Minnesota researchers decided that it was time to correct the laziness and created a new domesticated crop for the state: paddy-grown wild rice.

Ervin Oelke, another researcher at the University of Minnesota, began domesticating wild rice, using germplasm from 24 natural stands from throughout the state for most of his studies. The Ojibwe would contend that those natural stands belonged to them. Absent any tribal consent, Oelke and his researchers continued with their domestication. The impact of their work was fully realized with market analysis: the wholesale wild rice price dropped $4.44 per pound in 1967 to $2.68 per pound in 1976.

Wild Rice and Science
The International Wild Rice Association met in the basement of the Eldorado Casino in Reno, Nevada, in February 2003. Invited to discuss some of the concerns tribal nations have with the wild rice industry, I listened to University of Minnesota Extension Agent Raymond Porter present on the issues of agronomy and research. He also sought to dispel some of the criticism levied at the university by tribal representatives. Suggesting that the criticisms have been based, in part, on "misunderstanding and faulty conclusions," Raymond suggested that most of the issues raised by the tribes have been addressed by research and a number have been cleared up. Porter's essential argument was that the more the Native community understands about modern science and plant genomics, the more it will be happy with the research.

Porter's turf is the heart of Minnesota's cultivated wild rice research: an agricultural extension and experiment station in Grand Rapids, Minnesota. In 1963, the Bureau of Indian Affairs (keeping with Jenk's improved productivity strategy) provided funds to the station to begin work on wild rice. Subsequent funding increased beginning in 1964 and kept rising, with $100,000 a year allocated to wild rice research. By the 1990s, that amount increased even more. The U.S. Department of Agriculture awarded Porter a $237,171 grant for wild rice breeding and germplasm improvement, and other grants have continued to support the research.

Over years of research, the Minnesota Agricultural Extension office has created several strains of wild rice: 1968 Johnson, 1970 M1, 1972 M2, 1974 M3, 1978 Netum, 1983 Voyager, 1986 Meter, 1992 Franklin, and 2000 Petrowske Purple, all borne from the hands of University of Minnesota researchers. Are the varieties developed by the University of Minnesota researchers possibly contaminating the wild rice stands of the Anishinaabeg? Put it this way: there are around 6,000 bodies of water with significant wild rice beds in Minnesota, or around 60,000 acres of rice. And there are around 20,000 acres of cultivated wild rice paddies within close proximity of the many lakes of northern Minnesota. ,/p>
Pollen Drift and the Ducks

Anishinaabeg have long contended that paddy rice stands are contaminating the natural lake stands. Ronald Phillips, regents professor and McKnight Presidential Chair in Genomics at the University of Minnesota, claims there is little chance of cross pollination as long as approximately 660 feet separate the two kinds of wild rice. But research by the university extension office appears to be in keeping with criticism leveled at the university by the Ojibwe. In the summer of 2002, wild rice researchers studied possible pollen drift from paddy rice stands into wild stands. After a lot of different mathematical formulas, the bottom line is that there is a possibility that between one and five percent of the pollen from the test plots drifted up to two miles, and maybe further. Then there is the problem of the *zhiishiibig*—the ducks. There have been no systematic studies simulating duck and waterfowl movement in the wild rice area. Ducks and wild rice are a part of traditional Anishinaabeg stories, and likely will be in the future. Ducks and waterfowl do not differentiate between paddy rice plots and natural stands of wild rice; they move freely between both areas, carrying the rice from one into the other.

Wild Rice's Green Revolution

In the 1960s, paddy wild rice became a crop in Minnesota. Its production grew greatly in the 1970s, and Minnesota declared it the State Grain. Shortly thereafter, most people decided that to be in the wild rice industry, they needed to move to California, where they wouldn't have to contend with hail, wind, a fickle water supply, or inclement weather. By 1983, California was producing 8.5 million pounds, to Minnesota's 5 million pounds. In 2002 California produced 18 million pounds of paddy rice, while Minnesota's supply remained constant.

One would think that this quick shift to California would spell the end of the University of Minnesota's interest in the domesticated wild rice industry. But during the last five years the university has spent at least $1 million on its wild rice research programs—not including the budgets for their large wild rice breeding and genetics projects. This money, which comes mostly from the USDA, has been spent to benefit 20 paddy rice farmers, while Minnesota's 50,000 Indian people have been pushed aside once again.

Moving Forward

The Manoomin Ogitchidaag Coalition is composed of representatives from most of the Anishinaabeg bands in the region. In September 2003, the coalition made clear its demands to the University of Minnesota in a letter to Muscoplat's office: "a moratorium on genomic research and genetic research of wild rice at the University of Minnesota, to be effective December 31, 2004; protection of Anishinaabeg Intellectual Property Rights to Wild rice, including a ban on selling these rights; a cultural consultation program to be set in place by the University to examine the ethics of research on cross cultural issues; and mutually agreed upon beneficial research to be done on behalf of Anishinaabeg people, equal to that done on behalf of the cultivated wild rice industry." The university has yet to address these concerns.

One hundred years have passed since the head-measuring doctors came to the Anishinaabeg community. Academic freedom standards at that time may have been a bit lax, but the Anishinaabeg are concerned that the standards have not changed. Universities need to start recognizing that there is academic responsibility that goes along with their academic freedom. University of Minnesota researchers have stated that they will not genetically modify wild rice, which is a first step in guiding its research in the right direction. But there is much work to be done. The Anishinaabeg community is hopeful that the University of Minnesota will bring ethics into its relationships with indigenous people and others in the new millennium, so that we may stop the destructive patterns of research, and work toward a positive future for all of our children.

Winona LaDuke is founding director of the White Earth Land Recovery Project in Minnesota and program director of the Honor the Earth Fund.

The response to protect wild rice in Minnesota was the passing of an ordinance to prohibit the contamination of their traditional wild rice. In particular, the University of Minnesota was engaged in a program of genetically modifying rice, which posed a risk of contamination of the region's wild rice, across the bay.

FOND DU LAC BAND OF LAKE SUPERIOR CHIPPEWA

ORDINANCE #01/05

PROHIBITION OF GENETIC MODIFICATION OF MAHNOMEN

Adopted by Resolution #1036/05 of the Fond du Lac Reservation
Business Committee on February 3, 2005.

FOND DU LAC BAND OF LAKE SUPERIOR CHIPPEWA

ORDINANCE #_____

PROHIBITION OF GENETIC MODIFICATION OF MAHNOMEN

CHAPTER 1

AUTHORITY, PURPOSE AND SCOPE

Section 101   Authority

This Ordinance is enacted by the Fond du Lac Reservation Business Committee pursuant to the inherent sovereign authority of the Fond du Lac Fond du Lac Band of Lake Superior Chippewa, as recognized under the Treaty of LaPointe, 10 Stat. 1109; Section 16 of the Indian Reorganization Act, 25 U.S. C. S 476; the Indian SelfDetermination and Education Assistance Act, 25 U.S. C. S 450 et seq.;
Article VI of the Revised Constitution of the Minnesota Chippewa Tribe; and consistent with the purposes set forth under the Indian Religious Freedom Act, 42 U.S. C. § 1996.

Section 102   Purpose

The purpose of this Ordinance is to protect the cultural resources of the Fond du Lac Band through the prohibition of genetic modification of mahnomen (wild rice) within the Fond du Lac Reservation, or within the territories ceded to the United States under the Treaty of 1837, 7 Stat. 536, or under the Treaty of LaPointe, 10 Stat. 1109 ("ceded territories") , to the fullest extent of the Band' s authority.

Section 103   Findings

The Reservation Business Cotmittee recognizes that mahnomen playg an integral part of Anishinabe sustenance, culture and religion; that the preservation of mahnomen as a natural species is intimately related to continuity and vitality Of Anishinabe culture; that the genetic modification of mahnomen would irreversibly damage the maintenance of mahnomen as a natural species; and that the Reservation Business Committee must accordingly condemn, prohibit and oppose any program or activity which involves hybrid breeding, genetic mapping of the mahnomen rice genome, or any genetic modification of mahnomen as a natural species.

Section 104   Reservation of Rights

The Reservation Business Committee reserves the right to amend or repeal all or any part of thig Ordinance at any time. There shall be no vested private right of any kind created by this Ordinance. All the rights, privileges, or immunities conferred by this Ordinance or by acts done pursuant thereto shall exist subject to the power of the Reservation Business Committee. Nothing this Ordinance shall be construed to constitute a waiver of the sovereign immunity of the Fond du Lac Band or a consent to jurisdiction by any government or forum not expressly authorized to exercise jurisdiction under this Ordinance .

CHAPTER 2

DEFINITIONS AND INTERPRETATION

Section 201   Definitions

The following terms have the meanings given them.

a. Ceded territories means those territories ceded by the Fond du Lac Band under the treaties of 1837, 7 Stat. 536 and the Treaty of LaPointe, 10 Stat. 1109, over which the Band retains usufructuary rights regarding the harvest of mahnomen.

B. Fond du raac Band means the Fond du Lac Band of Lake Superior Chippewa.

b. Fond du Lac, Reservation means all land owned by the Fond du Lac Band or lying within the boundaries of the Fond du Lac Reservation.

d. means the elected governing body of the Fond du Lac

e. Genetically modified mahnomen or rice means mahnomen or wild rice

(1) altered at the molecular or cellular level by means that are not possible under natural conditions, including but not limited to recombinant DNA and RNA techniques, cell fusion, microencapsulation, macroencapgulation, gene deletion and doubling, introducing a foreign gene, and changing the positions of genes, other than a means consisting exclusively of breeding, conjugation , fermentation, hybridization, in vitro fertilization, or tissue culture the alteration, through the deletion or addition, to the genetic identity of mahnomen o wild rice; or

(2) made through sexual or asexual reproduction, o both, involving an organism described in subsection (1) of this section, if the mahnomen or wild rice possesses any of the altered cellular or molecular characteristics the organism so described.

f. Mahnomen or wild rice means the naturally grown species of mahnomen or wild rice whose genetic composition has not been altered by human manipulation.

Section 202   Interpretation

The provisions of this Ordinance shall be interpreted and administered in a manner which is intended to prevent the introduction of genetically modified mahnomen onto the Fond du Lac Reservation or into the ceded territories of the Fond du Lac.

The introduction, possession or cultivation of genetically modified mahnomen within the Fond du Lac Reservation or by any individual subject to this Ordinance within the Ceded Territories is prohibited.

Chapter 3
Prohibited Actions

Section 301   Prohibition of Gathering Mahnomen for the Purposes of Genetic Modification
The gathering of Mahnomen within the Fond du Lac Reservation or by any individual subject to this Ordinance within the Ceded Territories for the purpose of undertaking genetic modification of the species is prohibited.

Section 302   Prohibition of the Introduction, Possession, or Cultivation of Genetically Modified Mahnomen
The introduction, possession or cultivation of genetically modified Mahnomen within the Fond du Lac Reservation or by any individual subject to this ordinance within the Ceded Territories is prohibited.

Section 303   Prohibition of Cropp Pollination of Natural Mahnomen

The cross-pollination of genetically modified mahnomen with natural mahnomen within the Fond du Lac Reservation or by any individual subject to this Ordinance within the Ceded Territories is prohibited.

Chapter 4

ENFORCEMENT & PENALTIES

Section 401   Enforcement

The provisions of this Ordinance shall be enforced by any conservation officer of the Fond du Lac Band. Violations shall be subject to the original jurisdiction of the Fond du Lac Tribal Court.

Section 402   Penalties

Any violation of this Ordinance shall be subject to the following penalties :

a.   Mandatory appearance before the Fond du Lac Tribal Court ;

b.   fine of not less than $500; and

c.   Seizure of any genetically modified mahnomen, which shall be destroyed by the Fond du Lac Conservation Department after adjudication; and

Seizure of any instruments or devices which are directly used in undertaking any activity which is prohibited under this Ordinance.

CHAPTER 5

AMENDMENT OR REPEAL

Section 501   Amendment or Repeal

This Ordinance, and any provision herein, may be amended or repealed by resolution of the Fond du Lac Reservation Business Committee.

CERTIFICATION

We do hereby certify that the foregoing Ordinance #01/05 was duly presented and adopted by Resolution #1036/05 by a vote of 3 for, 0

against, 0 silent, with a quorum of 4 being present at a Special
Meeting of the Fond du Lac Reservation Business Committee held on
February 3, 2005 on the Fond du Lac Reservation.

Peter J. Defoe, Chairman

Vin R. DuBuis, Sr. Sec. Treas.

Fond du Lac Reservation
Business Committee

1720 Big Lake Rd.
Cloquet, MN 55720
Phone (218) 879-4593
Fax (218) 879-4146

RESOLUTION # 1036/05

The Fond du Lac Reservation Business Committee, on behalf of the Fond du Lac Band of Lake Superior Chippewa, hereby enacts the following Resolution:

WHEREAS , the Fond du Lac Reservation is a sovereignty, created by the Treaty of September 30, 1 54, 10 Stat. 1109, as the permanent home of the Fond du Lac Band of Lake Superior Chippewa, which possesses the inherent jurisdiction and authority to exercise regulatory control Secretary Treasurer within the boundaries of the Fond du Lac Kevin R. Dupuis, Sr.

WHEREAS , the Reservation Business Committee recognizes that mahnomen is an integral part of Anishinabe sustenance, culture and religion; that the preservation of mahnomen as a natural species is intimately relate to continuity and vitality of Anishnabe culture; that the genetic modification of mahnomen would irreversibly damage the maintenance of mahnomen as a natural species ; and

WHEREAS , the Reservation Business Committee has determined it to be necessary and in the best interests of the Fond du Lac Band to enact an ordinance protecting thig cultural resource through the prohibition of genetic modification Of mahnomen (wild rice) within the Fond du Lac Reservation, or within the territories ceded to the Unitëd States nder the Treaty of 1837, Stat. 536, or unde the Treaty of LaPointe, 10 Stat. 1109, to the fullest extent of the Band's authority.

WHEREAS , the Reservation Business Committee has determined it to be necessary and in the best interests of the Fond du Lac Band to enact an ordinance protecting thig cultural resource through the prohibition of genetic modification Of mahnomen (wild rice) within the Fond du Lac Reservation, or within the territories ceded to the Unitëd States under the Treaty of 1837, Stat. 536, or unde the Treaty of LaPointe, 10 Stat. 1109, to the fullest extent of the Band's authority;

NOW THEREFORE BE IT RESOLVED, that the Fond du Lac Reservation Business Committee does hereby adopt and enact Fond du Lac Ordinance #01/05, entitled "Prohibition of Genetic Modification of Mahnomen," for the purpose of protecting this cultural resource through the prohibition of genetic modification of mahnomen (wild rice) within the Fond du Lac Reservation, or within the territories ceded to the United States under the Treaty of 1837, 7 Stat. 536, or under the Treaty of LaPointe, 10 Stat. 1109, to the fullest extent of the Band's authority.

CERTIFICATION

We do hereby certify that the foregoing Resolution was duly presented and acted upon by a vote of 3 for, 0 against, 0 silent, with a quorum of 4 being present at a Special Meeting of the Fond du Lac Reservation Business Committee held on February 2, 2005 on the Fond du Lac Reservation.

Peter J. Defoe
Chairman

Kevin R. Dupuis, Sr.
Secretary/Treasurer

laws:12R012905

FOND DU LAC, R.B.C.

The Fond du Lac Chippewa have continued to respect their ceremonies and traditions of rice collection, but pressures from urbanization and environmental interest groups continues to threaten their sovereign control over their traditional crops.

9.1.3   Indigenous Food Sovereignty

The displacement and genocide of Native Americans in the U.S. (as well as globally) has also led to the loss of food sovereignty by tribes. This has occurred over centuries of disruption, resulting in the loss of food sovereignty over the diet and resources available to tribes as well as the ceremony and process of seed preservation and heritage. In addition, the seeds have been taken from the community and used in developing commercially patented varieties that are no longer shared with the communities from which they were derived (The Hawaiian Islands and Pacific Islands Taro root, is a good example, where the root was taken from the societies that cultivated and then genetically engineered to make it patentable and exclusive, without any involvement from the indigenous societies who had cultivated it for centuries.)

Article
The United Nations backs seed sovereignty in landmark small-scale farmers' rights declaration
By Timothy Wise
January 18, 2019

On Dec. 17, the United Nations General Assembly took a quiet but historic vote, approving the Declaration on the Rights of Peasants and other People Working in Rural Areas by a vote of 121-8 with 52 abstentions. The declaration, the product of some 17 years of diplomatic work led by the international peasant alliance La Via Campesina, formally extends human rights protections to farmers whose "seed sovereignty" is threatened by government and corporate practices.

"As peasants we need the protection and respect for our values and for our role in society in achieving food sovereignty," said Via Campesina coordinator Elizabeth Mpofu after the vote. Most developing countries voted in favor of the resolution, while many developed country representatives abstained. The only "no" votes came from the United States, United Kingdom, Australia, New Zealand, Hungary, Israel and Sweden.

"To have an internationally recognized instrument at the highest level of governance that was written by and for peasants from every continent is a tremendous achievement," said Jessie MacInnis of Canada's National Farmers Union. The challenge, of course, is to mobilize small-scale farmers to claim those rights, which are threatened by efforts to impose rich-country crop breeding regulations onto less developed countries, where the vast majority of food is grown by peasant farmers using seeds they save and exchange.

Seed sovereignty in Zambia

The loss of seed diversity is a national problem in Zambia. "We found a lot of erosion of local seed varieties," Juliet Nangamba, program director for the Community Technology Development Trust, told me in her Lusaka office.

She is working with the regional <u>Seed Knowledge Initiative (SKI)</u> to identify farmer seed systems and prevent the disappearance of local varieties. "Even crops that were common just 10 years ago are gone." Most have been displaced by maize, which is heavily subsidized by the government. She's from Southern Province, and she said their survey found very little presence of finger millet, a nutritious, drought-tolerant grain far better adapted to the region's growing conditions.

We found a lot of erosion of local seed varieties. Even crops that were common just 10 years ago are gone.

Farmers are taking action. Mary Tembo welcomed us to her farm near Chongwe in rural Zambia. Trained several years ago by <u>Kasisi Agricultural Training Center</u> in organic agriculture, Tembo is part of the SKI network, which is growing out native crops so seed is available to local farmers. Tembo pulled some chairs into the shade of a mango tree to escape the near-100-degree Fahrenheit heat, an unseasonable reminder of Southern Africa's changing climate. Rains were late, as they had been several of the last few years. Farmers had prepared their land for planting but were waiting for a rainy season they could believe in.

Tembo didn't seem worried. She still had some of her land in government-sponsored hybrid maize and chemical fertilizer, especially when she was lucky enough to get a government subsidy. But most of her land was in diverse native crops, chemical free for 10 years.

"I see improvements from organic," she explained, as Kasisi's Austin Chalala translated for me from the local Nyanja language. "It takes more work, but we are now used to it." The work involves more careful management of a diverse range of crops planted in ways that conserve and rebuild the soil: crop rotations; intercropping; conservation farming with minimal plowing; and the regular incorporation of crop residues and composted manure to build soil fertility. She has six pigs, seven goats, and 25 chickens, which she says gives her enough manure for the farm.

She was most proud of her seeds. She disappeared into the darkness of her small home. I was surprised when she emerged with a large fertilizer bag. She untied the top of the bag and began to pull out her stores of homegrown organic seeds. She laughed when I explained my surprise. She laid them out before us, a dazzling array: finger millet; orange maize; Bambara nuts; cowpea; sorghum; soybeans; mung beans; three kinds of groundnuts; popcorn; common beans. All had been saved from her previous harvest. The contribution of chemical fertilizer to these crops was, clearly, just the bag.

She explained that some would be sold for seed. There is a growing market for these common crops that have all but disappeared with the government's obsessive promotion of maize. Some she would share with the 50 other farmer members of the local SKI network. And some she and her family happily would consume. Crop diversity is certainly good for the soil, she said, but it's even better for the body.

Peasant rights crucial to climate adaptation

We visited three other Kasisi-trained farmers. All sang the praises of organic production and its diversity of native crops. All said their diets had improved dramatically, and they are much more food-secure than when they planted only maize. Diverse crops are the perfect hedge against a fickle climate. If the maize fails, as it has in recent years, other crops survive to feed farmers' families, providing a broader range of nutrients. Many traditional crops are more drought-tolerant than maize.

Another farmer we visited already had planted, optimistically, before the rains arrived. She showed us her fields, dry and with few shoots emerging. With her toe, she cleared some dirt from one furrow to reveal small green leaves, alive in the dry heat. "Millet," she said proudly. With a range of crops, she said, "the farmer can never go wrong."

The declaration gives farmers a potentially powerful international tool to defend themselves from the onslaught of policies and initiatives to replace native seeds with commercial varieties.

I found the same determination in Malawi, where the new Farm-Saved Seed Network (FASSNet) is building awareness and working with government on a "Farmers' Rights" bill to complement a controversial Seed Bill, which deals only with commercial seeds. A parallel process is advancing legislation on the right to food and nutrition. Both efforts should get a shot in the arm with the U.N.'s Peasants' Rights declaration.

The declaration gives such farmers a potentially powerful international tool to defend themselves from the onslaught of policies and initiatives, led by multinational seed companies, to replace native seeds with commercial varieties, the kind farmers have to buy every year.

Kasisi's Chalala told me that narrative is fierce in Zambia, with government representatives telling farmers such as Tembo that because her seeds are not certified by the government, they should be referred to only as "grain."

Eroding protection from GMOs

As if to illustrate the ongoing threats to farm-saved seed, that same week in Zambia controversy erupted over two actions by the government's National Biosafety Board to weaken the country's proud and clear stance against the use of genetically modified crops. The board quietly had granted approval for a supermarket chain to import and sell three products with GMOs, a move promptly criticized by the <u>Zambian National Farmers Union</u>.

Then it was revealed that the board secretly was drawing up regulations for the future planting of GM crops in the country, again in defiance of the government's approved policies. The <u>Zambian Alliance for Agroecology and Biodiversity</u> quickly <u>denounced the initiative</u>.

The U.N. declaration makes such actions a violation of peasants' rights. Now the task is to put that new tool in farmers' hands. "As with other rights, the vision and potential of the Peasant Rights Declaration will only be realized if people organize to claim these rights and to implement them in national and local institutions," argued University of Pittsburgh sociologists

Jackie Smith and Caitlin Schroering in <u>Common Dreams.</u> "Human rights don't 'trickle down' — they rise up!"

A/HRC/WG.15/3/2
Human Rights Council
Open-ended intergovernmental working group on the rights of peasants and other people working in rural areas
Third session
17–20 May 2016

Draft declaration on the rights of peasants and other people working in rural areas

presented by
the Chair-Rapporteur of the working group
The Human Rights Council,

Affirming that peasants and other people working in rural areas are equal to all other people and, in the exercise of their rights, should be free from any form of discrimination, including discrimination based on race, colour, sex, language, religion, political or other opinion, national or social origin, property, wealth, birth or other status,

Recognizing the past, present and future contributions of peasants and other people working in rural areas in all regions of the world to conserving and improving biodiversity and to ensuring food sovereignty, which are fundamental to attaining the internationally agreed development goals,

Convinced that peasants and other people working in rural areas should be provided with the means to promote and undertake environmentally sustainable practices of agricultural production that support and are in harmony with Mother Earth, including the biological and natural ability of ecosystems to adapt and regenerate through natural processes and cycles,

Concerned that peasants and other people working in rural areas suffer disproportionately from poverty and malnutrition and from the burdens caused by environmental degradation and climate change, and that an increasing number of peasants and other people working in rural areas are forcibly evicted or displaced every year to make way for large-scale development projects,

Stressing that peasant women and other rural women perform a disproportionate share of unpaid work and often do not have equal access to land, productive resources, financial services, information, employment or social protection,

Deeply concerned about the pervasiveness of violence against rural women and girls in all its forms and manifestations worldwide,

Stressing that several factors make it difficult for small-scale fishers and fish workers to make their voices heard, to defend their human rights and tenure rights, and to secure the sustainable use of the fishery resources on which they depend,

Recognizing that access to land, water, seeds and other natural resources is an increasing challenge for rural people, and stressing the importance of improving access to productive resources and investment in appropriate rural development, including agroecological approaches,

Considering the hazardous and exploitative conditions under which labourers in agriculture, fisheries and other activities have to work, often lacking living wages and social protection,

Deeply concerned that human rights defenders working on land and natural resources issues face a high risk of being subject to different forms of intimidation and of violations of their physical integrity, including attempted killings, killings, attacks, assault and ill-treatment, criminalization and excessive use of force by the police and other private bodies during demonstrations,

Noting that peasants and other people working in rural areas often face difficulties in gaining access to courts, police officers, prosecutors and lawyers to the extent that they are unable to seek immediate redress or protection from violence, abuse and exploitation,

Acknowledging that the Universal Declaration of Human Rights, the International Covenant on Economic, Social and Cultural Rights, the International Covenant on Civil and Political Rights, the Convention on the Elimination of All Forms of Discrimination against Women, the International Convention on the Eradication of Racial Discrimination, the Convention on the Protection of the Rights of All Migrant Workers and Members of Their Families and the Vienna Declaration and Programme of Action affirm the universality, indivisibility and interdependence of all human rights, civil, cultural, economic, political and social,

Recalling that, in order to address the labour protection gaps and decent work deficits faced by peasants and other people working in rural areas, the

International Labour Organization has developed an extensive body of conventions and recommendations, and that these standards represent the minimum rights to which these workers are entitled,

Recognizing that, in order to guarantee peoples' food sovereignty, it is essential to respect, protect and promote the rights recognized in the present declaration,

Affirming that freedom of association is a key enabling right to ensure that peasants and other people working in rural areas can join together to have access to and freely exercise the rights contained in the present declaration,

Affirming also that, according to the United Nations Declaration on the Rights of Indigenous Peoples, indigenous peoples, including indigenous peasants and other indigenous people working in rural areas, have the right to self-determination in matters relating to their internal and local affairs,

Recalling the outcome of the World Conference on Agrarian Reform and Rural Development and the Peasants' Charter adopted thereat, in which the need for the formulation of appropriate national strategies for agrarian reform and rural development, and their integration with overall national development strategies, was emphasized,

Convinced of the need for greater protection of the human rights of peasants and other people working in rural areas, and for a coherent interpretation and application of existing international human rights norms and standards in this matter, Emphasizing that the United Nations has an important and continuing role to play in promoting and protecting the rights of peasants and other people working in rural areas,

Solemnly adopts the following declaration on the rights of peasants and other people working in rural areas:

1. Definition and fundamental principles
Article 1: Definition of peasants and other people working in rural areas
1. For the purposes of the present declaration, the term peasant means any woman or man who engages in – or who seeks to engage in – small-scale agricultural production for subsistence and/or for the market, and who relies significantly, though not necessarily exclusively, on family or household labour and other non-monetized ways of organizing labour.

2. The present declaration applies to any person engaged in artisanal or small-scale agriculture, the raising of livestock, pastoralism, fishing, forestry, hunting or gathering, and handicrafts related to agriculture or a related occupation in a rural area.

3. The present declaration also applies to indigenous peoples working on the land, transhumant and nomadic communities and the landless.

. . . .

14
Article 22: Right to seeds

1. Peasants of all regions of the world have made, and will continue to make, enormous contributions to the conservation and development of plant genetic resources, which constitute the basis of food and agricultural production throughout the world.

2. Peasants and other people working in rural areas have the right to conserve, use, maintain and develop their own seeds, crops and genetic resources, or those of their choice. They also have the right to decide on the crops they wish to cultivate.

3. Peasants and other people working in rural areas have a right to save, store, transport, exchange, donate, sell, use and re-use farm-saved seeds, crops and propagating material. States should take appropriate measures to respect, protect and fulfil this right.

4. States shall take measures to respect, protect and promote traditional knowledge relevant to plant genetic resources.

5. States should respect, protect and promote peasant seed systems, and recognize the validity of the seed certification systems used by peasants.

6. States should take steps to ensure that planting material of sufficient quality and quantity are available to peasants that need them at the right time for planting, and for an affordable price.

7. States should ensure that agricultural research and development is oriented towards the needs of peasants and other people working in rural areas. To this end, in accordance with article 12.3 above and with the right of peasants to participate in making decisions on
matters relating to the conservation and sustainable use of plant genetic resources, States should ensure that the experience and the needs of peasants are effectively reflected when priorities for agricultural research and development are defined.

Article 23: Right to biological diversity
1. States recognize the enormous contribution that local, indigenous peoples and peasants of all regions of the world have made and will continue to

make to the conservation and development of agricultural biodiversity, which constitutes the basis of food and agricultural production throughout the world.

2. Peasants and other people working in rural areas have, individually or collectively, the right to conserve, maintain and develop agricultural biodiversity, and the right to associated knowledge, including in crops and animal races. This includes the right to save, exchange, sell or give away the seeds, plants and animal breeds that they develop. States shall recognize the collective use of and right to agricultural biodiversity, and the right to associated knowledge established and managed by peasants and other people working in rural areas.

3. States shall ensure that the seeds and livestock systems of peasants are protected from genetic contamination, biopiracy and theft. Peasants and other people working in rural areas have the right to maintain their traditional agrarian, pastoral and agroecological systems upon which their subsistence and their renewal of agricultural biodiversity depend.

4. Peasants and other people working in rural areas have the right to exclude from intellectual property rights genetic resources, agricultural biological diversity and associated knowledge and technologies that are owned, discovered or developed by their own communities.

5. Peasants and other people working in rural areas have the right not to accept certification mechanisms established by transnational corporations. They have the right to use certification mechanisms established or adopted by their Government. Guarantee schemes run by peasant organizations with government support should be promoted and protected.

6. States shall ensure that peasants and other people working in rural areas are free to conserve and develop their knowledge in agriculture, fishing and the rearing of livestock.

7. Peasants and other people working in rural areas have the right to be protected from measures threatening biological diversity and traditional knowledge, including forms of intellectual property that might adversely affect their traditional knowledge and use of genetic resources.

8. Peasants and others working in rural areas have the right to participate in decisionmaking on matters related to the conservation and sustainable use of agricultural biodiversity.

Chapter 10

Intellectual Property and Agricultural Biotechnology

10.1.1 Intellectual Property and Agricultural Biotechnology

10.1.1.1 Patents in Biotechnology

Biotechnology patents in the United States follow statutory guidelines, judicial interpretations, and the guidelines and standards of the U.S. Patent and Trademark Office (USPTO). The issues in international patenting of biotechnology are addressed in Chapter Five at 5.2. supra.

The U.S. Supreme Court established three requirements for a biotechnology patent in the case, Diamond v. Chakrabarty, 447 U.S. 303 (1980), discussed in Chapter One, 1.4, supra.: that "anything under the sun that is made by man" is patentable subject matter in accordance with 35 U.S.C. § 101. 447 U.S. 303 at 309. The three requirements are: (1) that the plant or animal invention must be a non-naturally occurring substance; (2) that the invention have a substantial amount of human intervention; and (3) the in- vention must have some useful industrial applicability, and is included in the Manual of Patent Examination Procedure §2105.

In USPTO policy, patentable subject matter is described as "non-naturally occurring, non-human, multicellular organisms" which does not recognize human creations because of the application of the U.S. Constitution, Thirteenth Amendment, prohibiting slavery. Donald J. Quigg, Policy Announcement by Assistant Secretary and Commissioner of Patents and Trademarks, 69 J. PAT. & TRADEMARK OFF. Soc'y 328 (1987).

In 1995, Congress passed legislation to provide for an exemption for the non-obvious requirement for biotechnology patents. The non-obviousness statutory require- ment is that "the subject matter sought to be patented and the prior art are such that the subject matter as a whole would have been obvious at the time the invention was made to a person having ordinary skill in the art to which said subject matter pertains." 35 U.S.C. § 103(a)

(2004). Because of the nature of the development of biotechnology, and the case In re Maney, 499 F.2d 1289 (Ct. Cl., 1974) it appeared that the nonobvious requirement would prevent the patenting of biotechnology in the United States and thereby leave inventors of many biotechnology products without protection in other countries where it could be patented.

In re Maney involved a known process method, but a novel starting material, which was a new strain of bacteria, Streptomyces. This process produced a novel antibiotic, daunorubicin. The USPTO denied the patent because they argued that one skilled in the art would find obvious, the process of developing the antibiotic. However, the Court of Claims held that it was the "invention as a whole;' rather than each part of the invention that must be non-obvious. Further, they held that the novelty of the starting material was determinative to non-obviousness, not the end product, or in this case, the antibiotic.

In 1998, the USPTO announced that §101 carried a morality element which would be applied in the review of patent applications that included biotechnologies. Donald J. Quigg, Patent and Trademark Office Issues Statement on Patenting of Partial Human Life Forms, 10 No. 6 J. Proprietary Rts. 17 (1998).

The Biotechnology Patent Act of 1995

Biotechnology is defined much more broadly in science than it is defined in patent law and limits the processes of biotechnology in § 103(b) to:

(A)   A process of genetically altering or otherwise inducing a single- or multi- celled organism to-

(i)   express an exogenous nucleotide sequence,

(ii)   inhibit, eliminate, augment, or alter expression of an endogenous nucleotide sequence, or

(iii)   express a specific physiological characteristic not naturally associ- ated with said organism;

(B)   cell fusion procedures yielding a cell line that expresses a specific protein, such as a monoclonal antibody; and

(C)   a method of using a product produced by a process defined by subpara- graph (A) or (B), or a combination of subparagraphs (A) and (B).93

These two processes, genetic alteration and cell line production and the problems with this narrow definition of biotechnology processes is described in the following article:

Becca Alley, The Biotechnology Process Patent Act of 1995: Providing Unresolved and Un-recognized Dilemmas in U.S. Patent Law, 12 J. INTELL. PROP. L. 229 (Fall 2004).

Genetic Alteration.

Genetic alteration, in general, is the manipulation of genetic material, or deoxyribonucleic acid (DNA). All living cells possess DNA, which are complex molecules which code for the production of proteins. These proteins, in turn, drive all of the basic functions of life. Specifically, each DNA molecule is composed of two polynucleotides associated to form a double helix. On the inside of this helix is a series of nucleic acid base pairs. There are only four nucleic acid bases which always pair the same way: adenine with thymine and guanine with cytosine. The sequence of these base pairs carries the organism's genetic information, providing instructions for the production of proteins (via ribonucleic acid (RNA)). In particular, series of three bases, called codons, encode for twenty specific amino acids which join together in certain combinations to compose specific proteins. These proteins play a central role in regulating the cell's functions and in determining the physiological characteristics of the organ- ism as a whole.

The statute describes genetic alteration as those procedures which stimulate a living thing to (1) express an exogenous nucleotide sequence, (2) change the expression of an endogenous nucleotide sequence, or (3) express a physiological trait not naturally associated with the organism. "Expression" of a nucleotide sequence refers to the process of protein synthesis from the genetic code. Expression of an exogenous nucleotide sequence thus involves an organism responding, via protein synthesis, to genetic information originating outside the organism. This new genetic information may be incorporated into an organism's pre-existing DNA through a number of recombinant DNA techniques. For example, in gene splicing, scientists use proteins called restriction enzymes to cut DNA molecules at specific locations and then insert foreign DNA, from the same or different species, at these locations. Similarly, altering the expression of an endogenous nucleotide sequence refers to a process of inducing an organism to express its original genetic material differently by starting, ceasing, or otherwise adjusting the production of certain proteins.

The third type of genetic alteration within the statutory definition involves the expression of a new physiological characteristic. This category is significantly more expansive than the previous two, apparently covering processes which do not involve the manipulation of DNA and thus are not processes of genetic alteration in the scientific sense. Specifically, a new physiological characteristic broadly refers to any change in the normal functioning of a living organism. The exact scope of this clause is somewhat vague and depends upon the definition of the word "express;' which in the context of the statute may be interpreted either as a genetics term of art or in its generic sense.

As mentioned earlier, expression in the field of genetics refers to the process of synthesizing proteins from the genetic code. Applying this definition would limit the scope of clause (iii) to those physiological changes which result from altered protein synthesis due to adjustments in the genetic code. This interpretation, however, would render clause (iii) superfluous given that the previous two clauses already cover such genetic alterations. That is, at a basic level, clause (i) covers processes incorporating outside genetic information while clause (ii) covers all other genetic alterations, specifically those involving changes to the organ- ism's original DNA. Additionally, the statute refers to "a process of genetically altering or otherwise inducing" new physiological characteristics. Since, "otherwise inducing" cannot apply to either of the previous clauses (because changes in nucleotide sequences are, by definition, processes of genetic alteration), these words too would be rendered superfluous if not applied to clause (iii).

The difficulties surrounding the term of art definition suggest that "express" should be interpreted in its generic sense to denote an outward manifestation. Under this extremely broad-but perhaps necessary-interpretation, any procedure which stimulates an organism to manifest an unnatural physiological characteristic (i.e., to change its normal functioning) is a biotechnology process under the statute . This definition could include procedures, such as injecting an organism with an inorganic chemical compound, which are beyond the bounds of genetic alteration in the scientific world.

2.   The Production of Cell Lines.

The second statutory category of biotechnology process involves the production of cell lines. Cell lines are populations of cells cultured in vitro (i.e., outside a living organism) that are descended from a single primary culture. These cells have common characteristics, and for this reason, researchers frequently utilize cell lines to produce specific proteins. The statute expressly mentions monoclonal antibodies, which are immune proteins secreted by a clone of cells, as an example of such a protein. Because these proteins specifically bind to particular antigens (i.e., foreign agents, such as bacterial and viral molecules, which elicit an immune response), monoclonal antibodies are particularly useful in laboratory research, clinical diagnosis, and the treatment of disease. The statute limits the production of cell lines, however, to those which result from cell fusion procedures, leaving out other production methods.

Additionally, the statute fails to incorporate numerous procedures involving isolated cells and cell products, which scientists generally categorize as biotechnology processes. That is, part (A) of the statutory definition applies only to "single and multi-celled organisms" while part (B), which applies to isolated cells, is limited to the production of cell lines through cell fusion procedures. This indicates that all other processes involving isolated cells or cell products are excluded under the statute (with the exception of those defined by part (C), described below). In other words, the statutory definition leaves out various biotechnological procedures, such as isolation of enzymes from animal and plant sources, incorporation of amino acids in food products and pharmaceuticals, and even certain developments in stem cell research.

A summary of the requirements for a biotechnology patent below, are taken from Margaret M. Duncan, Kathleen Harris, Duncan Curley and Patrick D. Richards, McDermott, Will & Emery, "Legal Implications for Patenting Genomics and Proteomics" Proceedings of The Biotech Law & Litigation Summit, Palo Alto, California (April 30-May l, 2001).

10.1.1.2   Biotechnology Patents Applications Requirements

There are three patentability requirements for biotechnology patent applications: the utility requirement in 35 U.S.C. § 101; the written description requirement of 35 U.S.C.§ 112; and the enablement requirement of 35 U.S.C. § 112. Those three patent requirements are described below.

10.1.1.3   The Utility Requirement

35 U.S.C. §101. The utility requirement was established in Brenner v. Manson, 383 U.S. 519, 534 (1966) wherein the U.S. Supreme Court held that an invention must have a definite, immediate, and demonstrable utility to meet the utility requirement of§ 101. The USPTO applied the Brenner standards to biotechnology patent applications and re- quired human clinical data to demonstrate biotechnology invention utility. See, Ex parte Balzarini, 21 U.S.P.Q.2d 1892, 1897 (Bd. Pat. App. & Interferences 1991), until 1995. In 1995, the USPTO issued guidance for biotechnology patent utility. Utility Examination Guidelines, 60 Fed. Reg. 36,263 (1995).

The USPTO also issued a series of interim utility guidance for comment between 1995 and 1999 which addressed the rising concerns regarding the legality and morality of issuing gene patents. Revised Utility Examination Guidelines; Request for Com- ments, 64 Fed. Reg. 71,440 (1999); Revised Utility Examination Guidelines; Request for Comments, Correction, 65 Fed. Reg. 3,425 (2000). These guidelines required the applicant to "explicitly identify, unless already well-established, a specific, substantial, and credible utility" for the claimed invention. These guidelines were intended to pro- vide examiners a basis for rejecting a gene patent application disclosing only theoretical utility.

Final utility guidance was issued in January 5, 2001, Utility Examination Guide- lines, 66 Fed. Reg. 1,092 (2001). The final guidance requires that examiners "review the claims and the supporting written description to determine if the applicant has asserted for the claimed invention any 'specific and substantial utility' that is credible, based on the view of one of ordinary skill in the art and any record evidence." Failure to meet the utility requirements of the guidance will result in a rejection under § 101 for lack of utility and under § 112 '" 1 for failure to teach how to use the invention.

Still, the guidance is criticized for not establishing distinctions between the classic discovery verses invention. According to the USPTO, "an inventor's discovery of a gene can be the basis for a patent on the genetic composition isolated from it's natural state and processed through purifying steps that separate the gene form other molecules naturally associated with it." PTO Finalizes Guidelines For Examiners on Utility Requirement, 61 PAT. TRADEMARK & COPYRIGHT J. (BNA) 252 (January 12, 2001).

10.1.1.4   The Written Description Requirement. 35 U.S.C. § 112

The written description requirement is codified at 35 U.S.C. § 112 '"l, "Written Description" Requirement, 66 Fed. Reg. 1,099 (2001). The published guidance for examiners in evaluating biotechnology patents requires the following procedure: (1) compare what the applicant possesses and what the applicant claims; (2) determine whether there is sufficient written description to inform a skilled artisan that the applicant is in possession of the claimed invention as a whole; (3) for species claims, determine whether the application (i) includes a reduction to practice; (ii) is complete based on the drawings; or (iii) identifies sufficient distinguishing characteristics to show the applicant was in possession of the claimed invention; and (4) for genus claims, determine whether the application: (i) describes a representative number of species by reduction to practice, drawings, or disclosure of identifying characteristics; or (ii) disclosed functional characteristics correlated with structure or a combination of identifying characteristics that indicate the inventor was in possession of the claimed invention.

For example, these heightened written description requirements for biotechnology patents may not require the exact DNA sequence to meet the written description requirement, but it appears likely that the USPTO will only grant, and the Federal Circuit, U.S. Court of Appeals, will only enforce patent protection to the extent of the scope of the invention at the time of the invention.

The guidance indicate that, in general, as knowledge and skill in the relevant art improve, the written description requirements may begin to relax. See, Margaret Sampson, The Evolution of the Enablement and Written Description Requirement Under 35 U.S.C. 112 in the Area of Biotechnology, 15 BERKELEY TEctt.L.J. 1233, 1266 (2000).

10.1.1.5   The Enabling Requirement. 35 U.S.C. § 112

The Federal Circuit, U.S. Court of Appeals, has reinforced the enabling requirement by invalidating broad biotechnology claims requiring "undue experimentation." In 1999, in Enzo Biochem, Inc. v. Ca/gene, Inc., 188 F.3d 1362 (Fed. Cir. 1999), the Federal Circuit, U.S. Court of Appeals returned to the Wands factors from In re Wands, 858 F.2d 731 (Fed. Cir. 1988), in determining where there was "undue experimentation.

The Wands factors are: (1) the quantity of experimentation required; (2) the amount of guidance provided; (3) the presence or absence of working examples; (4) the nature of the invention; (5) the state of the prior art; (6) the relative skill of those in the art; (7) the predictability of the art; and (8) the breadth of the claims.

_____

10.1.2 Monsanto v. Schmeiser

10.1.2.1 Unique Problems in Patenting Biotechnology

Monsanto Canada, Inc. v. Schmeiser
File No. T-1593-98
Federal Court Trial Division
2001 ACWSJ LEXIS 2163 (March 29, 2001)

Judge MacKay

This is an action heard in Saskatoon, against the defendants, pursuant to the Patent Act,

R.S.C. 1985, c. P-4 (the" Act"), for alleged infringement of the plaintiffs' Canadian Letters

Patent No. 1,313,830. The infringement alleged is by the defendants using, reproducing and creating genes, cells and canola seeds and plants containing genes and cells claimed in the plaintiffs' patent, and by selling the canola seed they harvested, all without the consent or licence of the plaintiffs. The commercial product resulting from the plaintiffs' develop- ment, from its patent and licensing agreements, is known as "Roundup Ready Canola", a canola seed that is tolerant of glyphosate herbicides including the plaintiffs' "Roundup".

On consideration of the evidence adduced, and the submissions, oral and written, on behalf of the parties I conclude that the plaintiffs' action is allowed and some of the remedies they seek should be granted . These reasons set out the bases for my conclusions, in particular my finding that, on the balance of probabilities, the defendants in- fringed a number of the claims under the plaintiffs' Canadian patent number 1,313,830 by planting, in 1998, without leave or licence by the plaintiffs, canola fields with seed saved from the 1997 crop which seed was known, or ought to have been known by the defendants to be Roundup tolerant and when tested was found to contain the gene and cells claimed under the plaintiffs' patent. By selling the seed harvested in 1998 the defendants further infringed the plaintiffs' patent....

Introduction

The plaintiff Monsanto Canada Inc. ("Monsanto Canada") is incorporated under the laws of Canada, and has its principal place of business in Mississauga, Ontario. The plaintiff Monsanto Company ("Monsanto US") is incorporated under the laws of the state of Delaware, U.S.A., and has its principal place of business in St. Louis, Missouri,

U.S.A. Reference to both corporations in these reasons is made by the terms "Monsanto" or "the plaintiffs."

On February 23, 1993, Monsanto US was issued Canadian Letters Patent No. 1,313,830 ("the '830 patent") for an invention termed "Glyphosate-Resistant Plants." ...

The defendant, Percy Schmeiser ("Mr. Schmeiser"), is an individual who resides near Bruno, Saskatchewan, and who has farmed in that region for more than 50 years. The defendant, Schmeiser Enterprises Ltd., is a corporation organized under the laws of Saskatchewan. It has existed since 1960 in relation to a number of other businesses op- erated by Mr. Schmeiser, and it was assigned control of his farming business in 1996. The only shareholders and directors of the corporation are Mr. Schmeiser and his wife. Reference to both defendants in these reasons is made by the terms "Schmeiser" or "the defendants."

Mr. Schmeiser has been farming near Bruno in the Rural Municipality of Bayne, Saskatchewan, for approximately 50 years. He has grown canola since the 1950's. There, in 1998, the year giving rise to the plaintiffs' claim, his corporation farmed nine fields, in which 1030 acres were devoted exclusively to growing canola. In addition to his farm- ing, Mr. Schmeiser has an extensive history in municipal and provincial politics, and as a businessman and an adventurer.

The plaintiffs' claim alleges that in 1998 the defendants planted glyphosate-resistant seeds to grow a crop of canola, for harvest, having a gene or cell that is the subject of the plain- tiffs' patent. By so doing the defendants are said to use, reproduce and create genes, cells, plants and seeds containing the genes and cells claimed in the plaintiffs' patent. The parties agree that the defendants did not at any time sign a Technology Use Agreement ("TUA"), the plaintiffs' form of license for growers of the seed containing the patented gene....

The defendants do not deny the presence of Roundup Ready canola in their fields in 1998, but they urged at trial that neither Mr. Schmeiser nor Schmeiser Enterprises Ltd. have ever deliberately planted, or caused to be planted, any seeds licensed by the plain- tiffs containing the patented gene. The defendants further asserted that substantial damage and loss has been suffered by them because of the herbicide-resistant plants. It is said for them that it is not possible to control the growth of the Roundup Ready canola with normal herbicides, it interferes with crop selection, making it difficult to plant anything other than canola, and it requires the adoption of new farming practices. I note that despite this claim no counterclaim by the defendants is before the Court. They do urge that, even if the plaintiffs' patented gene is present in the canola grown by the defendants, that gene must be used, in the sense that the crop must be sprayed with the herbicide Roundup, before any infringement of the patent can be found.

The defendants urged at trial that by the unconfined release of the gene into the environment the plaintiffs have not controlled its spread, and did not intend to do so, and they have thus lost or waived their right to exercise an exclusive patent over the gene.

The defendants further asserted at trial that Canadian Patent No. 1,313,830 is, and always has been, invalid and void because:

(a) the alleged invention is a life; form intended for human consumption and is not the proper subject matter for a patent; it is self-propagating and can spread without human intervention;

(b) the patent was obtained for an illicit purpose of creating a noxious plant that would spread by natural means to the lands of innocent parties so as to entrap them with nui- sance patent infringement claims. I note that no evidence was adduced and no argument was directed at trial to the alleged illicit purpose; ...

The patent in issue, entitled "Glyphosate-Resistant Plants", concerns man-made genet- ically-engineered genes, and cells containing those genes which, when inserted in plants, in this case canola, make those plants resistant to glyphosate herbicides such as Monsanto's product sold under the trade-mark Roundup. Glyphosate herbicides inhibit the enzyme known as EPSPS, required to produce a particular amino acid essential for the growth and survival of a very broad range of plants. The herbicide so inhibits the enzyme EPSPS that most plants sprayed with Roundup or other glyphosates do not survive.

By laboratory developments scientists of Monsanto US created a genetic insert, known as RT73, which, when introduced into the DNA of canola cells by a transformation vector, produces a variety of canola with a high level of tolerance to glyphosate. Once the modified gene is inserted in the DNA of the plant cells, the plant, its stem, leaves, seeds, etc., contain the modified gene. The plant's progeny, growing from seed with the patented gene and cells, will largely be comprised of cells with the modified gene. Thus the offspring or seeds of Roundup Ready canola, which is mainly self-germinating, contain the modified gene so that they too are glyphosate-tolerant....

Glyphosate herbicides such as Roundup have been widely used in Canada for many years. Canola tolerant to glyphosate first became available commercially in Canada in 1996. It has been marketed under licensing arrangements through Monsanto Canada under Monsanto's trade-mark Roundup Ready Canola. In 1996 approximately 600 farmers in Canada planted Roundup Ready canola, on some 50,000 acres. By 2000, approximately 4.5 to 5 million acres of Roundup Ready canola were planted in Canada, by about 20,000 farmers, producing nearly 40% of canola grown in Canada....

Canola growing in western Canada is a great Canadian success story. Rape seed was grown on a relatively small scale for many years. Now with the development, largely by Canadian scientists, of high yield seed, now called canola, crops for oil for human consumption and meal for animal feed, provide the greatest annual value of all grain crops in Canada.

The advantage of Roundup Ready canola is that it is tolerant to the glyphosate herbicide Roundup which can be sprayed after the desired crop has emerged, killing other plants. This procedure is said to avoid any need to delay seeding for early weed spraying, to avoid the use of other special types of herbicides, and to eliminate the need for extensive tillage of the land, thus preserving moisture in the ground.

Because the progeny of glyphosate-resistant canola will contain the modified gene and will also be glyphosate-resistant, Monsanto developed a licensing arrangement to protect its patent, and its market, by limiting the opportunity of a grower, under licence, to sell or give seed to another or to retain it for his own use.

All of the plaintiffs' licensing arrangements in Canada are made by or on behalf of Monsanto Canada. It licenses commercial seed growers to grow Roundup Ready canola for seed purposes. Farmers are required to attend a Grower Enrollment Meeting conducted by Monsanto representatives who describe the gene technology and the licensing terms for its use, A grower must be certified to use the gene technology by signing a Roundup Ready grower agreement. This entitles a farmer to purchase Roundup Ready canola seed from an authorized Monsanto agent, but to acquire seed the farmer must also sign a Technology Use Agreement provided by the retail seed agent acting for Monsanto Canada. Under the latter agreement, the farmer can use the seed for planting only one crop, to be sold for consumption to a commercial purchaser authorized by Monsanto. The farmer undertakes not to sell or give seed to any other third party and not to save seed for his own replanting or inventory. Under the TUA Monsanto has the right to inspect the fields of the contracting farmer and to take samples to verify compliance with the agreement.

Mr. Schmeiser's farming practices

As is apparently common practice for a number of canola farmers in the Bruno area, Mr. Schmeiser routinely saved a portion of the canola harvested on his property to serve as seed for the next generation of crops. Through this procedure, Mr. Schmeiser was able to avoid purchasing canola seed after 1993, until 1999, and over the years he believes he was able to develop his own strain of canola that was relatively resistant to various forms of diseases that tend to attack canola.

It is the defendants' usual practice to grow a conventional variety of canola known as Ar- gentine canola. They also grow wheat and peas, and in addition portions of his land are subject to summer fallow from time to time. For a number of years, Mr. Schmeiser has chosen to grow canola crops back-to-back in the same fields for a period of up to four years. At trial, he asserted that the advantage to such a farming practice is that one may then utilize the benefits of the fertilizer applied the year before, thereby using less and often creating a greater crop yield in the subsequent years. It is also the general practice of Mr. Schmeiser to time the cultivation of his land so as to avoid tilling potentially diseased plant remains into the soil and thereby reducing the possibility of certain diseases developing in new crops. Through this practice over the long-term the defendants say Mr. Schmeiser has been able to grow canola crops that are relatively free of weeds and the common diseases of blackleg and sclerotinia that plague canola. He claims his crops have been better-than-average yields in the Bruno, Saskatchewan area....

In the 1996 crop year, from which Mr. Schmeiser's 1998 seed was said to be derived through the 1997 crop, there were five other growers with farms in the Rural Municipality of Bayne No. 371 who grew Roundup Ready canola. It is the evidence of Aaron Mitchell, Biotechnology Manager, Research Development Department of Monsanto, at Saskatoon, that of the farms licensed to grown Roundup Ready canola in 1996 the clos- est field to the defendants' field number 2, from which seed was saved in 1997, was ap- proximately five miles.

I note that in 1996 one of the licensed farmers, Mr. Huber, a neighbour of Mr. Schmeiser, grew seed under license from Monsanto on a quarter section just north and west of, and diagonally adjacent to, Mr. Schmeiser's field No. 6. It was the evidence at trial of Mr. Schmeiser's hired man, Carlysle Moritz, that at the end of the 1996 crop year, a substantial swath of canola had blown from Mr. Huber's land onto field No. 6. There was no evidence that seed from Schmeiser's field No. 6 was saved in 1996 to be used as seed for his 1997 crop.

The evidence of Mr. Mitchell for Monsanto is that after both the 1996 and 1997 crop years, the crop was collected from licensed growers by commercial truckers who deliv- ered all of the canola to crushing plants in trucks with tight tarpaulins. In the case of the Bruno crop area, the crushing plants were located at Nipawin or Clavet.

Testing of Mr. Schmeiser's canola

Despite inconsistencies in the recollections of witnesses for the plaintiffs on the one hand, and for the defendants on the other, the chronology of events leading to the commencement of this action can be generally described.

In the summer of 1997, the plaintiffs, through Robinson Investigations, a private agency in Saskatoon, undertook random audits of canola crops growing in Saskatchewan. The farms were identified by Monsanto from among their licensed farmers, or from leads or tips suggesting that Roundup Ready seed might be growing on property of an unlicensed farmer, or from random inspections undertaken to audit a farming area. The defendants' farm was included in this audit process after an anonymous tip was received indicating that Roundup Ready canola was being grown in Schmeiser's fields, where it was not li- censed.

As we have noted Mr. Schmeiser testified that in 1997 he planted his canola crop with seed saved from 1996 which he believed came mainly from field number 1. Roundup resistant canola was first noticed in his crop in 1997, when Mr. Schmeiser and his hired hand, Carlysle Moritz, hand-sprayed Roundup around the power poles and in ditches along the road bordering fields l, 2, 3 and 4. These fields are adjacent to one another and are located along the east side of the main paved grid road that leads south to Bruno from these fields. This spraying was part of the regular farming practices of the defendants, to kill weeds and volunteer plants around power poles and in ditches. Several days after the spraying, Mr. Schmeiser noticed that a lame portion of the plants earlier sprayed by hand had survived the spraying with the Roundup herbicide.

In an attempt to determine why the plants had survived the herbicide spraying, Mr. Schmeiser conducted a test in field 2. Using his sprayer, he sprayed, with Roundup herbi- cide, a section of that field in a strip along the road. He made two passes with his sprayer set to spray 40 feet, the first weaving between and around the power poles, and the second beyond but adjacent to the first pass in the field, and parallel to the power poles. This was said by him to be some three to four acres in all, or "a good three acres". After some days, approximately 60% of the plants earlier sprayed had persisted and continued to grow.

Despite this result Mr. Schmeiser continued to work field 2, and, at harvest, Carlysle Moritz, on instruction from Mr. Schmeiser, swathed and combined field 2. He included swaths from the surviving canola seed along the roadside in the first load of seed in the combine which he emptied into an old Ford truck located in the field. That truck was covered with a tarp and later it was towed to one of Mr. Schmeiser's outbuildings at Bruno. In the spring of 1998 the seed from the old Ford truck was taken by Mr. Schmeiser in another truck to the Humboldt Flour Mill ("HFM") for treatment. After that, Mr. Schmeiser's testimony is that the treated seed was mixed with some; bin-run seed and fertilizer and then used for planting his 1998 canola crop.

Derbyshire samples, 1997 crop

Before the 1997 crop was harvested, acting for Robinson Investigations, on August 18, 1997, Mr. Wayne Derbyshire, after trying unsuccessfully to speak with Mr. Schmeiser at his garage and at his residence, took pod samples of canola from the west side, along the road allowance, beside field 2 and from the south and east sides along the road al- lowances bordering field 5. He testified he did not trespass on Schmeiser's land, taking his samples from the crop apparently planted, as Mr. Schmeiser does and many other farmers do, in the road allowance bordering his fields. Mr. Derbyshire placed the samples of pods from three or four plants in separate bags, marking them for identification by Mr. Schmeiser 's name, the date, his own file number and the number of the sample. The location of the sample gathering was described by Mr. Derbyshire in a document dated August 21, 1997, which, with the samples, was delivered to Robinson Investigations in Saskatoon on August 27, by courier. Until then the samples had been retained, sealed, in Mr. Derbyshire's car until his work in the Bruno area was completed on August 19....

At the University of Saskatchewan in the fall of 1997, four seeds of each sample were planted and two, three or four of the seeds germinated from each sample. When these reached the two or three leaf stage they were sprayed with Roundup herbicide. More than three weeks later all plants from five of these samples had survived the spraying....

Rather, in his view, the high percentage of glyphosate-tolerant plants, among those which had germinated, indicated they were grown from commercial Roundup Ready canola seed.

As a result of the 1997 test on samples of Schmeiser's canola, in March 1998, Mr. Robin- son, on instruction from Monsanto, visited Mr. Schmeiser in Bruno, and advised him that it was believed that Schmeiser had grown Roundup Ready canola the previous summer. Mr. Robinson testified he told

Mr. Schmeiser that he was representing Monsanto and that samples had been taken the previous summer. Mr. Schmeiser denies this was said.. ..

Sample in June 1995

In late July, 1998, Mr. E. L. Shwydiuk, a representative of Robinson Investigations, act- ing for Monsanto, collected random samples of leaves from several canola plants growing in the rights of way near the boundary of each of Schmeiser's nine fields. These were subjected by Mr. Shwydiuk to a "quick test", developed and used by Monsanto for de- tecting the presence of a protein found within Roundup Ready canola as a result of the inserted patented gene and cell. Each sample, from all the locations, tested positive for the presence of the tell-tale protein As a result of tests by Monsanto all of these samples were positive for the presence of the patented gene....

As earlier noted, the defendants did not purchase canola seed from 1993 until 1999. In 1999, because this action had been initiated, on the advice of their counsel the defendants destroyed all canola seed held from previous crops and purchased an entirely new inventory of seed for the planting of their 1999 canola crop, the source of which would be unquestioned. However, volunteer plants of Roundup Ready canola were said to be found within the 1999 canola fields grown by the defendants.

The issues

The issues arising in this action concern

-the admissibility of evidence of the tests conducted on samples of Schmeiser's canola,

-the validity of the plaintiffs' patent,

-possible waiver of patent rights by the plaintiffs,

- infringement of the patent, ...

I conclude that the samples taken under Court order in August 1998 were obtained in accord with the law. Evidence of tests using those samples is relevant to the issues before the Court and is admissible.

As for the samples taken in 1997 by Mr. Derbyshire, in the road allowances of fields and 5, and the samples obtained by the plaintiffs from HFM, it is urged that these were samples of the defendants' products, of their property, taken without their knowledge or approval. The same could be said of the nine leaf samples taken on July 30, 1998 by Mr. Shwydiuk, for the Robinson firm, which he selected from the public rights of way or road allowances bordering the nine fields on which Mr. Schmeiser's canola was growing. Taking the samples in all these cases is said to be unlawful, a conversion of the defendants' property, without permission. Even if the samples were taken from the public rights of way it is urged the plants were still the property of the defendants. It is urged that property in the samples taken by Messrs. Derbyshire and Shwydiuk, and the samples provided by HFM, originally withheld from Schmeiser for HFM's own purposes, was vested in the defendant corporation, and results of tests based on those samples should be excluded....

In my opinion, the evidence of tests conducted on all of the samples taken of the 1997 and 1993 canola crops of the corporate defendant is admissible. It is clearly relevant to the issues. It was not obtained illegally. I conclude that its admission would not bring the administration of justice into disrepute....

It is also urged that the sampling procedures were not designed to support scientific grow-out tests that could be accepted as indicating the extent of Roundup tolerant canola grown by the defendants in 1998, or in 1997. Moreover, the sampling was done by Robinson's investigators with police backgrounds and experience, but no reputed scientific qualifications, and the integrity of the samples, once collected, was in some cases said to be questionable.

These concerns require that the Court carefully weigh the evidence from any of the tests but, in my opinion, there is no basis, in this case, for disregarding all of the evidence from various tests. Particularly is this so where the evidence of more than one or two tests points to the same conclusions. I consider conclusions of fact that, in my opinion, may be drawn from evidence of the various tests, when I come to consider the issue of infringement, after considering argument concerning the validity of the plaintiffs' patent and concerning the loss or waiver of the plaintiffs' rights.

Validity of the plaintiffs' patent

The defendants question the validity of the plaintiffs' patent on the ground that the subject matter of the patent is not patentable. Further, it is urged that the enactment of the Plant Breeders' Rights Act, S.C. 1990, c.30 (the "PBRA") is a clear indication of Parliament's intent "that intellectual property rights pertaining to new plant varieties are to be governed by legislation other than the Patent Act and only to the extent permitted under the former Act". The PBRA preserves the right of a farmer to save and reuse seed. Monsanto does not deny that it seeks protection under the Patent Act for its intellectual property rights, to promote its commercial interests, including its interest to preclude by licensing agreements the saving of seed for use by farmers licensed to grow Roundup Ready canola.

Finally, the defendants say that the gene Monsanto claims protection for has been in- serted in many different registered varieties of canola and each canola plant is potentially different from others. At least within a particular variety those plants with the gene can- not be distinguished visually from those without, unless both are sprayed with Roundup herbicide. Moreover, the replication of the gene is not caused by human intervention but by natural means and it cannot be contained or controlled. For these reasons it is urged it is not the proper subject matter of a patent, and the patent should be declared invalid.

The defendants refer to the Patent Manual which describes Patent Office practice to re- gard as not patentable "subject matter for a process for producing a new genetic strain or variety of plant or animal, or the production thereof." (s. 12.03.0l(a))....

This manual is to be considered solely as a guide and should not be quoted as an au- thority. Authority must be found in the Patent Act, the Patent Rules, and in decisions of the Courts interpreting them.

The PBRA was intended to create a new form of intellectual property right in new plant varieties, as defined, for registered plant breeders....

In my opinion the PBRA was not intended to, and by its terms it does not, preclude reg- istration under the Patent Act of inventions that relate to plants, and that may lead to new varieties or characteristics of plants. The plaintiffs point to a similar issue raised under United States' statutes of the same general nature which was resolved in an analogous manner. The Court there concerned found no conflict in the application of the patent and plant breeders' legislation in that country. (See Pioneer Hi-Bred International Inc. v. J.E.M. Ag Supply Inc. (2000), 53 USPQ (2d) 140 (U.S.C.A., Fed.Crt.)).

The fact that the plaintiffs may have inserted the patented gene in a number of varieties of canola, each of which is different from the others, in my opinion, does not render the subject matter of the patent an improper subject for a patent. The patent is not granted in relation to any claim for a particular variety of canola, or indeed for canola plants ex- clusively. The subject matter is thus probably inappropriate, it seems to me, for registra- tion under the PBRA, but not inappropriate for registration under the Patent Act.

Moreover, the fact that replication of the gene may occur in the natural course of events, without human intervention after insertion of the gene in the original plant cells, and plants, produced for seed, and that this may result in differences between individual canola plants does not in itself preclude registration, under the Patent Act, of the invention, that is, creation of the gene and the process for inserting the gene. Not all progeny from pollen of Roundup Ready plants will be Roundup tolerant if outcrossing with Roundup susceptible plants occurs, but only use of those plants containing the gene can be subject to Monsanto's claims as patent holder.

In this case the Patent Office issued a patent to Monsanto US as owner of the patent. That patent is "valid in the absence of any evidence to the contrary" (the Act, s. 45).

The grant of the patent is consistent with the implications of the decision of Mr. Jus- tice Lamer, as he then was, for the Supreme Court of Canada in Pioneer Hi-Bred. In that case he dismissed an appeal from a decision of the Federal Court of Appeal that a new variety of soybean produced by cross-breeding (hybridization) was not patentable under the Patent Act . He found that the description of the plant was in- sufficient to qualify under that Act . In the course of that decision he distinguished between a product resulting from hybridization and a product resulting from a process for change in genetic material caused by human intervention within a gene. As I read his decision Lamer J. was careful to restrict his comments to the facts of the case, a product resulting from hybridization. The processes of genetic engineering, properly described, were not excluded from patent protection by implication of that decision.

In President and Fellows of Harvard College v. Canada (Commissioner of Patents), [1998] 3 F.C. 510 (F.C.T.D.), Mr. Justice Nation dismissed an appeal from a decision of the Commissioner of Patents denying an application for a patent for a transgenic mouse, which contained a gene artificially introduced into the chromosomes of the mammal at the embryonic stage. That decision was reversed by a majority decision of the Court of Appeal in President and Fellows of Harvard College v. Canada (Commissioner of Patents) .

The Harvard Mouse case is not of direct use in resolution of the matter before the Court. There the issue concerned patentability under the Act of a mammal, a higher life form, the oncomouse resulting from reproduction of mice, one of whom bears the gene introduced by invention to affect its susceptibility to cancerous growth. It was the claim to the mouse containing the genetically engineered material that the Commissioner had rejected but the Court of Appeal allowed.

It is essentially matters similar to those recognized by the patent granted originally to the applicant for the patent of the mouse that are the subjects of the claims patented in this case. Here it is the gene and the process for its insertion which can be reproduced and controlled by the inventor, and the cell derived from that process, that is the subject of the invention. The decision of the Trial Judge and of the Court of Appeal in the Harvard Mouse case implicitly support the grant of the patent to Monsanto.

The patent granted in this case would not appear to be revolutionary in recognizing, by the Patent Office, that certain life forms maybe patentable.

I sum up my conclusions in regard to the defendants' arguments concerning validity of the plaintiffs' patent. I am not persuaded on any of the grounds urged that the patent in issue is invalid....

Loss or waiver of the plaintiffs' patent rights

For the defendants it is urged Monsanto has no property interest in its gene, only intel- lectual property rights. While I acknowledge that the seed or plant containing the plain- tiffs' patented gene and cell may be owned in a legal sense by the farmer who has ac- quired the seed or plant, that "owner's" interest in the seed or plant is subject to the plaintiffs' patent rights, including the exclusive right to use or sell its gene or cell, and they alone may license others to use the invention.

Thus a farmer whose field contains seed or plants originating from seed spilled into them, or blown as seed, in swaths from a neighbour's land or even growing from germi- nation by pollen carried into his field from elsewhere by insects, birds, or by the wind, may own the seed or plants on his land even if he did not set about to plant them. He does not, however, own the right to the use of the patented gene, or of the seed or plant containing the patented gene or cell.

I do not agree that the situation is comparable to the "stray bull" cases that recognize that the progeny of stray bulls impregnating cows of another belong to that other, and that the owner of the straying bull may be liable in damages that may be caused to the owner of the cows. Further, the circumstances here are not akin to those cases that the defendants urge are part of the larger law of admixture, where property of A introduced by A without B's intervention to similar property of B from which it is indistinguishable, becomes the property of B. Monsanto does have ownership in its patented gene and cell and pursuant to the Act it has the exclusive use of its invention. That is an important factor which distinguishes this case from the others on which the defen- dants rely.

Here the defendants urge that having introduced its invention for unconfined release into the environment without control over its dispersion, the plaintiffs, as inventor and licensee have lost any claim to enforcement of their rights to exclusive use. It is said for the defendants that Monsanto obtained regulatory approval for the "uncon fined re- lease" into the environment of the patented gene pursuant to the Seeds Regulations,

C.R.C. c. 1400. Whether that is so is not significant in my view.

On the basis of the evidence of pictures adduced by Mr. Schmeiser, of stray plants and of plants in fields, in Bruno and its environs, it is urged that unconfined release and lack of control of Monsanto over the replication of the plants containing their patented gene clearly demonstrates extensive uncontrolled release of the plaintiffs' invention. Indeed it is urged this is so extensive that the spread of the invention cannot be controlled and Monsanto cannot claim the exclusive right to possess and use the invention. It is further urged that it was the plaintiffs' obligation to control its technology to ensure it did not spread and that Monsanto has not attempted to do so.

That assessment places much weight on photographs of stray plants in Bruno, said to have survived spraying with Roundup, in addition to photographs of canola in fields which is said to be of canola, some with the potential gene incorporated. With respect, the conclusion the defendants urge would ignore the evidence of the licensing arrange- ments developed by Monsanto in a thorough and determined manner to limit the spread of the gene. Those arrangements require agreement of growers not to sell the product derived from seed provided under a TUA except to authorized dealers, not to give it away and not to keep it for their own use even for reseeding. It ignores evidence of the plaintiffs' efforts to monitor the authorized growers, and any who might be con- sidered to be growing the product without authorization. It ignores the determined ef- forts to sample and test the crops of the defendants who were believed to be growing Roundup Ready canola without authorization. It ignores also the evidence of Mon- santo's efforts to remove plants from fields of other farmers who complained of unde- sired spread of Roundup Ready canola to their fields.

Indeed the weight of evidence in this case supports the conclusion that the plaintiffs un- dertook a variety of measures designed to control the unwanted spread of canola con- taining their patented gene and cell.

I am not persuaded that the plaintiffs have lost the right to claim exclusive use of their invention, or that they have waived any such claim. There clearly is no expressed waiver, and none can be implied from the conduct of the plaintiffs so far as that is a matter of record before the Court.. .
.

In my opinion the conduct of the plaintiffs does not support a conclusion that it has lost or waived its exclusive rights arising by statute as a result of the grant of its patent.

Infringement of the Patent

The plaintiffs claim that the defendants infringed Monsanto's '830 patent by growing, in 1998, seed that Mr. Schmeiser knew was from his 1997 crop and was from plants that were Roundup resistant. By so doing the defendants reproduced the patented gene and cells. The canola crop so grown in 1998 was harvested and sold by the defendants .

The evidence of Mr. Schmeiser is that seed for his 1998 crop was saved from seed har- vested in 1997 in field number 2 by his hired man Mr. Moritz. That seed was placed by Mr. Moritz in the old Ford truck, then located in field number 2, directly from the com- bine after it was harvested from the area of that field previously sprayed with Roundup by Mr. Schmeiser. That "testing" by him resulted, by his estimate, supported by Mr. Moritz, of about 60% of the sprayed canola plants surviving in the "good three acres" that he sprayed. The surviving plants were Roundup resistant and their seed constituted the source of seed stored in the old Ford truck.

Knowledge of the nature of that seed by Moritz, the hired hand, is attributable to Mr. Schmeiser and to the corporate defendant. Mr. Schmeiser must be presumed to know the nature of the seed stored in the truck by Mr. Moritz who acted under Schmeiser's general instructions in harvesting the crop....

Despite questions raised about particular aspects of the sampling and the handling of samples of the defendants' 1998 canola crop, subject to consideration of any defence raised, the balance of probabilities supports a conclusion that the growing and sale of Roundup tolerant canola by the defendants infringed the exclusive rights of the plain- tiffs to use the patented gene and cell. I reach that tentative conclusion having also con- cluded on a balance of probabilities that the samples taken from the borders of nine fields in July 1998 and three samples taken at random from within each field in August 1998 are representative of the entire crop, bearing in mind that all of the nine fields were planted with seed that was saved in 1997 in field number 2, which seed was known to be Roundup tolerant.

I turn to submissions of the defendants in reply to the claim for infringement . First, the defendants urge that there was no intention to infringe the patent. However, it is well settled that infringement is any act which interferes with the full enjoyment of the mo- nopoly rights of the patentee . . .

In the course of their defence, it was urged by defendants that the source of contamina- tion by Roundup resistant canola of their 1996 crop, from which seed was saved for 1997, was uncertain. Indeed so was the source of contamination in the 1997 crop.

A variety of possible sources were suggested, including cross field breeding by wind or in- sects, seed blown from passing trucks, or dropping from farm equipment, or swaths blown from neighbours' fields. All of these sources, it is urged, could be potential contributors to cross-breeding of Schmeiser's own canola or to deposit of seeds on his land without his consent. Mr. Borstmayer, who farmed on the same grid road but further north from Bruno than Mr. Schmeiser's fields numbers l, 2, 3 and 4, testified that in the winter of 1996-97 a bag of Roundup Ready canola seed had fallen from his truck in Bruno and bro- ken open, and some seed was lost before he put the broken bag back on his truck to be hauled past Schmeiser's fields to his own. Further, after harvesting his 1997 crop he trucked it to the elevator on the grid road to Bruno, past Schmeiser's fields, with at least two loads in an old truck with a loose tarp. He believes that on those journeys he lost some seed.

It may be that some Roundup Ready seed was carried to Mr. Schmeiser's field without his knowledge. Some such seed might have survived the winter to germinate in the spring of 1998. However, I am persuaded by evidence of Dr. Keith Downey, an expert witness appearing for the plaintiffs, that none of the suggested sources could reasonably explain the concentration or extent of Roundup Ready canola of a commercial quality evident from the results of tests on Schmeiser's crop. His view was supported in part by evidence of Dr. Barry Hertz, a mechanical engineer, whose evidence scientifically demonstrated the limited distance that canola seed blown from trucks in the road way could be expected to spread. I am persuaded on the basis of Dr. Downey's evidence that on a balance of probabilities none of the suggested possible sources of contamination of Schmeiser's crop was the basis for the substantial level of Roundup Ready canola grow- ing in field number 2 in 1997.

Yet the source of the Roundup resistant canola in the defendants' 1997 crop is really not significant for the resolution of the issue of infringement which relates to the 1998 crop. It is clear from Mr. Schmeiser himself that he retained seed grown in 1996 in field num- ber 1 to be his seed for the 1997 crop. In 1997 he was aware that the crop in field num- ber 2 showed a very high level of tolerance to Roundup herbicide and seed from that field was harvested, and retained for seed for 1998.

I find that in 1998 Mr. Schmeiser planted canola seed saved from his 1997 crop in his field number 2 which seed he knew or ought to have known was Roundup tolerant, and that seed was the primary source for seeding And for the defendants' crops in all nine fields of canola in 1998.

The principal defence raised by the defendants is that they did not use the patent be- cause they did not spray their 1998 canola crop with Roundup after it had commenced growing. Thus they say they did not make use of the invention as the inventor intended and so, did not use the patented gene or cell.

It is accepted, as the defendants urge, that the claims of a patent are to be construed purposefully. That does not mean that the utility of a patent defines or confines its purpose or its possible uses. It is the taking of the essence of the invention without leave or licence of the owner that constitutes infringement. Here the essence of the claims at issue in this case concerns the patented gene invented by Monsanto and the patented plant cells in which the gene may be found. The claims make no specific direction for or reliance upon the use, after germination of the plant containing the patented gene, of Roundup or other glyphosate herbicide as a part of the invention. The invention does improve glyphosate resistance of the plant that includes the patented gene and the cell, but that characteristic is unaffected by use or lack of use of glyphosate herbicides upon the plant once the seed germinates and the plant begins to grow.

Here the defendants grew canola in 1998 in nine fields, from seed saved from their 1997 crop, which seed Mr. Schmeiser knew or can be taken to have known was Roundup tolerant. That seed was grown and ultimately the crop was harvested and sold. In my opinion, whether or not that crop was sprayed with Roundup during its growing period is not important. Growth of the seed, reproducing the patented gene and cell, and sale of the harvested crop constitutes taking the essence of the plaintiffs' invention, using it, without permission. In so doing the defendants infringed upon the patent interests of the plaintiffs.

For the defendants it is urged that a finding of infringement will adversely affect the longstanding right of a farmer to save his own seed for use for another crop. In particular it is urged that those who do not purchase Roundup Ready canola seed but find the plant invading their land would be precluded from saving their own seed for use another year since their crop maybe contaminated without action by the farmer on whose land plants containing the patented gene are found.

That clearly is not Mr. Schmeiser's case in relation to his 1998 crop. I have found that he seeded that crop from seed saved in 1997 which he knew or ought to have known was Roundup tolerant, and samples of plants from that seed were found to contain the plaintiffs' patented claims for genes and cells. His infringement arises not simply from occasional or limited contamination of his Roundup susceptible canola by plants that are Roundup resistant. He planted his crop for 1998 with seed that he knew or ought to have known was Roundup tolerant.

Other farmers who found volunteer Roundup tolerant plants in their fields, two of whom testified at trial, called Monsanto and the undesired plants were thereafter re- moved by Monsanto at its expense.

In the result, I find on a balance of probabilities, and taking into account the evidence of Ms. Dixon about the results of genetic testing of the samples of the defendants' 1998 canola crop, that by growing seed known to be Roundup tolerant and selling the harvested seed, the defendants made use of the invention without permission of the plaintiffs.

Remedies or infringement

The plaintiffs claim the following relief for the infringement by the defendants: an in- junction; delivery up of any canola remaining from Schmeiser's 1998 crop; profits of

$105,000.00 for Monsanto US; damages of 515,450.00 for Monsanto Canada; exemplary damages of $25,000.00 and pre judgment and post judgment interest.

A declaration of validity of the patent

... The usual bases for alleging invalidity are not raised in this case. Nevertheless, insofar as the defendants challenge validity of the patent, the Court is prepared to issue such a declaration without foreclosing any possible claim on grounds not here considered, that the patent is invalid.

An injunction

While discretion to grant an injunction restraining further use or sale of the subject matter of the patent is expressly vested in the Court under s. 57 of the Act, the defendants here submit such relief, if it be to restrain the growing of Roundup Ready canola, would be impossible to comply with in light of the uncontrollable spread of the patented gene.

In my opinion, the plaintiffs are entitled to an injunction restraining action of the sort here found to constitute infringement. With this judgment the Court orders that pending settlement of the terms of judgment concerning an appropriate injunction, the defendants are enjoined from planting seed retained from their 1997 or 1998 canola crops, or any seed saved from plants which are known or ought to be known to be Roundup tolerant, and from selling or otherwise depriving the plaintiffs of their exclusive right to use plants which the defendants know or ought to know are Roundup tolerant, or using the seeds from such plants....

Personal liability of Mr. Schmeiser

While Mr. Schmeiser is a defendant in this action it is urged for the defendants that since the farming operations were legally those of the corporate defendant, it alone should be liable in any relief awarded and Mr. Schmeiser should not be personally liable....

I am not persuaded that Mr. Schmeiser's conduct, though deliberate and however uncooperative it appeared to the plaintiff, was such that personal liability in regard to dam- ages or interest is here warranted. Of course any claim to profits could only be in relation to the corporate defendant. As for the other orders here authorized, i.e. them function, the order for delivery up, should be directed to both defendants. Mr. Schmeiser is the directing mind and the active director of Schmeiser Enterprises. He may be made responsible for carrying out those orders. Judgment for damages or recovery of profits will be awarded against Schmeiser Enterprises only.

Conclusions

I find on a balance of probabilities that the growing by the defendants in 1998 of canola on nine fields, from seed saved in 1997 which was known or ought to have been known by them to be Roundup tolerant, and the harvesting and sale of that canola crop, in- fringed upon the plaintiffs' exclusive rights under Canadian patent number 1, 313, 830 in particular claims 1, 2, 5, 6, 22, 23, 27, 28 and 45 of the patent.

The plaintiffs' action for infringement is allowed and will be confirmed by Judgment to be filed after opportunity for counsel to consult, and, if appropriate, to make further submissions about the terms of Judgment to give effect to these Reasons and, in particular, to the relief which these Reasons provide are to be ordered to protect the plaintiffs' patent interests and to compensate them for the defendants' infringement of those interests.

Mr. Schmeiser challenged this outcome, and the Canada Supreme Court heard this case in 2004. The outcome was a positive one for Mr. Schmeiser, and as he wrote on his website: "Schmeiser views the decision as a draw as the Court determines Monsanto's patent is valid, but Schmeiser is not forced to pay Monsanto anything as he did not profit from the presence of RR canola in his fields " at http://www.percyschmeise.rcom/ (last visited Feb. 6, 2005).

The Canada Supreme Court decision follows.

Schmeiser v. Monsanto Canada Inc.

2004 sec 34

Supreme Court of Canada (May 21, 2004)

McLachlin C.J. and Major, Binnie, Deschamps and Fish JJ.; dissenting in part Iacobucci, Bastarache, Arbour,Lebel JJ.

The Chief Justice and Fish J.- Introduction

1 This case concerns a large scale, commercial farming operation that grew canola con- taining a patented cell and gene without obtaining licence or permission. The main issue is whether it thereby breached the Patent Act, R.S.C. 1985, c. P-4. We believe that it did.

In reaching this conclusion, we emphasize from the outset that we are not concerned here with the innocent discovery by farmers of "blow-by" patented plants on their land or in their cultivated fields. Nor are we concerned with the scope of the respondents' patent or the wisdom and social utility of the genetic modification of genes and cells- a practice authorized by Parliament under the Patent Act and its regulations. Our sole concern is with the application of established principles of patent law to the essentially undisputed facts of this case.

II.   The Salient Facts

Percy Schmeiser has farmed in Saskatchewan for more than 50 years. In 1996 he as- signed his farming business to a corporation in which he and his wife are the sole share- holders and directors. He and his corporation grow wheat, peas, and a large amount of canola.

In the 1990s, many farmers, including five farmers in Mr. Schmeiser's area, switched to Roundup Ready Canola, a canola variety containing genetically modified genes and cells that have been patented by Monsanto. Canola containing the patented genes and cells is resistant to a herbicide, Roundup, which kills all other plants, making it easier to control weeds. This eliminates the need for tillage and other herbicides.

It also avoids seeding delays to accommodate early weed spraying. Monsanto licenses farmers to use Roundup Ready Canola, at a cost of $15 per acre.

Schmeiser never purchased Roundup Ready Canola nor did he obtain a licence to plant it. Yet, in 1998, tests revealed that 95 to 98 percent of his 1,000 acres of canola crop was made up of Roundup Ready plants.

The origin of the plants is unclear. They may have been derived from Roundup Ready seed that blew onto or near Schmeiser's land, and was then collected from plants that survived after Schmeiser sprayed Roundup herbicide around the power poles and in the ditches along the roadway bordering four of his fields. The fact that these plants sur- vived the spraying indicated that they contained the patented gene and cell. The trial judge found that "none of the suggested sources [proposed by Schmeiser] could reason- ably explain the concentration or extent of Roundup Ready canola of a commercial quality" ultimately present in Schmeiser's crop (Monsanto Canada Inc . v. Schmeiser (2001), 202 F.T.R. 78, at para. ll8).

The issues on this appeal are whether Schmeiser infringed Monsanto's patent, and if so, what remedies Monsanto may claim.

III.   Analysis

A.   The Patent: Its Scope and Validity

The trial judge found the patent to be valid. He found that it did not offend the Plant Breeders' Rights Act, S.C. 1990, c. 20, and held that the difficulty of distinguishing canola plants containing the patented gene and cell from those without it did not preclude patenting the gene. The trial judge also rejected the argument that the gene and cell are unpatentable because they can be replicated without human intervention or control.

The scope of the patent is largely uncontroversial.

Everyone agrees that Monsanto did not claim protection for the genetically modified plant itself, but rather for the genes and the modified cells that make up the plant. Unlike our colleague, Arbour J., we do not believe this fact requires reading a proviso into the claims that would provide patent protection to the genes and cells only when in an isolated laboratory form.

The appellant Schmeiser argues that the subject matter claimed in the patent is un- patentable. While acknowledging that Monsanto claims protection only over a gene and a cell, Schmeiser contends that the result of extending such protection is to restrict use of a plant and a seed. This result, the argument goes, ought to render the subject matter unpatentable, following the reasoning of the majority of this Court in Harvard College v. Canada (Commissioner of Patents), [2002] 4 S.C.R. 45, 2002 SCC 76 ("Harvard Mouse"). In that case, plants and seeds were found to be unpatentable "higher life forms."

This case is different from Harvard Mouse, where the patent refused was for a mammal. The Patent Commissioner, moreover, had allowed other claims, which were not at issue before the Court in that case, notably a plasmid and a somatic cell culture. The claims at issue in this case, for a gene and a cell, are somewhat analogous, suggesting that to find a gene and a cell to be patentable is in fact consistent with both the majority and the mi- nority holdings in Harvard Mouse. Further, all members of the Court in Harvard Mouse noted in obiter that a fertilized, genetically altered oncomouse egg would be patentable subject matter, regardless of its ultimate anticipated development into a mouse.

Whether or not patent protection for the gene and the cell extends to activities involv- ing the plant is not relevant to the patent's validity. It relates only to the factual circum- stances in which infringement will be found to have taken place, as we shall explain below. Monsanto's patent has already been issued, and the onus is thus on Schmeiser to show that the Commissioner erred in allowing the patent. He has failed to discharge that onus. We therefore conclude that the patent is valid.

B.   Did Schmeiser "Make" or "Construct" the Patented Gene and Cell, Thus Infringing the Patent?

The Patent Act confers on the patent owner "the exclusive right, privilege and liberty of making, constructing and using the invention and selling it to others to be used": s. 42. Monsanto argues that when Schmeiser planted and cultivated Roundup Ready Canola seed, he necessarily infringed their patent by making the gene or cell.

We are not inclined to the view that Schmeiser "made" the cell within the meaning of s. 42 of the Patent Act. Neither Schmeiser nor his corporation created or constructed the gene, the expression vector, a plant transformation vector, or plant cells into which the chimeric gene has been inserted.

It is unnecessary, however, to express a decided opinion on this point, since we have in any event concluded that Schmeiser infringed s. 42 by "using" the patented cell and gene.

C.   Did Schmeiser "Use" the Patented Gene or Cell, Thus Infringing the Patent?

(1)   The Law on "Use"

The central question on this appeal is whether Schmeiser, by collecting, saving and planting seeds containing Monsanto's patented gene and cell, "used" that gene and cell.

The onus of proving infringement lies on the plaintiff, Monsanto.

Infringement is generally a question of fact. In most patent infringement cases, once the claim has been construed it is clear on the facts whether infringement has taken place: one need only compare the thing made or sold by the defendant with the claims as con- strued. Patent infringement cases that turn on "use" are more unusual. In those rare cases where a dispute arises on this issue, as in this case, judicial interpretation of the meaning of "use" in . .. the Act may be required.

Determining the meaning of "use" under s. 42 is essentially a matter of statutory construction. The starting point is the plain meaning of the word, in this case "use" or "exploiter." The Concise Oxford Dictionary defines "use" as "cause to act or serve for a pur- pose; bring into service; avail oneself of": The Concise Oxford Dictionary of Current English (9th ed.1995), at p. 1545. This denotes utilization for a purpose. The French word "exploiter" is even clearer. It denotes utilization with a view to production or ad- vantage: "tirer parti de (une chose), en vue d'une production ou dans un but lucratif; [.. .] [u]tiliser d'une maniere advantageuse . . .": Le Nouveau Petit Robert (2003), at p. 1004.

Three well-established rules or practices of statutory interpretation assist us further. First, the inquiry into the meaning of "use" under the Patent Act must be purposive, grounded in an understanding of the reasons for which patent protection is accorded. Second, the inquiry must be contextual, giving consideration to the other words of the provision. Fi- nally, the inquiry must be attentive to the wisdom of the case law. We will discuss each of these aids to interpretation briefly, and then apply them to the facts of this case.

We return first to the rule of purposive construction. Identifying whether there has been infringement by use, like construing the claim, must be approached by the route of purposive construction, "purposive construction is capable of expanding or limiting a literal [textual claim]": Similarly, it is capable of influencing what amounts to "use" in a given case.

The guiding principle is that patent law ought to provide the inventor with "protection for that which he has actually in good faith invented". Applied to "use;' the question be- comes: did the defendant's activity deprive the inventor in whole or in part, directly or indirectly, of full enjoyment of the monopoly conferred by law?

A purposive approach is complemented by a contextual examination of s. 42 of the Patent Act, which shows that the patentee's monopoly generally protects its business interests. Professor D. Vaver, in Intellectual Property Law: Copyright, Patents, Trade-marks (1997), suggests that the common thread among "(making, constructing and using the invention and selling it to others to be used) . .. is that the activity is usually for commercial pur- poses-to make a profit or to further the actor's business interests ... " (p.151). This is particularly consistent with the French version of s. 42, which uses the word " exploiter ".

As a practical matter, inventors are normally deprived of the fruits of their invention and the full enjoyment of their monopoly when another person, without licence or per- mission, uses the invention to further a business interest . Where the defendant's im- pugned activities furthered its own commercial interests, we should therefore be partic- ularly alert to the possibility that the defendant has committed an infringing use.

With respect for the contrary view of Arbour J., this does not require inventors to describe in their specifications a commercial advantage or utility for their inventions. Even in the absence of commercial exploitation, the patent holder is entitled to protection. However, a defendant's commercial activities involving the patented object will be particularly likely to constitute an infringing use. This is so because if there is a commercial benefit to be de- rived from the invention, a contextual analysis of s. 42 indicates that it belongs to the patent holder. The contextual analysis of the section thus complements- and confirms- the conclusion drawn from its purposive analysis. It is the reverse side of the same coin.

We turn now to the case law, the third aid to interpretation. Here we derive guidance from what courts in the past have considered to be use. As we shall see, precedent confirms the approach proposed above and it is of assistance as well in resolving some of the more specific questions raised by this case.

First, case law provides guidance as to whether patent protection extends to situations where the patented invention is contained within something else used by the defendant. This is relevant to the appellants' submission that growing plants did not amount to "using" their patented genes and cells.

Infringement through use is thus possible even where the patented invention is part of, or composes, a broader unpatented structure or process. This is, as Professor Vaver states, an expansive rule. It is, however, firmly rooted in the principle that the main purpose of patent protection is to prevent others from depriving the inventor, even in part and even indirectly, of the monopoly that the law intends to be theirs: only the in- ventor is entitled, by virtue of the patent and as a matter of law, to the full enjoyment of the monopoly conferred.

This confirms the centrality of the question that flows from a purposive interpretation of the Patent Act: did the defendant by his acts or conduct, deprive the inventor, in whole or in part, directly or indirectly, of the advantage of the patented invention?

In determining whether the defendant "used" the patented invention, one compares the object of the patent with what the defendant did and asks whether the defendant's ac- tions involved that object.

In fact, the patented invention need not be deployed precisely for its intended purpose in order for its object to be involved in the defendant's activity....

The general rule is that the defendant's intention is irrelevant to a finding of infringement. The issue is "what the defendant does, not what he intends': And the governing principle is whether the defendant, by his actions, activities or conduct, appropriated the patented invention, thus depriving the inventor, in whole or part, directly or indirectly, of the full enjoyment of the monopoly the patent grants.

However, intention becomes relevant where the defence invoked is possession without use. Where the alleged use consists of exploitation of the invention's "stand-by" utility, as discussed above, it is relevant whether the defendant intended to exploit the invention should the need arise.

The onus of proving infringement would become impractical and unduly burdensome in cases of possession were the patent holder required to demonstrate the defendant's intention to infringe. As Professor Vaver explains, "mere possession may not be use, but a business that possesses a patented product for trade may be presumed either to have used it or to intend to use it, unless it shows the contrary"(supra, at p. 151 (emphasis added)).

Thus, a defendant in possession of a patented invention in commercial circumstances may rebut the presumption of use by bringing credible evidence that the invention was neither used, nor intended to be used, even by exploiting its stand-by utility.

The court does not inquire into whether the patented invention in fact assisted the defendant or increased its profits.

The defendant's benefit or profit from the activity may be relevant at the stage of remedy, but not in determining infringement.

These propositions may be seen to emerge from the foregoing discussion of "use" under the Patent Act:

1   "Use" or " exploiter." in their ordinary dictionary meaning, denote utilization with a view to production or advantage.

308

2   The basic principle in determining whether the defendant has "used" a patented invention is whether the inventor has been deprived, in whole or in part, directly or indirectly, of the full enjoyment of the monopoly conferred by the patent.

3   If there is a commercial benefit to be derived from the invention, it belongs to the patent holder.

4   It is no bar to a finding of infringement that the patented object or process is a part of or composes a broader unpatented structure or process, provided the patented invention is significant or important to the defendant's activities that involve the unpatented structure.

5   Possession of a patented object or an object incorporating a patented feature may constitute "use" of the object's stand-by or insurance utility and thus constitute infringement.

6   Possession, at least in commercial circumstances, raises a rebuttable presumption of "use."

7   While intention is generally irrelevant to determining whether there has been "use" and hence infringement, the absence of intention to employ or gain any advantage from the invention may be relevant to rebutting the presumption of use raised by possession.

(2)   Application of the Law

In summary, it is clear on the findings of the trial judge that the appellants saved, planted, harvested and sold the crop from plants containing the gene and plant cell patented by Monsanto. The issue is whether this conduct amounted to "use" of Monsanto's invention-the glyphosate-resistant gene and cell.

The preliminary question is whether this conduct falls within the meaning of "use" or "exploiter."

We earlier concluded that these words, taken together, connote utilization with a view to production or advantage. Saving and planting seed, then harvesting and selling the resultant plants containing the patented cells and genes appears, on a common sense view, to constitute "utilization" of the patented material for production and advantage, within the meaning of s. 42.

We turn next to whether the other considerations relevant to "use" support this preliminary conclusion.

In this regard, the first and fundamental question is whether Monsanto was deprived in whole or in part, directly or indirectly, of the full enjoyment of the monopoly that the patent confers. And the answer is "yes."

Monsanto's patent gives it a monopoly over the patented gene and cell. The patent's object is production of a plant which is resistant to Roundup herbicide. Monsanto's monopoly enabled it to charge a licensing fee of $15 per acre to farmers wishing to grow canola plants with the patented genes and cells. The appellants cultivated 1030 acres of plants with these patented properties without paying Monsanto for the right to do so. By cultivating a plant containing the patented gene and composed of the patented cells without licence, the appellants thus deprived Monsanto of the full enjoyment of its monopoly.

The complementary question is whether the appellants employed or possessed the patented invention in the context of their commercial or business interests. The initial answer must again be "yes."

One of the appellants' businesses was growing canola. It used seeds containing the patented qualities in that business. Subject to the appellants' argument discussed below that they did not use the patented invention itself (whether because they used only the plant or because they did not spray with Roundup), the appellants' involvement with the disputed canola is clearly commercial in nature.

The answers to the two questions of principle that lie at the heart of "use" under the Patent Act both thus suggest that the trial judge and the Court of Appeal were correct in finding that the appellants "used" the protected invention and hence infringed Monsanto's patent. It is helpful as well, however, to consider the insights gained from the case law discussed above and their impact on arguments raised against this conclusion .

First, it is suggested that because Monsanto's claims are for genes and cells rather than for plants, it follows that infringement by use will only occur where a defendant uses the genes or cells in their isolated, laboratory form. This argument appears not to have been advanced in any detail at trial or on appeal, but is the position taken by our colleague, Arbour J.

It is uncontested that Monsanto's patented claim is only for the gene and cell that it developed. This, however, is the beginning and not the end of the inquiry. The more difficult question-and the nub of this case-is whether, by cultivating plants containing the cell and gene, the appellants used the patented components of those plants. The position taken by Arbour J. assumes that this inquiry is redundant and that the only way a patent may be infringed is to use the patented invention in isolation.

This position flies in the face of century-old patent law, which holds that where a defendant's commercial or business activity involves a thing of which a patented part is a significant or important component, infringement is established. It is no defence to say that the thing actually used was not patented, but only one of its components.

Professor Vaver, supra, observes that this is an "expansive doctrine." This is so because otherwise the inventor would be deprived of the full enjoyment of the monopoly that the law of patent confers on him or her. It is rare that patented components or processes are used in isolation; without this principle, an infringer could use the invention to his advantage, and take shelter in the excuse that he or she was not using the invention in isolation.

Provided the patented invention is a significant aspect of the defendant's activity, the defendant will be held to have "used" the invention and violated the patent. If Mr. Schmeiser's activities with Roundup Ready Canola plants amounted to use interfering with Monsanto's full enjoyment of their monopoly on the gene and cell, those activities infringed the patent. Infringement does not require use of the gene or cell in isolation .

Second, Mr. Schmeiser argued at trial that he should not be held to have "used" Monsanto's invention because he never took commercial advantage of the special utility that invention offered-resistance to Roundup herbicide. He testified that he never used Roundup herbicide as an aid to cultivation.

(That he used it in 1996 in his initial gathering of the Roundup Ready seed is clear.)

The trial judge dismissed this argument. He pointed out, at para. 122, that it "is the taking of the essence of the invention ... that constitutes infringement;' and that by growing and selling the Roundup Ready crop Mr. Schmeiser took that invention. Consequently, in the judge's view, "whether or not that crop was sprayed with Roundup ... [was] not important" (para. 123).

Perhaps the appellants' failure to spray with Roundup herbicide is a way of attempting to rebut the presumption of use that flows from possession. However, the appellants have failed to rebut the presumption.

Their argument fails to account for the stand-by or insurance utility of the properties of the patented genes and cells. Whether or not a farmer sprays with Roundup herbicide, cultivating canola containing the patented genes and cells provides stand-by utility. The farmer benefits from that advantage from the outset: if there is reason to spray in the future, the farmer may proceed to do so.

Although not directly at issue in this case, cultivating Roundup Ready Canola also presents future revenue opportunities to "brown-bag" the product to other farmers unwilling to pay the licence fee, thus depriving Monsanto of the full enjoyment of their monopoly.

Further, the appellants did not provide sufficient evidence to rebut the presumption of use. It may well be that defendant farmers could rebut the presumption by showing that they never intended to cultivate plants containing the patented genes and cells. They might perhaps prove that the continued presence of the patented gene on their land was accidental and unwelcome, for example, by showing that they acted quickly to arrange for its removal, and that its concentration was consistent with that to be expected from unsolicited "blow-by" canola. Knowledge of infringement is never a necessary component of infringement.

However, a defendant's conduct on becoming aware of the presence of the patented invention may assist in rebutting the presumption of use arising from possession.

However, the appellants in this case actively cultivated canola containing the patented invention as part of their business operations. Mr. Schmeiser complained that the original plants came onto his land without his intervention. However, he did not at all explain why he sprayed Roundup to isolate the Roundup Ready plants he found on his land; why he then harvested the plants and segregated the seeds, saved them, and kept them for seed; why he next planted them; and why, through this husbandry, he ended up with 1030 acres of Roundup Ready Canola which would otherwise have cost him

$15,000. In these circumstances, the presumption of use flowing from possession stands unrebutted. Third, as in their submissions on validity, the appellants seek to rely on the decision of the majority of this Court in Harvard Mouse. They contend that the patent should be given a narrow scope for infringement purposes, since the plants reproduce through the laws of nature rather than through human intervention. Thus, they argue, propagation of Roundup Ready Canola without a licence cannot be a "use" by them because plants are living things that grow by themselves.

This is also the perspective adopted by Arbour J. In support of the proposition that infringement of gene claims occurs only in a laboratory setting, she cites Kirin Amgen Inc. v. Hoechst Marion Roussel Ltd., (2002) E.W.J. No. 3792 (QL), [2002] EWCA Civ. 1096 (C.A.). That case dealt with a protein useful in the diagnosis and treatment of blood disorders. The English court construed the claims to exclude the naturally occurring form of the DNA sequence in a human cell. However, this was done to accord with the provisions of a regulatory scheme that has no parallel in Canada: Article 5 of the European Parliament's Directive 98/44/EC, which regulates patentability of biotechnological inventions. It states that the discovery of elements of the human body, including genes, is not patentable, although such elements are patentable when isolated or otherwise produced through technical means. The legislature has not enacted a comparable statutory scheme in Canada to narrow the scope of patent construction. Thus, Kirin Amgen is not applicable to the case before this Court.

The appellants' argument also ignores the role human beings play in agricultural propagation. Farming is a commercial enterprise in which farmers sow and cultivate the plants which prove most efficient and profitable. Plant science has been with us since long before Mendel. Human beings since time immemorial have striven to produce more efficient plants. Huge investments of energy and money have been poured into the quest for better seeds and better plants. One way in which that investment is protected is through the Patent Act giving investors a monopoly when they create a novel and useful invention in the realm of plant science, such as genetically modified genes and cells.

Finally, many inventions make use of natural processes in order to work. For ex- ample, many valid patents have referred to various yeasts, which would have no practical utility at all without "natural forces." See Re: Application of Abitibi Co. (1982), 62 C.P.R. (2d) 81 (Pat. App. Bd.), in which the inventive step consisted of acclimatizing a known species of yeast from domestic sewage to a new environment, where it would then through its natural operation act to purify waste from pulp plants. The issue is not the perhaps adventitious arrival of Roundup Ready on Mr. Schmeiser's land in 1998. What is at stake in this case is sowing and cultivation, which necessarily involves deliberate and careful activity on the part of the farmer. The appellants suggest that when a farmer such as Mr. Schmeiser actively cultivates a crop with particular properties through activities such as testing, isolating, treating, and planting the desired seed and tending the crops until harvest, the result is a crop which has merely "grown itself." Such a suggestion denies the realities of modern agriculture.

Inventions in the field of agriculture may give rise to concerns not raised in other fields-moral concerns about whether it is right to manipulate genes in order to obtain better weed control or higher yields.

It is open to Parliament to consider these concerns and amend the Patent Act should it find them persuasive. Our task, however, is to interpret and apply the Patent Act as it stands, in accordance with settled principles. Under the present Act, an invention in the domain of agriculture is as deserving of protection as an invention in the domain of mechanical science. Where Parliament has not seen fit to distinguish between inventions concerning plants and other inventions, neither should the courts.

Invoking the concepts of implied licence and waiver, the appellants argue that this Court should grant an exemption from infringement to "innocent bystanders." The simple answer to this contention is that on the facts found by the trial judge, Mr. Schmeiser was not an innocent bystander; rather, he actively cultivated Roundup Ready Canola. Had he been a mere "innocent bystander," he could have refuted the presumption of use arising from his possession of the patented gene and cell. More broadly, to the extent this submission rests on policy arguments about the particular dangers of biotechnology inventions, these, as discussed, find no support in the Patent Act as it stands today. Again, if Parliament wishes to respond legislatively to biotechnology inventions concerning plants, it is free to do so. Thus far it has not chosen to do so.

The appellants argue, finally, that Monsanto's activities tread on the ancient common law property rights of farmers to keep that which comes onto their land. Just as a farmer owns the progeny of a "stray bull" which wanders onto his land, so Mr. Schmeiser argues he owns the progeny of the Roundup Ready Canola that came onto his field. However, the issue is not property rights, but patent protection. Ownership is no defence to a breach of the Patent Act.

We conclude that the trial judge and Court of Appeal were correct in concluding that the appellants "used" Monsanto's patented gene and cell and hence infringed the Patent Act.

D.   Remedy

The trial judge granted injunctive relief and awarded Monsanto an accounting of the profits made by the respondents through growing Roundup Ready Canola, which he ultimately quantified at $19,832.

The record is not clear on precisely how this sum was arrived at; that it was awarded by the trial judge on account of profits is, however, undisputed.

The Court of Appeal upheld that order on the same basis and the issue is whether it erred in this regard.

The Patent Act permits two alternative types of remedy: damages and an accounting of profits.

Damages represent the inventor's loss, which may include the patent holder's lost profits from sales or lost royalty payments. An accounting of profits, by contrast, is measured by the profits made by the infringer, rather than the amount lost by the inventor. Here, damages are not available, in view of Monsanto's election to seek an accounting of profits.

It is settled law that the inventor is only entitled to that portion of the infringer's profit which is causally attributable to the invention.

The preferred means of calculating an accounting of profits is what has been termed the value based or "differential profit" approach, where profits are allocated according to the value contributed to the defendant's wares by the patent. A comparison is to be made between the defendant's profit attributable to the invention and his profit had he used the best non-infringing option. . . .

The difficulty with the trial judge's award is that it does not identify any causal connection between the profits the appellants were found to have earned through growing Roundup Ready Canola and the invention. On the facts found, the appellants made no profits as a result of the invention.

Their profits were precisely what they would have been had they planted and harvested ordinary canola. They sold the Roundup Ready Canola they grew in 1998 for feed, and thus obtained no premium for the fact that it was Roundup Ready Canola. Nor did they gain any agricultural advantage from the herbicide resistant nature of the canola, since no find- ing was made that they sprayed with Roundup herbicide to reduce weeds. The appellants' profits arose solely from qualities of their crop that cannot be attributed to the invention.

On this evidence, the appellants earned no profit from the invention and Monsanto is entitled to nothing on their claim of account.

IV.   Conclusion

We would allow the appeal in part, setting aside the award for account of profit. In all other respects we would confirm the order of the trial judge. In view of this mixed result, we would order that each party bear its own costs throughout.

The reasons of Iacobucci, Bastarache, Arbour and LeBel JJ. were delivered by ARBOUR J. (DISSENTING IN PART)-

I.   Introduction

This case was decided in the courts below without the benefit of this Court's decision in Harvard College v. Canada (Commissioner of Patents), [2002] 4 S.C.R. 45, 2002 SCC 76. The heart of the issue is whether the Federal Court of Appeal's decision can stand in light of our decision in that case.

More specifically, the trial judge interpreted the scope of the Monsanto patent without the benefit of the holding in Harvard College, supra, that higher life forms, including plants, are not patentable. Both lower court decisions "allo[w] Monsanto to do indirectly what Canadian patent law has not allowed them to do directly: namely, to acquire patent protection over whole plants".

Such a result is hard to reconcile with the majority decision in Harvard College, supra. It would also invalidate the Patent Office's long-standing policy of not granting exclusive rights, expressed in a patent grant, over higher life forms, that was upheld in Harvard College, supra: Patent Office, Manual of Patent Office Practice (1998 "Patent Office Manual"), at para. 16.05.

The two central issues here, the scope of Monsanto's patent and whether agricultural production of Roundup Ready Canola constitutes an infringing use, are determined by a purposive construction of the patent claims and the proper application of the majority decision in Harvard College, supra. Monsanto is on the horns of a dilemma; a narrow construction of its claims renders the claims valid but not infringed, the broader construction renders the claims invalid.

In light of Harvard College, supra, I conclude that the patent claims here cannot be interpreted to extend patent protection over whole plants and that there was no infringing use. I need not review, and take no issue with the factual overview of the case provided in my colleagues' reasons.

II.   Analysis

A.   The Decision in Harvard College

The issue in Harvard College, supra, was whether a mouse that was genetically modified to make it susceptible to cancer was the valid subject matter for a patent claim. The majority found that higher life forms were not "compositions of matter." Plants were clearly included in the category of higher life forms: e.g., Harvard College, supra, at para. 199. Accordingly, plants do not fit within the definition of an "invention":

Patent Act, R.S.C. 1985, c. P-4, s. 2.

The majority approved the line drawn by the Patent Office between unpatentable higher life forms, patentable lower life forms, and patentable processes for engineering trans- genic higher life forms in the laboratory: Harvard College, supra, at para. 199. That line is described in the Patent Office Manual, supra, at para. 16.05:

Higher life forms are not patentable subject matter. However, a process for producing a higher life form may be patentable provided the process requires significant technical intervention by man and is not essentially a natural biological process which occurs ac- cording to the laws of nature ...

The line was clearly enunciated in Re Application of Abitibi Co. (1982), 62 C.P.R. (2d) 81 (Pat. App. Bd.), at p. 89; patents apply to:

... all micro-organisms, yeasts, moulds, fungi, bacteria, actinomycetes, unicellular algae, cell lines, viruses or protozoa; in fact to all life forms which are produced en masse as chemical compounds are prepared, and are formed in such large numbers that any measurable quantity will possess uniform properties and characteristics.

Thus, in Harvard College, supra, claims for a genetically modified plasmid and the process claims to genetically modify a mouse so that it became susceptible to cancer were found to be valid. Claims for the mouse itself were found to be invalid by the Patent Commissioner and that finding was upheld by this Court. No other claims were at issue in Harvard College; transgenic mammalian eggs (single cells) were not claimed, although the majority suggested in obiter that such a claim may be the valid subject matter of a patent claim .

B.   The Patent Claims

Monsanto's Canadian Patent No. 1,313,830 is entitled "Glyphosate-Resistant Plants" (see Appendix).

The use is evident on the face of the claims, namely glyphosate resistance that a person skilled in the art would understand to mean the conferring of resistance to a glyphosate herbicide, such as "Roundup".

The Patent contained a series of hierarchical claims. The method claims are separate. The claims in the patent may be split into five general categories:

(1)   the chimeric gene, claims 1-7, that does not exist in nature and is constructed through human intervention of three components;

(2)   the cloning or expression vector, claims 8-14 (a vector is a DNA molecule into which another DNA segment has been integrated);

(3)   the plant transformation vector, claims 15-21, 52;

(4)   the glyphosate-resistant plant cell containing the chimeric gene, claims 22-28 and claims 43-51; and

(5)   the method for constructing (1)-(4) and, in the laboratory, regenerating a plant from the plant cell containing the chimeric gene, claims 29-42.

317

All of the differentiated cells in the regenerated plant contain the chimeric gene, which will be passed to offspring of the plants through natural reproduction. How- ever, as recognized by my colleagues, there is no claim for the regenerated plant or its progeny.

C.   Purposive Construction of the Claims

The first and pivotal step in an infringement action is the purposive construction of the patent claims: Whirlpool Corp. v. Cameo Inc., [2000] 2 S.C.R. 1067, 2000 SCC 67, at para. 43. The claims construction will set the scope of the patent claims, which, in turn, resolves the two issues in this case: validity and infringing use. However, Monsanto's patent claims cannot be construed with an eye to either infringement or the appellants' defence to infringement, invalidity: Whirlpool, supra.

Purposive construction delineates the scope of the invention. It identifies what the inventor considered to be the essential elements of the invention: Whirlpool, supra, at para. 45.

My colleagues emphasize the commercial value of the exclusive rights to the patentee as the primary consideration in distilling the "essential elements" of the patent claims. However, commercial interests are not the only considerations. There are three further themes to purposive construction of patent claims. I will address each of these in turn.

(1)   Fairness and Predictability

Fairness to the public is a recurring theme in jurisprudence on claims construction be- cause of the severe economic consequences of patent infringement. The scope of the patent protection should be both "fair" and "reasonably predictable". "Predictability is achieved by tying the patentee to its claims; fairness is achieved by interpreting those claims in an informed and purposive way".

(2)   What Is Not Claimed Is Disclaimed

The classic rule is "what is not claimed is considered disclaimed.". The inventor may not get exclusive rights to an invention that was not part of the public disclosure of the invention. The public must be able to predict the activities that will infringe on the exclusive rights granted to the patentee. So long as the claims are interpreted fairly and knowledgeably, if the patentee has limited the claims, then the public is entitled to rely on that limitation. An inventor cannot enlarge the scope of the grant of exclusive rights beyond that which has been specified.

However, the full specification may be looked at to discern the scope of the claims. The claims are invalid if they are broader than the disclosures.

(3)   The Person Skilled in the Art

Patent claims must be interpreted from the point of view of the hypothetical worker skilled in the art, who has been described by Binnie J. as a: hypothetical person possessing the ordinary skill and knowledge of the particular art to which the invention relates, and a mind willing to understand a specification that is addressed to him. This hypothetical person has sometimes been equated with the "reasonable man" used as a standard in negligence cases. He is assumed to be a man who is going to try to achieve success and not one who is looking for difficulties or seeking failure.

A reasonable person skilled in the art, however, must also be taken to know the state of the law as it relates to the subject matter of his or her invention This interpretation is fair and predictable because the public must equally be entitled to rely on this Court's jurisprudence in determining the scope of patent claims. [T]he English Court of Appeal considered the testimony of opposing experts (persons skilled in the art) and narrowed a patent claim over a naturally occurring DNA sequence (EPO gene) so that it excluded that DNA sequence in its natural and therefore unpatentable form. In doing so, the court stated at para. 60:

The patentee could not monopolise the gene per se as that existed in nature. The patentee therefore monopolised the DNA sequence encoding for DNA when isolated and in that respect was suitable for use to express EPO in a host cell. As of 1984 such a monopoly would have seemed to give fair protection. To seek to monopolise use of the sequence when not isolated by inserting a construct into a human cell would provide a monopoly not properly supported by the description in the specification. We also believe that third parties could reasonably expect that if they did not use a DNA sequence for insertion into a host cell, there would be no infringement. [Emphasis added.]

In conclusion, a person skilled in the art, upon filing of Monsanto's patent, could not reasonably have expected that the exclusive rights for gene, cell, vector, and method claims extended exclusive rights over unpatentable plants and their offspring.

(4)   Conclusion on the Scope of Monsanto's Claims

Accordingly, a purposive construction that limits this claim to its "essential elements," considering both the plain language of the claim and the specifications, leads me to the conclusion that the gene patent claims and the plant cell claims should not be construed to grant exclusive rights over the plant and all of its offspri ng.

It is clear from the specification that Monsanto's patent claims do not extend to plants, seeds, and crops. It is also clear that the gene claim does not extend patent protection to the plant. The plant cell claim ends at the point where the isolated plant cell containing the chimeric gene is placed into the growth medium for regeneration. Once the cell begins to multiply and differentiate into plant tissues, resulting in the growth of a plant, a claim should be made for the whole plant. However, the whole plant cannot be patented. Similarly, the method claim ends at the point of the regeneration of the transgenic founder plant but does not extend to methods for propagating that plant. It certainly does not extend to the offspring of the regener- ated plant.

In effect, the patent claims grant Monsanto a monopoly over the chimeric gene and the cell into which it is inserted and the method for doing so. Therefore, no other biotechnology company can use the chimeric gene to create a glyphosate-resistant plant cell that can then be regenerated into a glyphosate resistant plant.

D.   Validity

(1)   The Law on Validity Claims that would otherwise be valid may be limited by statutory provisions or by jurisprudence.

Subject matters that are specifically precluded by statute from patent protection are natural phenomena, laws of nature, and scientific principles: s. 27(8). Other subject matter has been excluded by judicial interpretation of s. 2 definitions of "invention" and "process" ands. 27(8). For example, the following have been excluded: computer programs if the discovery involved is a method of calculation; methods of medical treatment; higher life forms; business systems and methods and professional skills and methods; printed matter producing only an artistic intellectual or literary result; mere human conduct or mental steps, or instructions; and architectural plans. These ex- amples demonstrate that it is not unusual for courts and the Patent Office to interpret provisions of the Patent Act so as to exclude subject matter from patentability.

If a claim encompasses subject matter that is precluded from patentability, it is invalid.

(2)   Validity of Monsanto's Claims

Applying the purposive construction of Monsanto's product claims, that they do not ex- tend patent protection to plants, all of Monsanto's product claims are valid.

Monsanto's process claims are likewise valid. The method claims for making transgenic glyphosate-resistant plant cells should be valid because an invention may be a "process": Tennessee Eastman, supra. A process claim may be valid even where the subject matter it manufactures is not patentable, for example, because it is obvious: F. Hoffmann-Laroche & Co. v. Commissioner of Patents, [1955] S.C.R. 414; or it constitutes unpatentable subject matter: Harvard College, supra.

The second part of the method-the regeneration of the plant cell into a plant-may, however, seem more problematic. However, since this process involves substantial human intervention and does not follow the "laws of nature" as would natural asexual or sexual reproduction, I conclude that this part of the process would likewise be patentable. The Patent Commissioner in Harvard College, supra, found that the process of creating a transgenic cell culture that had the intermediate step of "allowing said embryo to develop into an adult animal" was patentable as a process claim. This conclusion is consistent with the policy of the Patent Office.

E.   Summary and Conclusion on Construction and Validity of the Claims

In short, properly construed, Monsanto's claims both for products and processes are valid. Neither extends patent protection to the plant itself, a higher life form incapable of patent protection. In order to avoid the claim extending to the whole plant, the plant cell claim cannot extend past the point where the genetically modified cell begins to multiply and differentiate into plant tissues, at which point the claim would be for every cell in the plant, i.e., for the plant itself.

Therefore, Monsanto's valid claims are solely for genetically modified chimeric genes and cells in the laboratory prior to regeneration-and for the attendant process for making the genetically modified plant.

F.   Infringement

Infringement is not defined in the Patent Act. To determine what constitutes infringement, recourse must be had to the common law, the statutory provisions that define the grant of rights to the inventor and the recourse to remedies, and, most importantly, the scope of the exclusive rights claimed in the patent.

The issue at this stage is whether the appellants used the invention so as to interfere with the exclusive rights of the patentee, keeping in mind that the scope of Monsanto's patent does not extend to plants. The public is entitled to rely on the reasonable expectation that unpatentable subject matter falls outside the scope of patent protection and its use does not constitute an infringement.

I will assume, as found by the courts below, that the appellants planted seeds containing Monsanto's patented gene and cell. I agree with my colleagues that the appellants did not make or construct the gene or cell contained in the canola crop and did not use Monsanto's patented process.

(1)   Statutory Interpretation of "Use" in Section 42 of the Patent Act

The relevant statutory provision is s. 42 of the Patent Act where, every patent granted under this Act shall contain the title or name of the invention, with a reference to the specification, and shall, subject to this Act, grant to the patentee and the patentee's legal representatives for the term of the patent, from the granting of the patent, the exclusive right, privilege and liberty of making, constructing and using the invention and selling it to others to be used, subject to adjudication in respect thereof before any court of competent jurisdiction.

I will use the same three principles of statutory interpretation as did my colleagues to construe the meaning of "use" in s. 42 of the Patent Act. These are a purposive interpretation of the word "use," a contextual analysis given the surrounding words in the pro- vision, and the case law.

A purposive construction of " use" suggests that "use" is limited by the subject matter of the invention, and that any acts for a purpose whether foreseen or not by the inventor may constitute an infringing use. The problem with defining "use" in the manner of my colleagues as commercial use is that the inventor is not obliged to describe the utility of the invention, the inventor must merely describe the invention so as to produce it. Utility need not include commercial utility, contrary to my colleagues' opinion.

The test for determining "use" is not whether the alleged user has deprived the patentee of the commercial benefits flowing from his invention, but whether the alleged user has deprived the patentee of his monopoly over the use of the invention as construed in the claims.

Applied here, the question is whether the appellants used Monsanto's genetically modified cells and genes as they existed in the laboratory prior to differentiation and propagation - or the process of genetic alteration. The question is not whether the appellants deprived Monsanto of some or all the commercial benefits of their invention.

(2)   The Law on Use

With respect, in my view, the case law does not support my colleagues' interpretation of use. Much of the jurisprudence on "use" and various analogies are unhelpful because of the unique properties of biological materials, especially higher life forms that can self-replicate and spread. The fact that self-replicating materials are difficult to place within the confines of the Patent Act was acknowledged by the Federal Court of Appeal, at para. 57: "it seems to me arguable that the patented Monsanto gene falls into a novel category. It is a patented invention found within a living plant that may, without human intervention, produce progeny containing the same invention."

It is well established that the use or sale of unpatented subject matter may still infringe a patent where the unpatented subject matter is made employing a patented process. This proposition does not assist the respondent, however. The appellants have not infringed the process claim because they have not used the claimed method to produce their canola crop.

The real question is whether a patented product (the gene or cell) extends patent protection to the unpatentable object into which it is incorporated. The respondents and the intervener, BIOTECanada, further contend that "[i]t is trite law that an un-patentable composition of matter can be an infringement by virtue of it incorporating patented material" (joint factum of BIOTECanada and the Canadian Seed Trade Association, at para. 39 (emphasis added)) but, like my colleagues, provided no authority on this point. In any event, there is no genuinely useful analogy between growing a plant in which every cell and every cell of all its progeny are remotely traceable to the genetically modified cell and contain the chimeric gene and putting a zipper in a garment, or tires on a car or constructing with Lego blocks. The analogies are particularly weak when it is considered that the plant can subsequently grow, reproduce, and spread with no further human intervention.

One option that was urged on us by the appellants was to incorporate a knowledge element into the definition of "use." Such a solution would be broadly applicable to other types of patents and lend uncertainty to a settled issue in Canadian patent law that intention is irrelevant to infringement.

Most people are not aware of the contents of patents but are effectively deemed to have knowledge.

What matters is what the person does. If the person's acts interfere with the exclusive rights granted by the patent, then there is infringement.

A truly innocent infringer may be able to rebut the presumption of use. However, that would likely prove difficult once the innocent infringer became aware that the genetically modified crop was present-or was likely to be present-on his or her land and continued to practice traditional farming methods, such as saving seed. The complexities and nuances of innocent bystander protection in the context of agricultural biotechnology should be expressly considered by Parliament because it can only be inadequately accommodated by the law on use.

(3)   Conclusion on Infringement

In the result, the lower courts erred not only in construing the claims to extend to plants and seed, but in construing "use" to include the use of subject matter disclaimed by the patentee, namely the plant.

The appellants as users were entitled to rely on the reasonable expectation that plants, as unpatentable subject matter, fall outside the scope of patent protection. Accordingly, the cultivation of plants containing the patented gene and cell does not constitute an infringement. The plants containing the patented gene can have no stand-by value or utility as my colleagues allege. To conclude otherwise would, in effect, confer patent protection on the plant.

Uses that would constitute an infringement include using the chimeric gene in its isolated form to create an expression or cloning vector or a transformation vector and using the transformation vector to create a transgenic plant cell. The use claimed for the plant cell extends to the isolated plant cell in a laboratory culture used to regenerate a "founder plant" but not to its offspring.

There is no claim for a "glyphosate-resistant" plant and all its offspring. Therefore saving, planting, or selling seed from glyphosate-resistant plants does not constitute an in- fringing use.

Obviously, as was done here, Monsanto can still license the sale of seeds that it produces from its patented invention and can impose contractual obligations on the licencee. Licensing allows the patent owner to impose conditions on the use of the plant, such as a prohibition on saving seeds, with the concomitant ability to sue the farmer for breach of contract if the farmer violates any of the terms of the licence.

G.   The Conclusion Is Consistent with Canada's International Obligations under the Agreement on Trade-Related Aspects of Intellectual Property Rights

In Harvard College, supra, both the majority and the minority called for Parliament's intervention on the issue of patenting higher life forms. As things stand, my conclusion on the scope of Monsanto's patent claims that is determinative of both validity and in- fringing use is not contrary to art. 27(1)

324

of TRIPS whereby Canada has agreed to make patents available for any invention without discrimination as to the field of technology.

The Canadian Biotechnology Advisory Committee (CBAC), Patenting of Higher Life Forms and Related Issues (June 2002) suggests that the contrary may, in fact, be the case. The use of biologically replicating organisms as a "vehicle" for genetic patents may overcompensate the patentee both in relation to what was invented, and to other areas of invention. CBAC, supra, at p. 12, explains the point as follows:

Because higher life forms can reproduce by themselves, the grant of a patent over a plant, seed or non-human animal covers not only the particular plant, seed or animal sold, but also all its progeny containing the patented invention for all generations until the expiry of the patent term (20 years from the priority date). In addition, much of the value of the higher life form, particularly with respect to animals, derives from the natural characteristics of the original organism and has nothing to do with the invention. In light of these unique characteristics of biological inventions, granting the patent holder exclusive rights that extend not only to the particular organism embodying the invention but also to all subsequent progeny of that organism represents a significant increase in the scope of rights offered to patent holders. It also represents a greater transfer of economic interests from the agricultural community to the biotechnology industry than exists in other fields of science.

My conclusion does not violate, and indeed is supported by art. 27(3)(b) of TRIPS, that states:

Article 27 ...

3. Members may also exclude from patentability: ...

(b) plants and animals other than micro-organisms, and essentially biological processes for the production of plants or animals other than non-biological and microbiological processes. However, Members shall provide for the protection of plant varieties either by patents or by an effective sui generis system of by any combination thereof. ...

Allowing gene and cell claims to extend patent protection to plants would render this provision of TRIPS meaningless. To find that possession of plants, as the embodiment of a gene or cell claim, constitute a "use" of that claim would have the same effect as patenting the plant. Therefore, my conclusion on both the scope of the claims and the scope of use is consistent with Canada's international obligations under TRIPS.

Canada has a sui generis system of protection for plants. The Plant Breeders' Rights Act,

S.C. 1990, c. 20, represents a nuanced statutory regime that takes into consideration the rights of both the developers of new plant varieties and users. There is nothing in the Plant Breeders' Rights Act that would exclude genetically modified new plant varieties, such as Roundup Ready Canola, from its purview. While the "rights available under the Plant Breeders' Rights Act fall well short of those conferred by patent, both in compre- hensiveness and in duration" (Harvard College, supra, at para. 63), they may be all that Monsanto is entitled to.

In light of my conclusion on the issue of infringement, it is unnecessary for me to con- sider the other issues on appeal.

III.   Disposition

I would allow the appeal with costs to the appellants throughout.

Appeal allowed in part, IACOBUCCI, BASTARACHE, ARBOUR and LEBEL JJ. dissenting in part.

10.2.1   Bowman v. Monsanto

Vernon Hugh BOWMAN, Petitioner v. MONSANTO COMPANY et al.

133 S.Ct. 1761 (2013)

Justice KAGAN delivered the opinion of the Court.

Under the doctrine of patent exhaustion, the authorized sale of a patented article gives the purchaser, or any subsequent owner, a right to use or resell that article. Such a sale, however, does not allow the purchaser to make new copies of the patented invention. The question in this case is whether a farmer who buys patented seeds may reproduce them through planting and harvesting without the patent holder's permission. We hold that he may not.

I

Respondent Monsanto invented a genetic modification that enables soybean plants to survive exposure to glyphosate, the active ingredient in many herbicides (including Monsanto's own Roundup). Monsanto markets soybean seed containing this altered genetic material as Roundup Ready seed. Farmers planting that seed can use a glyphosate-based herbicide to kill weeds without damaging their crops. Two patents issued to Monsanto cover various aspects of its Roundup Ready technology, including a seed incorporating the genetic alteration. See Supp.App. SA1–21 (U.S. Patent Nos. 5,352,605 and RE39, 247E); see also 657 F.3d 1341, 1343–1344 (C.A.Fed.2011).

Monsanto sells, and allows other companies to sell, Roundup Ready soybean seeds to growers who assent to a special licensing agreement. See App. 27a. That agreement permits a grower to plant the purchased seeds in one (and only one) season. He can then consume the resulting crop or sell it as a commodity, usually to a grain elevator or agricultural processor. See 657 F.3d, at 1344–1345. But under the agreement, the farmer may not save any of the harvested soybeans for replanting, nor may he supply them to anyone else for that purpose. These restrictions reflect the ease of producing new generations of Roundup Ready seed. Because glyphosate resistance comes from the seed's genetic material, that trait is passed on from the planted seed to the *1765 harvested soybeans: Indeed, a single Roundup Ready seed can grow a plant containing dozens of genetically identical beans, each of which, if replanted, can grow another such plant—and so on and so on. See App. 100a. The agreement's terms prevent the farmer from co-opting that process to produce his own Roundup Ready seeds, forcing him instead to buy from Monsanto each season.

Petitioner Vernon Bowman is a farmer in Indiana who, it is fair to say, appreciates Roundup Ready soybean seed. He purchased Roundup Ready each year, from a company affiliated with Monsanto, for his first crop of the season. In accord with the agreement just described, he used all of that seed for planting, and sold his entire crop to a grain elevator (which typically would resell it to an agricultural processor for human or animal consumption).

Bowman, however, devised a less orthodox approach for his second crop of each season. Because he thought such late-season planting "risky," he did not want to pay the premium price that Monsanto charges for Roundup Ready seed. Id., at 78a; see Brief for Petitioner 6. He therefore went to a grain elevator; purchased "commodity soybeans" intended for human or animal consumption; and planted them in his fields.1 Those soybeans came from prior harvests of other local farmers. And because most of those farmers also used Roundup Ready seed, Bowman could anticipate that many of the purchased soybeans would contain Monsanto's patented technology. When he applied a glyphosate-based herbicide to his fields, he confirmed that this was so; a significant proportion of the new plants survived the treatment,

327

and produced in their turn a new crop of soybeans with the Roundup Ready trait. Bowman saved seed from that crop to use in his late-season planting the next year—and then the next, and the next, until he had harvested eight crops in that way. Each year, that is, he planted saved seed from the year before (sometimes adding more soybeans bought from the grain elevator), sprayed his fields with glyphosate to kill weeds (and any non-resistant plants), and produced a new crop of glyphosate-resistant—i.e., Roundup Ready—soybeans.

After discovering this practice, Monsanto sued Bowman for infringing its patents on Roundup Ready seed. Bowman raised patent exhaustion as a defense, arguing that Monsanto could not control his use of the soybeans because they were the subject of a prior authorized sale (from local farmers to the grain elevator). The District Court rejected that argument, and awarded damages to Monsanto of $84,456. The Federal Circuit affirmed. It reasoned that patent exhaustion did not protect Bowman because he had "created a newly infringing article." 657 F.3d, at 1348. The "right to use" a patented article following an authorized sale, the court explained, "does not include the right to construct an essentially new article on the template of the original, for the right to make the article remains with the patentee." Ibid. (brackets and internal quotation marks omitted). Accordingly, Bowman could not " 'replicate' Monsanto's patented technology by planting it in the ground to create newly infringing genetic material, seeds, and plants." Ibid.

We granted certiorari to consider the important question of patent law raised in this case, 568 U.S. ----, 133 S.Ct. 420, 184 L.Ed.2d 251 (2012), and now affirm.

II

The doctrine of patent exhaustion limits a patentee's right to control what others can do with an article embodying or containing an invention.2 Under the doctrine, "the initial authorized sale of a patented item terminates all patent rights to that item." Quanta Computer, Inc. v. LG Electronics, Inc., 553 U.S. 617, 625, 128 S.Ct. 2109, 170 L.Ed.2d 996 (2008). And by "exhaust[ing] the [patentee's] monopoly" in that item, the sale confers on the purchaser, or any subsequent owner, "the right to use [or] sell" the thing as he sees fit. United States v. Univis Lens Co., 316 U.S. 241, 249–250, 62 S.Ct. 1088, 86 L.Ed. 1408 (1942). We have explained the basis for the doctrine as follows: "[T]he purpose of the patent law is fulfilled with respect to any particular article when the patentee has received his reward ... by the sale of the article"; once that "purpose is realized the patent law affords no basis for restraining the use and enjoyment of the thing sold." Id., at 251, 62 S.Ct. 1088.

Consistent with that rationale, the doctrine restricts a patentee's rights only as to the "particular article" sold, ibid.; it leaves untouched the patentee's ability to prevent a buyer from making new copies of the patented item. "[T]he purchaser of the [patented] machine ... does not acquire any right to construct another machine either for his own use or to be vended to another." Mitchell v. Hawley, 16 Wall. 544, 548, 21 L.Ed. 322 (1873); see Wilbur–Ellis Co. v. Kuther, 377 U.S. 422, 424, 84 S.Ct. 1561, 12 L.Ed.2d 419 (1964) (holding that a purchaser's "reconstruction" of a patented machine "would impinge on the patentee's right 'to exclude others from making' ... the article" (quoting 35 U.S.C. § 154 (1964 ed.))).

Rather, "a second creation" of the patented item "call[s] the monopoly, conferred by the patent grant, into play for a second time." Aro Mfg. Co. v. Convertible Top Replacement Co., 365 U.S. 336, 346, 81 S.Ct. 599, 5 L.Ed.2d 592 (1961). That is because the patent holder has "received his reward" only for the actual article sold, and not for subsequent recreations of it. Univis, 316 U.S., at 251, 62 S.Ct. 1088. If the purchaser of that article could make and sell endless copies, the patent would effectively protect the invention for just a single sale. Bowman himself disputes none of this analysis as a general matter: He forthrightly acknowledges the "well settled" principle "that the exhaustion doctrine does not extend to the right to 'make' a new product." Brief for Petitioner 37 (citing Aro, 365 U.S., at 346, 81 S.Ct. 599).

Unfortunately for Bowman, that principle decides this case against him. Under the patent exhaustion doctrine, Bowman could resell the patented soybeans he purchased from the grain elevator; so too he could consume the beans himself or feed them to his animals. Monsanto, although the patent holder, would have no business interfering in those uses of Roundup Ready beans. But the exhaustion doctrine does not enable Bowman to make additional patented soybeans without Monsanto's permission (either express or implied). And that is precisely what Bowman did. He took the soybeans he purchased home; planted them in his fields at the time he thought best; applied glyphosate to kill weeds (as well as any soy plants lacking the Roundup Ready trait); and finally harvested more (many more) beans than he started with. That is how "to 'make' a new product," to use Bowman's words, when the original product is a seed. Brief for Petitioner 37; see Webster's Third New International Dictionary 1363 (1961) ("make" means "cause to exist, occur, or appear," or more specifically, "plant and raise (a crop)"). Because Bowman thus reproduced Monsanto's patented invention, the exhaustion doctrine does not protect him.3

Were the matter otherwise, Monsanto's patent would provide scant benefit. After inventing the Roundup Ready trait, Monsanto would, to be sure, "receiv [e] [its] reward" for the first seeds it sells. Univis, 316 U.S., at 251, 62 S.Ct. 1088. But in short order, other seed companies could reproduce the product and market it to growers, thus depriving Monsanto of its monopoly. And farmers themselves need only buy the seed once, whether from Monsanto, a competitor, or (as here) a grain elevator. The grower could multiply his initial purchase, and then multiply that new creation, ad infinitum—each time profiting from the patented seed without compensating its inventor. Bowman's late-season plantings offer a prime illustration. After buying beans for a single harvest, Bowman saved enough seed each year to reduce or eliminate the need for additional purchases. Monsanto still held its patent, but received no gain from Bowman's annual production and sale of Roundup Ready soybeans. The exhaustion doctrine is limited to the "particular item" sold to avoid just such a mismatch between invention and reward.

Our holding today also follows from J.E.M. Ag Supply, Inc. v. Pioneer Hi–Bred Int'l, Inc., 534 U.S. 124, 122 S.Ct. 593, 151 L.Ed.2d 508 (2001). We considered there whether an inventor could get a patent on a seed or plant, or only a certificate issued under the Plant Variety Protection Act (PVPA), 7 U.S.C. § 2321 et seq. We decided a patent was available, rejecting the claim that the PVPA implicitly repealed the Patent Act's coverage of seeds and plants. On our view, the two statutes established different, but not conflicting schemes: The requirements for getting a patent "are more stringent than those for obtaining a PVP certificate, and the protections afforded" by a patent are correspondingly greater. J.E.M., 534 U.S., at 142, 122 S.Ct. 593. Most notable here, we explained that only a patent holder (not a certificate holder) could prohibit "[a] farmer who legally purchases and plants" a protected seed from saving harvested seed "for replanting." Id., at 140, 122 S.Ct. 593; see id., at 143, 122 S.Ct. 593 (noting that the Patent Act, unlike the PVPA, contains "no exemptio[n]" for "saving seed"). That statement is inconsistent with applying exhaustion to protect conduct like Bowman's. If a sale cut off the right to control a patented seed's progeny, then (contrary to J.E.M.) the patentee could not prevent the buyer from saving harvested seed. Indeed, the patentee could not stop the buyer from selling such seed, which even a PVP certificate owner (who, recall, is supposed to have fewer rights) can usually accomplish. See 7 U.S.C. §§ 2541, 2543. Those limitations would turn upside-down the statutory scheme J.E.M. described.

Bowman principally argues that exhaustion should apply here because seeds are meant to be planted. The exhaustion doctrine, he reminds us, typically prevents a patentee from controlling the use of a patented product following an authorized sale. And in planting Roundup Ready seeds, Bowman continues, he is merely using them in the normal way farmers do. Bowman thus concludes that allowing Monsanto to interfere with that use would "creat[e] an impermissible exception to the exhaustion doctrine" for patented seeds and other "self-replicating technologies." Brief for Petitioner 16.

But it is really Bowman who is asking for an unprecedented exception—to what he concedes is the "well settled" rule that "the exhaustion doctrine does not extend to the right to 'make' a new product." See supra, at 1766. Reproducing a patented article no doubt "uses" it after a fashion. But as already explained, we have always drawn the boundaries of the exhaustion doctrine to exclude that activity, so that the patentee retains an undiminished right to prohibit others from making the thing his patent protects. See, e.g., Cotton–Tie Co. v. Simmons, 106 U.S. 89, 93–94, 1 S.Ct. 52, 27 L.Ed. 79 (1882) (holding that a purchaser could not "use" the buckle from a patented cotton-bale tie to "make" a new tie). That is because, once again, if simple copying were a protected use, a patent would plummet in value after the first sale of the first item containing the invention. The undiluted patent monopoly, it might be said, would extend not for 20 years (as the Patent Act promises), but for only one transaction. And that would result in less incentive for innovation than Congress wanted. Hence our repeated insistence that exhaustion applies only to the particular item sold, and not to reproductions.

Nor do we think that rule will prevent farmers from making appropriate use of the Roundup Ready seed they buy. Bowman himself stands in a peculiarly poor position to assert such a claim. As noted earlier, the commodity soybeans he purchased were intended not for planting, but for consumption. See supra, at 1764 – 1765. Indeed, Bowman conceded in deposition testimony that he knew of no other farmer who employed beans bought from a grain elevator to grow a new crop. See App. 84a. So a non-replicating use of the commodity beans at issue here was not just available, but standard fare. And in the more ordinary case, when a farmer purchases Roundup Ready seed qua seed—that is, seed intended to grow a crop—he will be able to plant it. Monsanto, to be sure, conditions the farmer's ability to reproduce Roundup Ready; but it does not—could not realistically— preclude all planting. No sane farmer, after all, would buy the product without some ability to grow soybeans from it. And so Monsanto, predictably enough, sells Roundup Ready seed to farmers with a license to use it to make a crop. See supra, at 1764, 1767, n. 3. Applying our usual rule in this context therefore will allow farmers to benefit from Roundup Ready, even as it rewards Monsanto for its innovation.

Still, Bowman has another seeds-are-special argument: that soybeans naturally "self-replicate or 'sprout' unless stored in a controlled manner," and thus "it was the planted soybean, not Bowman" himself, *1769 that made replicas of Monsanto's patented invention. Brief for Petitioner 42; see Tr. of Oral Arg. 14 ("[F]armers, when they plant seeds, they don't exercise any control ... over their crop" or "over the creative process"). But we think that blame-the-bean defense tough to credit. Bowman was not a passive observer of his soybeans' multiplication; or put another way, the seeds he purchased (miraculous though they might be in other respects) did not spontaneously create eight successive soybean crops. As we have explained, supra at 1764 – 1765, Bowman devised and executed a novel way to harvest crops from Roundup Ready seeds without paying the usual premium. He purchased beans from a grain elevator anticipating that many would be Roundup Ready; applied a glyphosate-based herbicide in a way that culled any plants without the patented trait; and saved beans from the rest for the next season. He then planted those Roundup Ready beans at a chosen time; tended and treated them, including by exploiting their patented glyphosate-resistance; and harvested many more seeds, which he either marketed or saved to begin the next cycle. In all this, the bean surely figured. But it was Bowman, and not the bean, who controlled the reproduction (unto the eighth generation) of Monsanto's patented invention.

Our holding today is limited—addressing the situation before us, rather than every one involving a self-replicating product. We recognize that such inventions are becoming ever more prevalent, complex, and diverse. In another case, the article's self-replication might occur outside the purchaser's control. Or it might be a necessary but incidental step in using the item for another purpose. Cf. 17 U.S.C. § 117(a)(1) ("[I]t is not [a copyright] infringement for the owner of a copy of a computer program to make ... another copy or adaptation of that computer program provide[d] that such a new copy or adaptation is created as an essential step in the utilization of the computer program"). We need not address here whether or how the doctrine of patent exhaustion would apply in such circumstances. In the case at hand, Bowman planted Monsanto's patented soybeans solely to make and market replicas of them, thus depriving the company of the reward patent law provides for the sale of each article. Patent exhaustion provides no haven for that conduct. We accordingly affirm the judgment of the Court of Appeals for the Federal Circuit.

It is so ordered.

Footnotes

1. Grain elevators, as indicated above, purchase grain from farmers and sell it for consumption; under federal and state law, they generally cannot package or market their grain for use as agricultural seed. See 7 U.S.C. § 1571; Ind.Code § 15–15–1–32 (2012). But because soybeans are themselves seeds, nothing (except, as we shall see, the law) prevented Bowman from planting, rather than consuming, the product he bought from the grain elevator.

2. The Patent Act grants a patentee the "right to exclude others from making, using, offering for sale, or selling the invention." 35 U.S.C. § 154(a)(1); see § 271(a) ("[W]hoever without authority makes, uses, offers to sell, or sells any patented invention ... infringes the patent").

3. This conclusion applies however Bowman acquired Roundup Ready seed: The doctrine of patent exhaustion no more protected Bowman's reproduction of the seed he purchased for his first crop (from a Monsanto-affiliated seed company) than the beans he bought for his second (from a grain elevator). The difference between the two purchases was that the first—but not the second—came with a license from Monsanto to plant the seed and then harvest and market one crop of beans. We do not here confront a case in which Monsanto (or an affiliated seed company) sold Roundup Ready to a farmer without an express license agreement. For reasons we explain below, we think that case unlikely to arise. See infra, at 1768. And in the event it did, the farmer might reasonably claim that the sale came with an implied license to plant and harvest one soybean crop.

10.2.2   IP and Animals; Chakrabarty and NC Farm Partn v. Pig Improvement

The first genetics case decided by the U.S. Supreme Court involved the patentability of a living organism. In *Diamond v. Chakrabarty* the U.S. Supreme Court was faced with the question of whether a living organism created by human ingenuity could be patented.

Diamond v. Chakrabarty
447 U.S. 303 (1980)

Chief Justice Burger, delivered the opinion of the Court, in which Stewart, Blackmun, Rehnquist and Stevens, JJ, joined. Brennan, J. filed a dissenting opinion, in which White, Marshall and Powell, JJ joined.

Chief Justice Burger delivered the opinion of the Court.

We granted certiorari to determine whether a live, human-made micro-organism is patentable subject matter under 35 U. S. C. §§ 101.

I

In 1972, respondent Chakrabarty, a microbiologist, filed a patent application, assigned to the General Electric Co. The application asserted 36 claims related to Chakrabarty's invention of "a bacterium from the genus Pseudomonas containing therein at least two stable energy-generating plasmids, each of said plasmids providing a separate hydro- carbon degradative pathway."1 This human-made, genetically engineered bacterium is capable of breaking down multiple components of crude oil. Because of this property, which is possessed by no naturally occurring bacteria, Chakrabarty's invention is be- lieved to have significant value for the treatment of oil spills.2

1.   Plasmids are hereditary units physically separate from the chromosomes of the cell. In prior research, Chakrabarty and an associate discovered that plasmids control the oil degradation abilities of certain bacteria. In particular, the two researchers discovered plasmids capable of degrading cam- phor and octane, two components of crude oil. In the work represented by the patent application at issue here, Chakrabarty discovered a process by which four different plasmids, capable of degrading four different oil components, could be transferred to and maintained stably in a single Pseudomonas bacterium, which itself has no capacity for degrading oil.

2.   At present, biological control of oil spills requires the use of a mixture of naturally occurring bacteria, each capable of degrading one component of the oil complex. In this way, oil is decom- posed into simpler substances which can serve as food for aquatic life. However, for various reasons, only a portion of any such mixed culture survives to attack the oil spill. By breaking down multiple components of oil, Chakrabarty's micro-organism promises more efficient and rapid oil-spill con- trol.

Chakrabarty's patent claims were of three types: first, process claims for the method of producing the bacteria; second, claims for an inoculum comprised of a carrier material floating on water, such as straw, and the new bacteria; and third, claims to the bacteria thems elves. The patent examiner allowed the claims falling into the first two categories, but rejected claims for the bacteria. His decision rested on two grounds: (1) that micro- organisms are "products of nature," and (2) that as living things they are not patentable subject matter under 35 U. S. C. §§ 101.

Chakrabarty appealed the rejection of these claims to the Patent Office Board of Ap- peals, and the Board affirmed the examiner on the second ground.3 Relying on the leg- islative history of the 1930 Plant Patent Act, in which Congress extended patent protec- tion to certain asexually reproduced plants, the Board concluded that §§ 101 was not intended to cover living things such as these laboratory created micro-organisms....

II

The Constitution grants Congress broad power to legislate to "promote the Progress of Sci- ence and useful Arts, by securing for limited Times to Authors and Inventors the exclusive Right to their respective Writings and Discoveries:' Art. I, §§8, cl. 8. The patent laws pro- mote this progress by offering inventors exclusive rights for a limited period as an incentive for their inventiveness and research efforts. The authority of Congress is exercised in the hope that "[the] productive effort thereby fostered will have a positive effect on society through the introduction of new products and processes of manufacture into the economy, and the emanations by way of increased employment and better lives for our citizens."

The question before us in this case is a narrow one of statutory interpretation requiring us to construe 35 U. S. C. §§ 101, which provides:

"Whoever invents or discovers any new and useful process, machine, manufacture, or composition of matter, or any new and useful improvement thereof, may obtain a patent therefor, subject to the conditions and requirements of this title."

Specifically, we must determine whether respondent's micro-organism constitutes a "manufacture" or "composition of matter" within the meaning of the statute.

III

In cases of statutory construction we begin, of course, with the language of the statute . And "unless otherwise defined, words will be interpreted as taking their ordinary, con- temporary, common meaning." We have also cautioned that courts "should not read into the patent laws limitations and conditions which the legislature has not expressed."

Guided by these canons of construction, this Court has read the term "manufacture" in §§101 in accordance with its dictionary definition to mean "the production of articles for use from raw or prepared materials by giving to these materials new forms, qualities, properties, or combinations, whether by hand-labor or by machinery." Similarly, "com- position of matter" has been construed consistent with its common usage to include "all compositions of two or more substances and all composite articles, whether they be the results of chemical union, or of mechanical mixture, or whether they be gases, flu- ids, powders or solids:' In choosing such expansive terms as "manufacture" and "com- position of matter;' modified by the comprehensive "any;' Congress plainly contemplated that the patent laws would be given wide scope.

3.   The Board concluded that the new bacteria were not "products of nature," because Pseudomonas bacteria containing two or more different energy-generating plasmids are not naturally occurring.

The relevant legislative history also supports a broad construction. The Patent Act of 1793, authored by Thomas Jefferson, defined statutory subject matter as "any new and useful art, machine, manufacture, or composition of matter, or any new or useful improvement [t hereof]." Act of Feb. 21, 1793. The Act embodied Jefferson's philosophy that "ingenuity should receive a liberal encouragement." 5 Writings of Thomas Jefferson 75-76 (Washington ed. 1871). Subsequent patent statutes in 1836, 1870, and 1874 employed this same broad language. In 1952, when the patent laws were recodified, Con- gress replaced the word "art" with "process," but otherwise left Jefferson's language in- tact. The Committee Reports accompanying the 1952 Act inform us that Congress intended statutory subject matter to "include anything under the sun that is made by man." S. Rep. No. 1979, 82d Cong., 2d Sess., 5 (1952); H. R. Rep. No. 1923, 82d Cong., 2d Sess., 6 (1952).

This is not to suggest that§§ 101 has no limits or that it embraces every discovery. The laws of nature, physical phenomena, and abstract ideas have been held not patentable. Thus, a new mineral discovered in the earth or a new plant found in the wild is not patentable subject matter. Likewise,

Einstein could not patent his celebrated law that E=mc2; nor could Newton have patented the law of gravity. Such discoveries are "man- ifestations of ... nature, free to all men and reserved exclusively to none."

Judged in this light, respondent's micro-organism plainly qualifies as patentable subject matter. His claim is not to a hitherto unknown natural phenomenon, but to a nonnaturally occurring manufacture or composition of matter-a product of human ingenuity "having a distinctive name, character [and] use." The point is underscored dramatically by comparison of the invention here with that in Funk. There, the patentee had discovered that there existed in nature certain species of root-nodule bacteria which did not exert a mutually inhibitive effect on each other. He used that discovery to produce a mixed culture capable of inoculating the seeds of leguminous plants. Concluding that the patentee had discovered "only some of the handiwork of nature;' the Court ruled the product nonpatentable:

"Each of the species of root-nodule bacteria contained in the package infects the same group of leguminous plants which it always infected. No species acquires a different use. The combination of species produces no new bacteria, no change in the six species of bacteria, and no enlargement of the range of their utility. Each species has the same effect it always had. The bacteria perform in their natural way. Their use in combination does not improve in any way their natural functioning. They serve the ends nature originally provided and act quite independently of any effort of the patentee."

Here, by contrast, the patentee has produced a new bacterium with markedly different characteristics from any found in nature and one having the potential for significant utility. His discovery is not nature's handiwork, but his own; accordingly it is patentable subject matter under §§101.

IV
Two contrary arguments are advanced, neither of which we find persuasive.
(A)
... Prior to 1930, two factors were thought to remove plants from patent protection. The first was the belief that plants, even those artificially bred, were products of nature for purposes of the patent law. This position appears to have derived from the decision of the Patent Office in Ex parte Latimer, 1889, in which a patent claim for fiber found in the needle of the Pinus australis was rejected. The Commissioner reasoned that a contrary result would permit "patents [to] be obtained upon the trees of the forest and the plants of the earth, which of course would be unreasonable and

impossible." The Latimer case, it seems, came to "[set] forth the general stand taken in these matters" that plants were natural products not subject to patent protection.4 The second obstacle to patent protection for plants was the fact that plants were thought not amenable to the "written description" requirement of the patent law. Because new plants may differ from old only in color or perfume, differentiation by written description was often impossible.

In enacting the Plant Patent Act, Congress addressed both of these concerns. It explained at length its belief that the work of the plant breeder "in aid of nature" was patentable invention. And it relaxed the written description requirement in favor of "a description ... as complete as is reasonably possible." ... No Committee or Member of Congress, however, expressed the broader view, now urged by the petitioner, that the terms "manufacture" or "composition of matter" exclude living things.

Moreover, there is language in the House and Senate Committee Reports suggesting that to the extent Congress considered the matter it found the Secretary's dichotomy unpersuasive. The Reports observe:

"There is a clear and logical distinction between the discovery of a new variety of plant and of certain inanimate things, such, for example, as a new and useful natural mineral. The mineral is created wholly by nature unassisted by man. . .. On the other hand, a plant discovery resulting from cultivation is unique, isolated, and is not repeated by nature, nor can it be reproduced by nature unaided by man "

Congress thus recognized that the relevant distinction was not between living and inanimate things, but between products of nature, whether living or not, and human-made inventions. Here, respondent's micro-organism is the result of human ingenuity and re- search. Hence, the passage of the Plant Patent Act affords the Government no support.

Nor does the passage of the 1970 Plant Variety Protection Act support the Government's position. As the Government acknowledges, sexually reproduced plants were not included under the 1930 Act because new varieties could not be reproduced true-to-type through seedlings.

In particular, we find nothing in the exclusion of bacteria from plant variety protection to support the petitioner's position. The legislative history gives no reason for this exclusion. As the Court of Customs and Patent Appeals suggested, it may simply reflect congressional agreement with the result reached by that court in deciding In re Arzberger (1940), which held that bacteria were not plants for the purposes of the 1930 Act. Or it may reflect the fact that prior to 1970 the Patent Office had issued patents for bacteria under §§101.9 In any event, absent some clear indication that Congress "focused on [the] issues directly related to the one presently before the Court," there is no basis for reading into its actions an intent to modify the plain meaning of the words found in§§101.

4.   Writing three years after the passage of the 1930 Act, R. Cook, Editor of the Journal of Heredity, commented: "It is a little hard for plant men to understand why [Art. I, §§ 8] of the Constitution should not have been earlier construed to include the promotion of the art of plant breeding. The reason for this is probably to be found in the principle that natural products are not patentable!' Florists Exchange and Horticultural Tade World, July 15, 1933, p. 9.

9. In 1873, the Patent Office granted Louis Pasteur a patent on "yeast, free from organic germs of disease, as an article of manufacture!' And in 1967 and 1968, immediately prior to the passage of the Plant Variety Protection Act, that Office granted two patents which, as the petitioner concedes, state claims for living micro-organisms. See Reply Brief for Petitioner 3, and n. 2.

(B)
The petitioner's second argument is that micro-organisms cannot qualify as patentable subject matter until Congress expressly authorizes such protection. His position rests on the fact that genetic technology was unforeseen when Congress enacted §§101. From this it is argued that resolution of the patentability of inventions such as respondent's should be left to Congress. The legislative process, the petitioner argues, is best equipped to weigh the competing economic, social, and scientific considerations involved, and to determine whether living organisms produced by genetic engineering should receive patent protection. In support of this position, the petitioner relies on our recent holding in Parker v. Flook, 437 U.S. 584 (1978), and the statement that the judiciary "must proceed cautiously when ... asked to extend patent rights into areas wholly unforeseen by Congress."

It is, of course, correct that Congress, not the courts, must define the limits of patentability; but it is equally true that once Congress has spoken it is "the province and duty of the judicial department to say what the law is." Marbury v. Madison, 1 Cranch 137, 177 (1803). Congress has performed its constitutional role in defining patentable subject matter in§§101; we perform ours in construing the language Congress has employed. In so doing, our obligation is to take statutes as we find them, guided, if ambiguity appears, by the legislative history and statutory purpose. Here, we perceive no ambiguity. The subject-matter provisions of the patent law have been cast in broad terms to fulfill the constitutional and statutory goal of promoting "the Progress of Science and the useful Arts" with all that means for the social and economic benefits envisioned by Jefferson. Broad general language is not necessarily ambiguous when congressional objectives require broad terms....

Congress employed broad general language in drafting§§ 101 precisely because such inventions are often unforeseeable.

To buttress his argument, the petitioner, with the support of amicus, points to grave risks that may be generated by research endeavors such as respondent's. The briefs pre- sent a gruesome parade of horribles. Scientists, among them Nobel laureates, are quoted suggesting that genetic research may pose a serious threat to the human race, or, at the very least, that the dangers are far too substantial to permit such research to proceed apace at this time. We are told that genetic research and related technological de- velopments may spread pollution and disease, that it may result in a loss of genetic diversity, and that its practice may tend to depreciate the value of human life. These arguments are forcefully, even passionately, presented; they remind us that, at times, human ingenuity seems unable to control fully the forces it creates-that, with Hamlet, it is sometimes better "to bear those ills we have than fly to others that we know not of."

It is argued that this Court should weigh these potential hazards in considering whether respondent's invention is patentable subject matter under §§ 101. We disagree. The grant or denial of patents on micro-organisms is not likely to put an end to genetic re- search or to its attendant risks. The large amount of research that has already occurred when no researcher had sure knowledge that patent protection would be available suggests that legislative or judicial fiat as to patentability will not deter the scientific mind from probing into the unknown any more than Canute could command the tides. Whether respondent's claims are patentable may determine whether research efforts are accelerated by the hope of reward or slowed by want of incentives, but that is all.

What is more important is that we are without competence to entertain these arguments- either to brush them aside as fantasies generated by fear of the unknown, or to act on them. The choice we are urged to make is a matter of high policy for resolution within the legislative process after the kind of investigation, examination, and study that legislative bodies can provide and courts cannot. That process involves the balancing of competing values and interests, which in our democratic system is the business of elected representatives. Whatever their validity, the contentions now pressed on us should be addressed to the political branches of the Government, the Congress and the Executive, and not to the courts.11

We have emphasized in the recent past that "[our] individual appraisal of the wisdom or unwisdom of a particular [legislative] course ... is to be put aside in the process of interpreting a statute." TVA v. Hill, 437 U.S., at 194. Our task, rather, is the narrow one of determining what Congress meant by the words it used in the statute; once that is done our powers are exhausted. Congress is free to amend§§ 101 so as to exclude from patent protection organisms produced by genetic engineering. Or it may choose to craft a statute specifically designed for such living things. But, until Congress takes such action, this Court must construe the language of §§101 as it is. The language of that section fairly embraces respondent's invention.

Accordingly, the judgment of the Court of Customs and Patent Appeals is

Affirmed.

Dissent by Justice Brennan, with whom Justice White, Justice Marshall, and Justice Powell join, dissenting.

I agree with the Court that the question before us is a narrow one. Neither the future of scientific research, nor even the ability of respondent Chakrabarty to reap some monopoly profits from his pioneering work, is at stake. Patents on the processes by which he has produced and employed the new living organism are not contested. The only question we need decide is whether Congress, exercising its authority under Art. I, §§ 8, of the Constitution, intended that he be able to secure a monopoly on the living organ- ism itself, no matter how produced or how used. Because I believe the Court has misread the applicable legislation, I dissent.

The Court protests that its holding today is dictated by the broad language of§§101, which cannot "be confined to the 'particular [applications] contemplated by the legislators.'" [T]he Court's decision does not follow the unavoidable implications of the statute. Rather, it extends the patent system to cover living material even though Congress plainly has legislated in the belief that §§101 does not encompass living organ- isms. It is the role of

Congress, not this Court, to broaden or narrow the reach of the patent laws. This is especially true where, as here, the composition sought to be patented uniquely implicates matters of public concern.

11. We are not to be understood as suggesting that the political branches have been laggard in the consideration of the problems related to genetic research and technology. They have already taken action . In 1976, for example, the National Institutes of Health released guidelines for NIH-sponsored genetic research which established conditions under which such research could be per- formed. 41 Fed. Reg. 27902. In 1978 those guidelines were revised and relaxed. 43 Fed. Reg. 60080, 60108, 60134. And Committees of the Congress have held extensive hearings on these matters. See, e. g., Hearings on Genetic Engineering before the Subcommittee on Health of the Senate Committee on Labor and Public Welfare, 94th Cong., 1st Sess. (1975); Hearings before the Subcommittee on Science, Technology, and Space of the Senate Committee on Commerce, Science, and Transportation, 95th Cong., 1st Sess. (1977); Hearings on H. R. 4759 et al. before the Subcommittee on Health and the Environment of the House Committee on Interstate and Foreign Commerce, 95th Cong., 1st Sess. (1977).

Notes

1. A number of Amici curiae briefs were filed in the Chakrabarty case, in support of the patentability of life. However, one brief was filed in opposition by the Peoples Business Commission led by co-Director, Jeremy Rifkin. In part, they write :
The interest of the amicus herein is PBC's belief that the present cases are of critical importance to the potential development and direction of the burgeoning genetic engineering industry. Most financial and scientific observers concur that during the coming two decades, genetic engineering technologies will have a profit potential and social impact akin to the development of transistors and computer during the past twenty years. PBC contends that a ruling in favor of life form patents in Bergy or Chakrabarty would serve as a precedent in a host of related areas of genetic manipulation, most particularly in the field of recombinant DNA or "gene splicing". Such a ruling would significantly contribute to the profit potential of the genetic industry, thus generating a greater momentum in research and development of genetic engineering technologies.... It is PBC's contention that such a proliferation of genetically-based technologies is not in the public interest for a host of rea-sons. PBC believes that the ecological, evolutionary, ethical, philosophical, political and economic questions that surround the patenting of living organisms have been given insufficient consideration by the Congress, the country as a whole and the lower court in issuing its ruling in favor of such patents.

Specifically, the PBC goes on to describe the ecological and evolutionary disaster that might result from patenting life:

The General Electric Company Pseudomonas may well be a case in point. GE hopes to one day unleash its microorganism on an oil slick, thus preventing a tanker spill from polluting the shoreline. Environmentalists, however, are voicing concern about where the "oil eater" will go once the petroleum is consumed. . . . [W]hat if natural conditions turn out to be more complicated than the laboratory controlled environment? ... Once out of the laboratory, there is no recalling a life form.

The claimed threat to the environment of the "oil eaters" has not proven to be real, and in fact, most of the difficulty has been in keeping a large enough supply of the bacteria alive.

2.   Another amicus curiae brief was filed in support of the respondent, Chakrabarty, by Genetech, Inc. which cites the exciting contributions of biotechnology rather than the dire predictions of disaster suggested by the Jeremy Rifkin amicus in note one, supra:
The new biology holds enormous promise in application for the public good. Much tangible benefit is already in hand. Despite the contrary view of Amicus The People's Business Commission, it is the job of the Patent System to generate greater momentum in such research ... [G]rant of microorganism patent protection is required to avoid opportunities for cynical evasion of patent laws as they attach to processes....

––––––––––––––––

10.2.2.1   Trade Secrets as an Approach to Protecting Corporate Knowledge

Trade secrets includes formulas, patterns, programs, devices, methods, techniques, drawings, processes or other data that is sufficiently secret to derive economic value for not being generally known by others; and that efforts are made to keep it secret. This method of protecting corporate knowledge has the advantage of not being in the public domain through publication of a patent, if it was patentable material, thereby prevent- ing anyone from ever using the information, unlike a patent which has a limited period of protection to the property owner.

The next case opines that there cannot be a trade secret in animals.

North Carolina Farm Partnership v. Pig Improvement Company, Inc.
593 S.E.2d 126 (2004)

In 1996, North Carolina Farm Partnership (NCF), a North Carolina partnership, and PIC, a Wisconsin corporation, entered into a contract whereby NCF agreed to lease pigs and facilities in Warren County, North Carolina for pig breeding and nursery to PIC. At the expiration of the lease term, NCF was to retain possession of the pigs and the facilities, subject to the contractual options available to both parties on or before the termination of the lease.

Following expiration of the lease on 31 March 2000, NCF filed a complaint in Wake County, North Carolina on 27 July 2000 alleging breach of the lease terms by PIC. In its answer and counterclaim, PIC in turn alleged NCF breached the lease terms by continuing, "after termination of the lease, to use the progeny of [pigs] in the breeding herd as breeding stock in [NCF's] own herd and/or [by] transferr[ing] and/or s[elling] said progeny to other herds, rather than selling said progeny to slaughter as permitted in the lease." The answer and counterclaim also sought injunctive relief because "[t]he genetics incorporated into [PIC's] breeding animals are confidential, proprietary and secret information ."
The [c]ourt accepts PIC's contention, as supported by the evidence, that each pig contains unique genetics in its make-up and that the genetics and breeding processes which led to the breeding of the pigs containing such genetics are valuable intellectual property. However, this fact does not make a pig[ ] a trade secret. Because of the pig's genetic makeup, it may be a valuable pig, but it is not a trade secret.

On the contract issue, the trial court concluded NCF was not restricted in its use of the breeding herd left on the leased premises at the expiration of the lease.PIC does not cite, and our research did not reveal, any cases involving the application of trade secrets law to animals. Furthermore, PIC provided two affidavits containing general allegations but no specific scientific evidence to support those allegations. PIC's technical director in one affidavit states generally that PIC has used "molecular biological research and ... selective breeding" to develop favorable traits in pigs and that PIC's competitors could use the pure-line pigs in NCF's possession to duplicate those traits. The other affidavit, by a doctorate holder who provides no information on his specialty and other credentials, simply states that the breeding of great-grandparent female pigs in NCF's possession with pure-line boars would produce offspring with "one-half of the positive genetic qualities and characteristics" of the sow.

On the other hand, NCF provided a detailed affidavit of a North Carolina State University professor, explaining the current selection methodology for breeding swine, the feasibility of obtaining PIC pigs on the market, and the degree of difficulty competitors would face in attempting to discover and exploit favorable traits in PIC pigs. The professor, a published Professor of Animal Science and Genetics, has taught at the university since

1959 and been involved in research in the swine industry for more than thirty years. According to the professor: selective breeding is the exclusive method of genetic improvement in the swine industry and is not a secret; "[a] ny competitor could buy a[] sample of PIC product on the open market and test against these pigs"; and PIC's competitors would not be able to "work backwards to figure out what [PIC] did to develop [a] pig" or "to take the pigs in the possession of [NCF] and determine whether the PIC line was a superior line of pigs without first performing years of tests."

Affirmed.

————————————

Chapter 11

Torts and Agricultural Biotechnology

The possibility of intentional or unintentional torts including product liability is potentially an area to watch in agricultural biotechnology.

11.1.1   Torts and Biotechnology

11.1.1.1   Intentional Torts
Intentional torts with potential applicability to biotechnology issues include trespass, trespass to land, conversion, private nuisance and public nuisance. Torts have sought as remedies for damages in both human tissues as well as damages from genetically engineered crops. The first is a landmark case in establishing that human tissues are not property. It analyzes the theories of trespass and conversion for profiting on unique tis- sue taken from a patient without his consent, or remuneration for their commercialization. The second case raises the issues of conversion, private nuisance and public nuisance, in that unique damages can be done by genetically engineered crops in contaminating other crops which become economic losses.

The intentional torts have not proven to be successful legal tools for recovery from damages from the products and practices of biotechnology. The following article suggests that among the intentional torts, trespass to land and conversion may be the most promising.

Excerpt from, Symposium: Biotechnology and the Law: Biotechnology's Challenge to the Law of Torts, 32 MCGEORGE L. REv. 221 (Fall 2000).

There may be liability for intentional torts in the biotechnology context. The two intentional torts most likely to arise are trespass to land and conversion.

A.   Trespass to Land

Use of genetically engineered crops creates a significant risk of trespass to land. Trespass to land arises where a defendant intentionally enters the land of an- other or intentionally causes something to enter the land of another. Although intent is required, it is the intent to enter the land, not the intent to trespass, that is key. Thus, if a defendant enters the plaintiff's land reasonably believing that she has permission to do so, or even under a reasonable belief that the property is hers, she will be liable for trespass to land.

In the biotechnology context, if the defendant knows that it is substantially certain that seeds from her pesticide-resistant plants will find their way on to the plaintiff's property, she can be liable for trespass to land. Further, she is liable for all harm that ensues as a result of the trespass. Genetically engineered crops pose a real risk of trespass to land liability if they cross-pollinate with neighboring plants or otherwise contaminate the land of adjoining land owners.

B.   Conversion

The intentional tort that thus far has received the most attention in the biotechnology context is the tort of conversion. Conversion arises when a defendant intentionally exercises "dominion and control over a chattel which so seriously interferes with the right of another to control it that the actor may justly be required to pay the other the full value of the chattel." Although an intentional tort, as with trespass to land, it is simply the intent to do the act- here the exercise of dominion and control-that gives rise to liability.

In Re Starlink Corn Products Liability Litigation
212 F. Supp. 2d 828 (N.D. Ill. 2002)

Memorandum Opinion and Order by Judge James B. Moran

This controversy arises from the discovery of genetically modified corn in various food products. Plaintiffs disseminated a product that contaminated the entire United States' corn supply, increasing their costs and depressing corn prices. Plaintiffs have filed a 57- count master second amended consolidated class action complaint, alleging common law claims for negligence, strict liability, private nuisance, public nuisance and conversion on behalf of a nationwide class of corn farmers.... Defendants filed a motion to dismiss, arguing that the Federal Insecticide,

Fungicide and Rodenticide Act (FIFRA), 7 U.S.C. §§ 136 et seq., preempts plaintiffs' state law claims, that the economic loss doc- trine bars any recovery, and that the complaint fails to state a claim under any of plain- tiffs' purported legal theories. For the following reasons, defendants' motion to dismiss is granted in part and denied in part.

BACKGROUND

Aventis genetically engineered a corn seed to produce a protein known as Cry9C that is toxic to certain insects. The seeds are marketed under the brand name StarLink. Garst is a licensee who produced and distributed Starlink seeds. Aventis applied to register Star- link with the EPA, which is responsible for regulating insecticides under FIFRA, 7 U.S.C. §§ 136 et seq. The EPA noted that Cry9C had several attributes similar to known human allergens, and issued only a limited registration, permitting Starlink use for such purposes as animal feed, ethanol production and seed increase, but prohibiting its use for human consumption. Consequently, segregating it from non-StarLink corn, which was fit for human consumption, became of utmost importance. A little background about normal practices for cultivating, harvesting and distributing corn demonstrates the extensive steps necessary to prevent StarLink corn from entering the food supply.

Corn replicates by the transfer of pollen from one corn plant to another, including cross-pollination from one breed to another. Once airborne, corn pollen can drift over considerable distances, meaning that different corn varieties within a farm, and from neighboring farms, regularly cross-breed. With few exceptions, there are not procedures in place to segregate types of corn. Different corn breeds within an individual farm are commingled at the harvesting stage. Corn from hundreds of thousands of farms is then further commingled as it is gathered, stored and shipped through a system of local, re- gional and terminal grain elevators. Elevators, storage and transportation facilities are generally not equipped to test and segregate corn varieties. The commingled corn is then marketed and traded as a fungible commodity.

In light of these general practices in the corn industry, the EPA required special procedures with respect to StarLink. These included mandatory segregation methods to prevent Star- Link from commingling with other corn in cultivation, harvesting, handling, storage and transport, and a 660-foot "buffer zone" around StarLink corn crops to prevent cross-polli- nation with non-StarLink corn plants. The limited registration also made Aventis respon- sible for ensuring these restrictions were implemented, obligating it (a) to inform farmers of the EPA's requirements for the planting, cultivation and use of StarLink; (b) to instruct farmers growing StarLink how to store and dispose of the StarLink seeds, seed bags, and plant detritus; and (c)) to ensure that all farmers purchasing StarLink seeds signed a con- tract binding them to these terms before permitting them to grow StarLink corn.

StarLink was distributed throughout the United States from approximately May 1998 through October 2000. The limited registration initially limited StarLink cultivation to 120,000 acres. In January 1999, Aventis petitioned the EPA to raise this limit to 2.5 mil- lion acres. The EPA agreed, subject to an amended registration that required Aventis to

(a) inform purchasers (i.e. "Growers") at the time of StarLink seed corn sales, of the need to direct StarLink harvest to domestic feed and industrial non-food uses only;

(b) require all Growers to sign a "Grower Agreement" outlining field manage- ment requirements and stating the limits on StarLink corn use;

(c) deliver a Grower Guide, restating the provisions stated in the Grower Agreement, with all seed;

(d) provide all Growers with access to a confidential list of feed outlets and elevators that direct grain to domestic feed and industrial uses;

(e) write to Growers prior to planting, reminding them of the domestic and in-dustrial use requirements for StarLink corn;

(f) write to Growers prior to harvest, reminding them of the domestic and industrial use requirements for StarLink corn;

(g) conduct a statistically sound follow-up survey of Growers following har-vest, to monitor compliance with the Grower Agreement.

Over this 29-month period, StarLink cultivation expanded from 10,000 acres to 350,000 acres.

In October 2000, after numerous reports that human food products had tested positive for Cry9C, a wave of manufacturers issued recalls for their corn products . On October 12, 2000, Aventis, at EPA's urging, applied to cancel the limited registration, effective February 20, 2001. Fear of StarLink contamination nonetheless continues to affect corn markets. Many U.S. food producers have stopped using U.S. corn, replacing it with imported corn or corn substitutes. South Korea, Japan and other foreign countries have terminated or substantially limited imports of U.S. corn. Grain elevators and transport providers are now mandating expensive testing on all corn shipments .

Plaintiffs allege that the widespread StarLink contamination of the U.S. corn supply is a result of defendants' failure to comply with the EPA's requirements. Aventis did not include the EPA-mandated label on some StarLink packages, did not notify, instruct and remind StarLink farmers of the restrictions on StarLink use, proper segregation methods and buffer zone requirements, and did not require StarLink farmers to sign the obligatory contracts . Prior to the 2000 growing season Aventis allegedly instructed its seed representatives that it was unnecessary for them to advise StarLink farmers to segregate their StarLink crop or create buffer zones because Aventis believed the EPA would amend the registration to permit StarLink use for human consumption. In July 2001, however, an EPA Scientific Advisory Panel reaffirmed its previous position on StarLink's allergenic qualities. Further, the FDA has declared StarLink to be an adulterant under the Food, Drug and Cosmetic Act. . . .

II. Economic Loss Doctrine

This rule limits the types of damages plaintiffs may recover in tort. Physical injuries to persons or property are compensable; solely economic injuries are not. The difficult question is defining what constitutes an "economic" injury....

Non-StarLink corn crops are damaged when they are pollinated by StarLink corn. The pollen causes these corn plants to develop the Cry9C protein and renders what would otherwise be a valuable food crop unfit for human consumption. Non-StarLink corn is also damaged when it is commingled with StarLink corn. Once mixed, there is no way to re-segregate the corn into its edible and inedible parts. The entire batch is considered tainted and can only be used for the domestic and industrial purposes for which Star- Link is approved. None of that supply can ever be used for human food.

There are at least four different points along the supply chain at which StarLink could have entered the food corn supply, all of which are consistent with the complaint: (1) plaintiffs unknowingly purchased seed containing the Cry9C protein, i.e. their suppliers' inventory had been contaminated; (2) plaintiffs' crops were contaminated by pollen from StarLink corn on a neighboring farm; (3) plaintiffs' harvest was contaminated by commingling with StarLink corn in a transport or storage facility; and (4) food manufacturers commingled the corn within their raw material storage or processing activities. The first situation would fall within the economic loss doctrine. Plaintiffs could have negotiated contractual protection from their suppliers and simply did not get what they had bargained for. In the fourth, plaintiffs would have suffered no harm to their property because the corn was commingled after they had relinquished their ownership interest in it. Scenarios 2 and 3, however, present viable claims for harm to their crops. [Resolving the complaint's ambiguous phraseology in plaintiffs' favor, we find that they have sufficiently alleged that their crops were contaminated at some point within that chain.]

The StarLink situation does not fit neatly into traditional economic loss doctrine analysis. Plaintiffs here had no commercial dealings with defendants or defendants' customers. This is more than a lack of direct privity, and not a situation where a party could have negotiated warranty or indemnity protection and chose

351

not to. Plaintiffs had no opportunity to negotiate contractual protection with anyone . Still, as the access cases aptly demonstrate, the economic loss doctrine has grown beyond its original freedom- of-contract based policy justifications. Farmers' expectations of what they will receive for their crops are just that, expectations. Absent a physical injury, plaintiffs cannot re- cover for drops in market prices. Nor can they recover for any additional costs, such as testing procedures, imposed by the marketplace. But if there was some physical harm to plaintiffs' corn crop, the lack of a transaction with defendants affects what will be considered "other property." [This includes corn commingled at grain elevators because plaintiffs retain ownership rights to corn stored there. Each contributing farmer owns a pro rata share of the entire, now tainted, supply.] Assuming plaintiffs did not buy corn seeds with the Cry9C protein, it cannot be said that a defective part of their crop in-jured the whole, that a defective product was integrated into a system or that the harm to their crop was a foreseeable consequence of the seeds' failure to perform . These facts are distinguishable from Hapka, 458 N.W.2d at 688 (holding farmer who purchased diseased seeds could not recover for harm to rest of crop). Plaintiffs' seeds, as purchased, were adequate . The StarLink contaminant was wholly external.

Nor does the StarLink controversy present the unlimited or speculative damage concerns common in access cases. There are a finite number of potential plaintiffs-only non-StarLink corn farmers-who can claim injury. This may be a sizeable group, and the damages may be tremendous, but the fact that defendants are alleged to have directly harmed a large number of plaintiffs is not a defense. StarLink's effects on commercial corn farmers are distinct and qualitatively different from society at large. And damages are easily measured through price changes because corn is a regularly traded commodity with a readily measurable market. Further, as discussed above, the contamination of plaintiffs' corn supply is a physical injury.

To the extent plaintiffs allege that their crops were themselves contaminated, either by cross-pollination in the fields or by commingling later in the distribution chain, they have adequately stated a claim for harm to property. Once plaintiffs have established this harm they may be entitled to compensation for certain economic losses....

IV. Conversion

Conversion is defined as "an intentional exercise of dominion or control over a chattel which so seriously interferes with the right of another to control it that the actor may justly be required to pay the other the full value of the chattel." Restatement (Second) of Torts § 222A. Plaintiffs argue that defendants' role in contaminating the corn supply amounts to a conversion of their property. We disagree.

The defining element of conversion, the one that distinguishes it from a trespass to chattels, is the extent of interference with the owner's property rights. If the damage is minor, in duration or severity, plaintiff may only recover for the diminished value. But if the damage is sufficiently severe, plaintiff may recover full value. Conversion is akin to a forced judicial sale. The defendant pays full value for the chattel, and receives title to it. Restatement § 222A comment c. Here, plaintiffs have not alleged that defendants destroyed their crops or deprived them of possession. Plaintiffs retained possession and still had total control over the corn. Most, if not all of it, was ultimately sold to third parties. The only damages were a lower price, for which plaintiffs could be compensated without forcing a sale.

It is possible to convert a chattel by altering it, without completely destroying it. In particular, commingling fungible goods so that their identity is lost can constitute a con- version. Restatement § 226 comment e. To do so, however, the perpetrator must alter the chattel in a way that is "so material as to change the identity of the chattel or its essential character." Restatement § 226 comment d. At worst, StarLink contamination changed plaintiffs' yield from being corn fit for human consumption to corn fit only for domestic or industrial use. Plaintiffs do not claim they were growing the corn to eat themselves, but for sale on the commodity markets. The crops were still viable for the purpose for which plaintiffs would normally use them, for sale on the open market. That the market had become less hospitable does not change the product's essential character. As above, the severity of the alteration is indicated by the decrease in market price. This could arguably constitute a trespass to chattels, but does not rise to the level of conversion .

Lastly, negligence cannot support a conversion claim. It requires intent . Restatement § 224. The complaint alleges that defendants did not take adequate precautions to ensure that StarLink corn was adequately segregated. Nowhere do plaintiffs claim that defendants intentionally commingled StarLink and non-StarLink corn, or deliberately contaminated the food supply. Even if defendants negligently failed to prevent cross- pollination and commingling, they would not be liable for conversion.

V. Nuisance
A. Private [Nuisance]
The complaint alleges that defendants created a private nuisance by distributing corn seeds with the Cry9C protein, knowing that they would cross-pollinate with neighboring corn crops. [The private nuisance claims appear to be premised exclusively on cross- pollination in the fields, not commingling later in the distribution chain.]

A private nuisance is a nontrespassory invasion of another's interest in the private use and enjoyment of land." Restatement (Second) of Torts § 821D. We agree that drifting pollen can constitute an invasion, and that contaminating neighbors' crops interferes with their enjoyment of the land. The issue is whether

353

defendants are responsible for contamination caused by their product beyond the point of sale.

Commingling could not constitute a private nuisance because it does not involve an invasion of any private interests in land. By contrast, the public nuisance claims, discussed below, may be premised on commingling because "unlike a private nuisance, a public nuisance does not necessarily involve interference with use or enjoyment of land." Restatement §821B comment h.

Defendants argue that they cannot be liable for any nuisance caused by StarLink because they were no longer in control of the seeds once they were sold to farmers. But one can be liable for nuisance "not only when he carries on the activity but also when he participates to a substantial extent in carrying it on." Restatement § 834. Plaintiffs maintain that defendants' design of the StarLink technology, distribution of the seeds and, most importantly, their failure to fulfill their EPA-mandated duties, constitutes substantial participation.

The paradigm private nuisance case involves a suit between two neighboring landowners, one of whom alleges that the other's activities are somehow interfering with the first's enjoyment of the land. Suing the manufacturer of the product that the neighbor was using appears to be an extension of nuisance law into an area normally regulated by product liability. But there is precedent for such an application under certain circumstances, and it does fit within the definition of a nuisance....

Suppose, however, that [the manufacturer] had not taken steps to alert customers of the risks of the product, or intentionally marketed the product to customers who it knew or should have known would dispose of [it] in a manner that would harm the environment. Nothing in the opinion in City of Bloomington would preclude the imposition of liability on the manufacturer under those facts. . . .

This brings us to the case at bar, which is much closer to mainstream nuisance doctrine than either the asbestos or gun cases. In the asbestos cases, the plaintiffs had themselves purchased the product, consented to having it installed on their property and then sued the manufacturer when it turned out to be harmful. There was no invasion of a neighboring property and plaintiffs had exclusive access to the nuisance-causing agent. Here, plain- tiffs did not purchase StarLink seeds, and have alleged that pollen from neighboring farms did enter their premises. Aside from the presence of an invasion, the fact that the alleged nuisance occurred on another's property means that, unlike asbestos purchasers, plaintiffs had no ability to access or control the nuisance themselves. In the gun cases, manufacturers successfully argued that they should not be held responsible for third parties' inten- tional misuse of their products. Here, however, plaintiffs have not alleged that StarLink farmers defied the manufacturers' instructions, but rather that the instructions themselves violated the EPA's mandates. Moreover, the gun cases alleged a public nuisance and did not implicate plaintiffs' ability to enjoy land or anyone's unreasonable use of land. Private nuisance jurisprudence has always focused on the use and enjoyment of land. Plaintiffs here have alleged that they are unable to enjoy the profits of their land (selling food corn), because of an unreasonable activity on neighboring land (growing StarLink corn).

Another critical factor here is the impact of the limited registration, which negates many of the concerns courts have expressed about holding manufacturers liable for post-sale nuisances. For example, they emphasized that the manufacturers did not have any control over how the purchasers had used their products, or any access to abate the nuisance. Aventis, on the other hand, had an affirmative duty to enforce StarLink farmers' compliance with the Grower Agreements. This arguably gave Aventis some measure of control over StarLink's use, as well as a means to abate any nuisance caused by its misuse. This mirrors Page County Appliance Center, supra, where the court found the manufacturer's ongoing service contract with the purchaser gave defendant enough access and control to create a question of fact as to its contribution to the nuisance. Aventis' duties under the limited registration were, by comparison, even more extensive. Similarly, defendants' failure to give StarLink farmers the warnings mandated by the limited registration, and (ultimately incorrect) representations that StarLink need not be segregated because the EPA was going to approve it for human consumption, are also arguably the type of culpable conduct relied upon ...

In summary, of the states involved here Iowa, Wisconsin and Illinois have all held a manufacturer liable for a nuisance related to its product beyond the point of sale....

11.1.2   Trespass, Revisit- Johnson v. Paynesville

Supreme Court of Minnesota.
Oluf JOHNSON, et al., Respondents, v. PAYNESVILLE FARMERS UNION
COOPERATIVE OIL COMPANY, Appellant.
Nos. A10–1596, A10–2135.
Decided: August 01, 2012

OPINION
This action involves alleged pesticide contamination of organic farm fields in central Minnesota. Appellant Paynesville Farmers Union Cooperative Oil Company ("Cooperative") is a member owned farm products and services provider that, among other things, applies pesticides to farm fields. Respondents Oluf and Debra Johnson ("Johnsons") are organic farmers. The Johnsons claim that while the Cooperative was spraying pesticide onto conventionally farmed fields adjacent to the Johnsons' fields, some pesticide drifted onto and contaminated the Johnsons' organic fields. The Johnsons sued the Cooperative on theories including trespass, nuisance, and negligence

per se and sought damages and injunctive relief. The Johnsons claim that the pesticide drift caused them: (1) economic damages because they had to take the contaminated fields out of organic production for 3 years pursuant to 7 C.F.R. § 205.202(b) (2012), (2) economic damages because they had to destroy some crops, (3) inconvenience, and (4) adverse health effects. The district court granted summary judgment to the Cooperative and dismissed all of the Johnsons' claims. The court of appeals reversed. Because we conclude that the Johnsons' trespass claim and claims for damages based on 7 C.F.R. § 205.202(b), fail as a matter of law, we reverse the court of appeals' reinstatement of those claims. But because the district court failed to consider whether the Johnsons' non trespass claims that were not based on 7 C.F.R. § 205.202(b), could survive summary judgment, we affirm the court of appeals' reinstatement of those claims and remand for proceedings consistent with this opinion.

Before discussing the factual background of this case, it is helpful to briefly summarize the organic farming regulations at issue. American organic farming is regulated by the Organic Foods Production Act of 1990, 7 U.S.C. §§ 6501–6523 (2006) ("OFPA"), and the associated federal regulations in the National Organic Program, 7 C.F.R. § 205 (2012) ("NOP"). One of the purposes of the OFPA is "to establish national standards governing the marketing of certain agricultural products as organically produced products." 7 U.S.C. § 6501(1). The states may adopt the federal standards or they may impose "more restrictive requirements governing" products sold as organic. 7 U.S.C. § 6507(b)(1). Minnesota has adopted the OFPA and the NOP as its state organic farming law. Minn.Stat. § 31.925 (2010) (adopting the OFPA and the NOP "as the organic food production law and rules in this state").

Under the OFPA and the NOP regulations, a producer cannot market its crops as "organic," and receive the premium price paid for organic products, unless the producer is "certified" by an organic certifying agent. 7 U.S.C. § 6503(d) (stating that the OFPA is implemented by certifying agents authorized through the Secretary of Agriculture); 7 C.F.R. § 205.100, .102 (describing which products can carry the "organic" label). And in order to receive certification, a producer must comply with the NOP. 7 C.F.R. § 205.400. Among numerous other requirements, the NOP provides that land from which crops are intended to be sold as organic must "[h]ave had no prohibited substances . applied to it for a period of 3 years immediately preceding harvest of the crop." 7 C.F.R. § 205.202(b).1

Once producers obtain certification to sell products as organic, the OFPA and NOP provide guidelines for certified organic farming operations to ensure continued compliance. See 7 U.S.C. § 6511. Under these guidelines, if a prohibited substance is detected on a product sold or labeled as organic, the certifying agent must conduct an investigation to determine whether there has been a violation of the federal requirements. See 7 U.S.C. § 6511(c)(1). If the investigation indicates that the residue detected on the organic product was "the result of intentional application of a prohibited substance" or the residue is "present at levels that are greater than" federal regulations prescribe, the product cannot be sold as organic. 7 U.S.C. § 6511(c)(2). Under the NOP regulations, crops may not be sold as organic if the crops are shown to have a prohibited substance on them at levels that are greater than 5 percent of the Environmental Protection Agency's tolerance level for that substance. 7 C.F.R. § 205.671

With this regulatory scheme in mind, we turn to the incidents that gave rise to this lawsuit.

In June 2007, the Johnsons filed a complaint with the Minnesota Department of Agriculture ("MDA"), alleging that the Cooperative had contaminated one of their transitional soybean fields2 through pesticide drift. The subsequent MDA investigation verified that on June 15, 2007, a date when winds were blowing toward the Johnsons' fields at 9 to 21 miles per hour, the Cooperative sprayed Status (diflufenzopyr and dicamba) and Roundup Original (glyphosate) onto a conventional farmer's field immediately adjacent to one of the Johnsons' transitional soybean fields. The MDA informed the Johnsons that there was no tolerance for diflufenzopyr in soybeans (organic, transitional, or conventional) and that, pending chemical testing, the MDA would "determine if there [would] be any harvest prohibitions" on the Johnsons' soybeans. After receiving the results of the chemical testing, the MDA informed the parties that test results revealed that the chemical dicamba was present, but below detection levels. The MDA also reported that the chemicals diflufenzopyr and glyphosate were not present. Because only one of the three chemicals was present based on its testing, the MDA concluded that "it can not be proven if the detections were from drift." And even though the testing did not find diflufenzopyr, the MDA still required that the Johnsons plow down a small portion of the soybeans growing in the field because of "the presence of dicamba" and based on the "visual damage" observed to this crop. In response to this MDA directive, the Johnsons destroyed approximately 10 acres of their soybean crop.

The Johnsons also reported the alleged pesticide drift to their organic certifying agent, the Organic Crop Improvement Association (OCIA), as they were required to do under the NOP. See 7 C.F.R. § 205.400(f)(1). In an August 27, 2007 letter, the OCIA stated that there may have been chemical drift onto a transitional soybean field and that chemical testing was being done. The Johnsons were also told that "[i]f the analysis indicate[d] contamination," they would have to "take this land back to the beginning of 36–month transition." Based on the OCIA's letter, and the dicamba found by the MDA, the Johnsons took the transitional soybean field back to the beginning of the 3–year transition process. In other words, the Johnsons did not market soybeans harvested from this field as organic for an additional 3 years.

On July 3, 2008, the Johnsons reported another incident of alleged contamination to the MDA. In this report, the Johnsons alleged that there was pesticide drift onto one of their transitional alfalfa fields after the Cooperative applied Roundup Power Max and Select Max (containing the chemicals glyphosate and clethodium) to a neighboring conventional farmer's field. The MDA investigator did not observe any plant injury, but chemical testing revealed a minimal amount of glyphosate in the Johnsons' transitional alfalfa. The Johnsons reported another incident of drift on August 1, 2008. The MDA "did not observe any plant injury to the alfalfa field or plants, grass and weeds," but chemical testing revealed the presence, at minimal levels, of chloropyrifos, the active ingredient in another pesticide, Lorsban Advanced. The MDA concluded that drift from the Cooperative's spraying caused both of the positive test results. After receiving these test results, the Johnsons took the affected alfalfa field out of organic production for an additional 3 years. The Johnsons took this action because they believed that the presence of any amount of pesticide on their organic fields prohibited them from selling crops harvested from these fields as organic.

Based on the presence of pesticides in their fields, the Johnsons filed this lawsuit against the Cooperative, alleging trespass, nuisance, negligence per se, and battery. They sought damages and a permanent injunction prohibiting the Cooperative from spraying pesticides within a half mile of the Johnsons' fields.3 The Johnsons claimed the following types of damages: (1) loss of profits because they had to take the fields onto which pesticide drifted out of organic production for 3 years; (2) loss of profits because they had to destroy approximately 10 acres of soybeans; (3) inconvenience due to increased weeding, pollution remediation, and NOP reporting responsibilities; and (4) adverse health effects.

The district court granted, in part, the Johnsons' motion for a temporary injunction on June 26, 2009, requiring the Cooperative to give the Johnsons notice before it sprayed pesticides on land adjoining the Johnsons' organic farm. Subsequently, the Cooperative moved for summary judgment, and the Johnsons moved to amend their complaint to include claims based on the two 2008 incidents and a claim for punitive damages. After a hearing, the district court granted the Cooperative summary judgment on all of the Johnsons' claims, denied the Johnsons' motion to amend, and vacated the temporary injunction.

The district court concluded that the Johnsons' trespass claim failed as a matter of law, relying on the court of appeals decision in Wendinger v. Forst Farms Inc., 662 N.W.2d 546, 550 (Minn.App.2003), which held that Minnesota does not recognize trespass by particulate matter.5 The district court also concluded that all of the Johnsons' negligence per se and nuisance claims failed as a matter of law because the Johnsons lacked evidence of damages. This determination was based on the court's conclusion that because there was no evidence that any chemical on the Johnsons' crops exceeded the 5 percent tolerance level in 7 C.F.R. § 205.671, the Johnsons could have sold their crops as organic and therefore the Johnsons did not prove damages. Because the Johnsons did not have any "evidence of damages based on the NOP regulations," the court concluded that all of the Johnsons' claims must be dismissed and the temporary injunction vacated. And because the court concluded that the Johnsons' claims arising from the 2008 incidents would necessarily fail as a matter of law under the same analysis, the court denied the Johnsons' motion to amend their complaint to include claims based on the 2008 incidents.

The court of appeals reversed and remanded. Johnson v. Paynesville Farmers Union Coop. Oil Co., 802 N.W.2d 383 (Minn.App.2011). As to the trespass claim, the court of appeals concluded that the district court "read too much into" Wendinger. Id. at 387. The court of appeals stated that its decision in Wendinger should not be read "to define a unique category of physical substances that can never constitute a trespass." Id. at 388. Instead of focusing on the intangible nature of pesticide drift, the court of appeals focused on the harm caused by it, stating that pesticide drift will "affect the composition of the land." Id. Relying on cases from other jurisdictions that were explicitly distinguished in Wendinger, the court of appeals held that pesticide drift "can interfere with possession" and therefore "a trespass action can arise from a chemical pesticide being deposited in [discernible] and consequential amounts onto one agricultural property as the result of errant overspray during application directed at another." Id. at 389.

As to the negligence per se and nuisance claims based on 7 C.F.R. § 205.202(b), the court of appeals disagreed with the district court's interpretation of the NOP regulations. Johnson, 802 N.W.2d at 390–91. The court of appeals held that the phrase "applied to it" in section 205.202(b) included situations in which pesticides unintentionally came into contact with organic fields. 802 N.W.2d at 390. Based on this conclusion, the court reasoned that the presence of any amount of pesticide on the Johnsons' fields rendered the Johnsons noncompliant with 7 C.F.R. § 205.202(b), and therefore that OCIA had discretion to decertify the Johnsons' fields. 802 N.W.2d at 391 (citing 7 C.F.R. § 205.662(a), (c) (providing that "any noncompliance" with the NOP can lead to decertification)). And because the presence of pesticide on the Johnsons' fields allegedly caused those fields to be decertified, the court of appeals held that the Johnsons had viable claims for damages based on 7 C.F.R. § 205.202(b). 802 N.W.2d at 391. The court of appeals also concluded that the district court erred in failing to separately analyze or discuss the

Johnsons' claims that were not based on trespass or on 7 C.F.R. § 205.202(b), before dismissing all of the Johnsons' claims, and that the district court had abused its discretion in denying the Johnsons' motion to amend their complaint to include claims based on the 2008 incidents. 802 N.W.2d at 391–92.

We granted the Cooperative's petition for review, and on appeal, the Cooperative argues that (1) the Johnsons' trespass claim fails as a matter of law; (2) all of the Johnsons' claims fail as a matter of law because the Johnsons have not shown damages; (3) the district court did not err when it denied the Johnsons' motion to amend their complaint; and (4) the district court did not err when it denied the Johnsons a permanent injunction. We consider each of these issues in turn.

. . .

A.

We turn first to the portion of the Johnsons' nuisance and negligence per se claims that are based on 7 C.F.R. § 205.202(b). The Johnsons argue that they had to remove certain fields from organic production for 3 years because pesticides were "applied to" those fields in violation of 7 C.F.R. § 205.202(b). The Johnsons contend that the phrase "applied to it" in the regulation, read in conjunction with other sections of the NOP, means that any application of pesticides to a field, whether intentional or not, requires that the field be taken out of organic production for 3 years.11 Based on this reading, the Johnsons assert that they were required to take their soybean field back to the beginning of the 3–year transition period because of the 2007 pesticide drift.12As a result, the Johnsons claim they lost the ability to market crops from that field as organic, and therefore lost the opportunity to seek the premium prices commanded by organic products.

For its part, the Cooperative argues that the phrase "applied to it" in 7 C.F.R. § 205.202(b), unambiguously means that the organic farmer intentionally applied the prohibited substance to the field. Because the Johnsons did not apply pesticides to the field, the Cooperative argues that section 205.202(b) does not restrict the Johnsons' sale of organic products. In the alternative, the Cooperative argues that if section 205.202(b) is ambiguous, analysis of the relevant canons of construction confirms its interpretation.

The district court adopted the interpretation of the NOP regulation that the Cooperative advances. But the court of appeals reversed, holding that the phrase "applied to it" "implicitly includes unintentional pesticide drift," and that therefore OCIA had discretion to decertify the Johnsons' soybean field under section 205.202(b). Johnson, 802 N.W.2d at 390. And because there was discretion to decertify, the court of appeals concluded that the Johnsons had offered sufficient evidence to survive summary judgment. Id. at

391. We agree with the district court that section 205.202(b) does not regulate the Cooperative's pesticide drift.

In order to resolve the interpretation question presented, we must construe the regulation at issue—7 C.F.R. § 205.202(b). Our first task is to determine whether the regulation is ambiguous. E .g., In re Cities of Annandale & Maple Lake, 731 N.W.2d 502, 516 (Minn.2007) (considering whether a federal regulation was ambiguous). If it is not ambiguous, we apply the plain and ordinary meaning of the words used. See Exelon Generation Co. LLC v. Local 15 Int'l Bhd. Of Elec. Workers, 676 F.3d 566, 570 (7th Cir.2012) (stating that the same rules of construction apply to federal administrative rules as to statutes); Citizens Advocating Responsible Dev. v. Kandiyohi Cnty. Bd. of Comm'rs, 713 N.W.2d 817, 828 n. 9 (Minn.2006) (noting that administrative regulations are governed by the same rules of construction that apply to statutes); cf. Caminetti v. United States, 242 U.S. 470, 485, 37 S.Ct. 192, 61 L.Ed. 442 (1917) (noting that when the meaning of a statute "is plain . the sole function of the courts is to enforce it according to its terms"). In deciding whether the regulation is ambiguous, however, we do not construe the regulation in isolation. Rather, we are to examine the federal regulation in context. See, e.g., Caraco Pharm. Labs., Ltd. v. Novo Nordisk A/S, ---U.S. ----, 132 S.Ct. 1670, 1680, 182 L.Ed.2d 678 (2012) (noting that courts are to consider questions of statutory interpretation by looking at phrases in the context of the entire statute).

The OFPA provides important context for interpretation of the regulation because the NOP regulations were drafted to "carry out" the provisions of the OFPA. 7 U.S.C. § 6521(a). The OFPA focuses on the producers and handlers of the products that are marketed and sold as organic. See 7 U.S.C. § 6503(a) (directing the Secretary of Agriculture to "establish an organic certification program for producers and handlers of agricultural products"). For example, producers must prepare a plan for the operation of their farms in order to obtain certification to sell their products as organic. See 7 U.S.C. §§ 6504, 6513. They must also certify on an annual basis that they have not sold products labeled as organic "except in accordance" with the OFPA, and producers must allow the certifying agent an "on-site inspection" of their farm every year. 7 U.S.C. § 6506(a)(4),(5). Producers also must keep records for 5 years "concerning the production . of agricultural products sold . as organically produced." 7 U.S.C. § 6511(d).

In addition to these general provisions, the OFPA also establishes certain crop production practices that are prohibited when producers seek to sell products as organic. One of these specific practices provides that in order to be sold as organic, the product must "not be produced on land to which any prohibited substances, including synthetic chemicals, have been applied during the 3 years immediately preceding the harvest of the agricultural products." 7 U.S.C. § 6504(2). The OFPA also specifically provides that producers of organic products "shall not apply materials to . seeds or seedlings that are contrary to, or inconsistent with, the applicable organic certification program." 7 U.S.C. § 6508(a).

When we read the phrase "applied to it" in 7 C.F.R. § 205.202(b), within the context of the OFPA's focus on regulating the practices of the producer of organic products, we conclude that this phrase unambiguously regulates behavior by the producer. In other words, in order for products to be sold as organic, the organic farmer must not have applied prohibited substances to the field from which the product was harvested for a period of 3 years preceding the harvest.13

The Johnsons urge us, however, to construe the phrase "applied to it" to include actions of third parties, such as the pesticide drift that resulted from the Cooperative's spraying activity at issue here. The Johnsons base their construction on the use of the word "application" in 7 C.F.R. § 205.202(c) and 7 C.F.R. § 205.400(f)(1). Section 205.202(c) provides that any field from which crops are intended to be sold as organic must have distinct boundaries and buffer zones to prevent "unintended application of a prohibited substance." Section 205.400 details the requirements that a producer must meet in order to gain organic certification. Among other things, section 205.400 requires a producer to "[i]mmediately notify the certifying agent concerning any: [a]pplication, including drift, of a prohibited substance to any field . that is part of an [organic] operation." 7 C.F.R. § 205.400(f)(1). Because these regulations specifically include "unintended" applications and "drift" as types of applications, the Johnsons argue that the phrase "applied to it" in section 205.202(b) must similarly be read to include the Cooperative's pesticide drift. We disagree.

As is true for the OFPA and the NOP as a whole, section 205.202(c) is also directed at the producer of organic products, not third parties. In this section, the NOP requires that producers who have been certified as organic create buffers between the fields from which organic products will be harvested and other fields. This provision therefore does not support the conclusion that section 205.202(b) should be read to cover conduct by third parties.

Similarly, section 205.400 does not support the Johnsons' proposed construction of section 205.202(b). In this section, "drift" is the subject of a specific regulation. Section 205.400 confirms that when the NOP regulates "drift," that intention is made explicitly clear. But section 205.202(b) does not regulate "drift"; instead, it provides that prohibited substances are not to be "applied to" organic fields. The use of different words in the two provisions supports the conclusion that the sections address different behavior. See

Burlington N. & Santa Fe Ry. Co. v. White, 548 U.S. 53, 62–63, 126 S.Ct. 2405, 165 L.Ed.2d 345 (2006) ("[T]he question is whether Congress intended its different words to make a legal difference. We normally presume that, where words differ as they differ here, Congress acts intentionally and purposely in the disparate inclusion or exclusion." (citation omitted) (internal quotation marks omitted)). The compliance provision in the OFPA statute—7 U.S.C. § 6511—and the corresponding NOP regulation—7 C.F.R. § 205.671–confirm this interpretation.

The compliance provision requires, as a way to enforce the requirements in the OFPA, that "the certifying agent . utilize a system of residue testing to test products sold . as organically produced." 7 U.S.C. § 6511(a). If the agent "determines" that a product intended to be sold as organic "contains any [detectible] pesticide," the producer may be required "to prove that any prohibited substance was not applied to" that product. 7 U.S.C. § 6511(c)(1). Should the agent determine that the residue came from the "intentional application of a prohibited substance," the product may not be sold as organic. 7 U.S.C. § 6511(c)(2)(A). In addition, if "unavoidable residual environmental contamination" is present on the product "at levels that are greater than" those set for the substance at issue, the product may not be sold as organic. 7 U.S.C. § 6511(c)(2)(B). The OFPA thus contemplates that organic products with some amount of prohibited substance residue on them may be marketed and sold as organic. Specifically, if the residue is caused by "environmental contamination," but does not exceed the requisite levels, the product may continue to be sold as organic. Id.

The NOP regulation that specifically implements this compliance provision in the statute—7 C.F.R. § 205.671—confirms this interpretation. Section 205.671 addresses the disqualifying level for "unavoidable residual environmental contamination" referenced in section 6511 of the OFPA. Section 205.671 provides that a crop cannot be sold as organic "[w]hen residue testing detects prohibited substances at levels that are greater than 5 percent of the Environmental Protection Agency's [EPA] tolerance for the specific residue." 7 C.F.R. § 205.671. Under the plain terms of section 205.671, therefore, crops can be sold as organic even if testing shows prohibited substances on those crops as long as the amounts detected do not exceed 5 percent of EPA limits. But if, as the Johnsons contend, any application— including drift—were prohibited by section 205.202(b), then section 205.671 would be superfluous.

As the Johnsons read section 205.202(b), any amount of pesticide, no matter how it came into contact with the field, would require that the field be taken out of organic production for 3 years. There would accordingly be no organic crops left that would be covered under section 205.671 of the NOP or 7 U.S.C. § 6511(c)(2). And the OFPA and NOP would not need a provision allowing crops with minimum levels of pesticide on them (i.e., less than 5 percent) to be sold as organic because such crops would necessarily have been harvested from fields ineligible for organic production. We are not to adopt an interpretation that renders one section of the regulatory scheme a nullity. See Markham v. Cabell, 326 U.S. 404, 409, 66 S.Ct. 193, 90 L.Ed. 165 (1945) (stating that a law will not be strictly read if such reading "results in the emasculation or deletion of a provision which a less literal reading would preserve."). Because the Johnsons' interpretation nullifies part of the OFPA and the NOP, that interpretation is not reasonable, and we decline to adopt it. We instead conclude that "applied to it" used in section 205.202(b), when read in the context of the OFPA and the NOP regulations as a whole, unambiguously refers to prohibited substances that the producer intentionally puts on a field from which crops are intended to be sold as organic.

When the regulation is read in the context of the NOP and the OFPA as a whole and given the statutory scheme's focus on regulating the practices of producers, we conclude that section 205.202(b) does not cover the Cooperative's pesticide drift. Rather, this section governs an organic producer's intentional application of prohibited substances onto fields from which organic products will be harvested .

Having concluded that "applied to it" refers to situations where the producer has applied prohibited substances to the field, we must consider whether the district court correctly dismissed the Johnsons' nuisance and negligence per se claims based on 7 C.F.R. § 205.202(b). While the district court, both parties, and the court of appeals characterize the dismissal as one based on a lack of prima facie evidence of damages, the Johnsons clearly made a prima facie showing of damages; they actually took their soybean field back to the beginning of the 3–year transition period and lost the opportunity to market crops from that field as organic during that time period. The question therefore is not one of damages but is more properly framed as a question of causation. Cambern v. Hubbling, 307 Minn. 168, 171, 238 N.W.2d 622, 624 (1976) ("If the trial court's rule is correct, it is not to be reversed solely because its stated reason was not correct."). And "[w]hile the existence of [causation] is usually a question of fact for the jury, 'when reasonable minds could reach only one conclusion,' it is a question of law." Lietz v. N. States Power Co., 718 N.W.2d 865, 872 (Minn.2006) (quoting Canada v. McCarthy, 567 N.W.2d 496, 506 (Minn.1997)). In other words, the question presented is whether the Johnsons created an issue for trial that the Cooperative's pesticide drift required the Johnsons to remove their field from organic production due to 7 C.F.R. § 205.202(b). We conclude that they did not.

Construing the evidence in the light most favorable to the Johnsons, their certifying agent, OCIA, directed them to take their soybean fields out of organic production for 3 years. But any such directive was inconsistent with the plain language of 7 C.F.R. § 205 .202(b). It was also inconsistent with the OFPA because the Johnsons presented no evidence that any residue exceeded the 5 percent tolerance level in 7 C.F.R. § 205.671. The certifying agent's erroneous interpretation of section 205.202(b) and the OFPA was the proximate cause of the Johnsons' injury, but the Johnsons cannot hold the Cooperative liable for the certifying agent's erroneous interpretation of the law. The Johnsons' remedy for the certifying agent's error was an appeal of that determination because it was "inconsistent with the" OFPA. 7 U.S.C. § 6520(a)(2).

Under the plain language of 7 C.F.R. § 205.202(b), a third party's pesticide drift cannot cause a field to lose organic certification. The Cooperative's pesticide drift therefore could not proximately cause the Johnsons' soybean field to be taken out of organic production for 3 years. See Flom v. Flom, 291 N.W.2d 914, 917 (Minn.1980) (noting that to satisfy the element of proximate cause there must be a showing that the defendant's "conduct was a substantial factor in bringing about the injury"). Because the Cooperative was not, and could not be, the proximate cause of the Johnsons' damage, we hold that the district court properly granted summary judgment to the Cooperative on the Johnsons' nuisance and negligence per se claims based on section 205 .202(b).

. . .

IV.

In summary, we conclude that the Johnsons' trespass claim, and nuisance and negligence per se claims based on 7 C.F.R. § 205.202(b), fail as a matter of law. To the extent that the court of appeals' decision would reinstate those claims and allow the Johnsons to amend their complaint to include those claims for the 2008 incidents of pesticide drift, we reverse. But we conclude that the district court erred in (1) dismissing the Johnsons' nuisance and negligence per se claims to the extent those claims are not based on 7 C.F.R. § 205.202(b), and (2) denying the Johnsons' motion to amend their complaint to include claims for the 2008 incidents to the extent those claims are not based on trespass or 7 C.F.R. § 205.202(b).

Affirmed in part, reversed in part, and remanded.

11.1.3   Torts – Revisit to StarLink

This study of agricultural biotechnology law began with an introduction through the Starlink case. The case turned on the violation of a federal environmental statute, FIFRA, and led to reforms of the approval of genetically modified crops for animal and human consumption.

In this section, we revisit Starlink and look at the tort claims that were made in the case. Although the tort claims may not have succeeded in this case, they may be instructive for future cases.

In Re Starlink Corn Products Liability Litigation
212 F. Supp. 2d 828 (N.D. Ill., E. Div., 2002)

Memorandum Opinion and Order by Judge James B. Moran

This controversy arises from the discovery of genetically modified corn in various food products. Plaintiffs disseminated a product that contaminated the entire United States' corn supply, increasing their costs and depressing corn prices. Plaintiffs have filed a 57-count master second amended consolidated class action complaint, alleging common law claims for negligence, strict liability, private nuisance, public nuisance and conversion on behalf of a nationwide class of corn farmers. . . . Defendants filed a motion to dismiss, arguing that the Federal Insecticide, Fungicide and Rodenticide Act (FIFRA), 7 U.S.C. §§ 136 *et seq.*, preempts plaintiffs' state law claims, that the economic loss doctrine bars any recovery, and that the complaint fails to state a claim under any of plaintiffs' purported legal theories. For the following reasons, defendants' motion to dismiss is granted in part and denied in part.

BACKGROUND
Aventis genetically engineered a corn seed to produce a protein known as Cry9C that is toxic to certain insects. The seeds are marketed under the brand name StarLink. Garst is a licensee who produced and distributed Starlink seeds. Aventis applied to register Starlink with the EPA, which is responsible for regulating insecticides under FIFRA, 7 U.S.C. §§ 136 *et seq.* The EPA noted that Cry9C had several attributes similar to known human allergens, and issued only a limited registration, permitting Starlink use for such purposes as animal feed, ethanol production and seed increase, but prohibiting its use for human consumption. Consequently, segregating it from non-StarLink corn, which was fit for human consumption, became of utmost importance. A little background about normal practices for cultivating, harvesting and distributing corn demonstrates the extensive steps necessary to prevent StarLink corn from entering the food supply. Corn replicates by the transfer of pollen from one corn plant to another, including cross-pollination from one breed to another. Once airborne, corn pollen can drift over considerable distances, meaning that different corn varieties within a farm, and from neighboring farms, regularly cross-breed.

With few exceptions, there are not procedures in place to segregate types of corn. Different corn breeds within an individual farm are commingled at the harvesting stage. Corn from hundreds of thousands of farms is then further commingled as it is gathered, stored and shipped through a system of local, regional and terminal grain elevators. Elevators, storage and transportation facilities are generally not equipped to test and segregate corn varieties. The commingled corn is then marketed and traded as a fungible commodity.

In light of these general practices in the corn industry, the EPA required special procedures with respect to StarLink. These included mandatory segregation methods to prevent StarLink from commingling with other corn in cultivation, harvesting, handling, storage and transport, and a 660-foot "buffer zone" around StarLink corn crops to prevent cross-pollination with non-StarLink corn plants. The limited registration also made Aventis responsible for ensuring these restrictions were implemented, obligating it (a) to inform farmers of the EPA's requirements for the planting, cultivation and use of StarLink; (b) to instruct farmers growing StarLink how to store and dispose of the StarLink seeds, seed bags, and plant detritus; and (c) to ensure that all farmers purchasing StarLink seeds signed a contract binding them to these terms before permitting them to grow StarLink corn.StarLink was distributed throughout the United States from approximately May 1998 through October 2000. The limited registration initially limited StarLink cultivation to 120,000 acres.

In January 1999, Aventis petitioned the EPA to raise this limit to 2.5 million acres. The EPA agreed, subject to an amended registration that required Aventis to (a) inform purchasers (i.e. "Growers") at the time of StarLink seed corn sales, of the need to direct StarLink harvest to domestic feed and industrial non-food uses only;(b) require all Growers to sign a "Grower Agreement" outlining field management requirements and stating the limits on StarLink corn use;(c) deliver a Grower Guide, restating the provisions stated in the Grower Agreement, with all seed;(d) provide all Growers with access to a confidential list of feed outlets and elevators that direct grain to domestic feed and industrial uses;(e) write to Growers prior to planting, reminding them of the domestic and industrial use requirements for StarLink corn;(f) write to Growers prior to harvest, reminding them of the domestic and industrial use requirements for StarLink corn;(g) conduct a statistically sound follow-up survey of Growers following harvest, to monitor compliance with the Grower Agreement.

Over this 29-month period, StarLink cultivation expanded from 10,000 acres to 350,000 acres. In October 2000, after numerous reports that human food products had tested positive for Cry9C, a wave of manufacturers issued recalls for their corn products. On October 12, 2000, Aventis, at EPA's urging, applied to cancel the limited registration, effective February 20, 2001. Fear of StarLink contamination nonetheless continues to affect corn markets. Many U.S. food producers have stopped using U.S. corn, replacing it with imported corn or corn substitutes. South Korea, Japan and other foreign countries have terminated or substantially limited imports of U.S. corn. Grain elevators and transport providers are now mandating expensive testing on all corn shipments. Plaintiffs allege that the widespread StarLink contamination of the U.S. corn supply is a result of defendants' failure to comply with the EPA's requirements. Aventis did not include the EPA-mandated label on some StarLink packages, did not notify, instruct and remind StarLink farmers of the restrictions on StarLink use, proper segregation methods and buffer zone requirements, and did not require StarLink farmers to sign the obligatory contracts. Prior to the 2000 growing season Aventis allegedly instructed its seed representatives that it was unnecessary for them to advise StarLink farmers to segregate their StarLink crop or create buffer zones because Aventis believed the EPA would amend the registration to permit StarLink use for human consumption.

In July 2001, however, an EPA Scientific Advisory Panel reaffirmed its previous position on StarLink's allergenic qualities. Further, the FDA has declared StarLink to be an adulterant under the Food, Drug and Cosmetic Act..
. . .

II. Economic Loss Doctrine

This rule limits the types of damages plaintiffs may recover in tort. Physical injuries to persons or property are compensable; solely economic injuries are not. The difficult question is defining what constitutes an "economic" injury. . . .

Non-StarLink corn crops are damaged when they are pollinated by StarLink corn. The pollen causes these corn plants to develop the Cry9C protein and renders what would otherwise be a valuable food crop unfit for human consumption. Non-StarLink corn is also damaged when it is commingled with StarLink corn. Once mixed, there is no way to re-segregate the **corn** into its edible and inedible parts. The entire batch is considered tainted and can only be used for the domestic and industrial purposes for which StarLink is approved. None of that supply can ever be used for human food. There are at least four different points along the supply chain at which StarLink could have entered the food corn supply, all of which are consistent with the complaint: (1) plaintiffs unknowingly purchased seed containing the Cry9C protein, *i.e.* their suppliers' inventory had been contaminated; (2) plaintiffs' crops were contaminated by pollen from StarLink corn on a neighboring farm; (3) plaintiffs' harvest was contaminated by commingling with StarLink corn in a transport or storage facility; and (4) food manufacturers commingled the corn within their raw material storage or processing activities.

The first situation would fall within the economic loss doctrine. Plaintiffs could have negotiated contractual protection from their suppliers and simply did not get what they had bargained for. In the fourth, plaintiffs would have suffered no harm to their property because the corn was commingled after they had relinquished their ownership interest in it. Scenarios 2 and 3, however, present viable claims for harm to their crops. [Resolving the complaint's ambiguous phraseology in plaintiffs' favor, we find that they have sufficiently alleged that their crops were contaminated at some point within that chain.]

The StarLink situation does not fit neatly into traditional economic loss doctrine analysis. Plaintiffs here had no commercial dealings with defendants or defendants' customers. This is more than a lack of direct privity, and not a situation where a party could have negotiated warranty or indemnity protection and chose not to. Plaintiffs had no opportunity to negotiate contractual protection with anyone. Still, as the access cases aptly demonstrate, the economic loss doctrine has grown beyond its original freedom-of-contract based policy justifications. Farmers' expectations of what they will receive for their crops are just that, expectations. Absent a physical injury, plaintiffs cannot recover for drops in market prices. Nor can they recover for any additional costs, such as testing procedures, imposed by the marketplace. But if there was some physical harm to plaintiffs' corn crop, the lack of a transaction with defendants affects what will be considered "other property." [This includes corn commingled at grain elevators because plaintiffs retain ownership rights to corn stored there. Each contributing farmer owns a pro rata share of the entire, now tainted, supply.]

Assuming plaintiffs did not buy corn seeds with the Cry9C protein, it cannot be said that a defective part of their crop injured the whole, that a defective product was integrated into a system or that the harm to their crop was a foreseeable consequence of the seeds' failure to perform. These facts are distinguishable from Hapka, 458 N.W.2d at 688 (holding farmer who purchased diseased seeds could not recover for harm to rest of crop). Plaintiffs' seeds, as purchased, were adequate. The StarLink contaminant was wholly external.

Nor does the StarLink controversy present the unlimited or speculative damage concerns common in access cases. There are a finite number of potential plaintiffs -- only non-StarLink corn farmers -- who can claim injury. This may be a sizeable group, and the damages may be tremendous, but the fact that defendants are alleged to have directly harmed a large number of plaintiffs is not a defense. StarLink's effects on commercial corn farmers are distinct and qualitatively different from society at large. And damages are easily measured through price changes because corn is a regularly traded commodity with a readily measurable market. Further, as discussed above, the contamination of plaintiffs' corn supply is a physical injury. To the extent plaintiffs allege that their crops were themselves contaminated, either by cross-pollination in the fields or by commingling later in the distribution chain, they have adequately stated a claim for harm to property. Once plaintiffs have established this harm they may be entitled to compensation for certain economic losses.

III. Negligence

Defendants challenge three separate elements: duty, proximate cause and damages. Although cast in terms of a balance between foreseeability, reasonableness and public policy, the essence of their argument is remoteness -- any effect StarLink may have had on corn markets is too far removed from defendants' conduct. Defendants contend that the causal relationship involved six distinct steps: (1) the EPA approved the registration for Cry9C; (2) seed companies incorporated the StarLink technology into seed corn; (3) growers purchased StarLink seeds; (4) the StarLink seeds/corn was handled in such a way as to allow cross-pollination and commingling; (5) the tainted corn was introduced into the mainstream corn supply, leading to food product recalls; and (6) the discovery of StarLink in the main food supply hurt corn prices.In presenting their version of the causal chain, however, defendants have imposed their own construction on the complaint.

On a motion to dismiss we must not only accept plaintiffs' version, but also any set of facts consistent with it. First, defendants' argument used their own characterization of Aventis' role, or lack thereof, in bringing StarLink to market. Aventis denies any involvement in numerous steps leading to the widespread StarLink contamination. This is a simple factual dispute. The complaint plainly alleges that Aventis (or its predecessors) were involved in developing and licensing StarLink. Moreover, it alleges that pursuant to the limited registration Aventis was responsible for monitoring and enforcing compliance by StarLink farmers. For now we must accept plaintiffs' version of Aventis' involvement in introducing StarLink into the food supply.We must also collapse defendants' purported chain from the other end. Although they attempt to characterize the complaint as asserting some remote duty to preserve the market price of **corn,** the duty alleged is to prevent contamination. The effects on corn markets are merely a way to measure the damages. As we discussed above, we read the complaint to allege direct harm to plaintiffs' corn.

Defendants are correct that the complaint does not make this charge specifically, but it is a set of facts that is consistent with plaintiffs' allegations about the impact on the **corn** system as a whole. At this stage of litigation we must construe this ambiguity in plaintiffs' favor. Presuming Aventis' more active involvement with StarLink, and presuming further that the latter physically harmed plaintiffs' corn, the chain becomes substantially shorter. Aventis had a duty to ensure that StarLink did not enter the human food supply, and their failure to do so caused plaintiffs' corn to be contaminated.

Lastly, Aventis argues that even if plaintiffs suffered direct harm to their corn, its SES program would fully compensate them. Plaintiffs have alleged otherwise, and for now, that is sufficient.

IV. Conversion

Conversion is defined as "an intentional exercise of dominion or control over a chattel which so seriously interferes with the right of another to control it that the actor may justly be required to pay the other the full value of the chattel." Restatement (Second) of Torts § 222A. Plaintiffs argue that defendants' role in contaminating the corn supply amounts to a conversion of their property.

We disagree.

The defining element of conversion, the one that distinguishes it from a trespass to chattels, is the extent of interference with the owner's property rights. If the damage is minor, in duration or severity, plaintiff may only recover for the diminished value. But if the damage is sufficiently severe, plaintiff may recover full value. Conversion is akin to a forced judicial sale. The defendant pays full value for the chattel, and receives title to it.

Restatement § 222A comment c. Here, plaintiffs have not alleged that defendants destroyed their crops or deprived them of possession. Plaintiffs retained possession and still had total control over the **corn.** Most, if not all of it, was ultimately sold to third parties. The only damages were a lower price, for which plaintiffs could be compensated without forcing a sale. It is possible to convert a chattel by altering it, without completely destroying it. In particular, commingling fungible goods so that their identity is lost can constitute a conversion. Restatement § 226 comment e. To do so, however, the perpetrator must alter the chattel in a way that is "so material as to change the identity of the chattel or its essential character." Restatement § 226 comment d. At worst, StarLink contamination changed plaintiffs' yield from being corn fit for human consumption to corn fit only for domestic or industrial use. Plaintiffs do not claim they were growing the corn to eat themselves, but for sale on the commodity markets. The crops were still viable for the purpose for which plaintiffs would normally use them, for sale on the open market. That the market had become less hospitable does not change the product's essential character. As above, the severity of the alteration is indicated by the decrease in market price. This could arguably constitute a trespass to chattels, but does not rise to the level of conversion.

Lastly, negligence cannot support a conversion claim. It requires intent. Restatement § 224. The complaint alleges that defendants did not take adequate precautions to ensure that StarLink corn was adequately segregated. Nowhere do plaintiffs claim that defendants intentionally commingled StarLink and non-StarLink corn, or deliberately contaminated the food supply. Even if defendants negligently failed to prevent cross-pollination and commingling, they would not be liable for conversion.

V. Nuisance
A. Private

The complaint alleges that defendants created a private nuisance by distributing corn seeds with the Cry9C protein, knowing that they would cross-pollinate with neighboring corn crops. [The private nuisance claims appear to be premised exclusively on cross-pollination in the fields, not commingling later in the distribution chain.]

A private nuisance is a nontrespassory invasion of another's interest in the private use and enjoyment of land." Restatement (Second) of Torts § 821D. We agree that drifting pollen can constitute an invasion, and that contaminating neighbors' crops interferes with their enjoyment of the land. The issue is whether defendants are responsible for contamination caused by their product beyond the point of sale.

Commingling could not constitute a private nuisance because it does not involve an invasion of any private interests in land. By contrast, the public nuisance claims, discussed below, may be premised on commingling because "unlike a private nuisance, a public nuisance does not necessarily involve interference with use or enjoyment of land." Restatement § 821B comment h.Defendants argue that they cannot be liable for any nuisance caused by StarLink because they were no longer in control of the seeds once they were sold to farmers. But one can be liable for nuisance "not only when he carries on the activity but also when he participates to a substantial extent in carrying it on." Restatement § 834. Plaintiffs maintain that defendants' design of the StarLink technology, distribution of the seeds and, most importantly, their failure to fulfill their EPA-mandated duties, constitutes substantial participation.

The paradigm private nuisance case involves a suit between two neighboring landowners, one of whom alleges that the other's activities are somehow interfering with the first's enjoyment of the land. Suing the manufacturer of the product that the neighbor was using appears to be an extension of nuisance law into an area normally regulated by product liability. But there is precedent for such an application under certain circumstances, and it does fit within the definition of a nuisance. . . .Suppose, however, that [the manufacturer] had not taken steps to alert customers of the risks of the product, or intentionally marketed the product to customers who it knew or should have known would dispose of [it] in a manner that would harm the environment. Nothing in the opinion in City of Bloomington would preclude the imposition of liability on the manufacturer under those facts. . . .

This brings us to the case at bar, which is much closer to mainstream nuisance doctrine than either the asbestos or gun cases. In the asbestos cases, the plaintiffs had themselves purchased the product, consented to having it installed on their property and then sued the manufacturer when it turned out to be harmful. There was no invasion of a neighboring property and plaintiffs had exclusive access to the nuisance-causing agent. Here, plaintiffs did not purchase StarLink seeds, and have alleged that pollen from neighboring farms did enter their premises.

Aside from the presence of an invasion, the fact that the alleged nuisance occurred on another's property means that, unlike asbestos purchasers, plaintiffs had no ability to access or control the nuisance themselves. In the gun cases, manufacturers successfully argued that they should not be held responsible for third parties' intentional misuse of their products. Here, however, plaintiffs have not alleged that StarLink farmers defied the manufacturers' instructions, but rather that the instructions themselves violated the EPA's mandates. Moreover, the gun cases alleged a public nuisance and did not implicate plaintiffs' ability to enjoy land or anyone's unreasonable use of land. Private nuisance jurisprudence has always focused on the use and enjoyment of land.

Plaintiffs here have alleged that they are unable to enjoy the profits of their land (selling food corn), because of an unreasonable activity on neighboring land (growing StarLink corn). Another critical factor here is the impact of the limited registration, which negates many of the concerns courts have expressed about holding manufacturers liable for post-sale nuisances. For example, they emphasized that the manufacturers did not have any control over how the purchasers had used their products, or any access to abate the nuisance. Aventis, on the other hand, had an affirmative duty to enforce StarLink farmers' compliance with the Grower Agreements. This arguably gave Aventis some measure of control over StarLink's use, as well as a means to abate any nuisance caused by its misuse. This mirrors Page County Appliance Center, *supra,* where the court found the manufacturer's ongoing service contract with the purchaser gave defendant enough access and control to create a question of fact as to its contribution to the nuisance. Aventis' duties under the limited registration were, by comparison, even more extensive. Similarly, defendants' failure to give StarLink farmers the warnings mandated by the limited registration, and (ultimately incorrect) representations that StarLink need not be segregated because the EPA was going to approve it for human consumption, are also arguably the type of culpable conduct relied upon...In summary, of the states involved here Iowa, Wisconsin and Illinois have all held a manufacturer liable for a nuisance related to its product beyond the point of sale....The lack of state precedent matching these precise facts does not preclude us from applying widely accepted Restatement law to new factual situations. Residue from a product drifting across property lines presents a typical nuisance claim. All parties who substantially contribute to the nuisance are liable. The unique obligations imposed by the limited registration arguably put Aventis in a position to control the nuisance.

On a motion to dismiss we may not speculate whether the as yet undeveloped facts will constitute substantial contribution. To the extent the allegations comport with our preemption analysis above, they do state a valid claim for private nuisance.

B. Public [Nuisance]

Plaintiffs also assert that StarLink's contamination of the general food corn supply constitutes a public nuisance. Beyond defendants' argument that they lacked control over the alleged nuisance, discussed above, they assert that plaintiffs cannot establish special harm. At the outset, we note the limited depth of review courts typically undertake on a motion to dismiss a public nuisance claim.

The pleading requirements are not strenuous because the 'concept of common law public nuisance elude[s] precise definition.' ... The unreasonableness of the defendant's actions and the substantialness of the right invasion, which lead to the determination of nuisance, are questions of fact for the jury. 'To state a claim, plaintiffs must allege "an unreasonable interference with a right common to the general public." Restatement § 821B(1). The Restatement sweeps broadly in defining a "public right," including "the public health, the public safety, the public peace, the public comfort or the public convenience." Restatement § 821B(2)(a). Contamination of the food supply implicates health, safety, comfort and convenience, and certainly satisfies this permissive standard.

To state a private action for public nuisance, plaintiffs must also demonstrate that they have been harmed differently than the general public. Restatement § 821C. The harm must be of a different type, not merely a difference in severity or imposing a disproportionate share of the burden on plaintiffs. Among the Restatement's specific examples are physical harm to chattels, § 821C comment d, and pecuniary loss to businesses, § 821C comment h. Both are present here.

The closest analogy and most pertinent discussion is in Burgess v. M/V Tamano, 370 F. Supp. 247, 250 (D. Me. 1973). There, commercial fisherman alleged that an oil spill harmed local waters and marine life. The court found that although fishing the waters was a right of the general public, it affected commercial fishermen differently because they depended on it for their livelihood. This was consistent with the general principle that pecuniary loss to the plaintiff will be regarded as different in kind 'where the plaintiff has an established business making commercial use of the public right with which the defendant interferes ...." *Id., quoting* Prosser, Law of Torts, § 88 at 590 (4th ed. 1971). Here, plaintiffs are commercial corn farmers. While the general public has a right to safe food, plaintiffs depend on the integrity of the corn supply for their livelihood.

Defendants maintain that because plaintiffs purport to represent a group so numerous as a nationwide class of corn farmers, their damages cannot be considered special or unique. But the special damages requirement does not limit the absolute number of parties affected so much as it restricts the types of harm that are compensable. Class actions and special damages are not mutually exclusive. Commercial corn farmers, as a group, are affected differently than the general public.

CONCLUSION
For the foregoing reasons, defendants' motion to dismiss is granted with respect to the claims for conversion . . . . The motion is denied with respect to the claims for negligence *per se,* public nuisance, private nuisance . . . . The negligence and strict liability claims are dismissed to the extent they rely on a failure to warn, but may proceed under the theories outlined above.

Chapter 12

Cultured Meat, Organs and Xenotransplantation

12.1.1   Cultured meat

The first patent in the United States and internationally for cultured meat was awarded in 1999 to Van Eelen, a citizen of The Netherlands. But he was not able to produce what would be the world's first laboratory-created hamburger until 2013.

In 2015, Memphis Meats was founded with a goal of feeding 10 billion people by 2050 (http://www.memphismeats.com/about), using the cell culture method to produce meat.

There are two types of cultured meat production processes. The first is the cell-culture approach that requires a scaffold or framework to start the cells growing. The second method is the self-organization or tissue culture method that mimics the look and texture of meat.

Most advocates for cultured meat point out that animals are not killed with this method. Those who advocate against cultured meat, do so because it may suggest cannibalism for those cell cultures that being with human cells; or it may be against some religious beliefs.

Cultured meat is regulated by the U.S. Department of Agriculture and the Wholesome Meat Act, specifically defines "animal food product" (21 USC§§ 601) but the "meat food product" definition for exempts products that "historically have not been considered by consumers as products of the meat food industry" and "are not represented as meat food products," so whether the public considers it meat may determine jurisdiction under this definition. The definition for "food additives" does not seem to cover this product.

In 2018, Memphis Meats joined with in a letter to the President asking for clarification of the biotechnology regulatory framework as it applies to cultured meat regulation. Here is an excerpt of their letter:

August 23, 2018

President Donald J. Trump
The White House
1600 Pennsylvania Avenue NW
Washington, DC 20500

Dear Mr. President:

Memphis Meats and the North American Meat Institute respectfully request that your Administration clarify the regulatory framework for cell-based meat and poultry products, based on the existing comprehensive system that ensures U.S. consumers enjoy the safest and most affordable food in the world.

Existing law and practice, as well as longstanding precedent, demonstrate that both the U.S. Food and Drug Administration (FDA) and the U.S. Department of Agriculture (USDA) have roles to play in regulating cell-based meat and poultry products. To ensure the regulatory system protects consumers while fostering innovation, it is imperative that the agencies coordinate and collaborate in their efforts, consistent with established policy. . . .

In November 2018, the FDA and USDA issued a joint statement on working together to regulate cultured meat:

FDA STATEMENT
Statement from USDA Secretary Perdue and FDA Commissioner Gottlieb on the regulation of cell-cultured food products from cell lines of livestock and poultry

For Immediate Release:
    November 16, 2018
Statement From:
    Commissioner of Food and Drugs - Food and Drug Administration
    Scott Gottlieb M.D.

    Last month, the U.S. Department of Agriculture and the U.S. Food and Drug Administration held a public meeting to discuss the use of livestock and poultry cell lines to develop cell-cultured food products. At this meeting, stakeholders shared valuable perspectives on the regulation needed to both foster these innovative food products and maintain the highest standards of public health. The public comment period will be extended and will remain open through December 26, 2018.

After several thoughtful discussions between our two Agencies that incorporated this stakeholder feedback, we have concluded that both the USDA and the FDA should jointly oversee the production of cell-cultured food products derived from livestock and poultry. Drawing on the expertise of both USDA and FDA, the Agencies are today announcing agreement on a joint regulatory framework wherein FDA oversees cell collection, cell banks, and cell growth and differentiation. A transition from FDA to USDA oversight will occur during the cell harvest stage. USDA will then oversee the production and labeling of food products derived from the cells of livestock and poultry. And, the Agencies are actively refining the technical details of the framework, including robust collaboration and information sharing between the agencies to allow each to carry out our respective roles.

This regulatory framework will leverage both the FDA's experience regulating cell-culture technology and living biosystems and the USDA's expertise in regulating livestock and poultry products for human consumption. USDA and FDA are confident that this regulatory framework can be successfully implemented and assure the safety of these products. Because our agencies have the statutory authority necessary to appropriately regulate cell-cultured food products derived from livestock and poultry the Administration does not believe that legislation on this topic is necessary.

In March 2019, the FDA and USDA established a joint relationship in the regulation of cultured meat which was a first step in giving some meaningful notice to the regulated community about which agencies would be regulating this area. Formal Agreement Between FDA and USDA Regarding Oversight of Human Food Produced Using Animal Cell Technology Derived from Cell Lines of USDA-amenable Species, March 7, 2019, available at *https://www.fda.gov/food/domestic-interagency-agreements-food/formal-agreement-between-fda-and-usda-regarding-oversight-human-food-produced-using-animal-cell.*

By October 7, 2020, the FDA published a statement about their jurisdiction over cultured meat and calling for comments on whether cultured meat should be labeled [(85 Fed. Reg. 63277-63280 (Oct. 7, 2020)at https://www.federalregister.gov/documents/2020/10/07/2020-22140/labeling-of-foods-comprised-of-or-containing-cultured-seafood-cells-request-for-information]:

FDA Jurisdiction Over Cultured Animal Cells
Efforts are underway to develop various food products comprised of or containing cultured animal cells, including cells from livestock, poultry, and seafood [1] species, using a process often referred to as animal cell culture technology. Animal cell culture technology involves the controlled growth of animal cells, their subsequent differentiation into various cell types, and their harvesting and processing into food. Once produced, the harvested cells could potentially be processed into or combined with other foods and marketed in the same, or similar, manner as conventionally produced meat, poultry, and seafood. In this document we refer to these foods as "foods

comprised of or containing cultured animal cells." Many companies, both domestic and foreign, are developing products using this technology. Given these technological advances, it is appropriate to consider what actions, if any, may be needed to ensure the safe production and accurate labeling of these products.

FDA will be involved in the regulation of foods generated by animal cell culture technology consistent with our current legal authorities. We are responsible for implementing and enforcing the Federal Food, Drug, and Cosmetic Act (FD&C Act) (21 U.S.C. 301 et seq.), the Public Health Service Act (42 U.S.C. 201 et seq.), and the Fair Packaging and Labeling Act (15 U.S.C. 1451 et seq.). In carrying out our responsibilities under these laws, we maintain responsibility for ensuring that food is safe and not misbranded.

B. Relevant Misbranding Provisions Under the FD&C Act

This document primarily pertains to representations about the identity of foods comprised of or containing cultured seafood cells. Such representations include the name of the food and descriptions about its nature, source, or characteristics. There are Start Printed Page 63279several provisions in the FD&C Act under which food may be misbranded with respect to representations about identity. In general, the representations made or suggested must not cause the labeling to be misleading, either affirmatively or by omission of material facts (21 U.S.C. 343(a)(1) and 321(n)). The FD&C Act prohibits offering a food for sale under the name of another food (21 U.S.C. 343(b)). It requires the labels of non-standardized foods to bear the common or usual name of the food if such a name exists (21 U.S.C. 343(i)(1)). Common or usual names are generally established by common usage, though in some cases may be established by regulation pursuant to the principles in 21 CFR 102.5(a)-(c) (see 21 CFR 102.5(d)). In the absence of a common or usual name or other name established by federal law or regulation, food sold in packaged form is required to be labeled with an accurate description of the food or a fanciful name commonly used by the public (§ 101.3(b)(3) (21 CFR 101.3(b)(3))). Such description or name must not be false or misleading (21 U.S.C. 343(a)(1)) and is referred to as the statement of identity (§ 101.3(b)). Finally, the FD&C Act provides that words or statements required to appear on the label or labeling be in such terms as to render them likely to be understood by the ordinary individual under customary conditions of purchase and use (21 U.S.C. 343(f)).

C. FDA-USDA Agreement Regarding Oversight of Human Food Produced Using Animal Cell Technology Derived From Cell Lines of USDA-Amenable Species

In November 2018, FDA and the U.S. Department of Agriculture (USDA) formally announced that they will jointly oversee the production of cultured cell food products derived from livestock and poultry (Ref. 1). On March 7,

2019, FDA and USDA signed an agreement that described each entity's intended roles with respect to the oversight of human food produced using animal cell culture technology, derived from cell lines of those species [2] covered under the Federal Meat Inspection Act (FMIA) (21 U.S.C. 601 *et seq.*) and the Poultry Products Inspection Act (PPIA) (21 U.S.C. 451 *et seq.*) (Ref. 2). In summary, FDA will oversee the collection, growth and differentiation of livestock and poultry cells until cell harvest. A transition from FDA to USDA's Food Safety and Inspection Service oversight will occur during the cell harvest stage. USDA then will oversee the processing, packaging, and labeling of the resulting food products derived from the cultured cells of livestock and poultry. FDA will continue to regulate foods comprised of or containing cultured animal cells from other species under FDA's jurisdiction, such as seafood species other than Siluriformes fish. In the FDA-USDA agreement, FDA and USDA have agreed to develop joint principles for product labeling and claims to ensure that products are labeled consistently and transparently.

The questions for comment give us some insight into the type of regulation that FDA is considering for labeling:

II. Issues for Consideration and Request for Information

We invite comment in response to the questions below. Our use of the term "cultured seafood cells" in these questions is intended to distinguish between the foods, which are the subject of this document, and conventionally produced seafood. It is not intended to establish or suggest nomenclature for labeling purposes. The names and descriptions in food labeling should be based on consumer understanding and usage as described in section I.B. We invite comment, particularly data and other evidence, about: (1) Names or statements of identity for foods comprised of or containing cultured seafood cells; (2) consumer understanding of terms that have been suggested for the names or statements of identity of foods comprised of or containing cultured seafood cells; and (3) how to assess material differences between the foods that are the subject of this document and conventionally produced foods. In responding to these questions, please identify the question by its associated letter and number (such as "2(a)") so that we can associate your response with a specific question.

1. Should the name or statement of identity of foods comprised of or containing cultured seafood cells inform consumers about how the animal cells were produced? Please explain your reasoning.

2. What terms should be in the name or statement of identity of a food comprised of or containing cultured seafood cells to convey the nature or source of the food to consumers? (For example, possible terms could be "cell cultured" or "cell based" or "cell cultivated.") Please explain your reasoning and provide any studies or data about consumer understanding of such terms.

a. How do these terms inform consumers of the nature or source of the food?
b. If foods comprised of or containing cultured seafood cells were to be labeled with the term "culture" or "cultured" in their names or statements of identity (*e.g.*, "cell culture[d]"), would labeling differentiation be necessary to distinguish these products from other types of foods where the term "culture" or "cultured" is used (such as "aquaculture")? Please explain your reasoning and provide any studies or data about consumer understanding of such terms.

3. The names of many conventionally produced seafood products have been established by common usage or by statute or regulation. Names are also recommended for seafood species in *The Seafood List*.[3] In FDA's view, foods comprised of or containing cultured seafood cells are not yet in the marketplace and, therefore, do not have common or usual names established by common usage.
a. If you disagree with FDA's view, what are these names and what evidence demonstrates that the names are commonly used and understood by the American public for foods derived from cultured animal cells?
b. Should names for conventionally produced seafood products established by common usage, statute, or regulation Start Printed Page 63280be included in the names or statements of identity of food derived from cultured seafood cells? Please explain your reasoning.
c. If so, is additional qualifying language necessary? What qualifying terms or phrases would be appropriate? Please explain your reasoning.
d. Do these names, with or without qualifying language, clearly distinguish foods derived from seafood cell culture from conventionally produced seafood? Please explain your reasoning.
e. Should FDA update *The Seafood List* to include foods comprised of or containing cultured seafood cells? Please explain your reasoning.

4. Should terms that specify a certain type of seafood (such as "fillet" or "steak") be included in or accompany the name or statement of identity of foods comprised of or containing cultured animal cells?
a. Under what circumstances should these terms be used? What information would they convey to consumers? For example, would such terms convey the physical form or appearance of the food? Please explain your reasoning. Additionally, please provide any studies or data about consumer understanding of such terms when used to describe foods comprised of or containing cultured seafood cells.
b. Would these terms be misleading to consumers? Please explain your reasoning and provide any supporting studies or data.

5. When comparing conventionally produced seafood to foods comprised of or containing cultured seafood cells, what attributes (such as nutrition, taste, texture, or aroma) vary between the foods and should FDA consider to be

material to consumers' purchasing and consumption decisions? Please explain your reasoning.

a. Are there other characteristics beyond nutritional attributes or organoleptic properties that may be material differences? These could relate either to cellular constituents or characteristics influenced by the cell culture production process. Please be specific in your response and explain your reasoning.

The cattle industry is particularly interested in making sure that cultured meat is labeled so that their products can be distinguished in the marketplace. It is likely that some form of labeling will be used on cultured meat as the FDA continues to collect comments on these areas that will likely be subject to some form of distinguishing labeling.

12.1.2   Xenotransplantation

The critical shortage of organs for transplantation in humans has led to the need for cross-species transplantation, or xenotransplanation. The species most suitable for human xenotransplantation is the pig and the miniature pig and so it is the most likely candidate as a source for organs, including heart and kidneys. Nonhuman primates have done well over a period of years with these xenotransplants.

In 1996, the Public Health Service (PHS) published a "Draft Public Health Service (PHS) Guideline on Infectious Disease Issues in Xenotransplantation" (61 FR 49920, September 23, 1996) that was revised and issued on January 29, 2001 (66 FR 8120), based on public comments received and advances in fields relating to xenotransplantation[1] (hereafter referred to as "PHS Guideline"). This FDA guidance document reiterates many of the concepts in the PHS Guideline but, in addition, includes specific advice, regarding all aspects of xenotransplantation product development and production and xenotransplantation clinical trials. [

The FDA regulates xenotranplantation. In 2003, the FDA completed a review of the safety of xenotransplantation and concluded that much improvement has been made in cell and organ xenografting that adds to the research for xenotransplanation. FDA has provided a definition for xenotransplanation in their 2003 guidance [(68 Fed. Reg. 16542-16543 (Apr. 2003) at Source Animal, Product, Preclinical, and Clinical Issues Concerning the Use of Xenotransplantation Products in Humans https://www.fda.gov/regulatory-information/search-fda-guidance-documents/source-animal-product-preclinical-and-clinical-issues-concerning-use-xenotransplantation-products]:

> ... xenotransplantation refers to any procedure that involves the transplantation, implantation, or infusion into a human recipient of either (a) live cells, tissues, or organs from a nonhuman animal source; or (b) human body fluids, cells, tissues, or organs that have had ex vivo contact with live nonhuman animal cells, tissues, or organs.

The risk of the transfer of retroviruses and other microorganisms has been a concern since the 1990s. In 2003, the FDA and WHO developed consensus documents for the management of this risk, the Second Global Consultation on Regulatory Requirements for Xenotransplantation Clinical Trials.

The high risk of rejection of the organ has been partly mitigated by the genetic engineering of pigs that are designed for organ sources. This technique is becoming increasingly better. A scientific article summarized the state of xenotransplantation:

> The remarkable clinical success of transplantation over the past several decades has paradoxically led to an increasing shortage of transplantable human organs, by increasing the waiting list of patients aware that transplants could save their lives. Although there are other, competing technologies also under development, xenotransplantation is likely to the best near-term solution for this organ shortage. Many of the obstacles that have previously inhibited progress in xenotransplantation have now been overcome through GE of pigs to make their organs more compatible with human immune systems and physiology. Even with these modifications, however, it is not yet clear that the use of clinically-acceptable levels of immunosuppression could permit xenograft survivals similar to those of allografts. To achieve this goal, tolerance may be required. Additional GE of pigs to improve the likelihood of tolerance induction to pigs is also underway. Judicious combinations of modifying host immunity and genetically engineering swine donors is likely to lead to clinical success of xenotransplantation in the near future.
>
> Sykes, Megan, and David H Sachs. "Transplanting organs from pigs to humans." Science immunology vol. 4,41 (2019): eaau6298. doi:10.1126/sciimmunol.aau6298 .

The Transplant waiting list.

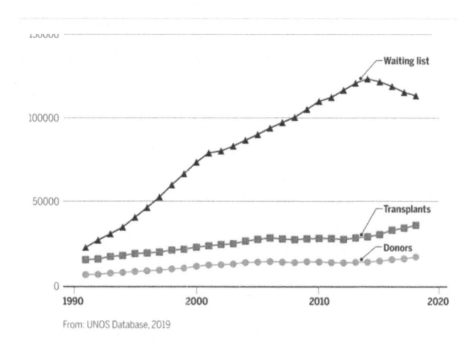

From: UNOS Database, 2019

The xenotransplantation of organs is regulated by the FDA.

Chapter 13

International Law and Agricultural Biotechnology

13.1.1   International Law and the United Nations

13.1.1.1   The Founder of International Law

Hugo Grotius (1583-1645) was a philosopher who conceptualized the world as a collection of nation-states and is known as the Father of International Law. He attended law school at Leiden University in Holland and was ultimately made Attorney General of Holland. Two of his most notable works are the publications, the Law of the Sea ('Mare Liberum') and the Law of War and Peace ('De Iure Belli Ac Pacis'). He observed and concluded that the sea was shared in common with all countries and belonged to no one country. As was the fate of many philosophers with creative ideas, he was tried at The Hague Prison Gate for his religious views about the existence of God being independent of natural law and humankind. As a result he was exiled at Loevenstein Castle.

13.1.1.2   The United Nations

The forum for global collective action is today, the United Nations. Prior to the founding of the United Nations in 1945, the League of Nations had been the global body for collaborative thought. Because not every nation was a part of the League of Nations and it had no real authority, it was failing to fulfill the vision of a global forum.

The United Nations own description states:

When States become Members of the United Nations, they agree to accept the obligations of the UN Charter, an international treaty that sets out basic principles of international relations. According to the Charter, the UN has four purposes: to maintain international peace and security; to develop friendly relations among nations; to cooperate in solving international problems and in promoting respect for human rights; and to be a centre for harmonizing the actions of nations.

The United Nations was created in 1945 to prevent "the scourge of war" as described in the preamble of the UN Charter. In establishing the United Nations , Chapter 3 of the Charter established the principal organs of the UN: (1) General Assembly; (2) Security Council; (3) Economic and Social Council; (4) Trustee Council; (5) International Court of Justice and (6) Secretariat.

The Security Council is the organ with the most extensive powers outlined in Chapters 5-8 of the UN Charter. In contrast, the General Assembly is made up of every nation-state member and can "make recommendations" which is outlined in Art. 10. The Security Council can make decisions which are adopted by the provisions of Chapter 7, and they become binding on all states. The Security Council is comprised of five permanent members and ten (four seats were added in 1963-65) rotating, non-permanent members. The five permanent members are: China; France; Soviet Union, now the Russian Federation; the United Kingdom; and the United States. The ten non-permanent members are elected for two-year terms by the General Assembly.

Although Japan, Germany, India and Brazil have emerged as major world players since 1945, historically, the original permanent members of the Security Council remain the same. However, these countries which have grown in world power want a greater role in global governance.

13.1.1.3   The UN International Court of Justice (ICJ)

The International Court of Justice (ICJ) interprets treaties and other documents. The traditional sources of law for the ICJ which are binding sources of law are: (1) international conventions; (2) international custom; and (3) general principles of law. Subsidiary sources for guidance include judicial decisions and the teachings of the most highly qualified publicists of the various nations.

13.1.1.4   International Governmental Organizations (IGOs)

International governmental organizations are neither states nor purely non-state actors. These are "Public international Organizations" and are typically created by multilateral international agreements and member states participate in governance. The United Nations is an example of an IGO.

Other types of international organizations include non-governmental organizations (NGOs) which observe IGOs and other international activities; nation-states are governments; and multinational corporations can also be important players in United Nations activities.

In summary, the United Nations was created after World War II and is governed by its UN Charter. It's primary objective is to keep peace and also functions to regulate international relations including free trade. The United Nations is a forum for negotiation and collaborative action and is the forum where international issues in emerging technologies are often raised because of the potential impact on humanity. Genetically modified organisms, human cloning and biological weapons are three such case studies that will be examined.

13.1.2 International Trade and GATT

13.1.2.1 International Law—Part 4, Free Trade Agreements and resistance to emerging technologies—the GMO example

The World Trade Organization was created in 1995 to administer the General Agreement on Tariffs and Trade (GATT), a multilateral agreement regulating international trade. The purpose of GATT is the "substantial reduction of tariffs and other trade barriers and the elimination of preferences, on a reciprocal and mutually advantageous basis." The GATT was originally signed in 1947 by 23 nations and took effect on January 1, 1948. It was adopted into the 1994 trade agreement with some modifications but the original GATT was adopted. As part of the agreement, the World Trade Organization was created in 1995. The World Trade Organization (WTO) deals with the global rules of trade between nations and its main function is to ensure that trade flows as smoothly, predictably and freely as possible.

The Preamble of the General Agreement on Tariffs and Trade (GATT) states the purpose of GATT which is for the "substantial reduction of tariffs and other trade barriers and the elimination of preferences, on a reciprocal and mutually advantageous basis."

13.1.2.2 The GMO Example in GATT

Genetically modified crops are increasing at a rate of 3-4% each year as a percent of crops grown. "In 2014, 82% (90.7 million hectares) of the 111 million hectares of the soybean planted globally were biotech (Figure 3). Biotech cotton was planted to 25.1 million hectares, which is 68% of the 37 million hectares of global cotton. Of the 184 million hectares of global maize planted in 2014, 30% or 55.2 million hectares were biotech maize. Finally, herbicide tolerant biotech canola was planted in 9 million hectares or 25% of the 36 million hectares of canola grown globally in 2014."[1]
Some estimates expect the demand for food to rise 70-100% by 2050, with the world's population reaching nine billion,[2] and increasing varieties of crops slowing their rate of increasing yields. The need for genetically modified crops with greater yields could not be more vital, yet the European Union has consistently blocked the sale of genetically modified foods from the United States and other countries. Also of note, there is no scientific evidence that genetically modified foods are harmful to humans in any way.

If GATT was designed for free trade and reduction of trade barriers, then how does the European Union manage to block the sale of American crops in the European Union where, because of this block, European farmers enjoy a monopoly?

---

[1] https://isaaa.org/resources/publications/pocketk/16/default.asp .
[2] http://www.technologyreview.com/featuredstory/522596/why-we-will-need-genetically-modified-foods/ .

The European Union is relying on GATT XX(b) and the Sanitary and Phytosanitary Rules (SPS) as well as the GATT XX(b) TBT Agreement, Technical barriers to trade (TBT). GATT Article XX on General Exceptions provides for a number of specific instances in which WTO members may be exempted from GATT rules, including section (b) which allows any member to be exempt from barriers to trade where "necessary to protect human health".

The text of GATT XX(b) reads:

Subject to the requirement that such measures are not applied in a manner which would constitute a means of arbitrary or unjustifiable discrimination between countries where the same conditions prevail, or a disguised restriction on international trade, nothing in this Agreement [the GATT] shall be construed to prevent the adoption or enforcement by any contracting party of measures: ...

(b) necessary to protect human, animal or plant life or health;...

To implement this article, the Sanitary and Phytosanitary Rules (SPS) and Agreement was developed to ensure that protectionism was not the motivation for barriers to trade. The Technical Barriers to Trade (TBT) agreement and committee is established to review those barriers based on the exceptions to also ensure that there is no protectionism motivating the barrier and to ensure that these TBT do not create unnecessary obstacles to trade. In fact, the Sanitary and Phytosanitary Rules require that barriers to trade based on protecting human health should be based on science and a science-based risk assessment.

The GATT text describes what is a risk assessment:

4. Risk assessment — The evaluation of the likelihood of entry, establishment or spread of a pest or disease within the territory of an importing Member according to the sanitary or phytosanitary measures which might be applied, and of the associated potential biological and economic consequences; or the evaluation of the potential for adverse effects on human or animal health arising from the presence of additives, contaminants, toxins or disease-causing organisms in food, beverages or feedstuffs.

However, there is no scientific evidence that genetically modified organisms have any risk to human health at all – or to the environment in Art. XX(g). To substitute for this uncertainty, the European Union has invoked the "precautionary principle" as a principle in international law which has a legitimate application where there is scientific uncertainty. The "precautionary principle", is a "safety first" approach to address scientific uncertainty. To some extent, Article 5.7 of the SPS Agreement addresses this, but some governments have said outside the WTO that they would like the principle strengthened. However, at the time of writing no proposal had been received. It is also unclear whether this would be handled under the SPS Agreement or through some other means.

The "precautionary principle" has been accepted as a temporary measure pending further investigation and research into any risks to human health that GMOs might have.

At the TBT meeting in July 2015, the representatives from China noted their support for stronger GMO protections and proposed regulatory changes. The summary of the action of China follows:

July 2015 TBT Meeting Highlights

China — proposed amendments of GMO approval procedure

The Committee discussed China's proposed regulatory change related to biotech products. China recently notified the WTO about the proposed amendments of its safety assessment of agricultural genetically modified organisms (GMOs) (see G/SPS/N/CHN/881). Paraguay and the United States welcomed China's notification, but noted the negative impact such a regulatory procedure could have on international trade. According to the United States, the delays and lack of transparency in China's current biotech approval process remain a serious trade concern for exporters, and the proposed amendment could further prolong and complicate the approval process. In response, China said that the draft revision aims to enhance the safety assessment of agricultural GMOs, and invited WTO members to comment on the proposed revision.

Whether protectionism is at issue here, remains to be a difficult issue to uncover.

13.1.2.3   The Precautionary Principle

Where there is uncertainty and irreversible consequences, the precautionary principle has been used to prevent any possibility of future harm. It requires only that the harm be scientifically plausible, not probable. It has become customary law, if not a principle of international law. Although it is not scientific because scientific evidence is lacking, it has been accepted as a temporary measure for the EU in the rejection of GMOs being imported into the EU.

Given the rapidly rising demand for food in the world which is certain to increase to 2050, the spectre of continuing to resist this emerging technology is questionable, in the face of no development of scientific evidence that there is any harm to human health or the environment. The SPS rules allowed for a broad precautionary principle to substitute temporarily for scientific-based decisionmaking, and future emerging technologies can be expected to be met with the same legal arguments in conformity with the precedent of the GMO case.

In summary, the GATT objective is to reduce barriers to free trade and GATT XX(b) is an exception to free trade based on risks to human health. GATT XX(g) provides for exceptions based on risks to the environment. The Sanitary and Phytosanitary Agreement sets out guidelines for GATT XX(b), and the Technical Barriers to Trade Agreement approves barriers based on all of the above. The precautionary principle has been accepted temporarily in the face of scientific uncertainty but with scientific plausibility of risk.

13.1.3   The Convention on Biological Diversity

13.1.3.1.   Introduction to Biodiversity and the Convention on Biological Diversity (CBD)

In the 1970s, the realization that biodiversity must be addressed internationally led to a dialogue which concluded that all members of the biological community were important to sustaining the environment, and the preservation of just a few species was inadequate to protect the world's ecosystems. For example, the clubbing of baby seals for the fur trade stirred the ire of the public, and efforts to stop the practice were coordinated. While the endearing marine mammals could excite the public, a more comprehensive effort was required to prevent the loss of biodiversity.

Biodiversity is the complex web of life that exists and sustains the members of its scope. To protect biodiversity, equal concern for both ant and anteater, rhinoceros beetle and the rhinoceros maintains all of the members of the community. An emphasis on biodiversity rather than simply conservation, has changed the focus of environmental protection. The threat to biodiversity occurs when one of the members of the ecosystem is eliminated causing a degradation to the ecosystem in unanticipated ways, or a series of events lead to the degradation of the environment. In order to monitor threats to an ecosystem, the population and health of a species important to an ecosystem, i.e., sentinel species, can be monitored. Frogs have been identified as sentinel species and recent worldwide decline of their numbers has been watched by the environmental community with great concern for the sustainability of the world's ecosystems.

E.O. Wilson, a highly regarded scientist, has estimated that the absolute number of species falls between 5 million and 30 million. Only about 1 ½ million species have been identified and described. This describes *species diversity*. Overall species richness decreases with latitude— the further from the equator, the less the diversity. The higher altitudes also have less species diversity. Isolation and inbreeding results in a loss of biodiversity sometimes.

Genetic diversity is the sum of genetic information contained in the genes of individual species. Number of genes ranges from 1,000 in bacteria to 400,000 in many flowering plants, and less than a million in humans — less than originally believed until the mapping of the human genome was completed in 2000.

Ecosystem diversity refers to the richness of habitats, biotic communities and ecological processes.

Sustainable development v. conservation. An illustration of the contrast between these concepts is the conflict on the ivory trade. The argument from Africa was that the control of the elephant trade in ivory would result in the long-term protection of the elephant, because killing elephants for ivory could be best controlled by monitoring and allowing some harvesting, rather than attempting a complete ban, which would result in large scale poaching. On the other hand, the conservation ethic, requires that wildlife not be killed for something like ivory as a commodity. In this case, conservation ethic may have led to complete destruction of the elephant whereas sustainable development practices would lead to cultivation of the elephant for ivory harvesting.

13.1.3.2 The Convention on Biological Diversity
History and Background of the Convention on Biological
Diversity (CBD)

In 1982, on the Tenth year anniversary of the Stockholm Declaration, the United Nations General Assembly passed the World Charter on Nature, which had no binding force. From 1984 to 1989, the United Nations revised a set of draft articles which would be the foundation of the proposed treaty on biodiversity. The articles were ultimately rejected by the General Assembly, but the action brought attention to the issue and led to the establishment of a working group in the United Nations Environment Program in 1987. Early in the working group discussions, a plan to encompass all wildlife treaties under one treaty was considered, but it was considered probably too difficult politically to succeed. It was also evident that the South would accept terms that focused on biodiversity, rather than a treaty with a conservation focus, only. Formal negotiations for a Convention on Biological Diversity began in 1991 with the formation of the Intergovernmental Negotiating Committee (INC), with a goal of preparing the final document in time for the UNCED Earth Summit in Rio de Janeiro, Brazil in June 1992. The great pressure to finish the convention led to some conflicting and unclear language, but it succeeded in meeting the time deadline and was presented at the Earth Summit, finished the last day, and signed two weeks later at UNCED. It entered into force just eighteen months later on December 29, 1993.

The actions taken at United States at the Earth Summit reveal why the United States was perceived as presenting a hardline refusal to sign the Convention. Administrator Reilly was the delegate for the Summit, and in the course of his visit he sent a memorandum to President George H.W. Bush, which immediately leaked to the press at the meeting, and resulted in bad publicity for the US. The financial part of the agreement was controversial, and the financial mechanism required that the North provide new, and additional funding to assist in biodiversity conservation. As a result of this leaked memorandum and refusal to amend the financial part of the agreement, the U.S. did not sign the agreement.

However, early in his term, President William Clinton signed the Convention, but the U.S. Senate did not ratify the treaty. In spite of President Clinton's urging that no new legislation would need to be passed, if the Convention was ratified, the U.S. Senate still refused to ratify it. As a result, the United States is not a signatory to the Convention on

Biological Diversity, because the U.S. Senate failed to ratify the CBD.

13.1.2.4.   Structure of the Convention on Biological Diversity

The Convention on Biological Diversity addresses six important issues in its concept of protecting biological diversity on an international basis in the Preamble and later in Article Six. First, the establishment of the common concern of mankind establishes the agreement between the parties to proceed with other specific issues. The preamble of the CBD begins the first disassembly of the concept of a "common heritage" which suggests that all resources are free and available to any country, from any country, and the South objected to this language. Developed countries of the North, believed that "common heritage" might lead to a requirement for technology transfer to the Southern developing countries. This was resolved by describing biological diversity as a "common concern of mankind."

Second, the aspect of common but differentiated responsibilities is established. The language reads: "Acknowledging further that special provision is required to meet the needs of developing countries, including the provision of new and additional financial resources and appropriate access to relevant technologies." Third, the precautionary principle is set forth as a guiding principle for actions taken by the parties: "Nothing also that where this is a threat of significant reduction or loss of biological diversity, lack of full scientific certainty should not be used as a reason for postponing measures to avoid or minimize such a threat."

Fourth, the concept of intergenerational equity is agreed upon, with the language: "Determined to conserve and sustainably use biological diversity for the benefit of present and future generations." And fifth, the right to develop is expressed as "recognizing that economic and social development and poverty eradication are the first and overriding priorities of developing countries. Finally, the sixth issue is the affirmation of the sovereignty of nations to act within their borders for their interests is addressed in Article Six: "States have . . . the sovereign right to exploit their own resources pursuant to their own environmental policies . . .".

Article one, sets for the objections which are: conservation of biological diversity, sustainable use, equitable sharing of benefits arising from utilization of genetic resources, appropriate access, appropriate transfer, appropriate funding. This addressed concerns of both the North and the South.

The definitions help to interpret the Convention:

genetic resources — " genetic material of actual or potential value."
genetic material — "any material of plant, animal, microbial or other origin containing functional units of heredity"
sustainable use — "the use of components of biological diversity in ways and at a rate that does not lead to the long-term decline of biological diversity, thereby maintaining its potential to meet the needs and aspirations of

present and future generations."

ecosystem — a dynamic complex of plant, animal and micro-organism communities and their non-living environment interacting as a functional unit.

Article six, General Measures of Conservation and Sustainable Use requires that nations develop national plans and strategies for biodiversity.

Article seven, Identification and Monitoring requires the identity of components of biological diversity and processes and develop a system to monitor, maintain and organize the information.

Article eight, In-situ Conservation, establishes the desireability of a system of protected areas, not necessarily on the framework of a national parks system, but based upon the unique areas of each country.

Article nine, Ex-situ conservation, is intended to complement in-situ measures, and established t he preference for ex-situ conservation to be in the country of origin, although, not necessarily in the country of origin.

Article ten, Sustainable Use of Components of Biological Diversity, integrates national decision making between the private sector and governmental authorities, with an objective of avoiding adverse environmental impacts. It reads: "(c) Protect and encourage customary use of biological resources in accordance with traditional cultural practices that are compatible with conservation or sustainable use requirements."

Article 14, Impact Assessment and Minimizing Adverse Impacts, in (1)(A) specifically provides that a NEPA-like process be adopted by each Party, and in (2) that Parties will study issues of redress, liability, restoration and compensation for damage to biological diversity except where such liability is a purely a domestic matter.

Articles 15, 16, 17, 18 and 19 address biological trade and the biosafety protocol.

Articles 22 and 23 address the relationship with other conventions an d the role of the Conference of Parties (COP).

Article 25, Subsidiary Body on Scientific, Technical and Technological Advice, provides for *(1) A subsidiary body for the provision of scientific, technical and technological advice . . . with timely advice relating to the implementation of this Convention. This Body shall be open to participation by all Parties and shall be multidisciplinary. It shall comprise government representative competent in the relevant field of expertise. It shall report regularly to the Conference of the Parties on all aspects of its work; and (2) Under the authority of and in accordance with guidelines laid down by the Conference of the Parties, and upon its request, this body shall:*

(A) Provide scientific and technical assessments of the status of biological diversity;

(B) Prepare scientific and technical assessments of the effects of types of measures taken in accordance with the provisions of this Convention;

(C) Identify innovative, efficient and state-of-the-art technologies and know-how relating to the conservation and sustainable use of biological diversity and advise on the ways and means of promoting development and/or transferring such technologies;

(D) Provide advice on scientific programmes and international cooperation in research and development related to conservation and sustainable use of biological diversity; and

(E) Respond to scientific, technical, technological and methodological questions that the Conference of the Parties and its subsidiary bodies may put to the body....

Article 26, provides for the development of reports on measures and their effectiveness which have been taken for the implementation of the provisions of the CBD.

Article 27, addresses the settlement of disputes, which is to be done through negotiation, and if that fails, through the mediation of a third party. If these first two methods fail the Parties agree to accept *one or both of the following means of dispute settlement as compulsory:*

(A) arbitration in accordance with the procedure laid down in Part 1 of Annex II

(B) Submission of the dispute to the International Court of Justice.

Article 8(j)

Article 8 (j) of the Convention provides that:
"Each contracting Party shall, as far as possible and as appropriate: Subject to national legislation, respect, preserve and maintain knowledge, innovations and practices of indigenous and local communities embodying traditional lifestyles relevant for the conservation and sustainable use of biological diversity and promote their wider application with the approval and involvement of the holders of such knowledge, innovations and practices and encourage the equitable sharing of the benefits arising from the utilization of such knowledge, innovations and practices"

The Convention of the parties addressed specifically the mandate of Article 8(j) and its related provisions:

In 1997, in Decision III/14, the COP held a five-day workshop on Traditional Knowledge and Biological Diversity, Madrid, Spain, November 1997. The COP realized that to implement Article 8(j), that the traditional knowledge, innovations and practices of indigenous and local communities should be examined in the context of other international agreements, in particular, the World Trade Organization's Agreement on Trade-related Aspects of Intellectual Property. (Decision III/17). Thereafter, an ad hoc open-ended inter-sessional working group on Article 8(j) was established with a mandate to (1) provide advice on the application of legal and other appropriate forms of protection for traditional knowledge; (2) to provide advice to the COP related to the implementation of Article 8(j)

396

and related provisions; (3) to develop a program of work; and (4) to provide advice to the COP on measures to strengthen cooperation and suggest mechanisms to increase cooperation among indigenous local communities at the international level.

The principal decision on the implementation of Article 8(j) was in Decision V/16, adopted at the fifth COP meeting in Nairobi, Kenya, May, 2000. Here, the parties agreed to the following provisions:

(1) the extension of the mandate of the Ad Hoc Working Group on Article 8(j); (2) promotion of the full and effective participation of indigenous and local communities, and particularly that of women, in implementing the Convention; (3) protection of the traditional knowledge, innovations and practices of indigenous and local communities related to the conservation of biodiversity and the sustainable use of natural resources; and (4) adoption of a programme of work for the Working Group.

Article 15. Access to Genetic Resources

The Convention on Biological Diversity, Article 15. "Access to Genetic Resources" reads as follows:

1. Recognizing the sovereign rights of States over their natural resources, the authority to determine access to genetic resources rests with the national governments and is subject to national legislation.

2. Each Contracting Party shall endeavour to create conditions to facilitate access to genetic resources for environmentally sound uses by other Contracting Parties and not to impose restrictions that run counter to the objectives of this Convention.

3. For the purpose of this Convention, the genetic resources being provided by a Contracting Party, as referred to in this Article and

Articles 16 and 19, are only those that are provided by Contracting Parties that are countries of origin of such resources or by the Parties that have acquired the genetic resources in accordance with this Convention.

4. Access, where granted, shall be on mutually agreed terms and subject to the provisions of this Article.

5. Access to genetic resources shall be subject to prior informed consent of the Contracting Party providing such resources, unless otherwise determined by that Party.

6. Each Contracting Party shall endeavour to develop and carry out scientific research based on genetic resources provided by other Contracting Parties with the full participation of, and where possible in, such Contracting Parties.

7. Each Contracting Party shall take legislative, administrative or policy measures, as appropriate, and in accordance with Articles 16 and 19 and, where necessary,

through the financial mechanism established by Articles 20 and 21 with the aim of sharing in a fair and equitable way the results of research and development and the benefits arising from the commercial and other utilization of genetic resources with the Contracting Party providing such resources. Such sharing shall be upon mutually agreed terms.

Access and benefit sharing is the guiding framework for bioprospecting by pharmaceutical companies and other institutions in their search to isolate chemical compounds from genetic resources to develop and commercialize new drugs. The difficulty in implementing this section of the CBD has been the international framework for recognition of traditional knowledge and genetic resources as intellectual property which could the provide protection for indigenous communities and developing nations. The following sections outline and examine these aspects of genetic resources and commercialization.

13.1.3.5   Bioprospecting and International Biopiracy

Access and benefit-sharing is the international term of reference for utilizing the biological resources for the good of all humankind in an equitable way.

The first company to pioneer the effort to make bioprospecting equitable for all parties was Merck Pharmaceutical Company, pioneering a novel effort in 1991 to include in bioprospecting in Costa Rica, and agreement with the Costa Rican Institute for Biodiversity. The contract provided that 10% of any budget for a research contract and 50% of any financial benefits will be donated to the National Parks Fund, provides for an advance payment for bioprospecting. The objective of the agreement is to develop new drugs form chemicals found in wild plants, insects and micro-organisms. Merck will own rights of any patented material, but will establish an Institute in Costa Rica and provide equipment and training to the Institute

The agreement was renewed in 1994.

In Indian, the Neem tree controversy raised objections to western biopiracy of traditional knowledge when W. R. Grace isolated the molecular compound in the Neem tree to patent.   The company was issued a patent in June 1992 for its invention.   In March 1994, W.R. Grace registered Neemix as a pesticide with EPA in accordance with FIFRA.

A coalition of 200 organizations from 35 different nations challenged the patent and filed a petition with the U.S. Patent and Trademark Office seeking to invalidate the patent. The challenge was ultimately dismissed.   However, the European Patent Office revoked the W.R. Grace patent [Decision Revoking European Patent No. 0436257 (Eur. Patent Off. Feb 13, 2001)].

The anti-malarial drug, quinine, was patented based on observations that chewing the bark of South American Cinchona trees was a practice of peoples of Peru in the

Eighteenth century which prevented them from getting malaria.

The San people of Africa, agreed to sell their interests in the hoodia cactus, Hoodia gordoniis, which was known among the San people as an appetite suppressant.

International protocols based on the Convention for Biological Diversity and the Inter-American Draft Declaration on the Rights of Indigenous Peoples, provide for bioprospecting that is equitable for both the pharmaceutical companies and the indigenous peoples. There is no international crime for biopiracy, but it describes the unethical practice of appropriating property of others and has taken on a meaning in international dialogues.

13.1.3.6 International approaches to bioprosecting

Two treaties directly address access and benefit-sharing: the Convention on Biological Diversity and the FAO International Treaty on Plant Genetic Resources for Food and Agriculture. Other treaties with intellectual property issues relating to access and benefit-sharing such as WIPO treaties and the WTO TRIPs agreement. There are several international legal instruments which govern this process summarized below from CBD UNEP/CBD/WG-ABS/3/2, 10 November 2004:

13.1.3.7 Convention on Biological Diversity

The Convention on Biological Diversity through Article 8(j) , 10 and 23, address the protection of traditional practices, the use of indigenous knowledge in the process of bioprosecting is being addressed by the Conference of the Parties. Guidelines have been developed for use by private sector companies seeking to explore the natural resources and traditional knowledge of a country.

<u>Article 10.</u> Sustainable Use Of Components of Biological Diversity
(c) Protect and encourage customary use of biological resources in accordance with traditional cultural practices that are compatible with conservation or sustainable use requirements;

13.1.3.8 FAO International Treaty on Plant Genetic Resources for Food and Agriculture

The FAO Treaty was adopted by the Food and Agriculture Organization of the United Nations (FAO) in November 2001 and entered into force November 29, 2004. 61 countries and the European Union ratified the treaty. The objective is, "the conservation and sustainable use of plant genetic resources for food and agriculture and the fair and equitable sharing of benefits derived from their use, in harmony with the Convention on Biological Diversity for sustainable agriculture and food security."

The mechanism for implementation is a Material Transfer Agreement (MTA) which is adopted by the country's governing body, which will set out the conditions for access to genetic resources and benefit-sharing. The treaty provides for benefit sharing through payment of monetary benefits, information exchange, access to and transfer of technology and capacity building.

13.1.3.9   WTO Agreement on Trade-related Aspects of Intellectual Property Rights

The TRIPS agreement came into force on January 1, 1995 from the Uruguay round of multilateral trade negotiations.   The main objective is to ensure that intellectual property rights do not become an impediment to legitimate trade.   Article 7 of the agreement sets out as one of its objectives that the protection and enforcement of intellectual property rights should contribute to the promotion of technological innovation and the transfer and dissemination of technology, to the mutual advantage of producers and users of technological knowledge and in a manner conducive to social and economic welfare, and to a balance of rights and obligations.

The agreement establishes the minimum standards of protection to be provided by Members in each of the main areas of intellectual property covered by the TRIPs Agreement.   It also addresses remedies for the enforcement of intellectual property rights and makes disputes between WTO members subject to the WTO dispute-settlement procedures. The Agreement also provides for the applicability of basic GATT principles such as favored nation status.

Patentability under TRIPs requires in article 27(1) that patents shall be available for inventions that are "new, involve an inventive step and are capable of industrial application."   Article 27, para. 3(b) provides that Members may exclude from patentability, plants, animals and other micro-organisms and biological processes for the production of plants and animals.   However, if any nation chooses to exclude plants, they must provide an effective sui generis system of protection.

The Doha Declaration, Paragraph 19, requires that the TRIPS Council should examine the relationship between the TRIPS Agreement and the Convention on Biological Diversity, the protection of traditional knowledge and folklore.

TRIPS does not require patent applicants to disclose the origin of genetic resources and associated traditional knowledge in patent applications where the subject matter of the application is based on genetic resources or related traditional knowledge; nor does it require prior informed consent from the sources of that knowledge.

WIPO has begun to address these issues through the Patent Law Treaty (PLT); the draft Substantive Patent Law Treaty (SPLT); the reform of the Patent Cooperation Treaty (PCT) and the Intergovernmental Committee on Intellectual Property and Genetic Resources, Traditional Knowledge and Folklore (IGC).   WIPO will continue to consider amendments to the Patent Law Treaty and the Substantive Patent Law Treaty to address the deficiencies in addressing genetic resources and traditional knowledge intellectual property rights.

13.1.3.10   International Convention for the Protection of New Varieties of Plants

The Convention was signed in Paris in 1961 and entered into force in 1968.   The purpose is "to ensure that the members of the union acknowledge the achievement of breeders of new varieties of plants, by granting to them an intellectual property right, on the basis of a set of clearly defined principles," forming a sui generis type of protection. The 1991 Act of the UPOV Convention entered into force in 1998, its objective being to encourage the development of new plant varieties, and avoiding barriers from intellectual property rights in traditional knowledge that might prevent carrying out this objective. The Convention provides a sui generis type of protection by its purpose "to ensure that the Members of the Union acknowledge the achievement of breeders of new varieties of plants, by granting to them an intellectual property right, on the basis of a set of clearly defined principles." To be eligible for protection under the Convention varieties have to be "(i)distinct from existing, commonly known varieties; (ii) sufficiently uniform; (iii) stable; and (iv) new in the sense that they must not have been commercialized prior to certain dates established by reference to the date of the application for protection.

The protection is in the form of a "breeder's right," for the development of new species.   However, the protection of the breeder's right is limited by two exceptions: (1) the first exception known as the "breeder's exemption" optimizes variety improvement by ensuring the germplasm sources remain available to other breeders; and (2) the second exemption is known as the "farmer's exemption" continues the practice of allowing farmers to keep their seed for the purpose of resowing.

13.1.3.11 Convention on International Trade in Endangered Species of Wild Fauna and Flora

CITES entered into force in 1975, with the purpose of regulating international trade in flora and fauna to ensure that trade does not threaten the survival of these species. The same system of permits might be used to regulate the identification of origin and ownership of biological materials exported and imported between member countries.

13.1.3.12 The Antarctic Treaty

The Antarctic Treaty was signed on Dec 1, 1959 and entered into force on June 23, 1961 for the purpose of regulating relations among states in the Antarctic.

The purpose is to ensure "in the interests of all mankind that Antarctica shall continue forever to be used exclusively for peaceful purposes and shall not become the scene or object of international discord." The Scientific Committee on Antarctic Research (SCAR), the Committee for Environmental Protection (CEP) and the Antarctic Treaty Consultative Meeting (ATCM) are addressing the concern of unregulated bioprosecting in the region.

13.1.3.13   Universal Declaration of Human Rights

Adopted by the General Assemble of the United Nations on Dec 10, 1948, with the objective "as a common standard of achievement for all peoples and all nations to promote respect for these rights and freedoms and by progressive measures, national and international, to secure their universal and effective recognition and observance."

Art 29 (1) states that "everyone has duties to the community in which alone the free and full development of his personality is possible."

13.1.3.14   International Covenant on Economic, Social and Cultural Rights
Was adopted Dec 16, 1966 and entered into force on March 23, 1976.
Article 1, para. 2, states:
All peoples may, for their own ends, freely dispose of their natural wealth and resources without prejudice to any obligations arising out of international economic cooperation, bused upon the principle of mutual benefit, and international law. In no case may a people be deprived of its own means of subsistence.

13.1.3.15.   Regional agreements:
Regional approaches can be utilized because of similar needs and conditions for access and benefit-sharing. Competition between countries and tribal nations in a region would be minimized, "forum shopping" by companies would be eliminated and bioprosecting companies would have more predictability in the process.

1.   Andean Pact decision 391 on the Common Regime on Access to Genetic Resources
2.   Draft Central American Agreement on Access to Genetic Resources and Bio-chemicals and related Traditional Knowledge
3.   Draft ASEAN Framework Agreement on Access to Biological and Genetic Resources
4.   African Model Law for the Protection of the Rights of Local Communities, Farmers and Breeders and for the Regulation of Access to Biological Resources.
5.   Draft Pacific Model Law

13.2.2   International Codes of Conduct for Bioprospecting

13.2.2.1   International Codes of Conduct for Bioprospecting
There are two codes of conduct. "The Micro-organisms Sustainable Use and Access Regulation International Code of Conduct" and the "Bonn Guidelines on Access to Genetic Resources and Fair and Equitable Sharing of the Benefits Arising out of their Utilization" [(Montreal: Secretariat of the Convention on Biological Diversity (2002)], which were written to address specifically Articles 8(j), 10(c), 15, 16 and 19 of the Convention on Biological Diversity.

13.2.2.2   The Micro-organisms Sustainable Use and Access Regulation International Code of Conduct (MOSAICC)

The Belgian Co-ordinated Collections of Micro-organisms (BCCM) initiated the coordinated action to develop the MOSAICC guidelines with the support of the Directorate General XII for Science, Research and Development of the European Commission.   In November 2000, the MOSAICC document was developed.   The MOSAICC document states the following about its purpose and principles:

MOSAICC is a voluntary Code of Conduct. It is developed to facilitate access to microbial genetic resources (MGRs) and to help partners to make appropriate agreements when transferring MGRs, in the framework of the Convention on Biological Diversity (CBD)2 and other applicable rules of international3 and national laws. MOSAICC is a tool to support the implementation of the CBD at the microbial level; it can also serve as a model when dealing with genetic resources other than MGRs. Access to MGRs is a prerequisite for the advancement of microbiology and world-wide sustainable development. Furthermore, monitoring the transfer of MGRs is necessary to identify the individuals or groups that are entitled to be scientifically or financially rewarded for their contribution to the conservation and sustainable use of the MGRs. Therefore, MOSAICC combines the need for easy transfer of MGRs and the need to monitor the transfer of MGRs. It proposes a system that works through two operating principles:
1. The in situ origin of the MGRs is identified via initial **Prior Informed Consent (PIC)** procedure providing authorisation for sampling. The in situ origin of the MGRs is always mentioned when transfer occurs.
2. The transfer of MGRs is monitored and occurs under **Material Transfer Agreement (MTA)** which terms are defined by both recipient and provider. MTA is a generic term that covers either a very short shipment document, a simple standard delivery notice, a standard invoice containing minimal standard requirements or a more detailed specific contract including tailor-made mutually agreed terms. According to the use and intended distribution of the MGRs, mutually agreed terms can be short or very detailed.

MOSAICC recommends that compensation for access to genetic resources should be "partly dedicated to technical and scientific co-operation programmes" and include "initial, up-front payments . . . made before or after accessing the MGRs, but this always independently of the possible, successful commercial use of the MGRs. MOSAICC recommends to calculate the importance of the initial payments in terms of the actual involvement of the provider in the delivery of the MGRs." Further, the guidance suggests, "milestones payments . . related to the progress made in the development of a product or process that could be commercialised," as we;; as "royalty payments . . .fully dependent on the successful commercial use of the MGRs concerned."
[http://www.belspo.be/bccm/mosaicc.]

The following form letter is recommended by MOSAICC for the beginning of a prior informed consent process:

_____

(Date)
(Name and address of the PIC-provider)
Dear (...........),
According to article 15 of the Convention on Biological Diversity (CBD) stating that «the authority to determine access to genetic resources rests with the national governments and

is subject to national legislation » and that «Each Contracting Party shall endeavour to create conditions to facilitate access to genetic resources for environmentally sound uses by other Contracting Parties and not to impose restrictions that run counter to the objectives of this Convention », as well that «access to genetic resources shall be subject to prior informed consent of the Contracting Party providing such resources »; and, as ratified by (Name of the Country where one wants to access MGRs), I would like to acquire access to (Name of the field survey area), as well as to its genetic resources, with your prior informed consent (PIC), during the period and under the conditions specified in annex.

To this end, I have annexed a model form of PIC-certificate to be used if you agree to provide me with such a PIC according to the principles and rules laid down in the CBD.

(closing salutation)
(Name, address and signature of the PIC-applicant)

The second part of the MOSAICC guidance requires a material transfer agreement, and the following form letter is provided in the guidance:

(*Name and address of the CBD PIC-provider*) (*Date*)
Dear (*Name of the PIC-applicant*),
      In reply to your PIC-application of (*date of written demand*), having as a reference (*reference*), and as annexed; as well as, according to article 15 of the Convention on Biological Diversity (CBD) stating that «*the authority to determine access to genetic resources rests with the national governments and is subject to national legislation* » and that «*Each Contracting Party shall endeavour to create conditions to facilitate access to genetic resources for environmentally sound uses by other Contracting Parties and not to impose restrictions that run counter to the objectives of this Convention* », as well that «*access to genetic resources shall be subject to prior informed consent of the Contracting Party providing such resources* »; and, as ratified by (*Name of the Country providing the MGRs*), on (*Date of ratification*);as well as, in conformity with the national laws and rules referred to in annex; We, the undersigned, being (within the framework of the CBD)*, on behalf of (*Name of the country providing the MGRs*), the competent authority for surveying *in-situ* access to the genetic resources of (*Name of the geographical area of competence*), have the pleasure to provide you, exclusively for the annexed PIC-application, with the required PIC. This PIC for access to *in-situ* MGRs from (*Name of the field survey area*) grants access to this area from (*date*) to (*date*). This PIC is not transferable from one organisation to another without written agreement of the undersigned authority.
      (*closing salutation*)
      (*Place and date of issue, official administrative seals and signature of*

the CBD PIC-provider.)

_____

13.2.2.2.   Bonn Guidelines on Access to Genetic Resources and Fair and
Equitable Sharing of the Benefits Arising out of their Utilization

The Bonn Guidelines were developed by the leadership of the Secretariat of the
Convention on Biological Diversity in 2002.   The scope of the Bonn Guidelines extends to
"All genetic resources and associated traditional knowledge, innovations and practices
covered by the Convention on Biological Diversity and benefits arising from the
commercial and other utilization of such resources should be covered by the guidelines,
with the exclusion of human genetic resources."

The Bonn Guidelines establish a set of principles for prior informed consent before
beginning any bioprospecting activities:

1. The basic principles of a prior informed consent system should include:
(a) Legal certainty and clarity;
(b) Access to genetic resources should be facilitated at minimum cost;
(c) Restrictions on access to genetic resources should be transparent, based
on legal grounds, and not run counter to the objectives of the Convention;
(d) Consent of the relevant competent national authority(ies) in the provider
country. The consent of relevant stakeholders, such as indigenous and
local communities, as appropriate to the circumstances and subject to
domestic law, should also be obtained.

2.   Elements of a prior informed consent system may include:
(a) Competent authority(ies) granting or providing for evidence of prior
informed consent;
(b) Timing and deadlines;
(c) Specification of use;
(d) Procedures for obtaining prior informed consent;
(e) Mechanism for consultation of relevant stakeholders;
(f) Process.

The Guidelines provide for a process for obtaining prior informed consent:

An application for access could require the following information to be
provided, in order for the competent authority to determine whether or not
access to a genetic resource should be granted. This list is indicative and should
be adapted to national circumstances:
(a) Legal entity and affiliation of the applicant and/or collector and contact
person when the applicant is an institution;
(b) Type and quantity of genetic resources to which access is sought;

(c) Starting date and duration of the activity;

(d) Geographical prospecting area;

(e) Evaluation of how the access activity may impact on conservation and sustainable use of biodiversity, to determine the relative costs and benefits of granting access;

(f) Accurate information regarding intended use (e.g.: taxonomy, collection, research, commercialization);

(g) Identification of where the research and development will take place;

(h) Information on how the research and development is to be carried out;

(i) Identification of local bodies for collaboration in research and development;

(j) Possible third party involvement;

(k) Purpose of the collection, research and expected results;

(l) Kinds/types of benefits that could come from obtaining access to the resource, including benefits from derivatives and products arising from the commercial and other utilization of the genetic resource;

(m) Indication of benefit-sharing arrangements;

(n) Budget;

(o) Treatment of confidential information.

37. Permission to access genetic resources does not necessarily imply permission to use associated knowledge and vice versa.

38. Applications for access to genetic resources through prior informed consent and decisions by the competent authority(ies) to grant access to genetic resources or not shall be documented in written form.

39. The competent authority could grant access by issuing a permit or licence or following other appropriate procedures. A national registration system could be used to record the issuance of all permits or licences,on the basis of duly completed application forms.

40. The procedures for obtaining an access permit/licence should be transparent and accessible by any interested party.

13.2.2,4   International Intellectual Property and Biotechnology

Patent Protection in the United States

In the United States a patent issued by the U.S. Patent Office will grant the right for 20 years from the date of application to exclude everyone from making, using or selling the patented invention without permission of the holder of the patent.   The United States grants patent based on the principle of "first to invent" not "first to file" as do many other countries.

Infringement on U.S. held patents in other countries can be prosecuted in U.S. courts for injunctive relief and damages through several enforcement mechanisms. "Exclusion orders" are issued by the International Trade Commission under Sec. 337 of the Tariff Act of 1930, and are enforced by the U.S. Customs Service, where there are foreign made infringing articles.

Patent Protection in other countries

There are two major types of patenting systems in the governments of the world, which are registration and examination. Some countries grant patents upon "registration" without making an initial inquiry about patentability of the invention, such as France. The validity of such a patent grant is not questioned until there is an infringement or a need to defend the patent, and only then is it determined whether it is a patentable invention. Under the system of "examination" there is a careful examination and inquiry into the prior art and statutory criteria on patentability, as in the United States and Germany. A "deferred examination" may also be part of the process, giving notice to the public to oppose the patent. The validity of patents granted under an examination system are much more likely to survive a patentability examination in court if it must be defended or if there is an infringement claim.

In comparison to the United States, one major difference in patent protection in other countries is the difference in timing that is presented by the "first to invent" which could come much earlier than the "first to file", and present conflicting patents, both valid in both countries.

For patent protection in other countries, patent applications must be filed in those countries and are governed by the domestic law of each country. A decision that a patent is invalid in one country is not binding on any other country, nor is the recognition of a patent in one country binding on another.

13.2.2.4   International Patenting

For international patenting, it is important to know that patents are protected territorially, not internationally. Patents are granted according to national law. There is no international patent protection, which requires patents to be filed in each country. There is some limited protection provided by the Paris Convention through the World Intellectual Property Organization (WIPO) at Geneva. A "right of priority" is granted through this organization to a patent holder if they file in foreign jurisdictions within twelve months of the filing of the original patent in the first country. However, even this protection may not overcome the differences in the "first to file" jurisdictions for United States patentees seeking international protection.

There is another international mechanism which is intended to make the patent application process more uniform and to provide protection for at least a limited international scope. Approximately forty countries have joined in The Patent Cooperation Treaty (PCT) which allows one patent filing to be done once under the PCT which will include a number of selected countries. The offices, designated as International Searching Authorities (ISA) where this filing can be done under the PCT include the national patent offices of the United States, Russia, Sweden, Japan and the European Patent Office at Munich and The Hague. The PCT offices provide that the patent applicant may see a preliminary examination and seek a non-binding opinion on the questions of novelty, non-obviousness and utility. This initial filing, together with the international search report is filed with each national patent office where the patentee is seeking protection. The individual countries establish their own substantive requirements for patentability and remedies for infringement, although in many countries without extensive patent systems, the report of the PCT may carry great weight.

13.2.2.5. International Trade and Biotechnology

Exporting biotechnologies
Unlike many products in international trade, the import and export of many biotechnologies are regulated by the U.S. Department of Commerce. A determination of whether the biotechnology being exported is on a list maintained through the U.S. Department of Commerce, Bureau of Export Administration, which administers non-defense and dual-use products in commerce. These Export Administration Regulations (EAR) may require a permit for the export of biotechnologies or biological material, or their export may be prohibited, if for example the biological material could be used as a biological weapon and is being sent to a country listed as one which should not receive those types of technologies.

13.2.2.6   The Cartegena Biosafety Protocol
More than 130 countries adopted the Biosafety Protocol on January 29, 2000, in Montreal, Canada and is named for the extraordinary Conference of the Parties to the Convention on Biological Diversity (CBD) in Cartagena in 1999. The objective of the Cartegena Biosafety Protocol to the Convention on Biological Diversity is to contribute to the safe international transfer, handling and use of living modified organisms (LMOs) and to avoid adverse effects on the conservation and sustainable use of biodiversity without burdening the world food trade.

The Biosafety Protocol, Art. 15 specifies procedures for the handling, transport, packing and identification of living modified organisms (LMOs). Shipments must be identified by traits and characteristics of the organism, include instructions for safe handling and shipment and a point of contact for further information or in the event of an emergency. In addition, the shipment must include a declaration that the transboundary movement is being conducted in compliance with the requirements of the Biosafety Protocol.

Labeling within the meaning of the Protocol has come to mean that the requirements of the Protocol must be included on the label. The Protocol requires the Parties to provide public information about safe-handling of LMOs, through the Biosafety Clearing House.

13.2.2.6   International Security

The Biological Weapons Convention of 1972

In the 1960s many countries ended their offensive military programs in biological weapons, including the United Kingdom, the United States (1969) and France (1972).   In 1972, the Biological and Toxin Weapons Convention was signed and entered into force in 1975.

The Biological Weapons Convention prohibits the development, production, stokpiling and acquisition of biolgoical atents or toxins that "have no justification for prophylactic, protective or other peaceful purposes." (Art. 1).   Signatories to the Convention committed to the destruction or conversion to peaceful purposes all agents, weapons, equipment and means of delivery within nine months of the treaty's entry into force (Art. 3).

The existence of biological weapons programs is still a very real threat, and several countries including Iran and South Korea are considered to be potentially working with biological agents for use as weapons.

13.2.2.6 .International Human Rights and Biotechnology

United Nations Treaty on Indigenous Peoples and Human Rights

Key articles of the Draft Declaration for biotechnology issues are as follows:

Article 7. [Indigenous people will have the right to prevent and seek redress for] any action which has the aim or effect of dispossessing them of their lands, territories or resources.

Article 24.   [Rights of indigenous people include] the right to the protection of vital medicinal plants, animals and minerals.

Article 29.   Indigenous peoples are entitled to the recognition of the full ownership, control and protection of their cultural and intellectual property. They have the right to special measures to control, develop and protect their sciences, technologies and cultural manifestations, including human and other genetic resources, seeds, medicines, knowledge of the properties of fauna and flora, oral traditions, literatures designs and visual and performing arts.

Article 30.   Indigenous peoples have the right . . . to require that States obtain their free and informed consent prior to the approval of any project affecting their lands, territories and other resources, particularly in connection with the development . . . of . . . resources.

The term "indigenous people" is one of the most controversial in the area, in terms of defining who that is. The term "indigenous peoples" in international contexts is defined by meeting all of a list of criteria. Required criteria are (1) self-identification as a distinct ethnic group; (2) historical experience of, or contingent vulnerability to, sever disruption, dislocation, or exploitation; (3) long connection with the region; (4) wish to retain a distinct identity. Other relevant criteria are (1) nondominance in the national (or regional) society; (2) close cultural affinity with a particular area of land or territories; (3) historic continuity (especially by descent) with prior occupants of land in the region; (4) socio-economic and cultural differences from the ambient population: (5) distinct objective characteristics: language, race, material or spiritual culture; and (6) regarded as indigenous by the ambient population or treated as such in legal and administrative arrangements. [Kingsbury].

Earlier definitions by the World Bank and IMO limited the scope of the definition of indigenous peoples to those who maintained traditional lifestyles, such as hunter-gatherer. Indigenous tribes in North America objected to this.

The World Bank has developed its own definition of indigenous peoples as: (a) a close attachment to ancestral territories and to the natural resources in these areas; (b) self-identification and identification by others as members of a distinct cultural group; (c) an indigenous language; (d) presence of customary social and political institutions; and (e) primarily subsistence-oriented production.

13.2.2.7 Human DNA

Human DNA is not within the scope of the Convention on Biological Diversity, and at the second Conference of the Parties, it was declared that human genetic diversity was not subject to the Biodiversity Convention.

The United States as well as at least 17 other countries were engaged in the human genome mapping project.   The mapping of the human genome was completed in 2000 by two private companies.   The Human Genome Project is funded by the U.S. federal government, and has been fraught with criticism, corruption and other problems since the beginning.   It was originally headed by Dr. Watson, of the Crick and Watson team who first modeled the double-helix of DNA.   When the federal government moved too slowly, one of the staff, Craig Ventner went out on his own to start a private endeavor to race to map the human genome.

Originally it was thought there were more than 100,000 genes in the human genome, but it was discovered that there were only about 30,000.   The genes of flowers, also were thought to be much greater in number, probably around 400,000; but it has been discovered that the number is closer to 30,000.

Chapter 14

The Future of Agricultural Biotechnology Law

From 10,000 years ago when the first tribes of the Balsas River Valley in south central Mexico began trying to enhance the yields of teosinte grass, they were trying to modify the genome of this wild grass that was to become modern corn. The methods have changed but the goal has remained the same – enhancing production for human use. We have improved our tools from early natural selection and then breeding selection, to the first genetic engineering by crop modification to the newest CRISPR tools that give us a scalpel instead of a machete to make adjustments.

One problem remains, and that is human acceptance of these changes. If we were there 10,000 years ago, we might have seen a tribal faction opposed to interfering with Mother Nature, carrying torches and warning those defiling nature they must stop. Resulting monocultures of those favorite high-producing varieties has set up a potential disaster for a crop plague that could wipe out the food supply for the world. The growing number of seed preservation banks (the Doomsday Bank) houses the varieties that we would need to start over, but not fast enough to stop a global starvation that might result.

Animals that are developed as pharmacological factories are just emerging without a lot of public awareness. Doubtless when the first disaster happens (like Starlink), there will be a setback in technology that might otherwise proceed quietly in the shadows of agriculture.

In intellectual property, it is important that the courts do not make the mistake of preventing the development of more inventions that are useful without unnecessarily creating roadblocks by protecting a natural genome. (This was a mistake that was almost made in the contentious Myriad case, until the U.S. Supreme Court opined in a vague way that may have prevented further attempts to patent the human genome.)

Further, the DIY community will continue to grow as the tools become more affordable and more widespread. Many in the DIY community began to develop therapeutics, vaccines and tests in the midst of the COVID-19 pandemic. FDA is continuing to try to find ways to communicate with that community just to stay abreast of the activities. The FBI continues to also be involved with this community to stay abreast of potential biosecurity threats.

The federal government has developed an updated biotechnology framework but it will continue operation based on Memoranda of Understanding between agencies as areas blur between regulated products and processes. The basis of regulating based on end product rather than process has been the policy of the U.S., and will hopefully continue.

Given the recent switch in a determination of statutory jurisdiction between the FDA and EPA statutes over the Oxitec mosquito signals that agencies are open to being flexible as they learn. The continuing relationship of the FDA and USDA in biopharma animals defining them as "drugs" may eventually give way to a different agency to regulate this emerging area of animal welfare and pharmacological animals.

In summary, the future of agricultural biotechnology is promising and certain to grow in ways we have not yet imagined. The following report was developed in 2005 by USDA with a group of experts addressing the future of biotechnology and agriculture. This report gives us three possible scenarios for the future, and we can look back on this report, and assess how well we did with future predictions.

Preparing for the Future
A report prepared by the USDA Advisory Committee
On Biotechnology and 21st Century Agriculture

The USDA Advisory Committee on Biotechnology and 21st Century Agriculture (AC21) has been charged with helping USDA and the Secretary of Agriculture understand how biotechnology will change agriculture and USDA's role over the course of the next decade. This is a daunting task. Agricultural biotechnology[1] sits at the crossroads of other debates on the future of American and world agriculture, on international trade relations, on biological diversity and the development of international instruments related to its preservation and exploitation, on the role of multinational corporations, and on how best to build public confidence in

---

[1] Biotechnology is a range of tools, including traditional breeding techniques, that: (1) alter living organisms (or part of organisms) to make or modify products; (2) improve plants or animals; or (3) develop microorganisms for specific uses. Much of the discussion of biotechnology in this report focuses on "products of modern biotechnology" and "transgenic (or genetically engineered) organisms" (or their products), namely organisms produced through genetic engineering or recombinant DNA processes, and products derived from them.

rapidly emerging technologies in general. And, as all this occurs, the science continues to advance rapidly.

Neither the AC21, nor anyone else, can say with certainty what U.S. agriculture will look like in a decade. But we can try to examine different scenarios. This does not imply that we are predicting or endorsing any given scenario,[2] but rather that we are trying to understand the implications of differing outcomes.

A range of external forces and factors, some of which can be identified today, will impact the future of technology adoption. To help understand the range of possibilities, we have divided our work into two major components. First, what are the key predetermined factors—the major driving forces— that will likely have a major impact on shaping the future? Second, what are the key uncertainties that may push future outcomes in one direction or another?

WHAT WE KNOW (OR THINK WE KNOW)

What are some key drivers likely to influence the next decade, regardless of other uncertainties?

The AC21 has honed in on the following:

An increasing world population, especially in poor, non-Western countries, is leading to growing global food and feed needs. World population is not expected to level off until mid-century. This will require increased productivity from agricultural lands and could increase encroachment on non-agricultural lands, especially if agricultural productivity (e.g. production per acre planted) does not keep pace with increases in global populations..[3]

Regional prosperity leads to increased meat consumption. As income in developing countries rises, there has been and will continue to be a substantial increase in world demand for commodity crops, especially for animal feed use. India and China are likely to be the key drivers of additional demand for US agricultural commodities.[4] Food sufficiency (or excess) in developed nations will continue to be a major challenge.

---

[2] Several authors have detailed the methodology of scenario planning, including Peter Schwartz, in *"The Art of the Long View."*

[3] Although population growth has slowed somewhat over the past decade it continues to expand in absolute numbers, particularly in the developing world. http://www.census.gov/ipc/prod/wp02/wp-02001.pdf

[4] http://www.agribusiness.asn.au/review/1998V6/chinameat.htm

There will be an aging Western population, relative to developing nations. This population will continue to exercise significant purchasing power. Countries will face growing demands on their medical system. Research and treatment-mitigation-prevention of chronic diseases will be ever more important. Many products will be launched in the attempt to maintain the health of this population. Massive Social Security and health care costs will become a substantial drain on national budgets, reducing resources for other sectors of the economy.

Farmers in the US and globally will continue to have broad options and make planting decisions based on the value of the products produced with their production systems on their farms. The cost of production coupled with commodity prices will drive farmer decisions on crops and seed varieties.

Increasing public concern with health and nutrition, and increasing scrutiny by consumers, especially in developed nations, will drive change in the food system. Many people are demanding ever more information about the food they're eating, stimulated in part by the wide availability of increasingly sophisticated information technologies. The combination of escalating interest in information and technological advancements will result in increasing traceability and sophisticated, multiple product channels from farm to shelf.

Faced with growing abundance and increasing variety of food products, consumers in wealthy countries will be become increasingly selective about the products they buy. There will be increasing consumer demands for convenience, information about ingredients, safety, and methods of production.

There will be a trend toward increased consumer interest in, and awareness of, methods of food production. Developed country marketplaces, in particular, will be crowded with production labels, some of which, like organic, may be based on third-party or government verification. Consumers will continue to rely on governments and regulatory agencies to assure the safety of our food and safety of our crops to the environment.

The food marketplace will continue to experience rapid changes in demand based on consumer perceptions of health. These trends— pro- or anti-meat, pro- or anti-carbohydrates, will continue to produce big swings in food choices.

Global malnutrition and hunger will continue to be a major issue. Despite aggregate global food sufficiency, global hunger, malnutrition, and insecurity will persist, with the most pervasive impact in the world's poor countries but also among disadvantaged populations in wealthy countries.

Obesity will increase in importance as an issue. In the US over 64% of males and 62% of females are obese or overweight.[5] The increasing trend toward obesity shows little signs of abating, and is one of the factors driving up the costs of medical care. Concerns about this trend are focusing attention on current western diets and lifestyle practices, and may lead to changes in those diets that could lead to changes in demand for certain foods.

The trends toward urbanization and agricultural mechanization will continue. Fewer people will be involved in producing crops. This trend is driven by commercial agriculture and encourages standardization and consolidation.

Knowledge is driving changes in the economies of all nations. The dissemination of technology will continue to create momentum for innovation. New technologies and the resulting products are being picked up by scientists and entrepreneurs in countries all over the world (with or without respect for intellectual property). These new ideas and capabilities will drive social and economic change within and beyond the sphere of the industrialized countries. On the individual level, the advantages of widely available information will be counterbalanced by the problems of information overload and the unreliability of widely disseminated information.

Life sciences research will continue to expand on both the basic and applied fronts. Exponential increases in biological information contained in gene and protein databases will continue, although the rate of new product deployment based on that information is not likely to match the exponential rate of information generation over the next decade. In medicine, genomics data may lead to new disease treatment strategies and identification of new drug targets. In agriculture, such information will lead to a growing set of new tools and products, including biosensors and diagnostics, to enhance productivity. The biomedical research establishment will remain a powerful interest group in the United States.

Global trade and economic policies will remain important drivers of agricultural policies. There will be increasing pressure in the World Trade Organization on developed nations to liberalize agricultural policies. Bilateral trade agreements will continue to proliferate. Concerns about biotechnology are very likely to be used by U.S. competitors as non-

---

[5] http://www.niddk.nih.gov/health/nutrit/pubs/statobes.htm#preval

technical trade barriers to modulate trade. Food will continue to be treated differently than other traded goods.

The United States will remain a dominant global power. The U.S. will retain its position as a leader in technological developments in medicine and agriculture. The U.S. will also continue to empower other nations and spread democracy, but our dominant world position will continue to breed resistance, resentment, and competition.

EU regulations and consumer preferences will continue to impact world agricultural production systems. The expanded European Union will remain a huge market for global agriculture.

Increasing "South-South" dialogue in trade and political forums will increase the influence of China and India on other developing nations and enhance their global clout. The next decade will see the emergence of China as a growing challenge to US dominance.

Water issues will become increasingly important domestically and internationally. There will be increasing pressure on fresh water supplies, and less water will be available for agricultural uses. Overall world fresh water quality will decline. Linkages between water conservation, new agricultural technologies, and no-till agriculture will become increasingly important.

Global climate change will become increasingly important. The quantities of CO_2 and other greenhouse gases in the atmosphere will increase, and the window of opportunity for preventing global climate change will close. International efforts will increasingly focus on slowing and mitigating changes underway. The increase in global CO_2 levels will be exacerbated by rapid industrialization in many developing countries, especially China. Response to global warming could lead to major changes in agricultural production patterns or energy policies.

Globally, there will be decreasing availability of arable land currently cultivated, due to urban encroachment, conservation needs, non-sustainable farming practices, and soil degradation. This will increase the pressure on agricultural productivity, open new lands that may be less suitable for agriculture and/or will continue to increase species extinction pressures, especially in developing countries.

The increasing price and diminishing supply of fossil fuels will become an ever more urgent concern for U.S. agriculture. Worries about fossil fuels, coupled with new technology advances, will drive the development of bio-based fuels. In addition, high energy prices could constrain the use of synthetic fertilizers in the U.S. and also pose a challenge for the long-term viability of new agricultural lands that are dependent on large fertilizer inputs.

Increased global trade and travel will continue to increase the potential for new emerging diseases as well as more rapid disease transmission for plants, animals, and humans. Changing agricultural systems, new lands opened to agriculture, and climate change create new opportunities for agricultural diseases. Human infectious diseases, including, prominently, AIDS, and perhaps malaria, tuberculosis, and influenza, will increase in importance as issues. Allergies (including food allergies) and asthma are also likely to increase.

Enormous new agricultural commodity production areas will come on line in South America, particularly in Brazil and Argentina. There will be tremendous pressure and structural change in the soybean market. This could have implications on the U.S. export of soybeans.

The agricultural commodity system will continue to be dominated by 4 crops: corn, soy, wheat, and rice. Tensions may develop as non-food uses for some or all of these crops compete with food and feed uses for agricultural land and resources.

The trends toward consolidation and globalization will continue. These trends will increase vertical integration along the food chain, and increase the use of monocultures in crop production on larger farms. Consolidation in the global food industry, and the increasing market power of large food retailers, such as Wal-Mart or McDonald's, will continue to exacerbate the domestic or worldwide influence of a few marketing decisions on the availability or use of transgenic-derived ingredients and products.

High levels of debt and large budget deficits will persist in industrialized nations. Resultant budgetary pressures will increase the importance of agricultural trade, historically a major contributor to the export side of the U.S. trade ledger.

WHAT IS MUCH LESS CERTAIN

While the list of things we don't know is necessarily far longer than the previous list, the AC21 would like to focus on some of the key uncertainties whose outcomes could directly shape the future for agricultural products, including biotechnology products.

Disruptive events.
A broad variety of events could have a strong positive or negative impact on the public's perception of the application of biotechnology to

agriculture. Potentially, these range from rapid global adoption and support for biotechnology from countries like China, Brazil, Russia, India, etc. and rapid production of biotechnology products to issues that could negatively impact biotechnology acceptance like acts of bioterrorism (directed toward agriculture or not) to the emergence of significant new agricultural diseases that cannot be controlled through conventional means. Regional famines could require significantly increasing food aid shipments. Accidents involving contamination of the food supply with a product(s) not intended or appropriate for use in food could have serious consequences.

Demographic uncertainties.

Increases in food and commodity consumption linked to world population are also tied to global wealth creation. Increasing world demand for food, especially meat, will be linked to the level of growth and wealth creation in key countries like China and India. Changes (whether short- or long-term) in dietary preferences in developed countries, e.g., low-carbohydrate diets, could also impact the demand for key agricultural commodities. Aging populations in developed countries may express changed dietary preferences: one could as easily expect to see increased demand for new, "health-improved" products, and/or a trend toward consumption of organic-based products, or to see no particular net shifts.

Political uncertainties.

Political and economic decisions by key trading partners or competitors can have a major impact on the ability of biotechnology products to be produced and sold competitively. The political stability of key market countries such as China and India could significantly impact agricultural trade. Further escalation of Middle East conflicts could also affect trade. Will the European Union, a decade from now, be increasing access for biotechnology-derived crop varieties and growing them as well? What will be the impacts on the use of transgenic varieties of implementing multilateral agreements, such as the Cartagena Protocol on Biosafety or future agreements under the World Trade Organization?

Technological and regulatory uncertainties.

The product landscape and the regulatory landscape for new transgenic-derived products are evolving. With an evolving regulatory system, it is uncertain how quickly new applications (as food, seeds, drugs, or new industrial compounds) will reach the marketplace, here or in other countries. Which products will make it to the U.S. or global marketplaces, who will reap the benefits, and where? Will new products developed using the wealth of new genomic information be transgenic varieties, or will they be non-transgenic varieties developed through knowledge-based, marker-assisted selection techniques? Will food safety issues arising in conventional, organic, biotech, or other new production systems lead to a need for new regulation? Will US farmers continue to be concerned about their ability to compete with farmers in South America and China?

Will concerns regarding the deployment of transgenic plants producing plant-based pharmaceuticals in food crops inhibit or severely restrict their cultivation? Will production of these or other products move offshore in response to economic or regulatory considerations? Will transgenic products with significant consumer pull, perhaps "nutriceutical products" or others, reach the marketplace in any quantity? To what extent will parallel technologies emerge that may compete with transgenic products for use in agriculture?

Environmental uncertainties

Will serious effects of global warming become pressing within the next decade? What will be the price of fuel or energy? Will agricultural systems be increasingly looked at as solutions to global problems, such as energy needs or global warming?

Consumer uncertainties

The public's receptiveness to increasingly novel products that may come to market is unknown. Such products could include transgenic animal-derived products, plant-derived food products engineered to offer specific health benefits to consumers, and plants and livestock producing pharmaceutical and industrial compounds. Will such products drive consumer acceptance or raise new concerns and/or resistance?

Will consumer opinion regarding biotechnology remain changeable, or will views harden? Will there be a consumer backlash against the market power of some large conglomerates? Will concern over the implication of other applications of new technologies, e.g., human cloning, spill over into perceptions related to the use of transgenic organisms in agriculture?

Agriculture and food system uncertainties.

How will agricultural land use change over the next decade? What proportion of agricultural land will continue to be used for food production versus other uses? Economics or technological innovations could drive significant expansion of crop production for bio-energy, industrial feedstock purposes, or other novel uses. Could such uses change the overall economics of commodity production? What will be the global distribution of large-scale bulk commodity production in a decade? Will new transgenic crops that are commercialized be mostly intended for bulk use or will there be increasing commercialization of products for niche markets?

Down the food chain, actions by major players in the food system could dramatically alter the landscape for new transgenic products. Food franchises, supermarket chains, and mega-retailers will evolve over the next decade. What will they look like, how much consolidation (or global expansion) will there be, what will the future companies look like, and what will be their attitudes towards products containing transgenic-derived ingredients and what ingredients will be generated that may influence consumer attitudes?

ENVISIONING A FEW POSSIBLE FUTURES

The numerous uncertainties above (and probably a host of others) could propel a myriad of possible futures, depending on how events play out regarding each of them. Neither the AC21 nor USDA is in a position to predict what will actually happen. However, the AC21 believes it is useful to provide examples of possible futures, which are intended to illustrate how resolution of key uncertainties in particular ways could shape the future for the use of transgenic organisms in agriculture and the work of USDA. The scenarios share the certainties, but how the uncertainties play out influence how the scenarios are shaped.

Each scenario is intended as a coherent description of what the world might look like a decade from now, after events driven by the certainties and some of the key uncertainties listed above play out.

These are _not_ predictions of the future, nor are probabilities or likelihoods assigned to them. They were created to provoke thought over a wide range of possibilities, so no single scenario should be considered in isolation.

Indeed, we can be relatively certain that when we look back a decade from now, none of the scenarios will have accurately represented what actually occurred in the interim. Nor do they represent the full range of conceivable outcomes.

However, they do demonstrate the sensitivity of agriculture and the food system to events that can tip the future in different ways, and, looked at together, provide an opportunity to extract additional knowledge about broader impacts into the future.

Here, then, are three scenarios we have created, among the many that could be developed. We have entitled them "Rosy Future," "Continental

Islands,", and "Biotech Goes Niche." Using and adding to the list of certainties and uncertainties, you can build your own scenarios.

Because each of these scenarios has implications for farm income, consumers, the environment, trade, private investment, USDA agendas, and resources, we advise you to read these scenarios without making value judgments or picking a favorite. Instead, we advise you to consider the consequences of each if the scenario or some version thereof came to pass. After outlining the three scenarios, we will pose a series of specific questions that could help you work out some of the implications.

I. "Rosy Future"

By 2015, life science research delivered beyond anyone's expectations. Like those involved in the information technology revolution, even those doing the research and investment were overwhelmed by the scale and speed of change. Among the new products were crops with increased yield, resistance to key stresses like drought, plants engineered for new energy uses, including production of biodiesel, and new food products that provide valuable health benefits. In addition, plants with various combinations of traits significantly increased the utility or impact of these new crops.

Agricultural biotechnology began being employed all over the world, not only in agricultural exporting countries. Research and development continued in the Western world and in those developing countries whose governments quickly recognized the opportunities and were able to provide an appropriate investment climate. European nations continued their development of new ag biotech uses for pharmaceutical, industrial, and energy products. European opposition to food uses decreased significantly as EU governments, non-governmental organizations, and consumers realized the value of increasing agricultural productivity on GDP and competitiveness.

More food could be produced on less land, which was fortunate because, as Chinese and Indian incomes rose, demand for animal feed exploded. Had the new transgenic products not come on line, meeting demand would have required bringing enormous amounts of new agricultural land under cultivation.

Farmers now faced a much more complex world with an even broader array of crop and seed variety options. Their acreage could now be used not just for food, feed, and fiber production, but also for chemical, pharmaceutical, and energy production. This meant that they could participate in, and had to understand and follow, a wider range of markets, financial instruments, and opportunities. Niche and small family farming became profitable because of the high value of some transgenic products grown on farms. Non-food uses for crops became increasingly economically important, but remained high value, low acre opportunities.

Overall farm and agribusiness income increased and there was ever less dependence on subsidies. Alternatives like converting biomass to energy meant there was now a floor price on grains. Why sell a bushel of corn for food or feed at the government loan rate if energy companies would pay more? In addition, because the increased number of agricultural biotechnology products and uses reduced the need for subsidies, trade wars became less of an issue.

An increasingly sophisticated and broad set of companies established partnerships with various segments of the agribusiness chain. Pharmaceutical companies used their new networks of seed producers to begin growing various medicines and vaccines. Some forms of animal husbandry became far more specialized, regulated, and profitable as areas like medical and materials production grew. Information, computing, and diagnostic companies became increasingly involved in this process. Energy companies began to invest in bio-based energy. Governments began permitting the establishment of carbon trading enterprises based on an increased focus on global warming. Farmers, particularly those using biotech products in no-till agriculture, began to capitalize on these new market opportunities.

As various conglomerates began to integrate technologies and outlets, mergers and acquisitions blossomed on a very broad scale. Bioinformation companies merged with financial companies. Mergers between seed companies and chemical-pharmaceutical companies continued. Some energy companies began developing broad portfolios of alliances and acquisitions outside the traditional energy business.

Companies began seeing more and more diverse business opportunities. Even with increased global competition, for U.S. companies the overall opportunity "pie" was growing faster than the increase in competition.

Some medicine-producing goats were worth hundreds of thousands of dollars and were cared for as carefully as human patients in a hospital. Highly specialized animal products for xenotransplantation[6] merged the most sophisticated laboratories and boutique farms.

Within the food system, a series of niche markets serving different "nutriceutical" needs provided farmers with far more specialized markets and opportunities. Foods engineered to help people lose weight or ward off certain diseases exploded off supermarket shelves. This created consumer pull for a wide range of new farm products and a much broader acceptance of biotechnology. Further integrating the grocery industry and food processors with projected crop needs became ever more important. As niche crops became more important, often a farmer's whole crop was sold prior to planting, as long as it met strict quality criteria. Some environmentalists throughout the developed world continued to worry that the increasing rate of new product introductions could lead to a serious accident, but so far this had not occurred.

Farmers adapting to the new technologies became more profitable regardless of farm size. Those who did not adapt had a harder time and were replaced by more technically sophisticated producers. For high value crops, production became highly vertically integrated, continuing existing trends in that direction.

Most of the innovations took place in major crops, but some improvements to minor crops took place and began to change cropping patterns in the U.S. and elsewhere.

Maintaining the integrity and traceability of the streams of products coming off the farm and into various supply chains including chemicals, energy, cosmetic, and food became ever more important. This meant that much of the production during the first years of this broad biotech revolution continued within the US market and expanded to other agricultural exporting countries. Countries with a long history of technologically intensive, greenhouse-based production, became formidable competitors for specific products. Higher margins and a need for tight control over all aspects of the food chain made the idea of moving production of the specialty applications of crop biotechnology to the developing world less attractive for U.S. companies.

---

[6] "Xenotransplantation" refers to transplantation of organs derived from other animal species for therapeutic purposes. As of 2004, there is active biotechnology research to "humanize" animal organs to make them less likely to be rejected by organ recipients.

Not all was positive however: changes in global consumption and production patterns – increased global demand for animal feed, increased demand for energy uses and continued population growth and urbanization - created its own set of pressures. As farmers increasingly used commodity crops for other uses besides food, commodity prices rose and there was increased clamor to bring ever more land under cultivation. Environmentalists throughout the developed world lobbied to limit this trend. Biotechnology was utilized as a tool to increase the efficient use of agricultural land. There was continuing concern over long-term environmental degradation resulting from the exclusive focus on output optimization. However, the overwhelming impact of biotech crops grown on large areas was to reduce the environmental impacts of agriculture. Less overall water, fuel, chemical pesticides and packaging were used compared to non-biotech agriculture, and soil erosion problems were reduced.

Governments adopted compatible regulatory systems, essential for development of, and trade in, new products. However, the poorest developing countries found themselves ever more marginalized. Much of the benefits and profits of this revolution went to those who had done the biotechnological research and provided sophisticated services. There was increased talk and concern of a life sciences divide as well as the digital divide.

While the increased number of new patented seeds, animals, and techniques reflected a broader acceptance of the importance of intellectual property, intellectual property remained a significant battleground between developed and developing countries. However, a few developing countries saw the future and joined the developed world with respect to these techniques. Some countries also began producing generic versions of popular products.

II. "Continental Islands"

New products of biotechnology continued to be developed and introduced into the marketplace. Farmers in a number of countries in the Americas and Asia continued to adopt biotech crops, based on significant positive economic impacts. Many of these new products were plant varieties with two or more new traits in a single variety, providing additional value for growers, and some new agronomic and consumer focused products have come to the market. Development of transgenic animals continued for niche applications, including xenotransplantation, but not for food uses. Given smaller markets, little investment was made in minor crop biotechnology.

The process for bringing transgenic agricultural products through the regulatory approval process to commercialization remained efficient in the U.S., Canada, and Argentina, and China, Mexico and Brazil joined their ranks. In some other countries with much slower regulatory processes, such as India, Australia, the European Union, and some African countries, additional products were only commercialized slowly. In other countries the approval processes remained non-existent or cumbersome.

Despite continued efforts, no international harmonization of regulations occurred and restrictive regulations continued to serve as trade barriers. Different countries or regions had varying regulatory systems and procedures. Labeling of biotechnology products varied by country and was non-standard.

The United States continued to be a major producer and distributor of biotechnology products. Other major growers and producers were Canada, Argentina, China, India, Brazil, and South Africa. One or more of these countries commercialized a major transgenic crop not commercialized in the U.S. Asia and the rest of Africa remained divided, with some countries accepting or promoting the technology, and others rejecting it (even as food aid).

The EU (including the accession countries) continued not to accept food products in general, though they accepted products for feed uses and approved some products for field testing and importation. Despite the approvals, though, no products were actually tested (except for very small-scale field trials) nor were many food products imported and offered for sale.

Commodities destined for food use and those for feed use continued to be handled differently in different continents or regions.

The impacts seen in the farming community varied from farmer to farmer, depending on whether their principal markets were domestic or export. The domestic market continued to utilize transgenic products. Some exporters continued to test for their absence since non-transgenic certified products could be sold at a premium to food manufacturers wanting to avoid labeling and other compliance issues. Premium contracts with growers were often used to meet these non-transgenic crop needs.

Along the agricultural food chain, the pattern was similar. Products containing ingredients derived from transgenic varieties were acceptable and widely used for domestic markets, while food products for export largely sourced for non-transgenic-derived ingredients. Multinational food companies also used non-transgenic ingredient sources where there was mandatory biotech food labeling, or used non-transgenic ingredient sourcing globally. Since much of the biotech corn, soy and cotton produced in the U.S. was destined for domestic markets or markets with approval of biotech crops, farmers continued to plant large amounts of biotech corn, cotton and soybeans and realize the associated economic returns. With an increased demand for ethanol, the demand for corn in the U.S. continued to increase, creating additional growth and consumption of biotech corn.

Research and development activities by multinational technology providers and developers focused more on basic research since the market for new transgenic products was limited, and there was more emphasis on leveraging genetic understanding into targeted breeding programs, etc. There was continued consolidation among technology providers, but little additional capital for expansion. Research and development activities by public universities now focused on basic research.

Consumers worldwide remained divided and/or ambivalent. Those in the U.S. and most of the Americas continued to accept products containing ingredients derived from the first generation of transgenic plants without special labeling. Those in the EU and some other parts of the world were either opposed to the technology (and supported mandatory labeling as a means of product avoidance) or were ambivalent. Consumers in other countries varied in their sentiments, depending on the views of their governments. The situation was most confused in Africa, given the dire need for food and given confusion regarding trade-related issues, especially with the EU.

There continued to be no negative health implications from transgenic-derived food products. Continued positive environmental impacts were realized in the U.S., particularly with respect to decreases in pesticide use and increases in conservation tillage.

International trade remained complicated given regulatory and acceptance differences. USDA, the State Department and other agencies continued to expend a significant amount of resources in fighting for biotechnology in the trade arena. Several other countries opposing the spread of the technology devoted comparable resources on the opposite side.

III. _"Biotech goes niche"_

After a splashy debut, genetically engineered crops products did not turn out to be major components of world commodity agriculture, but continued to thrive in important niche markets. The first two products of crop biotechnology--- Bt and herbicide tolerance products, widely adopted in the U.S., Canada, and South America, were not followed by other blockbuster products. Some major agricultural regions continued to reject genetically engineered crops.

No transgenic varieties of wheat were ever commercialized. None of the promised new traits—drought tolerance or cold tolerance—panned out for corn, soy, cotton, or canola. The first generation of adopters remained enthusiastic about herbicide-tolerant and insect resistant (Bt) crops but was gradually forced to turn away from them because of lack of global acceptance and increased use of marker assisted technologies for development of improved germplasm in conventional seeds, but not "transgenic crops".

The public did not accept the genetic engineering of animals for food uses, and given the technical difficulties associated with many of the modifications, there was no enthusiasm for commercializing genetically engineered animals for those uses. However, applications involving genetic engineering of animals for producing pharmaceuticals or tissues for xenotransplantation came on line.

The reasons for the fading away of transgenic products were complicated. First, the technology never overcame the barriers inherent in engineering useful traits involving multiple genes. Research costs remained high. The few products with claims to improved nutrition were never attractive enough to enjoy large price premiums. Without those price premiums it was hard to justify big investments in continued research and identity preservation schemes.

In the regulatory arena, mandatory food safety approval and transboundary movement requirements continued to increase as did the cost and time it took to go to market. There were some efforts amongst countries to harmonize requirements. However, the majority of countries developed their own regulatory systems based on local needs and market protection preferences. Consequently product developers had to deal with multiple diverse regulatory schemes in order to do international business. This was further complicated by farm-to-table traceability and labeling requirements and country-of-destination requirements imposed by the Cartagena Protocol on Biosafety and several other international treaties. Frequent detections of transgenes in both traditional and other transgenic crops posed interrelated policy challenges. Attempts to address those challenges with new approaches to adventitious presence, approved detection and sampling methods, and what constitutes a "novel" product never met with consensus.

Another part of the equation was consumer resistance. Consumers in the United States continued to be generally receptive or somewhat indifferent to transgenic crops, but consumers in many other countries remained opposed to the technology. In the increasingly interconnected global marketplace, international retail companies simply found it easier to source non-transgenic material. There was no consumer demand for genetically engineered products, so there seemed little reason for food companies to take on the extra burden of selling "GMOs" to customers who did not want them.

Food manufacturers, fast-food chains and mega-retail enterprises began specifying non-transgenic-sourced food ingredients and raw materials for their branded products. Many consumers failed to recognize potential benefits of the technology and questioned whether benefits from transgenic commodities were being directed to big business. Business economics demonstrated that new transgenics would only be profitable in the specialty "niche" market. Concerns grew stronger over the potential discovery of a pharmaceutical gene product in a food product. Although scientists said it did not present any human health risks, customers nevertheless tended to reach for other food options.

Although interest in new commodity transgenics faded, agricultural innovation continued. On the scientific front the complete genomes of the major food, feed and oil crops were made available through public databases to scientists, researchers, breeders and others in developed and developing economies. There was welcome progress in the ability to translate sequence information into agricultural improvements. Agricultural advances were facilitated by exponential growth of data delivered from various technologies, such as genomics, proteomics, gene expression assays, and bioinformatics.

Some innovations resulted from marker-assisted or traditional breeding. While the fruits of genomics were a while in coming, the mountains of data were eventually digested. Because traditional breeding could more readily accomplish selection for interacting sets of genes, the new products wound up providing a broader variety of traits than did genetic engineering. In addition, because they were traditionally bred, the new products could be brought to market with little regulatory oversight. However, some problematic new diseases, for which enhanced traditional approaches were not effective, emerged. Except for some groups focused on patenting and monopoly concerns, most of the new, innovative products escaped consumer opposition.

Some innovations depended on new non-biotech systems of agriculture and included new ways of enriching soil, protecting against pests and increasing yields. Many of these ideas were generated in the research done in support of organic and other new systems made possible by research funds diverted from investment in biotechnology products. With steady increases and double digit annual growth, these new food production systems rose to constitute 6 percent of total food production. Several large multinational food companies launched new product lines. Marker-assisted breeding programs became integrated with farmer and producer needs and were welcomed into these new systems.

Scientists did not abandon genetic engineering, but aimed their research at niche markets that generally did not involve the food system. The new genetically engineered products included a few energy crops, although most energy crops were produced using traditional or marker-assisted breeding. The production of pharmaceuticals in transgenic non-food crops also became a niche market. Two genetically engineered foods, for which developers were able to make compelling claims for prevention of heart disease and Alzheimer's, performed well in clinical trials and were expected to be commercialized soon. Companies redirected their efforts onto new niche markets, like energy-based or pharmaceutical products. These markets offered viable survival strategies for seed and technology companies.

The trade arena continued to be dynamic. China emerged as both a market and a competitor to the U.S. in the global commodity arena—huge and unpredictable. The demand for commodity products increased but so did global agricultural production as new areas in South America and Central Europe came on line. The result was an unpredictable seesaw of prices. There was growing concern globally that farmers in China were benefiting from the widespread use of biotechnology products in China without any regulatory oversight in the international markets. Some U.S.

biotech companies transferred their research and development efforts to China and other developing countries with more open trade policies and greater food security needs.

With regard to farm subsidies, deadlines for agreed-upon reductions in payments were not met. National and regional trade restrictions continued, as did high tariffs. Through two election cycles since the last Farm Bill, both the U.S. farm policy and the European Common Agriculture Policy remained surplus-friendly. A number of developing economies led by several small Asian and African countries continued to fight against subsidies in the WTO round of discussions by demanding that subsidies and protective tariffs be eliminated and markets opened to products grown in these developing economies. Global trade in agricultural products continued to be characterized by a maze of national/regional phytosanitary standards, but the adoption of genetic engineering technology faded as a factor in global competition..

Developing countries—the poorest countries of the world—remained poor, because the world community remained unable to help them develop the infrastructure, access to markets, and targeted agricultural research investments that would result in an agriculture that could increase incomes and exports.

Without a barrage of new transgenic products on the horizon, the State Department and USDA and other agencies did not need to expend resources in fighting for market access for commodities and other agricultural products generated through biotechnology in the trade arena, in Codex Alimentarius and in other arenas. Overall, the drop-off in introduction of new transgenic commodity crops decreased the U.S. policy focus on international acceptance of those crops, and consequently lessened global agricultural trade frictions. This freed up some resources for other purposes, including assistance to poor countries.

A decrease in biotechnology crop plantings resulted in a return to agricultural farm practices based on conventional crops. This resulted in an increase in overall volumes of insecticides and herbicides used to protect crops, and an increase in the use of energy and water in the manufacture, transport and application of these products. Additionally, soil erosion began to increase as more farmers used tillage in their fields.

You have now visited three very different worlds. Here are a few questions you might wish to consider for these and other scenarios you might envision. These questions are designed to provoke discussion and help prepare for an uncertain future.

1.   What is the economic impact of the scenario?
    - Competitive drivers
    - Economic growth
    - Trade development/exports
    - Farmer income and rural development
    - Market segmentation

2.   What is the impact of the scenario on the natural environment?

3.   What are the implications of the scenario for USDA?

    - Resources
    - Regulatory structure
    - Trade and promotion
    - Impacts on other government agency resources that could affect USDA
    - Public research agenda

4.   What are the implications of the scenario for consumers and for public acceptance?

5.   What are the implications of the scenario for addressing global food sufficiency/food security?

———————————

Acknowledgments

I want to acknowledge the contributions of my students at Texas Tech University over the years, to the development of this book. In particular, I am grateful to Joel Aldrich, my former research assistant and a Texas Tech University School of Law alumnus.

Thanks are in order to my faculty colleagues and Dean Nowlin at the Texas Tech University School of Law, for allowing me the time and support to complete this book.

Finally, I want to thank my children who continue to inspire me in no small way.

Made in the USA
Coppell, TX
29 December 2020